Privacy and Security Management Practices for Organizations

Supaprawat Siripipatthanakul
Manipal GlobalNxt University, Malaysia

IGI Global
Scientific Publishing
Publishing Tomorrow's Research Today

Vice President of Editorial	Melissa Wagner
Director of Acquisitions	Mikaela Felty
Director of Book Development	Jocelynn Hessler
Production Manager	Mike Brehm
Cover Design	Phillip Shickler

Published in the United States of America by
IGI Global Scientific Publishing
701 East Chocolate Avenue
Hershey, PA, 17033, USA
Tel: 717-533-8845
Fax: 717-533-7115
Website: https://www.igi-global.com E-mail: cust@igi-global.com

Library of Congress Cataloging-in-Publication Data

Names: Siripipatthanakul, Supaprawat, 1973- editor.
Title: Privacy and security management practices for organizations / edited by Supaprawat Siripipatthanakul.
Description: Hershey, PA : IGI Global Scientific Publishing, [2025] | Includes bibliographical references and index. | Summary: "This book explains how organizations can choose the proper control selection technique based on the situation. This flexibility is needed to address security and privacy issues and ensure organizations are completing their due diligence"-- Provided by publisher.
Identifiers: LCCN 2024055206 (print) | LCCN 2024055207 (ebook) | ISBN 9798369397206 (hardcover) | ISBN 9798369397213 (paperback) | ISBN 9798369397220 (ebook)
Subjects: LCSH: Personal information management. | Information technology--Management.
Classification: LCC HD30.2 .P745 2025 (print) | LCC HD30.2 (ebook) | DDC 658/.0558--dc23/eng/20250201
LC record available at https://lccn.loc.gov/2024055206
LC ebook record available at https://lccn.loc.gov/2024055207

British Cataloguing in Publication Data
A Cataloguing in Publication record for this book is available from the British Library.

Table of Contents

Detailed Table of Contents

This chapter covers the digital economy, privacy, and cybersecurity. Cyber protection, privacy, and data security address computer infections and cyberattacks. This study is a review article based on scholarly papers from valid sources, including Google Scholar, Scopus, and Web of Science (WOS), from 2020 to 2024. The findings show that digital privacy safeguards consumer data. Personal data, communication, and behavior are safe online. Shows internet data privacy rules. The data-driven society needs digital privacy. Digital platforms create vast amounts of personal data that could be misused, including financial and health records. Data theft is prevented via digital privacy. For democracy, we need digital privacy. Diverse viewpoints survive without manipulation. Digital privacy rules enhance customer trust and business reputation, enabling companies to compete more effectively.

This study examines email spam, WhatsApp, and Telegram in relation to Singaporean cybersecurity, financial security, and personal privacy. Use convenience sampling and descriptive statistics to analyze 157 online questionnaires. The results reveal privacy risks and high rates of phishing and unwanted messages. Younger digital users are more vulnerable to these threats, while higher-educated people are more aware and more likely to take precautions. The perceived privacy risks and requests for improved cybersecurity features show user anxiety. The report identifies platform security and user knowledge gaps, underscoring the need for enhanced cybersecurity, stricter regulatory oversight, and targeted public education. The proposals include enhancing encryption, implementing AI-driven spam detection, and revising Singapore's cybersecurity legislative framework. These safeguards

innovation, sustainability, ethics, and risk management. Key issues include cyber threats, technological infrastructure limitations, and employees' lack of cybersecurity literacy. Clear policies, employee training, and investments in advanced technologies such as encryption and intrusion detection must address these.

Data privacy and security are crucial to competitiveness in the information age, especially for Foreign Direct Investment (FDI) and firm-level competitive advantage. A systematic review and content analysis were conducted based on scientific publications. This chapter explains the intricate relationship between factor conditions, supporting industries, policies, and regulatory frameworks that contribute to its competitiveness in attracting Foreign Direct Investment (FDI). The institutional stability of data protection boosts employees' trust and reduces geopolitical and cybersecurity concerns. The approach enhances competitiveness in attracting technology-driven Foreign Direct Investment (FDI) and enables enterprises to maintain long-term profitability through secure and transparent data ecosystems. According to research, compelling data governance and privacy enable organizations to capitalize on market opportunities and mitigate risks. The chapter provides a framework for corporate leaders to integrate privacy, security, and FDI competitiveness in digital globalization.

This chapter discusses how technology and regulatory changes have complicated research privacy and security. Researchers must balance ethics and law while safeguarding personal data. The book emphasizes risk assessment and management throughout the research process to protect participant privacy and comply with data security standards. Safe data collection, storage, and sharing and privacy-enhancing technologies like anonymization and pseudonymization are key subjects. In order to maintain ethical and legal compliance, researchers and oversight agencies like Institutional Review Boards (IRBs) must work together. It also shows how proactive methods and information environment knowledge may build trust among participants, sponsors, and the public. It gives a thorough approach on balancing privacy, security, and research objectives in a data-driven world, protecting research integrity and stakeholder confidence.

Everyone knows about privacy rights and how to protect them in this digital era. This chapter explains the importance of being aware of privacy information when using ChatGPT. The systematic review was synthesized through content analysis of scholarly papers, which are reliable and valid sources, from Scopus, Web of Science (WOS), and Google Scholar, using purposive sampling based on English versions and primarily published between 2020 and 2025. Findings suggest that everyone must acknowledge the importance of privacy in their daily lives as the volume of personal information exchanged online continues to rise. Personal information disclosure can pose risks. Thus, users should be aware of them and take precautions. Users' understanding of service privacy settings and policies, the importance of privacy that raises privacy concerns, the quality and quantity of personal information they disclose, and the personal consequences of potential data breaches on the technological services for information privacy awareness and sharing when using ChatGPT.

Academics and politicians agree that airport infrastructure boosts regional economic development, connectivity, and competitiveness. Airport infrastructure in Northern Malaysia is essential for attracting Foreign Direct Investments (FDI), tourism, trade, and logistics. Due to its proximity to Indonesia and Thailand and economic strength, northern Malaysia is well-positioned to use airport development as a regional competitive advantage. For decades, Penang International Airport (PIA) has been Northern Malaysia's main domestic and international airport. Like many others in Malaysia, the airport suffers capacity issues, obsolete infrastructure, government funding constraints, limited growth opportunities, and the need for privacy and security management for sustainable adaptations. These reasons demonstrate the

Preface

INTRODUCTION

The digital revolution has improved firms' capacity to optimize operations and handle substantial volumes of data, including consumer information, health records, and financial documentation. Nevertheless, it is not wholly secure against the perils posed by cyber terrorists. Substantial harm may ensue following a cyber-attack, encompassing the exploitation of private information, identity theft, and financial fraud. Consequently, enterprises must implement safeguards for cloud environments and develop strategies for addressing data. The risk policy of an organization protects digital data from unlawful access, utilization, and disclosure. Data disruption, alteration, and eradication are likewise obstructed. Every organization needs data. Consequently, it requires safeguarding. Ensuring data confidentiality, integrity, and availability necessitates robust data security measures. Strong data security can protect assets, fulfill regulatory requirements, and preserve consumer confidence. Data security and privacy are occasionally muddled in discussions regarding data protection. Data protection organizations are capable of articulating their privacy and security protocols. This book elucidates how organizations can identify the optimal control selection methodology. This adaptability assists firms in addressing security and privacy vulnerabilities while fulfilling due diligence requirements. System security and privacy methods implement, evaluate, and oversee controls after control selection.

Privacy and Security Management Practices for Organizations discusses the impact of recent legislative modifications in data privacy, environmental standards, and labor restrictions on corporate strategies and management practices. Examples of the essentials of privacy and security management practices are crucial for online marketplaces, remote work, cyber terrorism, etc. It is an invaluable resource for corporate executives, managers, cybersecurity experts, data scientists, researchers, scholars, and academics. The many academic areas covered in privacy and security management practices include but are not limited to Banking Systems, Cloud Computing, Computer Science, Cyber Terrorism, Cybersecurity, Digital Economy, FinTech, Logistics Information Systems, Online Marketplaces, Privacy Information Sharing, Public Organizations, Remote Working, and Security Management.

The book includes eight chapters that could empower academic leaders and strategic planners for privacy and security management to encourage researchers to adopt collaboration, creativity, communication, and critical thinking among researchers, organizations, and industries.

Chapter 1: ***The Essentials of Privacy and Cybersecurity in the Digital Economy*** by Parichat Jaipong (DBA Candidate) and Watthanasakon Rakpathum discusses privacy, cybersecurity, and the digital economy. Cybersecurity, privacy, and data security address computer viruses and cyberattacks. Digital privacy protects customer data, personal data, communication, and conduct online. Digital platforms generate massive amounts of personal data, including financial and health records, that could be exploited. Data theft is protected via digital privacy.

Chapter 2: ***Email Spam, WhatsApp, and Telegram Affect Privacy, Cybersecurity, Financial Security, and Personal Invasion - A Case Study in Singapore*** by Dr. Lewes Lim and Dr. Penpim Phuangsuwan discusses privacy risks, high phishing rates, and unwanted messages. Younger digital users are more vulnerable to these threats, while higher-educated people are more aware and likely to take precautions. The perceived privacy risks and requests for improved cybersecurity features show user anxiety. The platform security and user knowledge gaps underscore the need for enhanced cybersecurity, stricter regulatory oversight, and targeted public education. A way to strengthen encryption, implement-driven spam detection, and revise Singapore's cybersecurity legislative framework has been proposed to protect user privacy and reduce financial theft and data breaches in modern digital communication platforms.

Chapter 3: ***Security Management Practices in Social Sciences and Humanities: Safeguarding Research Integrity and Data*** by Dr. Andi Asrifan and Chirapat Kaewnaknaew discusses social science and humanities (SSH) security management for research integrity and ethical data handling. Due to its different ethnic and socioeconomic participants, SSH research requires confidentiality, informed consent, and anonymity. The chapter discusses how digitalization and online data collection have exacerbated cybersecurity threats like leaks and illegal access. Scholars must traverse numerous legal regimes and collaborate across boundaries in interdisciplinary and transnational SSH research. Use encryption, secure storage, and strict data management to safeguard sensitive data. The institutions should support comprehensive cybersecurity and ethical research policies and training. Security precautions are essential for public trust, study validity, and participant rights and well-being.

Chapter 4: ***Challenges and Management Practices in Protecting Employee Personal Data*** by Dr. Syamsul Hadi, Eni Purnasari, Dr. Riskin Hidayat, Dr. Ambar Lukitaningsih, Dr. Kusuma Chandra Kirana, and Dr. Supaprawat Siripipatthanakul discuss the key challenges in managing employee personal data in the digital transformation era and explores effective management practices to protect such data. Personal data management practices are closely linked to technological innovation, sustainability, ethics, and risk management. Key issues include cyber threats, technological infrastructure limitations, and employees' lack of cybersecurity literacy. Clear policies, employee training, and investments in advanced technologies such as encryption and intrusion detection must address these.

Chapter 5: ***The Determinants of FDI Attraction in Creating a Foreign Firm's Competitive Advantage: An Extended Model for Data Protection in Privacy and Security*** by Seng Loong (Stanley) Kok, and Dr. Patcharavadee Sriboonruang discusses the crucial of data privacy and security for competitiveness in the information age, especially for Foreign Direct Investment (FDI) and firm-level competitive advantage. A systematic review and content analysis were conducted based on scientific publications. This chapter explains the intricate relationship between factor conditions, supporting industries, policies, and regulatory frameworks contributing to its competitiveness in attracting Foreign Direct Investment (FDI). The institutional stability of data protection boosts employees' trust and reduces geopolitical and cybersecurity concerns. The approach enhances competitiveness in attracting technology-driven Foreign Direct Investment (FDI) and enables enterprises to maintain long-term profitability through secure and transparent data ecosystems. According to research, compelling data governance and privacy would allow organizations to capitalize on market opportunities and mitigate risks. The chapter provides a framework for corporate leaders to integrate privacy, security, and FDI competitiveness in digital globalization.

Chapter 6: ***Managing Privacy and Security in Research: Effective Practices and Strategies*** by Dr. Andi Asrifan, Dr. Supaprawat Siripipatthanakul, Dr. Mohammed H. Alaqad, Dr. Syamsuardi Saodi, and Dr. Sadaruddin Sadaruddin, discuss how technology and regulatory changes have complicated research privacy and security. Researchers must balance ethics and law while safeguarding personal data. Risk assessment and management throughout the research process to protect participant privacy and comply with data security standards is crucial. Safe data collection, storage, and sharing and privacy-enhancing technologies like anonymization and pseudonymization are key subjects. Researchers and oversight agencies like Institutional Review Boards (IRBs) must work together to maintain ethical and legal compliance. It also shows how proactive methods and information environment knowledge may build trust among participants, sponsors, and the public. It gives a thorough approach to balancing privacy, security, and research objectives in a data-driven world, protecting research integrity and stakeholder confidence.

Chapter 7: ***Privacy Information Awareness: A Case of ChatGPT Adoption*** by Chirapat Kaewnaknaew and Dr. Patcharavadee Sriboonruang discusses the importance of being aware of privacy information when using ChatGPT. Everyone must acknowledge the importance of privacy in their daily lives as the volume of personal information exchanged online continues to rise. Personal information disclosure can pose risks. Users should be aware of them and take precautions by understanding service privacy settings and policies, the importance of privacy that raises privacy concerns, the quality and quantity of personal information they disclose, and the personal consequences of potential data breaches on the technological services for information privacy awareness and sharing when using ChatGPT.

Chapter 8: ***Strategic Planning on Airport Infrastructure in the Northern Malaysia Region: The Relevance of Privacy and Cyber Security*** by Dr. Seng Loong (Stanley) Kok and Dr. Sutithep Siripipattanakul discusses how infrastructure boosts regional economic development, connectivity, and competitiveness. Airport infrastructure in Northern Malaysia is essential for attracting Foreign Direct Investments (FDI), tourism, trade, and logistics. Due to its proximity to Indonesia and Thailand and economic strength, northern Malaysia is well-positioned to use airport development as a regional competitive advantage. For decades, Penang International Airport (PIA) has been Northern Malaysia's main domestic and international airport. Like many others in Malaysia, the airport suffers capacity issues, obsolete infrastructure, government funding constraints, limited growth opportunities, and the need for privacy and security management for sustainable adaptations. There is an urgent necessity for a comprehensive airport development plan in Northern Malaysia to incorporate privacy and cyber security management for competitive advantage and sustainable development.

Through thoughtful collaboration among researchers and professors on these diverse themes, "Privacy and Security Management Practices for Organizations" provides academic leaders and strategic planners with ways to improve organizational privacy and security practices.

Introduction

This book, entitled "Privacy and Security Management Practices for Organizations," results from extensive research, collaborative effort, and unwavering commitment to the relevance of researchers, educators, and professors within the academic and research community. It exemplifies the joint efforts of many individuals and institutions that contributed their time and knowledge and helped with its research and development. After giving this journey some thought, I have realized that I was fortunate to be surrounded by a remarkable group of researchers and professors whose contributions were essential to producing this book.

I want to express my overwhelming thanks to the IGI Global Scientific Publishing team, whose unwavering support for our initiative served as the foundation upon which this book was built. Their professionalism, patience, and attention were indispensable throughout the production process, from the preliminary to the final phases. The help and skills they provided throughout the entire process, from the proposal to the final production, were essential in determining the ultimate result. Because of their dependability, experience, and meticulous attention to detail, the highest standards of academic publishing were consistently upheld throughout the process.

In addition, I would like to express my utmost gratitude to the remarkable collection of authors and co-authors (the researchers and professors) who contributed their incredible effort, hard work, and thoughts to this book. Each chapter is the result of their laborious efforts, and it has been a privilege to work with such a distinguished collection of academics, professionals, and experts during this project. The content has been significantly increased due to the desire to engage with the complex topics discussed in this book, share the experiences among researchers and professors, and add significant insights. The diverse range of perspectives and experiences presented across the chapters illustrates the expansive and international character of organizations' privacy and security management practices.

I am sincerely grateful for the contributions that collaborators have made. The dedication anyone has to making this work a true masterpiece, and their enthusiasm for the subject matter, are evident on every page.

Chapter 1
The Essentials of Privacy and Cybersecurity in the Digital Economy

Parichat Jaipong
https://orcid.org/0000-0002-9249-3169
Manipal GlobalNxt University, Malaysia

Watthanasakon Rakpathum
https://orcid.org/0009-0002-0118-043X
Navamindradhiraj University, Thailand

ABSTRACT

This chapter covers the digital economy, privacy, and cybersecurity. Cyberprotection, privacy, and data security address computer infections and cyberattacks. This study is a review article based on scholarly papers from valid sources, including Google Scholar, Scopus, and Web of Science (WOS), from 2020 to 2024. The findings show that digital privacy safeguards consumer data. Personal data, communication, and behavior are safe online. Shows internet data privacy rules. The data-driven society needs digital privacy. Digital platforms create vast amounts of personal data that could be misused, including financial and health records. Data theft is prevented via digital privacy. For democracy, we need digital privacy. Diverse viewpoints survive without manipulation. Digital privacy rules enhance customer trust and business reputation, enabling companies to compete more effectively.

DOI: 10.4018/979-8-3693-9720-6.ch001

1. INTRODUCTION

The rapid growth of technology in the 21st century has significantly transformed the global economy, leading to the emergence of the digital economy. This paradigm shift involves incorporating digital technologies in diverse economic activities, transforming business operations, governmental functions, and individual interactions. Over the last twenty-five years, numerous scientific publications have explored various aspects of the digital economy, aiming to comprehend its ramifications, dynamics, and the broader socio-economic transformations it has triggered. This review examines the notable scientific contributions from 2000 to 2024, interpreting the results and offering conclusions that enhance our understanding of this revolutionary phenomenon (Mihus & Gupta, 2023). The rapid advancement and broadening application of digital technology in the industry have increasingly brought cybersecurity concerns to the public's attention. Protecting the confidentiality and integrity of corporate data, safeguarding against unauthorized cyberattacks, and optimizing the effectiveness of cybersecurity insurance applications have emerged as critical concerns for organizations (Guo, 2023). Amid economic globalization, the digital economy has seen substantial growth. The digital economy is experiencing exponential growth, primarily in emerging countries. The Information Technology (IT) sector, which delivers essential digital services and products, is a fundamental anchor of the digital economy. The digital economy is characterized by economic output that is predominantly derived from digital technology, with business models centered on digital services and goods (Williams, 2021). The digital economy is emerging as a rapidly progressing sector, as evidenced by projections of double-digit annual growth rates worldwide. Political and economic issues influence this tendency to develop. Nonetheless, these characteristics originate from technical innovation, which is influenced by broader forces. This group of technologies encompasses digital affordances—actions that an organization or individual can undertake based on digital systems within their operational ecosystem. Datafication enhances the understanding of information retention, while digitization transforms all data value chains from traditional to digital formats. Virtualization involves the physical disassembly of processes, and generalization applies technologies and datasets in a manner not organized by origin through recombination and reprogramming (Williams, 2021).

The ramifications of any endeavor are outcomes of varying scales and the extent of implications. Widespread dispersion, the integration of developing nations, and the growing scope of implications are driving the rapid advancement of digitalized technology, significantly impacting the digital economy. One can understand the consequences as a disruption of current economic processes, sectors, and systems that influence contemporary user habits, organizational partnerships, and organizational structures. Thus, new economic systems, processes, and sectors emerge (Williams,

2021). For example, social interactions and transactional data drive financial markets, thereby accelerating the rapid advancement of developing technologies to align with supply and demand trends. In a domestic context, disseminating digital media (videos, music, images, and documents) through messaging platforms serves to augment disciplines such as information technology, sports, social sciences, education, and health. For instance, Internet of Things (IoT) devices facilitate the instantaneous and efficient transfer of data globally through the Internet of Everything (IoE) via cloud technology. In an industrial setting, smart sensors, application programming interfaces (APIs), and IoT networks enable remote work across global digital boundaries (Wylde et al., 2022). Businesses are hastening their digital transformation initiatives due to significant advantages. Cybersecurity has become a substantial concern for corporations, and to ensure business continuity, organizations must secure their digital transformation tools and assets. Consequently, enterprises implementing digital transformation must emphasize cybersecurity measures and guarantee the security of their systems against potential threats (Moller, 2020). Enterprises must ensure the protection of technical solutions against digital attacks, as cybercriminals may exploit flaws in digital technologies. Implementing encryption, authentication, and access control mechanisms can achieve cybersecurity by protecting data and networks from unauthorized access or hostile actions. Furthermore, enterprises should consider investing in cyber insurance policies that provide financial protection against losses resulting from a successful cyberattack on their networks. Another crucial issue is enhancing employees' understanding of cybersecurity assaults, as increased awareness leads to more reliable information security practices. Cyberattacks have increased significantly; therefore, companies must understand cybersecurity threats and the most effective strategies for comprehensive mitigation. These attacks typically aim to compromise, modify, or destroy sensitive information, extort financial gains from users, or disrupt standard corporate operations. Cybersecurity encompasses methods to protect computers and networks from unauthorized access and malicious actions, including data theft and destruction (Saeed, 2023). The necessity to protect consumers from the exploitation of their personal information, particularly in light of instances of illicit sale and acquisition of consumer data by FinTech applications, has influenced the global framework of data privacy legislation (Sinaga, 2021). This has led to the implementation of rigorous data protection legislation across multiple jurisdictions, designed to safeguard consumer rights to privacy, security, and safety in the digital economy (Stevani & Sudirman, 2021).

2. LITERATURE REVIEW

2.1 Digital Economy

The progression of the digital economy commences with the advancement of digital technologies. Scientific papers from the early 2000s emphasized the introduction and adoption of fundamental technologies, including the Internet, mobile devices, and the nascent phases of data analytics. These studies frequently examined the influence of these technologies on corporate operations, communication, and the rise of e-commerce. Over the years, the discourse evolved to encompass more sophisticated technologies, such as artificial intelligence (AI), blockchain, and the Internet of Things (IoT) (Mihus & Gupta, 2023). There are evolving definitions of the digital economy, as Jordan and Ellen (2009) assert that digital economies pose both threats and opportunities for development in the era of business intelligence (BI). Certain studies modify interpretations, such as recognizing digital economies outside intricate frameworks or understanding them as a "minimum concept," primarily as a method of execution. However, the majority of the research provides interpretations, some of which present contemporary definitions in a straightforward and unpretentious manner, such as "an economy characterized by digital initiatives." Definitions typically serve as a foundation and reflection of the movements and eras from which they emerge. The encompassed initiatives illustrate this. Preliminary definitions emphasize the internet, highlighting its emergence in the early 1990s as a significant facet of technical advancement inside the economy, notably in the Global North. Subsequent meanings incorporate innovative technologies, such as sensor networks, mobile networks, extensive data, and cloud computing. Alternatively, they focus on a broad view of digital activities, relying on simplistic concepts. We can visualize the historical foundation within the parameters of the definitions (Williams, 2021).

The phrase "digital economy" primarily refers to the recent and largely unfulfilled transformations across various economic sectors resulting from the digitalization of computer-assisted data. Therefore, the writers underscored the importance of considering factors beyond fundamental information ideologies. The digitalized economy evaluated and incorporated the web's capacity to facilitate business transactions. Writers and editors have integrated e-commerce into the digital economy, particularly during the internet boom. The definitions are categorized into elements based on the identification of four segments within digital economies: "Significantly digital services and goods: This category encompasses goods that can be delivered digitally and services where substantial portions are provided in a digital format, such as software sales, internet data services, hybrid digitalized services and goods, and online education, among others (Williams, 2021).

These are the primary prospects for the continued advancement of digital technologies.

1. Ongoing Integration of AI: The evolution of digital technology indicates an increased incorporation of artificial intelligence across multiple sectors. We expect artificial intelligence to help automate tasks, improve decision-making processes, and promote creativity.
2. The deployment of 5G technology will transform connections by facilitating accelerated data transfer, reducing latency, and promoting the extensive adoption of IoT devices. This will have a significant impact on sectors such as healthcare, transportation, and smart cities.
3. The potential applications of blockchain technology extend beyond cryptocurrency. Industries such as supply chain management, healthcare, and identity verification are exploring blockchain technology to enhance security, transparency, and efficiency.
4. Ethical and Regulatory Considerations: As digital technology becomes more prevalent, there is a growing emphasis on ethical considerations and regulatory frameworks. Conversations regarding data privacy, cybersecurity, and ethical AI are becoming increasingly significant.
5. Sustainability in Digital Innovation: We expect future digital advancements to prioritize sustainable methods. Initiatives aimed at mitigating technology's environmental impact, alongside green computing efforts, will influence the advancement of digital technologies during a period of increased environmental consciousness.

Digital commerce processes have facilitated the shift from traditional economic activities through three phases: pre-transaction, in-transaction, and post-transaction activities (Gopal et al., 2003). Numerous factors in industrialized nations have influenced the transaction costs at each level. Initially, consumers must acquire information regarding the maker of the products or commodities they intend to purchase for their market transactions. Whether influenced by relatives, friends, or social media, consumers bear the expense of pre-transaction research. In the digital economy, pre-transaction search costs have significantly diminished. Consumers can identify suitable manufacturers, retailers, and products online via the search engines available at their homes, rather than having to venture out themselves. Moreover, intelligent agent software assists users in product searches and pricing comparisons, enabling them to purchase more affordable and superior goods. Additionally, numerous online platforms offer product and commodity information, decreasing the costs for online purchasers seeking specific items (Kehal & Singh, 2005). This phenomenon is also becoming increasingly prevalent in Asian countries. Secondly, throughout the trade process, merchants may utilize extensive information about customers and their purchasing habits, whereas consumers may only negotiate with sellers based on the prices they display. This incurs bargaining expenses. In the digital economy, the competitive nature of online price comparisons complicates enterprises' ability to differentiate, thereby reducing negotiating costs in e-commerce. Consumers simply need to select the desired products, provide their personal information, and complete the ordering process. Third, the execution of transactions necessitates delivery and after-sales service, resulting in post-transaction expenses. The digital economy now categorizes computer software, e-books, digital newspapers, films, MP3 music, and other digital content as digital commodities. The ability to transfer them directly via a network is their most notable characteristic. Consequently, consumers can circumvent transaction expenses associated with shipping fees, a significant consequence of digitalization and a prevalent characteristic of global business today. Even though the traditional economy has evolved, economic activity still involves transaction expenses. An economy devoid of friction represents an ideal condition akin to the concept of perfect competition in economic theory. Although improvements in ICTs have reduced traditional transaction costs, problems persist. These include the costs of protecting intellectual property rights, network congestion, and cultural and regulatory issues that have become more important because of differences between regions (Li et al., 2019).

2.2 Cybersecurity

Numerous domestic and international firms have been enhancing their internal digitalization initiatives in recent years to establish a comprehensive, efficient, automated, and modernized system that aligns with contemporary development trends (Guo, 2023). The implementation of cybersecurity features enhances the efficient administration of Internet hardware and software operations, physical interfaces, and internal policy formulation. Network communication protocols, data access control, and cryptography (such as password encryption) are all facilitated by the ISO 27001 management system. These enhance secure communication methods, such as training for cybersecurity staff, and reduce the risk of network communication attacks from malicious actors (Rawindaran et al., 2021).

Methodologies utilize specific algorithms and analytical techniques on vast amounts of public, private, and sensitive data transmitted over digital networks to derive value from the vast quantity, variety, and accuracy of available data. This dramatically increases the risk of data breaches, viruses, and cyberattacks. Utilizing these technologies effectively to collect and process data from both public and private sectors, along with implementing practical user safety measures, may reveal issues and vulnerabilities that could increase the likelihood of individuals or groups becoming victims of cybercrime (Wylde et al., 2022).

A heightened focus on cybersecurity and the creation of digital trust has paralleled the expansion of the digital economy. Research articles examined the dynamic characteristics of cyber threats, the role of encryption, and the importance of establishing trust in online transactions. The evolution of cybersecurity and digital trust comprises four primary stages. The initial phase pertains to the emergence of cybersecurity challenges. In the early 2000s, cybersecurity research focused on understanding the fundamental threats and vulnerabilities within the emerging digital environment. Foundational studies, such as "Cybersecurity Threats: A Comprehensive Analysis" (2004), systematically evaluated common risks, including malware and network vulnerabilities. These initial efforts established the foundation for acknowledging the complex nature of cyber threats and the necessity for strong defense strategies. Dinev and Hart's research (2006) examined the elements affecting individuals' cybersecurity awareness, offering insights into the human aspect of cybersecurity. Understanding user behavior and perspectives is crucial for developing effective security solutions. The Evolution of Cyber Threats and Countermeasures The onset of the 2010s marked a new phase of cyber threats distinguished by heightened complexity, persistence, and the capacity for significant economic and societal consequences. As malevolent entities advanced their strategies, techniques, and processes, cybersecurity researchers and practitioners undertook a mission to comprehend, assess, and counter these emerging dangers. Axelsson's (2013) research investigated the utilization of machine learning in cybersecurity for anomaly detection. The findings underscored the capability of AI-driven methodologies to improve threat detection and response. Additional studies, including Alperovitch's (2011) study on Advanced Persistent Threats (APTs), highlight the covert and enduring characteristics of cyber threats. The results underscored the need for adaptive cybersecurity methods to combat sophisticated and targeted attacks. The third stage involves the emergence of cloud security and privacy concerns. The introduction of cloud computing marked a transformative shift in information technology, enabling enterprises to leverage scalable and adaptable infrastructure. This transition presented several challenges, primarily due to the security and privacy issues associated with entrusting sensitive data to cloud service providers. Literature, particularly Rittinghouse and Ransome's work (2016), supports this transition by examining the development of comprehensive security frameworks for cloud systems. The results underscored the necessity for stringent security protocols to safeguard data in the cloud. Finally, cybersecurity in the era of IoT and 5G: The convergence of the Internet of Things (IoT) with fifth-generation (5G) technology has ushered in a period of unprecedented connectedness and technological advancement. This overview encapsulates the complexities of safeguarding a high-speed, linked digital ecosystem, highlighting the difficulties, opportunities, and emerging techniques involved. Ghosh et al. (2021) examined the security ramifications of 5G networks. The findings emphasized the necessity for adaptive security architectures to mitigate the expanded attack surface resulting from the extensive implementation of 5G. Roman et al. (2013) conducted research that examined the distinct security concerns presented by the Internet of Things (IoT). The results underscored the necessity of safeguarding the networked devices that form the IoT ecosystem.

The principal developmental trends in cybersecurity and digital trust are:

1. The initial decade saw the transformation of the cyber threat landscape, characterized by the emergence of viruses, worms, and rudimentary malware. Cybersecurity emphasized conventional strategies, such as antivirus software and firewalls, throughout this period. The focus was on safeguarding individual devices against identified risks.
2. The second phase (2010-2015) was characterized by the emergence of sophisticated threats, particularly Advanced Persistent Threats (APTs), which targeted specific entities over an extended period. Cybersecurity solutions have been developed to identify and counter sophisticated threats. Proactive threat intelligence and behavioral analytics have become increasingly prominent methods for combating persistent and covert attacks.
3. The growth of cloud services from 2015 to 2020 gave rise to new security challenges and heightened concerns about data privacy. Cybersecurity strategies are specifically designed to protect data in cloud environments. Technologies that preserve privacy and robust security mechanisms are crucial for safeguarding digital assets in shared and distributed cloud environments.
4. The integration of Internet of Things (IoT) devices and the deployment of 5G networks from 2020 to 2024 have broadened the attack surface, presenting new security challenges. Ensuring the security of networked devices and mitigating the security ramifications of 5G networks has become imperative. Adaptive security architectures were necessary to manage the difficulties arising from the proliferation of connected devices and the accelerated pace of communication.
5. The Zero Trust security model and the projection of future threat landscapes (2020-2024) have characterized current trends. Cybersecurity strategies have transitioned to a zero-trust model, prioritizing continuous verification and the tenet of "never trust, always verify." Given the fluid and developing characteristics of cyber threats, proactive methodologies for addressing future threat environments have become essential.

Countermeasures in this domain invariably accompany emerging technologies designed to enhance cybersecurity and mitigate the impact of cyberattacks. Understanding these adversaries and conducting further research will help reduce or at least control the frequency of attacks.

Exist in any digital realm and environment from now on. Identifying funding deficiencies that the government can address to support SMEs through grants, subsidies, and similar financial assistance via diverse public sector policies is a crucial avenue to explore. All SME management and their personnel must possess awareness and training to understand both fundamental and potentially sophisticated aspects of cybersecurity (Wylde et al., 2022). Publications, such as Forrester Research's examination of the Zero Trust security model (2010), introduced a paradigm shift in cybersecurity. The results underscored the necessity of ongoing verification and the philosophy of "never trust, always verify" as fundamental to contemporary cybersecurity efforts. Choo et al. (2023) investigated future danger landscapes and emerging issues. The results underscored the evolving nature of cybersecurity threats requiring proactive and anticipatory cybersecurity strategies. Cybersecurity expenditures and cybercrimes are demonstrating a rising trend worldwide (Sharif, 2022). Haislip et al. (2019) highlighted the undervaluation of the economic impact of cybersecurity breaches, which extend beyond the immediate target and affect the relevant business through diminished returns and increased insurance expenses. Garg (2021) identified seven key advantages of investing in cybersecurity, encouraging firms to allocate resources toward cybersecurity initiatives. This encompasses safeguarding intellectual property, effectively addressing customer needs, reducing customer attrition, branding secure products, collaborating with secure providers within an integrated network, enhancing business reputation, and mitigating collateral damage within the industry. Lee (2021) introduced a risk management approach that emphasizes the ongoing enhancement of cybersecurity procedures and the cost-benefit analysis of cybersecurity investments. Numerous firms utilize the National Institute for Standards and Technology (NIST) Cybersecurity Framework for managing cybersecurity risks; however, the standard lacks a comprehensive cost-benefit analysis. Gordon et al. (2020) introduced the Gordon-Loeb model to identify the most successful NIST tier for a specific organization based on a cost-benefit analysis. Krutilla et al. (2021) refined the Gordon-Loeb model by incorporating the depreciation cost of cybersecurity assets, thereby influencing the cost-benefit analysis of cybersecurity projects. Simon and Omar (2020) emphasized that cybersecurity threats can impact organizations through attacks on their supply chain partners, thereby requiring cybersecurity investments to account for both coordinated and uncoordinated assaults. Uddin et al. (2020) emphasized that cybersecurity vulnerabilities harm organizational growth and performance, particularly in the banking industry, where operational risks have increased due to cyber threats. Curti et al. (2023) emphasized that cybersecurity attacks are escalating within the governmental sector, prompting governments to increase operational expenditures and total financial costs to mitigate these risks.

2.3 Data Privacy

The swift advancement of information technology, particularly within the financial services industry, where financial technology (FinTech) applications have gained prominence, has profoundly impacted the global evolution of data privacy legislation (Sinaga, 2021). The emergence of FinTech, characterized by the digitalization of financial services, including online payments, wealth management, insurance, and peer-to-peer lending, has prompted a reassessment of current legal frameworks to address new challenges related to data protection and privacy (Stevani & Sudirman, 2021). The recognition of the crucial role data plays in the FinTech sector, acting as both a driver for innovation and growth and a pathway for cybersecurity threats and privacy violations, has driven the development of this legislation. Dorfleitner, Hornuf, and Kreppmeier (2023) have developed a regulatory framework for data privacy to promote technological advancement and protect individual privacy rights. The ISO 27001 framework operates in combination with the General Data Protection Regulation (GDPR) Regulation (EU) 2016/679 and the Data Protection Act 2018 c. 12 (DPA) in enabling personal data governance and protocols throughout the digital jurisdictions of the UK and European Union (EU). When processing medical data, we conduct a compulsory Data Protection Impact Assessment (DPIA) to identify and evaluate risks. We adhere to eight fundamental principles, which include lawful and ethical data acquisition methods, data storage security and retention duration, equitable use, and the requirement to maintain data within designated locations and regions (Wylde et al., 2022). Implementing these legal frameworks and management systems could lead to the use of illegal tracking tools, such as 'cookies,' that employ AI, ML, and algorithmic analysis. This could make users unaware of the tracking functionalities and capabilities incorporated into the software for analytical and marketing purposes. Suppose users do not agree to be aware of and keep essential cookies for web navigation. In that case, business networks may be vulnerable to anti-forensic techniques, legal jurisdiction issues, system hardware failures, and Service Level Agreement (SLA) breaches. These problems can accumulate over time, making it more challenging to utilize IoT devices safely, legally, and in compliance with business requirements. In healthcare services, a supply chain policy that utilizes cryptography as a cybersecurity control mechanism provides the public, financial markets, business professionals, and legal representatives with transparency, agency protection, and accountability. This makes it easier for the directorate or client to take legal and clear actions or investigations. When applied retrospectively, this method ensures accountability for maintaining vigilance and resilience in cyberspace management. It emphasizes an operator's duty of care regarding confidential data breaches, their dissemination, and the consequences of exposing extensive confidential National Health Service (NHS) patient data (Balasubramanian et al., 2022).

In a global context, is it feasible to ethically and accurately gather data, including without consent, while ensuring clarity for successful data collection, resource allocation, and deployment strategies? A crucial aspect of the answer involves fostering public trust in technologies and advancing research on worldwide deployment tactics. This entails a comprehensive and ongoing evaluation of legal frameworks and outcomes among firms, organizations, and institutions for a long-term data privacy strategy. Strategies also encompass fostering confidence among groups and individuals over the integrity of their data in the cloud. Facilitating users' confident engagement through education and interaction with diverse groups and mental health issues is an excellent method for providing collective assurances. Data protection concepts and public engagement techniques varied substantially across various countries. To anticipate potential disasters or pandemics, accountability via public participation could facilitate the restoration of national and international trust. This development reflects a broader trend toward the global standardization of data privacy regulations, profoundly influenced by crucial legislative frameworks such as the European Union's General Data Protection Regulation (GDPR). Global benchmarks have established a foundation for comprehensive data protection legislation addressing the complexities of the contemporary digital landscape, including issues related to transnational data transfers, consent management, and the rights of data subjects (Dorfleitner, Hornuf, & Kreppmeier, 2023). The impact of these evolving data privacy laws on the FinTech sector has been profound, introducing challenges and opportunities. On the one hand, compliance with diverse and sometimes conflicting regulatory requirements across jurisdictions poses significant operational and financial burdens on FinTech companies. On the other hand, adherence to robust data protection standards can enhance consumer trust and competitiveness in the global market (Sinaga, 2021). We also need to design and promote a flexible global strategy that encompasses technical solutions, operational resource strategies, and policy development. This would enhance data protection objectives, build trust in government-monitored apps among the population, and ultimately provide a successful and robust global protection strategy (Wylde et al., 2022). Research by Dwork and Roth (2014) investigating privacy-preserving technologies addressed growing concerns about data privacy. The results contributed insights into cryptographic techniques and privacy-enhancing technologies. The potentially catastrophic occurrences of data sharing and criminality undermine the confidentiality and protections established by governments, businesses, and organizations. This leads to legal and ethical conflicts that can have substantial financial consequences, disrupting extensive business data architectures, infrastructures, networks, and services. Consequently, as society increasingly relies on the exchange and processing of personally identifiable information (PII) through the Internet of Things (IoT), trust in reputable institutions and government organizations, including broadcast and digital media outlets, becomes a central issue. When a user chooses to share social network, personal, and confidential information while shopping online, for example, they should be aware of the nature and intent of cybercriminality and have faith in the criminal justice system of the given territory (Wylde et al., 2022).

The global development of data privacy legislation marks a pivotal response to the challenges and opportunities presented by the digital transformation of financial services. With FinTech reshaping the economic landscape, crafting legal structures that safeguard personal information while fostering innovation is a crucial concern for lawmakers, regulatory bodies, and industry participants (Dorfleitner, Hornuf, & Kreppmeier, 2023). Moreover, the dynamic nature of the FinTech industry, characterized by rapid innovation and the continuous introduction of new technologies, requires that data privacy laws evolve in response to emerging threats and opportunities. This has led to ongoing legal and regulatory developments to ensure that data privacy protections remain adequate and relevant in the face of technological change (Stevani & Sudirman, 2021). The intersection of data privacy laws and financial technology (FinTech) companies is a critical area of focus in the digital age, where the rapid evolution of technology and the increasing reliance on big data and artificial intelligence (AI) have raised significant ethical and privacy concerns. FinTech companies, which leverage technology to offer innovative financial services, are at the forefront of this intersection, navigating the complex landscape of global data privacy regulations while striving to maintain customer trust and comply with legal standards. The ethical considerations at this junction include issues related to bias, discrimination, privacy, transparency, justice, ownership, and control of data. These concerns underscore the necessity for FinTech companies to implement measures that safeguard customer data against misuse and ensure compliance with data protection laws (Aldboush & Ferdous, 2023). The implementation of encryption techniques, transparent data collection and usage policies, customer opt-out options, and staff training on data protection are practical measures that companies can take to address these ethical considerations. The legal framework surrounding online financial transactions, particularly those facilitated by FinTech platforms, further complicates this intersection. The validity of online loan agreements, for instance, hinges on compliance with specific legal requirements, such as those outlined in the Civil Code and information technology laws, which govern electronic signatures and documents (Pradnyawati, Sukandia & Arini, 2021). Legal protections for creditors and consumers in the FinTech space must, therefore, encompass both preventive and repressive measures to ensure fair and secure online financial transactions. In navigating the intersection of data privacy laws and FinTech, companies must therefore engage in a continuous process of adaptation and innovation. This involves not only adhering to existing legal standards but also anticipating future regulatory developments and societal expectations regarding data privacy and ethical considerations. The goal is to build and maintain trust among consumers and stakeholders by demonstrating a commitment to ethical practices, transparency, and privacy protection in the digital financial ecosystem. Many constitutions, legislative documents, and international treaties emphasize the importance of privacy and data protection, which FinTech companies must consider to maintain the integrity of the financial system (Adeyoju, 2020). This regulatory environment is characterized by a patchwork of laws that vary significantly across jurisdictions, presenting a challenge for FinTech firms operating globally.

The strategic use of data has revolutionized financial technology (FinTech), bringing about a significant shift in the delivery and consumption of financial services. Data, serving as the lifeblood of the FinTech ecosystem, underpins the operational, strategic, and innovative facets of this dynamic sector. We cannot overstate the importance of data in FinTech, as it drives decision-making, enhances customer experiences, and fosters the development of new financial products and services. Security and trust form the cornerstone of the FinTech industry, with companies relying heavily on robust cybersecurity measures to protect sensitive financial information. Adopting Security Information and Event Management (SIEM) systems exemplifies the sector's commitment to safeguarding financial data against potential breaches, thereby maintaining the trust of customers who entrust FinTech firms with their personal and financial details (Jangampeta, 2022). This trust is crucial, as any failure in data security could undermine the foundation of customer confidence that FinTech companies heavily rely on. One of the primary challenges is the diversity and complexity of data privacy regulations across different jurisdictions. FinTech companies often operate globally, requiring them to comply with many laws that can vary significantly from one region to another. This regulatory fragmentation poses a significant operational burden, as companies must ensure their services comply with the regulations of all markets they serve. For example, the General Data Protection Regulation (GDPR) in the European Union establishes a high standard for data protection, with strict requirements for data processing and obtaining consumer consent. Adhering to such standards while maintaining the agility and innovation that characterize FinTech is daunting (Aldboush & Ferdous, 2023). Moreover, the dynamic nature of technology and regulation requires FinTech companies to remain vigilant and adaptable. New technologies can introduce unforeseen privacy concerns while regulatory landscapes evolve in response to emerging risks and societal expectations. This constant state of flux challenges FinTech firms to be proactive in their compliance efforts, often necessitating significant investments in legal expertise and data security infrastructure. The ethical considerations surrounding data use in FinTech further complicate compliance efforts. Issues of bias, discrimination, and transparency in AI-driven financial services underscore the need for ethical frameworks that extend beyond mere legal compliance. FinTech companies must navigate these ethical dilemmas to build trust with consumers and stakeholders, ensuring that their data use aligns with broader societal values (Aldboush & Ferdous, 2023). The opportunities created by data privacy laws for FinTech companies extend beyond compliance and trust-building. These regulations encourage the adoption of innovative technologies and practices that prioritize data security and ethical considerations. By aligning their operations with these legal standards, FinTech firms position themselves to spearhead the development of new financial products and services that cater to the evolving needs of digital consumers. Furthermore, the global nature of FinTech and the diversity of data privacy regulations across jurisdictions necessitate a more holistic approach to data protection for companies. This global perspective facilitates compliance and enables FinTech firms to cater to a broader audience, enhancing their competitiveness in the international market. Data privacy laws provide a framework within which FinTech companies can innovate responsibly, ensuring that their services are efficient, user-friendly, secure, and trustworthy. As the digital economy continues to grow, the relationship between FinTech and data privacy laws will undoubtedly evolve, offering new opportunities for companies to differentiate themselves through their commitment to protecting consumer data (Oyewole et al., 2024).

3. MATERIALS AND METHODS

A narrative synthesis was used in this systematic review. Narrative synthesis involves conducting a systematic review and synthesis of findings from multiple studies, relying heavily on words and text to summarize and explain the results (Limna, 2022). In this review, a narrative synthesis and a systematic literature review were conducted to identify cybersecurity and data privacy models through the documentary method and content analysis. The literature and data were obtained from the EBSCO, Google Scholar, Scopus, Web of Science, and ScienceDirect databases, all of which are published in English. They were peer-reviewed using purposive sampling, with data collection taking place between November 15th, 2024, and January 18th, 2025.

The chapter content was reviewed for reliability and validity by three experts, as recommended by Siripipatthanakul (2011). This article has been checked for plagiarism, with a percentage of less than 15%, following the studies by Siripipatthanakul (a, b, c; 2025) and Siripipatthanakul and Siripipattanakul (2025). The findings indicate that plagiarism accounts for approximately 2% and grammatical errors for 93%, as determined using Grammarly, by the recommendation of Phuangsuwan et al. (2025).

4. RESULTS

Numerous emerging trends and technologies are shaping the future of AI in cybersecurity while also addressing privacy concerns. A significant trend is the advancement of privacy-preserving machine learning methodologies. Researchers are exploring innovative approaches, such as secure multi-party computation (SMPC) and advanced homomorphic encryption algorithms, which enable work to be performed on encrypted data while maintaining privacy (Chen et al., 2021; Gentry, 2009). These technologies aim to enhance security while minimizing the exposure of confidential information. People have traditionally used signature-based detection to keep computers safe, which compares data to known attack patterns or signatures (Santos, 2020). This method has proven efficient against recognized dangers but encounters difficulties with novel, unidentified threats. Moreover, we have employed rule-based algorithms and heuristics to detect suspicious behaviors and potential vulnerabilities. These methodologies utilize established principles and patterns to identify anomalies in typical behavior. Nevertheless, conventional approaches encounter considerable obstacles. A significant drawback is their incapacity to identify zero-day attacks that exploit undiscovered vulnerabilities (Zhao et al., 2021). While signature-based systems are effective, they rely solely on the quality of their signatures. The system might not detect a new threat if it doesn't match any existing signatures. Moreover, conventional techniques often yield numerous false positives, leading to alert fatigue and reduced efficiency. Traditional systems are becoming increasingly ineffective at addressing the evolving threat landscape, as cyber threats are constantly evolving and more sophisticated methods of attack are being developed.

Figure 1. Grammarly for plagiarism checking

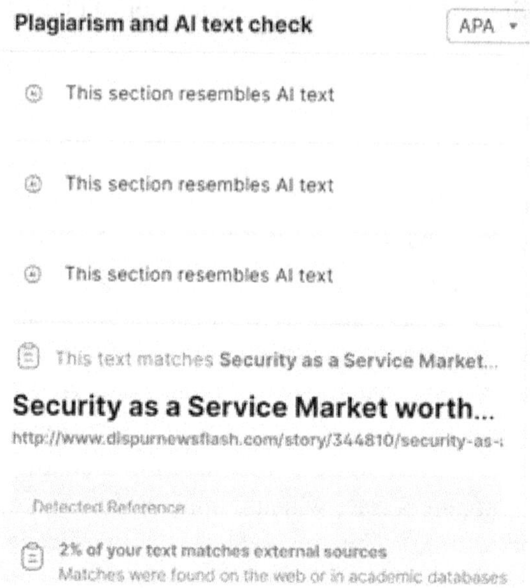

5. DISCUSSIONS

5.1 Influence of Artificial Intelligence (AI) on Data Privacy

Deep learning Artificial intelligence systems frequently depend on extensive datasets to operate efficiently. These systems collect data from diverse sources, encompassing human interactions, transactional records, and sensor inputs. Machine learning models trained on extensive datasets can analyze user behavior patterns to deliver personalized suggestions or identify abnormalities (Binns, 2018). Deep learning methods require a substantial amount of labeled data to train complex neural networks, which are essential for tasks such as image recognition and natural language processing. Site scraping, data aggregation, and direct user submissions are the standard data collection methods. AI systems frequently consolidate data from several sources to enhance precision and resilience (Zuboff, 2019). A recommendation system may integrate browsing history with demographic information to customize suggestions. This data-centric strategy enhances the performance of AI systems, but it also presents significant privacy risks, particularly regarding personal and sensitive information. Incorporating AI and deep learning into diverse applications presents multiple privacy threats. A primary issue is the risk of data breaches and unauthorized access to confidential information (Solove, 2021). Due to their complexity, deep learning models often utilize extensive datasets, making them attractive targets for attacks. If attackers gain access to these databases, they may recover personal information or reconstruct sensitive data previously believed to be anonymized (Shokri et al., 2017). A further issue pertains to data aggregation and profiling. Artificial intelligence algorithms can generate comprehensive profiles of individuals by combining data from multiple sources. This may improve user experience, but it also heightens the potential for intrusive profiling and surveillance (O'Flaherty, 2021). For example, a corporation may employ AI to analyze user behavior across multiple platforms, yielding comprehensive insights into an individual's habits, interests, and potentially sensitive data. Furthermore, AI systems often rely on extensive data collection for training, which raises concerns about consent and transparency (Tufekci, 2018). Users may be unaware of the data collection and utilization methods, which can result in potential privacy infringements.

5.2 Regulatory Compliance

In response to growing concerns about data privacy, numerous policies have been introduced to regulate the use of personal data by AI systems. The General Data Protection Regulation (GDPR), enacted by the European Union in 2018, is among the most extensive data protection laws. The GDPR requires enterprises to secure explicit consent from individuals before collecting or processing their data. It also confers individuals the right to access personal data, request amendments, and demand its eradication (European Parliament & Council of the European Union, 2016). The California Consumer Privacy Act (CCPA), effective as of January 2020, provides comparable safeguards for California residents. It enables consumers to ascertain the personal information being gathered, request its removal, and opt out of the sale of their data (California Legislative Information, 2018). Both the GDPR and the CCPA prioritize openness, data minimization, and accountability, mandating that enterprises adopt procedures for safeguarding personal data and ensuring compliance.

Another set of privacy rules is the Health Insurance Portability and Accountability Act (HIPAA) in the US, which protects the privacy of health information, and the Personal Information Protection and Electronic Documents Act (PIPEDA) in Canada, which sets rules for how personal data should be handled (U.S. Department of Health & Human Services, 2020; Government of Canada, 2018). These policies seek to mitigate privacy risks pertinent to various sectors and areas. Moreover, AI systems must navigate a complex legal framework to ensure compliance with privacy legislation. For example, the GDPR requires enterprises to conduct Data Protection Impact Assessments (DPIAs) before implementing AI systems that process substantial volumes of personal data. Data Protection Impact Assessments (DPIAs) help identify and mitigate privacy issues associated with data processing operations (Information Commissioner's Office, 2020). Additionally, AI systems must adhere to privacy-by-design principles, ensuring that data protection measures are integrated from the outset of the development process.

Furthermore, AI systems must provide functionalities that enable users to control their data preferences and assert their rights in accordance with these requirements (California Department of Justice, 2020). Compliance involves implementing robust security measures to protect data against unauthorized access and breaches. This encompasses encryption, access limits, and periodic security assessments. AI systems ought to implement data anonymization and pseudonymization methods to reduce the likelihood of re-identification (European Union Agency for Cybersecurity, 2023). In conclusion, while AI and deep learning have made substantial progress, they also pose significant challenges to privacy and data protection. Adherence to privacy legislation, such as GDPR and CCPA, is essential to address these challenges and ensure that AI systems are used responsibly and ethically.

5.3 Example of Successful Implementation

5.3.1 Google's Federated Learning Within Gboard

Google's Gboard keyboard utilizes federated learning to improve predictive text capabilities while protecting user privacy. Instead of transmitting users' typing data to Google's servers, federated learning enables users to train the model directly on their devices. The local models are regularly updated and consolidated, enabling Google to enhance the prediction algorithms without retrieving or retaining personal typing information. This method has significantly improved predictive text accuracy while maintaining strict data privacy standards (Hard et al., 2018).

5.3.2 Apple's Initiatives in Differential Privacy

Apple has employed differential privacy methods to improve user privacy in its iOS operating system. By integrating differential privacy into data-gathering methods, Apple guarantees that aggregate data insights are accessible without disclosing specific user information. For instance, Apple employs differential privacy to examine user activity patterns and enhance functionality, including emoji suggestions and app usage statistics, while safeguarding individual privacy (Apple, 2017).

5.3.3 Confidentiality-Safeguarding Health Data Examination

Strategies that preserve privacy are essential for analyzing sensitive patient data in the healthcare sector. An exemplary instance is the application of homomorphic encryption for the secure analysis of medical data. Researchers have utilized homomorphic encryption to do computations on encrypted health records, facilitating secure analysis of patient data while safeguarding sensitive information. This technology enables collaborative research and data sharing among healthcare professionals while ensuring patient privacy (Chen et al., 2021).

5.4 Advantages of Privacy Protection

5.4.1 Enhanced Privacy Protection

Differential privacy, federated learning, and homomorphic encryption are available privacy protection methods. These methods reduce the likelihood of data leakage or illegal access. Differential privacy protects each person's data contribution, federated learning reduces the risk of centralized data breaches, and homomorphic encryption enables calculations on encrypted data without requiring decryption.

5.4.2 Enabling Collaboration and Innovation

Privacy-enhancing technologies facilitate secure data sharing and collaboration among enterprises and research institutions. By safeguarding individual privacy, these methods foster collaboration in sectors such as healthcare and finance, allowing businesses to harness the benefits of AI while maintaining data confidentiality.

5.4.3 Adherence to Privacy Regulations

Employing privacy-preserving methodologies enables firms to adhere to regulations such as the GDPR and CCPA. Differential privacy, federated learning, and homomorphic encryption meet data protection and privacy regulations. This means that businesses can utilize AI technology while still complying with the law.

6. SUGGESTIONS

6.1 Foster Transparency and Accountability

Transparency and accountability must be fundamental to the creation and implementation of AI systems. Organizations must furnish explicit information regarding data-gathering methodologies, the application of AI algorithms, and the safeguards implemented to ensure privacy protection. Interacting with stakeholders and offering avenues for input and resolution helps foster confidence and mitigate worries (Solove, 2021).

6.2 Employ Privacy-Preserving Methodologies

To protect personal information when using deep learning for cybersecurity, companies should employ privacy-preserving methods such as federated learning, homomorphic encryption, and differential privacy. These methods prevent the leakage of private data during the training or deployment of AI models, adhering to privacy laws and best practices (Abadi et al., 2016; McMahan et al., 2017; Gentry, 2009).

6.3 Conduct Regular Privacy Impact Assessments

Regularly conducting privacy impact assessments (PIAs) is crucial for identifying potential privacy hazards associated with AI-driven cybersecurity solutions. The Information Commissioner's Office (ICO) states that PIAs enable the identification and resolution of privacy issues before new technologies are implemented, thereby ensuring that security protocols don't compromise individuals' privacy (ICO, 2020).

6.4 Allocate Resources to Research and Development

Investment in research and development is crucial for advancing privacy-preserving technology and striking a balance between security and privacy. Organizations must continually invest in research into novel solutions and collaborate with academic and industry partners to stay at the forefront of emerging technologies and best practices (Chen et al., 2021).

7. CONCLUSIONS

This chapter discusses cybersecurity, privacy, and the digital economy. Data security, privacy, and cyber defense address computer viruses and cyberattacks. This study is a review article that draws on reliable sources from academic publications published between 2020 and 2024, as indexed in Web of Science (WOS), Scopus, and Google Scholar. The results demonstrate that consumer data is protected by digital privacy. Online conversations, behaviors, and personal information are secure. Displays the regulations for internet data privacy. Digital privacy is essential in today's data-driven culture. Large volumes of personal data, including financial and medical records, are produced by digital platforms and may be exploited. Digital privacy prevents data theft. Digital privacy is essential to democracy. Different points of view endure without being manipulated. Regulations about digital privacy help businesses compete by enhancing consumer trust and company reputation.

The strategic application of data has revolutionized financial technology (FinTech), leading to a significant shift in the provision and utilization of financial services. Data, as the essential foundation of the FinTech ecosystem, supports the operational, strategic, and inventive aspects of this dynamic business. The significance of data in FinTech is paramount, as it informs decision-making, improves user experiences, and facilitates the creation of innovative financial products and services. Security and trust form the foundation of the FinTech sector, with firms relying heavily on stringent cybersecurity protocols to protect sensitive financial data.

Deep learning Artificial intelligence systems often rely on substantial datasets for optimal functionality. These systems aggregate data from several sources, including human interactions, transactional records, and sensor inputs. Machine learning models, developed using comprehensive datasets, can analyze user behavior patterns to provide personalized recommendations or identify anomalies. Deep learning techniques require a substantial amount of labeled data to train complex neural networks, which are essential for applications such as image recognition and natural language processing. Standard data collection methods include site scraping, data aggregation, and direct user submissions. AI systems often aggregate data from multiple sources to improve accuracy and robustness. A recommendation system may amalgamate browser history with demographic data to tailor suggestions. This data-driven approach enhances AI system performance, although it also poses significant privacy risks, particularly for personal and sensitive information. The integration of AI and deep learning into various applications poses numerous privacy risks. A principal concern is the threat of data breaches and illicit access to sensitive information. Due to their complexity, deep learning models often rely on large datasets, making them attractive targets for attacks. If attackers infiltrate these databases, they may get personal information or reconstruct sensitive material that was previously thought to be anonymized. Another concern is data aggregation and profiling. Artificial intelligence systems can create detailed profiles of individuals by integrating data from various sources. This may enhance user experience; nevertheless, it also increases the risk of intrusive profiling and surveillance. A firm may utilize AI to analyze user behavior across multiple platforms, generating extensive insights into an individual's habits, hobbies, and potentially sensitive information. Moreover, AI systems often rely on extensive data collection for training, which raises questions about consent and transparency. Users may lack awareness of data collection and usage practices, which can lead to privacy violations.

The following are the main developments in cybersecurity and digital trust:

1. The first decade saw the evolution of the cyber threat environment, characterized by the emergence of viruses, worms, and basic malware. Cybersecurity focused on traditional tactics, such as firewalls and antivirus software, during this time. Protecting individual gadgets from known hazards was the primary goal.
2. The emergence of sophisticated attacks, especially Advanced Persistent attacks (APTs), which targeted certain entities for an extended period, defined the second phase (2010-2015). Cybersecurity solutions have been developed to identify and prevent advanced attacks. Behavioral analytics and proactive threat intelligence have emerged as key strategies for thwarting persistent and stealthy attacks.
3. As cloud services expanded between 2015 and 2020, new security issues and data privacy concerns grew. Cybersecurity tactics are primarily designed to safeguard data in cloud environments. Strong security features and privacy-preserving technologies are crucial for safeguarding digital assets in distributed and shared cloud environments.
4. The deployment of 5G networks between 2020 and 2024, along with the integration of Internet of Things (IoT) devices, has expanded the attack surface and created new security issues. Protecting networked devices and managing the security implications of 5G networks is crucial. Adaptive security architectures were required to handle the challenges posed by the increase in connected devices and the rapid pace of communication.
5. The Zero Trust security model and the forecast of future threat landscapes (2020–2024) have defined current trends. A Zero-Trust approach has replaced previous cybersecurity techniques, emphasizing ongoing verification and the maxim “never trust, always verify.” Due to the dynamic and evolving nature of cyber threats, proactive approaches to future threat scenarios have become crucial.

Data privacy regulations offer FinTech businesses more than just compliance and trust-building opportunities. These rules promote the use of cutting-edge procedures and technology that prioritize data security and ethics. FinTech companies position themselves to lead the creation of new financial services and products that address the evolving demands of digital consumers by operating by these regulatory requirements. Furthermore, businesses are challenged to take a more comprehensive approach to data protection due to the global nature of FinTech and the variations in data privacy laws across jurisdictions. FinTech companies can serve a wider audience and comply more efficiently, thanks to this global perspective, making them more competitive in the global market. FinTech businesses can innovate responsibly within the framework provided by data privacy legislation, ensuring the effectiveness, usability, security, and reliability of their services. The relationship between FinTech and data privacy regulations will evolve as the digital economy expands, presenting new opportunities for businesses to differentiate themselves from the competition by securing customer data.

Digital technology drives economic growth in the digital economy, with a focus on digital services and goods. Global estimates of double-digit yearly growth suggest that the digital economy is expanding rapidly. Policy and economics affect this trend. These traits stem from technical innovation, which is impacted by more significant influences. This collection of technologies encompasses digital affordances—actions that an organization or individual can take using digital systems within their operational ecology. Digitization converts all data value chains to digital, whereas datafication improves information retention. Virtualization disassembles processes physically, and generalization recombines and reprograms technology and datasets without regard to order.

In an era where digital technologies drive economic growth and social progress, cybersecurity and privacy have become critical issues. In pursuing an inclusive digital economy, it is essential to ensure data privacy and cybersecurity for all, particularly for marginalized communities. These populations, often the most vulnerable, face distinct risks and challenges that necessitate specialized methods and solutions to safeguard them from digital threats. There is a significance of cybersecurity and privacy in promoting digital inclusion and outlining effective strategies to protect marginalized groups. The digital economy is fundamentally dependent on user trust and security. Cybersecurity, which encompasses strategies to protect digital systems, networks, and data from attacks, damage, and unauthorized access, is a crucial foundation of this trust. Privacy entails the protection of personal information and the assurance that individuals maintain authority over the collection, utilization, and dissemination of their data. The stakes are especially significant for marginalized communities, including low-income individuals, rural populations, and other vulnerable groups. These groups progressively utilize digital financial services, educational platforms, and health technology, rendering cybersecurity and privacy essential for their engagement in the digital economy. Facilitating the safe and confident use of digital technologies by these individuals is crucial for advancing digital inclusion and fostering equitable economic growth.

REFERENCES

Abadi, M., Chu, A., Goodfellow, I., McMahan, H. B., Mironov, I., Talwar, K., & Zhang, L. (2016, October). Deep learning with differential privacy. In *Proceedings of the 2016 ACM SIGSAC Conference on Computer and Communications Security* (pp. 308–318). DOI: 10.1145/2976749.2978318

Adeyoju, F. I. P. (2020). Financial Technology and Privacy: Evaluating the Approach to Consumer Data. *Available atSSRN* 3558810. https://doi.org/DOI: 10.2139/ssrn.3558810

Aldboush, H. H., & Ferdous, M. (2023). Building trust in fintech: An analysis of ethical and privacy considerations in the intersection of big data, ai, and customer trust. *International Journal of Financial Studies, 11*(3), 90. DOI: 10.3390/ijfs11030090

Alperovitch, D. (2011). *Revealed: Operation Shady RAT. McAfee Apple. Apple's approach to privacy.*

Axelsson, S. (2013). Intrusion detection systems: A survey and taxonomy. *Journal of Computer Networks*, *34*(4), 476–491.

Balasubramanian, R., Prakash, E., Khan, I., & Platts, J. (2021, May). Blockchain technology for healthcare. In *AMI 2021-The 5th Advances in Management and Innovation Conference 2021.*

Chen, X., Li, N., & Zhang, L. (2021). Privacy-preserving machine learning: A survey on techniques and applications. *IEEE Transactions on Knowledge and Data Engineering*, *33*(5), 1955–1971.

Choo, K. K. R., Liu, J., & Choo, R. (2023). A Comprehensive Review of Future Threat Landscapes in Cyberspace. *IEEE Transactions on Emerging Topics in Computing.*

Chukwunweike, J. N., Yussuf, M., Okusi, O., & Oluwatobi, T. (2024). The role of deep learning in ensuring privacy integrity and security: Applications in AI-driven cybersecurity solutions. *World Journal of Advanced Research and Reviews*, *23*(2), 2550.

Curti, F., Ivanov, I., Macchiavelli, M., & Zimmermann, T. (2023). City hall has been hacked! the financial costs of lax cybersecurity. SSRN *Electronic Journal.* DOI: 10.2139/ssrn.4465071

Dinev, T., & Hart, P. (2006). An extended privacy calculus model for e-commerce transactions. *Information Systems Research*, *17*(1), 61–80. DOI: 10.1287/isre.1060.0080

Dorfleitner, G., Hornuf, L., & Kreppmeier, J. (2023). Promise not fulfilled: FinTech, data privacy, and the GDPR. *Electronic Markets, 33*(1), 33. DOI: 10.1007/s12525-023-00622-x

Dwork, C., & Roth, A. (2014). The algorithmic foundations of differential privacy. Foundations and Trends® in Theoretical Computer Science, 9(3–4), 211-407.

European Parliament & Council of the European Union. (2016). *Regulation (EU) 2016/679 of the European Parliament and of the Council.*

Floridi, L., Cowls, J., Beltrametti, M., Chatila, R., Chazerand, P., Dignum, V., Luetge, C., Madelin, R., Pagallo, U., Rossi, F., Schafer, B., Valcke, P., & Vayena, E. (2018). AI4People—an ethical framework for a good AI society: Opportunities, risks, principles, and recommendations. *Minds and Machines, 28*(4), 689–707. DOI: 10.1007/s11023-018-9482-5 PMID: 30930541

Ghosh, A., Thomas, M., & Chakraborty, S. (2021). 5G and IoT security: Emerging threats and countermeasures. *Journal of Ambient Intelligence and Humanized Computing, 12*(5), 5033–5047.

Gopal, R. D., Ramesh, R., & Whinston, A. B. (2003). Microproducts in a digital economy: Trading small, gaining large. *International Journal of Electronic Commerce, 8*(2), 9–30. DOI: 10.1080/10864415.2003.11044292

Gordon, L. A., Loeb, M. P., & Zhou, L. (2020). Integrating cost–benefit analysis into the NIST Cybersecurity Framework via the Gordon–Loeb Model. *Journal of Cybersecurity, 6*(1), tyaa005.

Guo, Y. C. (2023). Development Opportunities, Challenges, and Strategies for Cybersecurity Insurance in the Digital Economy Era. *Global Economic Perspectives, 1*(3).

Haislip, J., Kolev, K., Pinsker, R., & Steffen, T. (2019, June). The economic cost of cybersecurity breaches: A broad-based analysis. In *Workshop on the economics of information security (WEIS)* (Vol. 1, p. 37).

Jangampeta, S. (2022). Financial data security and SIEM: Protecting Sensitive Financial Information in Banking and Fintech Systems. *Turkish Journal of Computer and Mathematics Education, 13*(2), 1185–1188. DOI: 10.61841/turcomat.v13i2.14414

Jordan, J., & Ellen, C. (2009). Business need, data and business intelligence. *Journal of Digital Asset Management, 5*(1), 10–20. DOI: 10.1057/dam.2008.53

Kehal, H. S., & Singh, V. P. (Eds.). (2005). *Digital Economy: impacts, influences, and challenges.* IGI Global. DOI: 10.4018/978-1-59140-363-0

Kindervag, J., & Balaouras, S. (2010). No more chewy centers: Introducing the zero trust model of information security. *Forestry Research*, *3*(1), 1–16.

Krutilla, K., Alexeev, A., Jardine, E., & Good, D. (2021). The benefits and costs of cybersecurity risk reduction: A dynamic extension of the Gordon and Loeb model. *Risk Analysis*, *41*(10), 1795–1808. DOI: 10.1111/risa.13713 PMID: 33586801

Lee, I. (2021). Cybersecurity: Risk management framework and investment cost analysis. *Business Horizons*, *64*(5), 659–671. DOI: 10.1016/j.bushor.2021.02.022

Li, K., Kim, D. J., Lang, K. R., Kauffman, R. J., & Naldi, M. (2020). How should we understand the digital economy in Asia? Critical assessment and research agenda. *Electronic Commerce Research and Applications*, *44*, 101004. DOI: 10.1016/j.elerap.2020.101004 PMID: 32922241

Li, Z., Lu, Q., Chen, S., Liu, Y., & Xu, X. (2019, May). A landscape of cryptocurrencies. In *2019 IEEE International Conference on Blockchain and Cryptocurrency (ICBC)* (pp. 165-166). IEEE. Available: DOI: 10.1109/BLOC.2019.8751469

Mihus, I., & Gupta, S. G. (2023). Exploring the foundations of the digital economy: an in-depth overview. *Business model innovation in the digital economy*, 6-37.

Möller, D. P. (2023). Cybersecurity in digital transformation. In *Guide to cybersecurity in digital transformation: Trends, methods, technologies, applications and best practices* (pp. 1–70). Springer Nature Switzerland. DOI: 10.1007/978-3-031-26845-8_1

O'Flaherty, K. (2024). The rise of AI-powered surveillance. The Guardian. Available from: [URL]. Accessed 2024 Aug 20.

Oyewole, A. T., Oguejiofor, B. B., Eneh, N. E., Akpuokwe, C. U., & Bakare, S. S.Adedoyin Tolulope OyewoleBisola Beatrice OguejioforNkechi Emmanuella EnehChidiogo Uzoamaka AkpuokweSeun Solomon Bakare. (2024). Data privacy laws and their impact on financial technology companies: A review. *Computer Science & IT Research Journal*, *5*(3), 628–650. DOI: 10.51594/csitrj.v5i3.911

Phuangsuwan, P., Siripipatthanakul, S., Praesri, S., & Rakpathum, W. (2025). The Relationship between Good Governance and Organizational Performance through the Mediating Role of Employee Satisfaction. *Journal of Governance and Regulation/Volume, 14*(1).

Pradnyawati, N. M. E., Sukandia, I. N., & Arini, D. G. D. (2021). Perjanjian Pinjaman Online Berbasis Financial Technology (Fintech). *Jurnal Konstruksi Hukum*, *2*(2), 320–325. DOI: 10.22225/jkh.2.2.3230.320-325

Rawindaran, N., Jayal, A., & Prakash, E. (2021). Artificial intelligence and machine learning within the context of cyber security used in the UK SME Sector. *Proceedings of the AMI.*

Regulation, P. (2016). Regulation (EU) 2016/679 of the European Parliament and of the Council. *Regulation, 679*, 2016.

Rittinghouse, J. W., & Ransome, J. F. (2016). *Cloud computing: Implementation, management, and security*. CRC Press.

Roman, R., Zhou, J., & Lopez, J. (2013). On the features and challenges of security and privacy in distributed internet of things. *Computer Networks, 57*(10), 2266–2279. DOI: 10.1016/j.comnet.2012.12.018

Saeed, S. (2023). A Customer-Centric View of E-Commerce Security and Privacy. *Applied Sciences (Basel, Switzerland), 13*(2), 1020. DOI: 10.3390/app13021020

Saeed, S. (2023). DigitalWorkplaces and Information Security Behavior of Business Employees: An Empirical Study of Saudi Arabia. *Sustainability (Basel), 15*(7), 6019. DOI: 10.3390/su15076019

Saeed, S., Altamimi, S. A., Alkayyal, N. A., Alshehri, E., & Alabbad, D. A. (2023). Digital transformation and cybersecurity challenges for businesses resilience: Issues and recommendations. *Sensors (Basel), 23*(15), 6666. DOI: 10.3390/s23156666 PMID: 37571451

Santos, J. R. (2020). Cybersecurity and the role of traditional methods. In: *Proceedings of the International Conference on Cybersecurity*; Mar 10-12, 2020; London, UK. IEEE. p. 43-58.

Sharif, M. H. U., & Mohammed, M. A.Md Haris Uddin SharifMehmood Ali Mohammed. (2022). A literature review of financial losses statistics for cyber security and future trend. *World J. Adv.Res. Rev., 15*(1), 138–156. DOI: 10.30574/wjarr.2022.15.1.0573

Shokri, R., Stronati, M., Song, L., & Shmatikov, V. (2017). Membership inference attacks against machine learning models. *IEEE Symposium on Security and Privacy*; San Jose, CA, USA. IEEE. p. 3-18 DOI: 10.1109/SP.2017.41

Simon, J., & Omar, A. (2020). Cybersecurity investments in the supply chain: Coordination and a strategic attacker. *European Journal of Operational Research, 282*(1), 161–171. DOI: 10.1016/j.ejor.2019.09.017

Sinaga, N. P. (2021). Perlindungan hukum bagi konsumen yang data pribadinya diperjualbelikan di aplikasi fintech peer-to-peer lending. *Nusantara Law and Opinion Journal, 2*(2), 156–167. Advance online publication. DOI: 10.51622/njlo.v2i02.366

Siripipatthanakul, S. (2011). Development of a Model for Administration of Student Dental Health Promotion Work for Basic Education Schools in Thailand. *International Journal of Learning, 17*(12), 137–150. DOI: 10.18848/1447-9494/CGP/v17i12/47373

Siripipatthanakul, S., Limna, P., Phuangsuwan, P., & Siripipattanakul, S. (2025a). Enhancing Student Satisfaction With Blended Learning Among Thai Higher Education Students. In Navigating Quality Assurance and Accreditation in Global Higher Education (pp. 293-312). IGI Global Scientific Publishing.

Siripipatthanakul, S., Limna, P., Phuangsuwan, P., & Siripipattanakul, S. (2025c). Enriching Satisfaction With Web-Based Learning (WBL) Among Higher Education Students in Thailand. In Building Organizational Capacity and Strategic Management in Academia (pp. 213-236). IGI Global.

Siripipatthanakul, S., Limna, P., Siripipattanakul, S., & Phuangsuwan, P. (2025b). Modelling Problem-Based Learning, Student Satisfaction, and Effectiveness Among Higher Education Students in Thailand. In International Academic Transformations and Cross-Border Collaborations (pp. 311-332). IGI Global Scientific Publishing.

Siripipatthanakul, S., & Siripipattanakul, S. (2025). Online Gambling of Higher Education Learners. In *International Academic Transformations and Cross-Border Collaborations* (pp. 377–400). IGI Global Scientific Publishing.

Solove, D. J. (2021). *Understanding privacy*. Harvard University Press.

Stevani, W., & Sudirman, L. (2021). Urgensi Perlindungan Data Pengguna Financial Technology terhadap Aksi Kejahatan Online di Indonesia. *Journal of Judicial Review, 23*(2), 197–216. DOI: 10.37253/jjr.v23i2.5028

Tufekci, Z. (2018). Algorithmic harms beyond Facebook and Google: Emergent challenges of computational agency. *Colorado Tech Law J., 13*(2), 203–218.

Uddin, M.H.; Ali, M.H.; Hassan, M.K. (2020). Cybersecurity hazards and financial system vulnerability: A synthesis of literature. Risk Manag. 22, 239–309. University; 2021.

U.S. Department of Health & Human Services. (1966). Health Insurance Portability and Accountability Act of 1996 (HIPAA). Available from. [URL], Retrieved August 20, 2024, from.

Williams, L. D. (2021). Concepts of Digital Economy and Industry 4.0 in Intelligent and information systems. *International Journal of Intelligent Networks*, *2*, 122–129. DOI: 10.1016/j.ijin.2021.09.002

Wylde, V., & Prakash, E. (2021). [Crisis: Is our personal data likely to be breached?]. *COVID*, •••, 19.

Wylde, V., Rawindaran, N., Lawrence, J., Balasubramanian, R., Prakash, E., Jayal, A., Khan, I., Hewage, C., & Platts, J. (2022). Cybersecurity, data privacy and blockchain: A review. *SN Computer Science*, *3*(2), 127. DOI: 10.1007/s42979-022-01020-4 PMID: 35036930

Zhao, H., Jiang, Q., & Yu, H. (2021). Zero-day attack detection and mitigation strategies. In: *Proceedings of the International Symposium on Information Technology*; 2021 Jul 12-14; Beijing, China. IEEE. p. 135-45

Zuboff, S. (2019). *The age of surveillance capitalism: The fight for a human future at the new frontier of power*. PublicAffairs.

Chapter 2
Email Spam, WhatsApp, and Telegram Affect Privacy, Cybersecurity, Financial Security, and Personal Invasion:
A Case Study in Singapore

Lewes Lim
https://orcid.org/0009-0006-3499-5079
Manipal GlobalNxt University, Malaysia

Penpim Phuangsuwan
https://orcid.org/0000-0003-2371-7998
University of Phayao, Thailand

ABSTRACT

This study examines email spam, WhatsApp, and Telegram in relation to Singaporean cybersecurity, financial security, and personal privacy. Use convenience sampling and descriptive statistics to analyze 157 online questionnaires. The results reveal privacy risks and high rates of phishing and unwanted messages. Younger digital users are more vulnerable to these threats, while higher-educated people are more aware and more likely to take precautions. The perceived privacy risks and requests for improved cybersecurity features show user anxiety. The report identifies platform security and user knowledge gaps, underscoring the need for enhanced cybersecurity, stricter regulatory oversight, and targeted public education. The proposals include enhancing encryption, implementing AI-driven spam detection,

DOI: 10.4018/979-8-3693-9720-6.ch002

and revising Singapore's cybersecurity legislative framework. These safeguards protect user privacy and reduce financial theft and data breaches in modern digital communication platforms.

1. INTRODUCTION

1.1 Research Question

Why do email spam, WhatsApp, and Telegram affect privacy, cybersecurity, financial security, and personal invasion?

1.2 Research Objective

This chapter identifies the privacy, cybersecurity, and financial security threats associated with the use of email, WhatsApp, and Telegram in Singapore. Cybercriminals employ various strategies and techniques to exploit vulnerabilities in digital communication platforms. Evaluate the awareness and preparedness of Singaporean users in identifying and managing digital risks associated with email, WhatsApp, and Telegram. Finally, strategies and optimal practices for enhancing cybersecurity measures and protecting users from cyberattacks on these platforms are discussed.

2. LITERATURE REVIEW

2.1 Emergence of Cyber Threats

The surge in email, WhatsApp, and Telegram use has paralleled a notable increase in cyber risks, particularly in email spam, phishing, and fraudulent activities targeting messaging platforms. Email spam, a longstanding problem, has evolved into more sophisticated types of cyberattacks, such as phishing scams that deceive users into disclosing sensitive information. A study on email spam detection highlighted the escalating sophistication of spam strategies, which increasingly exploit vulnerabilities in email systems. Blockchain technology has been proposed as a solution for spam detection, offering transparency and reduced manipulation. Nonetheless, despite progress in spam detection, phishing remains a significant threat. Phishing emails often mimic authentic institutions, such as banks or government bodies, to deceive consumers into disclosing personal data or financial information (Bae & Hong, 2023; Joglekar et al., 2024; Patil, 2024).

Likewise, messaging applications such as WhatsApp and Telegram have become targets for fraudsters seeking to exploit their extensive user bases. Notwithstanding its end-to-end encryption, WhatsApp has evolved into a fertile environment for fraudulent activities, encompassing counterfeit lotteries, investment scams, and impersonation fraud. Fraudsters frequently mimic trustworthy contacts to deceive victims into transferring funds or disclosing confidential information. Telegrams, which emphasize privacy, have also experienced an increase in cyberattacks, highlighting the dangers associated with Telegram's "secret chats" function. Although this feature offers robust encryption, it can be misused by criminals for clandestine activities. The rise of these risks on messaging platforms has raised substantial worries over user privacy, data security, and financial losses. The increasing complexity of these attacks requires strong cybersecurity protections across all digital communication platforms (Imron et al., 2023; Alibeigi & Munir, 2023; Kim et al., 2023).

2.2 Cybersecurity Threats on Email, WhatsApp, and Telegram

Cybersecurity threats on digital platforms such as email, WhatsApp, and Telegram have become increasingly sophisticated and frequent, posing significant risks to both individual users and organizations. Email, as one of the oldest digital communication tools, remains a primary target for phishing attacks, malware distribution, and identity theft. These attacks exploit vulnerabilities in email systems, often bypassing basic spam filters to reach users with malicious content. For instance, phishing emails, disguised as legitimate communications, aim to trick users into revealing sensitive information such as login credentials or financial data. As demonstrated, the deployment of machine learning-based phishing detection tools can significantly reduce the success rate of such attacks; however, the constantly evolving tactics of cybercriminals pose an ongoing challenge (Chowdhary et al., 2024).

Similarly, messaging applications such as WhatsApp and Telegram, which have millions of daily users worldwide, are vulnerable to cyber threats. Notwithstanding their end-to-end encryption capabilities, which provide a measure of security, both platforms have emerged as conducive environments for the proliferation of malware, spyware, and phishing schemes. Cybercriminals utilize WhatsApp and Telegram to disseminate links to malicious websites or to propagate destructive software masquerading as legitimate files. In certain instances, these applications are used in social engineering attacks, where users are coerced into revealing sensitive information or executing activities that compromise their security. Research highlights the need for enhanced cybersecurity protocols on these platforms, including multi-factor authentication and AI-driven threat detection systems, which can help mitigate the risks associated with these evolving threats (Thapaliya, 2024; Machora, 2024).

The magnitude of the problem is especially alarming in areas with significant Internet penetration, such as Singapore. Given the extensive use of email, WhatsApp, and Telegram for both personal and professional communications, any breach may lead to significant repercussions, including unauthorized access to personal information and financial losses. and corporate espionage in cybersecurity inside healthcare systems presents a pertinent comparison, illustrating that although encryption and AI tools can protect sensitive data, the ongoing evolution of cyber-attack techniques necessitates correspondingly advanced security mechanisms. Considering the significant risks, particularly for financial institutions and healthcare providers, the integration of AI-based cybersecurity solutions, as proposed, has become essential for identifying and thwarting these advanced threats (Wisdom et al., 2023; Chowdhary et al., 2024).

2.3 Financial Fraud and Digital Vulnerabilities

Financial fraud is a growing concern in the digital era, as hackers exploit the vulnerabilities of unsuspecting individuals through email, WhatsApp, and Telegram. Phishing is a widespread financial fraud technique in which perpetrators send misleading emails or messages to manipulate recipients into revealing confidential financial information, including bank account details or credit card numbers. Phishing attempts are becoming more complex, frequently mimicking official messages from financial institutions to enhance their authenticity. This type of fraud has resulted in considerable financial losses for both people and businesses (Shawky, 2023).

In addition to phishing, WhatsApp and Telegram have been employed for financial fraud, notably through deceptive investment schemes and Ponzi schemes. Cybercriminals establish groups or channels on these platforms to entice victims with assurances of substantial investment returns, subsequently vanishing after accumulating sufficient funds from unwary users. Such techniques are especially perilous as they manipulate the faith users have in the ostensibly private and secure characteristics of these messaging applications. The examination of cybersecurity vulnerabilities in communication networks underscores the necessity for enhanced regulatory monitoring and user education to safeguard individuals from financial theft (Thapaliya, 2024; Machora, 2024)

The ramifications of financial fraud on digital platforms extend beyond mere immediate monetary losses. The enduring repercussions encompass impaired credit ratings, legal disputes, and, in certain instances, identity theft, when perpetrators exploit the acquired financial data to impersonate victims and perpetrate additional offenses. This poses significant challenges for enterprises that rely heavily on email and messaging services for transactions and communication. The integration of AI and machine learning technologies, as demonstrated by their research on phishing detection, offers a viable approach for identifying and mitigating financial fraud. These tools can evaluate extensive data sets in real time, detecting anomalous patterns and behaviors that may indicate fraudulent activity. Nonetheless, a considerable disparity persists in the adoption of these technologies across various sectors, particularly in smaller enterprises and underdeveloped areas, where financial resources for implementing advanced cybersecurity solutions may be limited (Shawky, 2023; Wisdom et al., 2023; Chowdhary et al., 2024)

2.4 The Impact of Digital Spam on Psychological and Social Well-Being

The repercussions of digital spam, encompassing unsolicited emails and messages on platforms such as WhatsApp and Telegram, extend beyond cybersecurity and financial issues, affecting users' psychological and social well-being. Persistent exposure to spam messages, phishing attempts, and online fraud can result in heightened tension, anxiety, and a sense of vulnerability among users. It is noted that the prevalence and complexity of cyberattacks, primarily via phishing emails, can engender a continual sense of unease as users become uncertain about the authenticity of communications and the potential threats they may pose (Shawky, 2023).

Digital spam has a detrimental impact on social dynamics by eroding trust in online communication networks. Individuals frequently inundated with spam and phishing attempts may develop a reluctance to participate in digital platforms, which can impact their social relationships and digital literacy. This is especially troubling for older folks and individuals with little technological proficiency, who may already have anxiety around the use of internet communication technologies. Research on healthcare cybersecurity emphasizes the importance of establishing trust in digital systems to safeguard sensitive information and promote user engagement and confidence in digital platforms (Wisdom et al., 2023).

The psychological impact of digital spam is exacerbated by the rise in social engineering attacks, in which fraudsters deceive users into revealing personal information or taking actions that compromise their security. These assaults frequently exploit users' emotions, including fear, urgency, or curiosity, rendering them very effective in capitalizing on psychological vulnerabilities. For example, individuals may receive WhatsApp messages claiming that their bank accounts have been compromised, urging them to click on malicious links or disclose confidential information. The emotional turmoil resulting from these attacks can produce enduring consequences for users, culminating in heightened anxiety and an aversion to future engagement with online platforms (Shawky, 2023; Machora, 2024).

To mitigate the psychological and social impacts of digital spam, it is crucial to implement robust cybersecurity protocols that not only detect and counter cyber threats but also educate users on recognizing and responding to spam and phishing attempts. AI-driven systems that evaluate user behavior and communication patterns can effectively identify and filter suspect communications before they are received by the user, thereby alleviating the emotional strain associated with persistent cyberattacks. Furthermore, fostering digital literacy and awareness initiatives might enable users to adopt proactive measures in safeguarding their online privacy and security, hence improving their psychological well-being in the digital era (Thapaliya, 2024).

2.5 The Importance of Privacy, Cybersecurity, and Financial Security

According to the previous studies (Alibeigi & Munir, 2023; Bae & Hong, 2023; Kim et al., 2023), it confirms that; email, WhatsApp, and Telegram in Singapore, a technologically advanced nation with high internet penetration, in light of the growing threats to privacy, cybersecurity, and financial security. Singapore serves as an exemplary case study, owing to its position as a global financial center and its sophisticated digital infrastructure. The nation's substantial dependence on digital communication makes it especially vulnerable to cyberattacks, which carry significant consequences for both individuals and corporations. The financial industry in Singapore has experienced a rise in cyberattacks, including phishing schemes that target both financial institutions and consumers. These assaults can result in significant financial losses and compromises of sensitive information, underscoring the pressing necessity for improved cybersecurity regulations. Furthermore, Singapore's stringent regulatory framework offers a compelling context for evaluating the efficacy of current cybersecurity protocols. The nation's Personal Data Protection Act (PDPA) aims to protect individual data; however, the rise in phishing and message fraud suggests that additional measures may be necessary to combat the increasing sophistication of cyberattacks. The primary hazards associated with email, WhatsApp, and Telegram in Singapore, assessing users' awareness of these risks, and recommending strategies for their mitigation. The most critical privacy and security concerns were identified through comprehensive interviews with Singaporean users and cybersecurity professionals, offering insights into how individuals and businesses can enhance their protection

The significance of this chapter extends beyond Singapore, as its findings can be applied to other regions facing similar cybersecurity challenges. The increasing interconnectedness of global digital communication platforms means that cyberattacks are rarely confined to a single country. Thus, by addressing the privacy and cybersecurity risks in Singapore, this research could offer broader recommendations for improving digital security globally, especially in densely connected cities where digital platforms are integral to daily life

3. METHODOLOGY

This study employs a quantitative approach, based on a convenience sample of Singaporeans, to investigate the impact of email spam, WhatsApp, and Telegram on privacy, cybersecurity, financial security, and personal invasion. Online questionnaire surveys were collected through structured surveys administered to a diverse sample of respondents (n = 157), as detailed in Table 1, representing various demographic categories. The survey included five-point Likert scale questions to gauge perceptions of privacy risks, encounters with scammers, and cybersecurity awareness. Secondary data was collated from national and international research papers and reports to provide a broader context for the study, ensuring a well-rounded analysis of the existing literature. SPSS software was used for data analysis, enabling the statistical interpretation of the survey results, including descriptive statistics, correlation analysis, and path modeling, as illustrated in the correlation matrix and structural equation modeling (SEM) model. This approach enabled a comprehensive examination of the cybersecurity landscape across different user demographics and behaviors.

4. RESEULTS

Table 1. Demographic characteristics of respondents

Demographic Variable	Categories	Frequency (n=157)	Percentage
Gender	Male	50	31.8%
	Female	47	29.9%
	Other	60	38.2%
Age Group	18-25	42	26.8%
	26-35	36	22.9%
	36-45	32	20.4%
	46-55	27	17.2%
	56+	20	12.7%
Education	High School	25	15.9%
	Bachelor's	49	31.2%
	Master's	40	25.5%
	Doctorate's	43	27.4%
Occupation	Student	47	29.9%
	Professional	42	26.8%
	Self Employed	34	21.7%
	Unemployed	34	21.7%
Income Level	<30K	50	31.8%
	30-50K	40	25.5%
	50-70K	37	23.6%
	>70K	30	19.1%

The demographic profile in Table 1 reflects a balanced representation of respondents across various categories, including gender, age, education, occupation, and income level. The majority of respondents are young, with 49.7% falling within the 18-35 age bracket, highlighting a digitally engaged group that is more likely to use email, WhatsApp, and Telegram for personal and professional communication. The high level of education among respondents, with 27.4% holding Doctorates, suggests a relatively informed and potentially security-conscious sample. The variation in income levels offers insights into how digital platform usage and perceptions of privacy and cybersecurity threats may differ across socioeconomic backgrounds. This diverse sample provides a comprehensive understanding of the cybersecurity landscape and the risks perceived by various demographic groups.

Figure 2. Likert scale responses

Likert Scale Questions	Mean	SD	Minimum	Maximum
There is a high risk to privacy when using email, WhatsApp, and Telegram.	4.2	0.85	1	5
Potential scammers try to obtain your personal information through these platforms.	4.5	0.76	1	5
It is necessary to protect the information from scammers using email, WhatsApp, and Telegram.	4.1	0.91	1	5
It should be taken to improve cybersecurity.	4.6	0.79	1	5
It should be taken to enhance cybersecurity.	4.4	0.82	1	5

Figure 2 presents the Likert scale responses regarding privacy risks, encounters with scammers, and perceptions of cybersecurity measures. The mean scores indicate that most respondents perceive significant privacy risks when using email, WhatsApp, and Telegram, with a mean of 4.2 on a scale of 1 to 5. Furthermore, encounters with potential scammers are widespread, with an average score of 4.5, suggesting that more than 90% of respondents have experienced scamming attempts on these platforms. The responses also reveal a strong inclination toward adopting protective measures (mean of 4.1) and the necessity of cybersecurity improvements (mean of 4.6). These findings suggest that respondents are not only aware of the risks but are also proactive in addressing them, underlining the importance of enhanced security features on digital communication platforms.

5. DISCUSSIONS

The findings support previous studies as follows;

Bae and Hong (2023) examine the escalating danger landscape for digital financial services and the corresponding evolution of cybersecurity regulations in their work, entitled "A Work on Digital Financial Security Threats and Cybersecurity Regulations." The study aimed to highlight the principal security challenges within the digital banking sector, particularly as online transactions proliferate worldwide. The authors conducted a qualitative review of policy documents and cybersecurity incidents to elucidate the discrepancies between financial innovations and current regulatory frameworks. Their findings indicated that although digital financial platforms are significantly susceptible to cyberattacks, there is a lack of robust security regulations specifically designed for the financial industry. The finding underscores the necessity for dynamic, adaptable cybersecurity frameworks. Nevertheless, the study presents a research vacuum in assessing the real-time efficacy of these regulations across various jurisdictions.

Thapliyal et al. (2022), in their study on the Convergence of Artificial Intelligence and Cybersecurity, featuring a case study on email spam detection, seek to integrate AI technologies with conventional cybersecurity approaches. The research employed artificial intelligence methodologies, including machine learning, to address the issue of email spam detection, utilizing both qualitative and quantitative methods, such as case studies and algorithm performance assessments. The results indicate that AI-driven spam detection systems significantly decrease false positives compared to rule-based systems. The research found that artificial intelligence has significant potential for enhancing cybersecurity. The research revealed a deficiency in the real-time flexibility of these AI models when confronted with innovative spam tactics.

Alkkaya (2023) examines the convergence of health data and cybersecurity in the chapter "HES: A Case Study on Cybersecurity and Privacy Risks in Health Surveillance Systems." The research examines privacy issues associated with health surveillance systems, particularly in the context of increasing digitalization in healthcare. The authors analyzed the efficacy of current privacy policies through a case study of health surveillance systems in Turkey. Their findings reveal considerable hazards associated with data breaches and privacy infringements. The study concludes that, although health systems are progressing, there is a delay in implementing relevant security measures. The research vacuum exists due to the absence of cross-national studies evaluating the efficacy of health data privacy legislation in various nations.

Alkhdour et al. (2024) proposed a novel method for Identifying Email Spam Threats Utilizing LSTM-particle swarm Optimization Algorithms, which is a hybrid approach designed to enhance spam detection accuracy. The study aimed to enhance the efficacy of spam filters by integrating Long Short-Term Memory (LSTM) neural networks with Particle Swarm Optimization (PSO) algorithms. The authors conducted simulations and evaluated the model against established spam detection techniques. The results indicate that the hybrid model surpassed conventional spam filters in terms of both precision and efficiency. The research concludes that hybrid AI methodologies can offer a formidable answer for email security. Nonetheless, a research deficiency persists about the model's scalability in practical applications characterized by dynamic spam patterns.

Alibeigi and Munir (2023) analyzed the privacy issues associated with public health data in their chapter titled "Public Health Data and International Privacy Rules and Practices: A Case Study of Singapore." They emphasized international regulations and norms. The authors examined Singapore's privacy standards about international regulations, such as the GDPR and HIPAA. The findings indicated that Singapore's privacy legislation closely aligns with global standards; nonetheless, they highlighted deficiencies in enforcement, particularly within the private healthcare sector. The study found that enhanced international collaboration is crucial for protecting data across borders. This research identifies a gap in the lack of longitudinal studies assessing the long-term efficacy of these programs.

Hassan, Abatcha, and Dada (2024), in their work on the Ensemble Machine Learning Algorithm for Telegram Spam Detection, constructed an ensemble model to identify spam in Telegram communications. The aim was to address the growing issue of spam and phishing attacks on chat systems. The study assessed the efficacy of several models through a combination of machine learning techniques. Their research demonstrates that ensemble approaches markedly enhance spam detection rates while reducing false positives. The research determined that these models present a viable alternative for enhancing security in Telegram. A research vacuum persists regarding the necessity for real-time applications of these models to counteract evolving spam methods effectively.

Josten and Weis (2024) examine the efficacy of Bayesian spam filters in identifying spam emails modified using advanced language models (LLM-modified), emphasizing the issues posed by such emails. The aim was to evaluate the efficacy of Bayesian filters against these advanced spam variants. Through a simulation and comparison study, the scientists determined that Bayesian spam filters were comparatively inefficient against LLM-modified spam, underscoring the shifting nature of cyber threats. The study shows that whereas Bayesian filters are effective against conventional spam, they encounter difficulties with more intricate variants. The research gap pertains to the absence of adaptive spam filters capable of evolving in response to developing threats based on large language models (LLMs).

Venčkauskas et al. (2024) proposed a unique strategy in their Email Cyber Threat Intelligence Method that integrates domain ontology with machine learning for the detection of email threats. The aim was to enhance the contextual comprehension of cyber dangers in emails by utilizing domain-specific information. The authors utilized a mixed-methods approach, integrating qualitative domain study with quantitative machine-learning methodologies. Their findings indicate that this strategy enhances the precision of email threat identification compared to statistical models alone. The research concludes that domain ontology can augment machine learning in improving email security. The research gap exists in the application of this strategy to increasingly extensive and varied email datasets.

Antunes et al. (2021). In "Information Security and Cybersecurity Management: A Case Study with SMEs in Portugal," the escalating cybersecurity concerns confronting small and medium-sized enterprises (SMEs) in Portugal are emphasized. The study aimed to investigate how SMEs handle cybersecurity and information security, emphasizing their preparedness and the rules they adopt. The authors employed a mixed-methods approach, conducting surveys and interviews with SME managers to evaluate cybersecurity practices. The results indicated that numerous SMEs lack robust cybersecurity plans owing to financial limitations and insufficient competence. The report highlights the urgent need for improved accessibility to cybersecurity training and resources for small and medium-sized enterprises (SMEs). A notable research gap is the lack of longitudinal studies evaluating the long-term effectiveness of cybersecurity initiatives implemented by these SMEs.

Asiryan (2023), in the article *Legislative Practice of Singapore on the Use of Artificial Intelligence*, investigates the legal frameworks surrounding the use of artificial intelligence (AI) in Singapore. The objective of this research was to assess the adequacy of current AI legislation in ensuring cybersecurity, privacy, and ethical standards. The methodology included an analysis of Singaporean legislative documents and AI-related incidents. The findings suggest that while Singapore has made significant strides in AI governance, there remain gaps in areas such as data protection and transparency in AI applications. The study concludes that legislative reforms are needed to address emerging AI risks. However, the research gap lies in the need for comparative studies between Singapore and other AI-advanced nations.

Kankwende (2024) examines the essential difficulties of safeguarding digital assets against increasingly sophisticated cyberattacks in the text "Cybersecurity in the Modern Age: Protecting Digital Assets." The study aimed to evaluate the efficacy of existing cybersecurity measures and provide enhanced solutions for asset protection. The research, conducted through case studies and quantitative analysis, determined that conventional cybersecurity measures are insufficient in addressing emerging threats. The finding underscores the importance of incorporating modern technologies, such as artificial intelligence and blockchain, to enhance cybersecurity. The identified research gap is the lack of extensive real-world testing of these proposed technologies.

Dorairajan (2024) examines the correlation between an organization's cybersecurity framework and its overall performance in "Cybersecurity and Organizational Performance- the Interplay." The study aimed to determine whether enhanced cybersecurity leads to improved organizational performance. The author employed a quantitative methodology, administering surveys across multiple sectors, which indicated that organizations with strong cybersecurity frameworks tend to excel more frequently compared to those with weaker systems. The report asserts that cybersecurity must be regarded as a fundamental component of a company's strategy rather than merely a technical obligation. A notable gap is the lack of research on the impact of industry-specific cybersecurity requirements on performance.

Siew (2024), in the article "Strengthening Big Data Security and Privacy in Libraries: A Review of ISO Standards and Real-World Cyberattack Case Studies," examines the implementation of ISO standards to safeguard library systems from cyberattacks. The aim was to assess the efficacy of these guidelines in safeguarding big data and maintaining privacy within library systems. The analysis of real-world cyberattack case studies revealed that, although ISO standards provide a robust framework, many organizations still inadequately apply them. The research concludes that libraries must implement more aggressive and flexible cybersecurity strategies. The research gap exists in the necessity for additional sector-specific analyses assessing cybersecurity efficacy across various institutional types.

Fenton (2024), in the study titled "Preventing Catastrophic Cyber-Physical Attacks on the Global Maritime Transportation System: A Case Study of Hybrid Maritime Security in the Straits of Malacca and Singapore," analyzes the cybersecurity vulnerabilities inherent in marine transportation networks. The study aimed to evaluate the effectiveness of hybrid maritime security measures in addressing cyber-physical threats. The research, employing a case study methodology, found that existing security solutions are insufficient to address the complexities of cyber threats. The research finds that global collaboration is essential for enhancing marine cybersecurity. A research gap is evident due to the lack of large-scale simulations to evaluate the suggested hybrid security frameworks.

Abbas and Robbins (2024), in "Cybersecurity Protocols in Human Resources: Ensuring Legal Compliance and Ethical Standards," emphasize the significance of cybersecurity in managing human resources data. The aim was to examine how firms maintain adherence to legal and ethical norms in the management of sensitive employee information. The authors employed qualitative methodologies to examine diverse organizational protocols and conducted interviews with HR specialists. The results indicate that numerous firms continue to lack adequate cybersecurity measures, which can lead to potential data breaches. The report finds that there is an urgent necessity for enhanced integration of cybersecurity into HR procedures.

The identified research need is the absence of real-time monitoring solutions in HR cybersecurity.

Afzal (2024) examines the best practices of Digital Laws and digital justice, highlighting their contributions to equitable digital justice systems worldwide. The study aimed to evaluate the efficacy of existing digital legislation in safeguarding individual privacy and maintaining cybersecurity within court systems. The study revealed through comparative analysis that although digital regulations are being increasingly implemented, enforcement is inconsistent. The research concludes that consistent worldwide standards are essential for achieving digital justice. A research gap exists due to the absence of empirical studies investigating the long-term effects of digital legislation on judicial outcomes.

Wang (2024), confirm the difficulties of safeguarding personal information in the digital era. Enhanced strategies for safeguarding personal information online, taking into account existing legal regulations, demonstrate that existing policies are inadequate in mitigating data breaches. Enhanced rules and technical advancements are essential for safeguarding personal information. The identified research gap is the insufficient investigation into user behavior and its influence on the efficacy of personal information protection measures.

Imron et al. (2023) identify the significant dangers associated with online licensing procedures for nuclear materials in Indonesia. The potential cybersecurity vulnerabilities in digital systems that manage nuclear materials. The significant deficiencies in cybersecurity infrastructure jeopardized sensitive nuclear information. The authors determined that immediate adjustments in cybersecurity policy are essential; however, a research deficit persists in examining foreign best practices that can be tailored to Indonesia's specific context.

Patil (2024) investigated the innovative application of blockchain technology for the identification and prevention of email spam. The research aimed to enhance the efficacy and reliability of spam identification by leveraging the decentralized framework of blockchain technology. Blockchain-based spam filters were evaluated experimentally against conventional spam detection methods. The findings demonstrated that blockchain enhances transparency and mitigates the risks of manipulation in email communication. The conclusion highlighted blockchain's promise for protecting email systems; nevertheless, the study inadequately examined the scalability of this method, indicating a research need in its large-scale implementation.

Kim et al. (2023) introduced a content-based spam filtering system in their article, "PCSF: Privacy-Preserving Content-Based Spam Filter," which safeguards user privacy while enhancing spam detection. The research focused on incorporating privacy-preserving techniques into content filtering through the use of advanced encryption technologies. The research entailed evaluating the spam filter using authentic email datasets. The results indicated that the Privacy-Preserving Content-based Spam Filter (PCSF) markedly improves detection accuracy while safeguarding user privacy. The research found that privacy-preserving methodologies can be effectively integrated into spam detection systems. The investigation revealed a deficiency in tackling the growing spam strategies that may circumvent the filter.

Joglekar et al. (2024) analyzed the use of machine learning techniques to enhance the precision and effectiveness of email spam detection systems to create a resilient machine learning model capable of managing the increasingly complex intricacies of spam methodologies. The authors employed a quantitative methodology to evaluate multiple machine learning methods, such as support vector machines and neural networks, on extensive email datasets. Their research demonstrated that machine learning-based spam filters surpassed conventional methods in both accuracy and speed. The report recommended broader adoption of machine learning technologies in cybersecurity. The identified research gap was the insufficient emphasis on real-time performance and adaptation to emerging email attack vectors.

Kumar and Madan (2021) examined the privacy risks associated with the Aadhaar system, India's biometric identification database, in a study on Aadhaar privacy and personal security issues. The research aimed to assess the risks associated with personal data breaches and identity theft within the Aadhaar framework. A mixed-methods approach was utilized, incorporating surveys and interviews to collect data from users and experts. The results underscored considerable weaknesses in data management and security measures. The authors determined that further encryption and privacy protections are necessary for Aadhar. The research gap identified in the study pertains to the lack of a longitudinal investigation of the system's security as it adapts to ongoing technological advancements.

Herath and Herath (2006), in "Justifying Spam and E-mail Virus Security Investments: A Case Study," examined the economic justification for investing in email security measures against spam and viruses. The research aimed to assess the economic implications of email-related security breaches on enterprises. The authors assessed the return on investment of several email security systems using a cost-benefit analysis framework. The results indicated that proactive investment in cybersecurity yields substantial long-term savings by reducing the occurrence and impact of email-related attacks. The research determined that firms must prioritize email security within their cybersecurity strategy. Nonetheless, the analysis failed to address the indirect costs of email assaults, including reputational harm.

Aloumi et al. (2024) examined the determinants that impact customer trust and engagement with FinTech platforms in their chapter, "Factors Influencing Consumer Interactions with FinTech Services." The research aimed to identify primary factors, including privacy concerns and cybersecurity risks that deter customers from adopting FinTech services. The authors discovered, through surveys and case studies, that trust in data security and privacy regulations has a significant impact on user engagement with FinTech platforms. The research determined that improving transparency in data management and bolstering security protocols are essential for cultivating consumer confidence. A study vacuum was recognized in the cross-national analysis of FinTech security issues, particularly in emerging markets.

Badsha et al. (2019), in their conference paper "Privacy-Preserving Cyber Threat Information Sharing and Learning for Cyber Defense," examined methods for the secure exchange of cyber threat information among businesses while safeguarding sensitive data. The research aimed to develop privacy-preserving models for information dissemination using machine learning. The authors employed an experimental methodology to evaluate their models in controlled settings. The results indicated that their methodology successfully preserved privacy while enhancing the precision of cyber security systems. The research determined that collaborative cybersecurity initiatives can be improved by safe information exchange. A research gap persists in the practical application across several sectors.

Fenton (2024), in the study titled "Preventing Catastrophic Cyber-Physical Attacks on the Global Maritime Transportation System: A Case Study of Hybrid Maritime Security in the Straits of Malacca and Singapore," examined the cybersecurity dangers confronting global maritime transportation networks. The research aimed to identify weaknesses and propose security measures for mitigating hybrid cyber-physical attacks in a key maritime corridor. Employing a case study methodology, Fenton analyzed prior cyber-attacks and evaluated the robustness of existing security solutions. The results indicated that although certain advancements have occurred, substantial deficiencies persist in real-time threat identification and response. The research determined that a hybrid strategy, combining physical and cyber protection, is crucial for marine security. The research gap lies in evaluating these models across more extensive maritime routes.

Li (2024) examined the application and challenges of artificial intelligence (AI) in cybersecurity, focusing on both the prospects and obstacles of incorporating AI technology into cybersecurity frameworks—the research aimed to evaluate the effectiveness of AI in detecting and mitigating cyber threats. The authors discovered the benefits of AI in enhancing the speed and accuracy of threat identification through an examination of current AI-driven cybersecurity models. Nonetheless, the study highlighted shortcomings, including the susceptibility of AI systems to manipulation through adversarial attacks. The study found that although AI offers considerable advantages, further research is needed to enhance its resilience against advanced cyberattacks, highlighting a gap in the sector.

According to Thapliyal et al. (2023), Alibeigi & Munir (2023), and Josten & Weis (2024), notwithstanding considerable progress in cybersecurity technologies and regulatory structures, a substantial research deficiency persists in comprehending the intricate effects of email spam, WhatsApp, and Telegram on personal privacy and financial security, especially in a technologically advanced country such as Singapore. Current research has predominantly focused on specific facets of cybersecurity, such as AI-based spam detection and phishing schemes; however, there is a lack of comprehensive studies that examine the interrelated impacts of these platforms on user behavior, privacy violations, and financial crime. Furthermore, whereas prior studies have emphasized the importance of legislative frameworks such as the Personal Data Protection Act, there is a lack of research examining the effectiveness of these policies in safeguarding users from emerging threats on digital communication platforms. This study emphasizes the need for a comprehensive approach that combines user awareness, technology solutions, and regulatory compliance to mitigate the growing risks associated with digital communication.

Styoutomo & Ruldeviyani (2023) executed a study on the Information Security Awareness Enhancement Strategy employing the Fuzzy AHP Method alongside HAIS-Q and ISO/IEC 27001:2013: A Case Study of XYZ Financial Institution. This study aimed to develop a plan for enhancing information security awareness using the Fuzzy Analytical Hierarchy Process (FAHP) and the HAIS-Q, in accordance with the requirements of ISO/IEC 27001:2013. The methodology entailed gathering primary data from employees of XYZ Financial Institution, thereafter employing multi-criteria decision-making (MCDM) methodologies to assess security procedures. The results revealed a notable deficiency in employee awareness, suggesting that specialized training programs may effectively address these concerns. The study found that a comprehensive information security awareness plan, grounded in standardized guidelines, is crucial for safeguarding financial institutions against cyber threats. A research gap was identified in the limited scope of employee functions, suggesting that future studies should investigate broader organizational impacts.

Prokopowicz (2023) investigated the changing dynamics of cybercrime in the research project titled "How Does the Advancement of Generative Artificial Intelligence Technology Influence the Evolution of Cybercrime Methodologies and the Enhancement of Cybersecurity Systems?" This study highlighted the need to comprehend how generative AI is transforming cybercrime techniques and cybersecurity defense measures. The investigation primarily relied on secondary data sources, examining the current literature on developments in AI and cybercrime. The results indicated that generative AI has facilitated more advanced cyberattacks, hence complicating the detection and prevention of breaches by conventional cybersecurity techniques. The research determined that cybersecurity solutions must progress in tandem with AI developments to maintain their efficacy. The research gap highlights the deficiency of empirical evidence on AI-driven cyberattacks, necessitating future investigations centered on real-world case studies to corroborate theoretical conclusions.

Wang & Yishake (2024), in their presentation entitled "Along the Deep Interface of Digital Food: Islanding and Networking amidst the Territorialization of Uygur Cuisine," they examined the digitalization of culinary cultures, with an emphasis on Uygur cuisine. Although not explicitly focused on cybersecurity, the study provided significant insights into how digital platforms, such as social media and messaging applications, promote the dissemination of cultural norms while also presenting security threats related to personal data. The technique involved a qualitative investigation of online information and interactions related to Uygur cuisine, demonstrating how digital communication facilitates cultural exchange while also exposing vulnerabilities in privacy and data security. This convergence of culture and digital security raises significant questions about how platforms such as WhatsApp and Telegram, despite not being conventionally linked to cybercrime, may still serve as tools for surveillance or data exploitation. The identified research gap is the lack of comprehensive guidelines for protecting cultural data in digital environments.

Sharma et al. (2024) offer a comprehensive examination of cybersecurity concerns within the healthcare sector in their book, Understanding Cybersecurity Management in Healthcare: Challenges, Strategies, and Trends. This study examined the increasing incidence of cyberattacks targeting healthcare organizations, which has been intensified by the transition to digital healthcare management systems. The authors employed case studies and statistical research to examine cybersecurity trends in healthcare, highlighting patient data protection as a significant issue. They determined that a combination of advanced encryption technologies and employee training initiatives is crucial to mitigate these risks. The research revealed a deficiency in examining how smaller healthcare institutions with constrained resources might adopt successful cybersecurity techniques, indicating a need for additional investigation in this domain.

Lahtinen et al. (2021), investigated the integration of Brain-Computer Interfaces (BCIs) with Extended Reality (XR), emphasizing the future implications, privacy concerns, and security threats involved with this convergence. The research examined the privacy and data security issues associated with BCIs, highlighting the necessity for enhanced security measures due to the delicate nature of brain data. The research included experimental tests on BCI security, as well as analyses of privacy regulations and frameworks, including the General Data Protection Regulation (GDPR). The findings indicated that existing security protocols are inadequate for safeguarding brain data from unwanted access, necessitating the development of new, more effective cybersecurity safeguards. This study identified a research gap regarding the inadequate legal frameworks that regulate the use of BCIs, particularly regarding cross-border data transfers.

Shawky (2023) provides a comprehensive examination of the prevalent types of cyberattacks that have emerged in recent years in his article "13 Types of Cyberattacks You Should Know in 2023." The study emphasizes the significance of comprehending various attack techniques, including phishing, malware, and ransomware, to enhance defensive measures against them. This research aimed to increase awareness of the evolving dynamics of cyber threats in the contemporary digital landscape. Shawky employed secondary data and case studies to demonstrate the effects of these attacks on persons and organizations. The results underscore the necessity for enhanced cybersecurity frameworks and educational programs to help users identify potential threats. The study suggests that although technology solutions are vital, user knowledge and proactive action are crucial in reducing cyber dangers. The noted study gap is the insufficient emphasis on the responses of diverse populations to cyber threats, indicating that future studies should explore user-specific reactions to different cyberattacks.

Chowdhary et al. (2024) developed a machine learning-based technique for detecting phishing attempts in financial email interactions. It is significant due to the increasing incidence of phishing attempts targeting financial data, necessitating that financial institutions enhance their detection systems—the project aimed to develop an efficient instrument utilizing machine learning algorithms to identify phishing emails. The research employed a combination of primary data from actual phishing attempts and secondary data from prior studies. The results demonstrated a substantial success rate in identifying phishing emails, markedly decreasing the likelihood of financial fraud. The study stated that machine learning presents a promising opportunity for enhancing email security but indicated that the tool's efficacy may be improved by incorporating artificial intelligence. A significant study gap was identified, specifically the insufficient testing of the tool across various industries, which could be explored in future studies to generalize the findings.

Machora (2024) highlights cybersecurity and performance challenges in 4G LTE networks, aiming to mitigate growing concerns about security vulnerabilities in contemporary communication networks. Security issues associated with 4G LTE networks are prevalent in both personal and professional contexts. The research focused on examining network design and its related security vulnerabilities. The methodology integrated qualitative and quantitative methods, employing case studies and performance indicators to assess network risks. Although 4G LTE networks offer considerable performance advantages, they are vulnerable to multiple types of attacks, including man-in-the-middle and denial-of-service attacks. The study found that although existing security protocols in 4G LTE networks are sufficient for the majority of users, supplementary encryption and intrusion detection systems are essential to safeguard against more advanced threats. The identified study gap is the absence of real-time strategies for reducing such dangers, which future studies should address.

Wisdom et al. (2023) explored in their chapter "Mitigating Cyber Threats in Healthcare Systems: The Role of Artificial Intelligence and Machine Learning" the integration of AI and ML technologies to enhance cybersecurity in healthcare. This research is significant due to the increasing number of cyberattacks targeting sensitive healthcare data. The objective of this study was to explore how AI and ML can be leveraged to detect and prevent cyber threats in healthcare systems. The authors used a mixed-methods approach, incorporating case studies from hospitals and healthcare institutions that have implemented AI-driven cybersecurity measures. The findings showed that AI and ML significantly improve the detection of anomalies and potential threats in healthcare systems, thus reducing the incidence of data breaches. However, the study concluded that while these technologies offer substantial benefits, they must be continuously updated to stay ahead of emerging threats. A research gap identified was the limited implementation of these technologies in smaller healthcare institutions, which could be a focus of future studies.

Thapaliya (2024) examined the transformative impact of AI-driven cybersecurity solutions on financial sector management in his work, "Examining the Influence of AI-Driven Cybersecurity in Financial Sector Management." This study is significant because financial institutions are primary targets for cybercriminals, and AI-driven solutions provide innovative methods to safeguard sensitive financial information. The research aimed to assess the effectiveness of AI-based cybersecurity tools in detecting and mitigating cyber threats within the banking industry. The technique encompassed a synthesis of survey data from financial organizations and a secondary data analysis of current AI technologies employed in cybersecurity. The results demonstrated that AI significantly enhances the efficacy of threat detection systems, particularly in real-time surveillance and response. The research determined that although AI presents intriguing solutions for the financial sector, its implementation entails hurdles, including the necessity for substantial computational resources and specialized skills. A research gap identified is the insufficient emphasis on how small financial institutions with limited resources can implement AI-driven cybersecurity systems, indicating that future research should focus on cost-effective AI solutions.

6. CONCLUSIONS

This study's findings underscore the urgent need for enhanced security protocols on email, WhatsApp, and Telegram to address the growing threats of privacy breaches, cybersecurity concerns, and financial theft. The positive correlation between perceived privacy threats and the desire for enhanced cybersecurity measures suggests that users are becoming increasingly aware of the vulnerabilities inherent in these platforms. The disparity between awareness and action, as illustrated by the limited correlation between cybersecurity awareness and the implementation of protective measures, underscores the need for more comprehensive user education campaigns. Furthermore, platform providers must allocate resources toward AI-based threat detection systems, sophisticated encryption protocols, and multi-factor authentication to mitigate the dangers of privacy violations and financial fraud. Regulatory authorities, including those in Singapore, must continue to revise their cybersecurity regulations to ensure that digital communication platforms adhere to rigorous data protection standards and provide users with essential tools to protect their personal information. Their collective endeavors will be essential in establishing a more secure digital landscape for people in Singapore and beyond. Email spam, WhatsApp, and Telegram: Privacy, cybersecurity, financial security, and personal invasion in Singapore; the findings highlight that these platforms, although crucial for personal and professional communication, are significantly vulnerable to threats including phishing attacks, malware dissemination, and unsolicited communications that result in privacy violations and financial detriment. The demographic research indicated that younger, digitally active users are more susceptible to these dangers, mostly due to their heightened interaction with these platforms. Moreover, individuals with advanced educational qualifications exhibited heightened awareness of cybersecurity threats and were more proactive in implementing defensive strategies. The relationship between perceived privacy threats and the demand for enhanced cybersecurity measures highlights the growing concern among users, underscoring the need for both individual and institutional actions. The analysis revealed that interactions with scammers are prevalent, with most respondents having encountered attempts to solicit personal information via email, WhatsApp, or Telegram. Despite the implementation of protective measures by numerous respondents, the elevated frequency of these instances indicates that the current security features on these platforms are inadequate. The study's correlation matrix reveals that users who frequently encounter fraudsters are more likely to adopt defensive responses; however, this does not necessarily translate into increased concerns about privacy issues. This disconnection suggests that, although consumers acknowledge and react to scams, they may not fully comprehend the broader privacy implications, including data breaches and identity theft. Consequently, there is an imperative need for enhanced platform security, user education, and more rigorous regulatory oversight to address these concerns comprehensively. The findings underscore an urgent necessity for platform providers and policymakers to mitigate the vulnerabilities inherent in digital communication systems.

7. LIMITATIONS AND RECOMMENDATIONS

This chapter examines the impact of email spam, WhatsApp, and Telegram on privacy, cybersecurity, and financial security in Singapore, providing valuable insights. However, it possesses certain limitations. A notable disadvantage is the reliance on self-reported data via questionnaires, which may introduce biases such as underreporting or overestimation of security incidents. Furthermore, although the study employs a diverse sample, its focus on a single nation may limit the applicability of the results to other regions where digital communication and cybersecurity regulations differ. The study's cross-sectional design limits the capacity to analyze long-term patterns in cybersecurity behavior. Notwithstanding these constraints, the study possesses significant ramifications for both practice and policy. It highlights the need for improved user education on cybersecurity threats, particularly in recognizing phishing and spam. Moreover, it emphasizes the necessity of utilizing AI-driven security solutions and enhancing regulatory frameworks to protect individuals against emerging digital risks. Future studies should conduct longitudinal research across multiple geographies and utilize real-time data analysis to gain a more comprehensive understanding of these challenges. The study's findings provide many essential recommendations to decrease the hazards connected with email spam, WhatsApp, and Telegram in Singapore. Initially, platform providers ought to allocate resources toward sophisticated cybersecurity technologies, including artificial intelligence and machine learning, to enhance the identification of phishing attempts, malware, and various types of spam. Prior research indicates that the implementation of AI-based spam filters can markedly decrease the frequency of unsolicited communications. End-to-end encryption, although currently implemented, should be augmented by multi-factor authentication to protect user data. Furthermore, platforms must emphasize transparency in their privacy policies, guaranteeing that users are thoroughly informed on the storage, sharing, and protection of their data. Enhanced encryption mechanisms and more transparent user consent procedures would further mitigate the risks of personal intrusion and data breaches. The Singaporean government should enhance current cybersecurity regulations, notably the Personal Data Protection Act (PDPA), to guarantee that digital platforms adhere to rigorous data protection standards. Stricter sanctions should be imposed on platforms that fail to protect user data adequately. Furthermore, public awareness initiatives emphasizing digital hygiene and cybersecurity protocols are essential. Educational initiatives aimed at enhancing user understanding of privacy hazards, phishing schemes, and cybersecurity threats should be implemented at both community and national levels, with a primary focus on vulnerable populations, including youth and the elderly. Collaboration between foreign cybersecurity agencies and Singapore's regulatory authorities will be essential in mitigating cross-border digital risks. Disseminating

REFERENCES

Abbas, Z., & Robbins, S. (2024). Cybersecurity protocols in human resources: Ensuring legal compliance and ethical standards. *ResearchGate*. https://doi.org/DOI: 10.13140/RG.2.2.17080.76809

Afzal, J. (2024). Best practice of digital laws and digital justice. In Zhang, X., & Liu, S. (Eds.), *Global Digital Laws and Justice* (pp. 105–121). Springer., DOI: 10.1007/978-981-97-7106-6_5

Akkaya, F. D. (2023). HES: A case study on cybersecurity and privacy risks in health surveillance systems. *In L. Santiago & M. Chen (Eds.), Cybersecurity Challenges in Health Systems* (pp. 112-137). IGI Global. DOI: 10.4018/978-1-6684-9018-1.ch006

Alibeigi, A., & Munir, A. B. (2023). Public health data and international privacy rules and practices: A case study of Singapore. In Xu, X., & Liu, Y. (Eds.), *Digital Health Governance* (pp. 57–77). Springer., DOI: 10.1007/978-3-031-39841-4_4

Alkhdour, T., Alrawashdeh, R., Almaiah, M. A., Al-Ali, R., & Salloum, S. A. (2024). A new technique for detecting email spam risks using LSTM-particle swarm optimization algorithms. *Journal of Information Security and Applications*, *65*, 103–119.

Aloumi, D., Malik, S., Alkhaldi, A., & de Pablos, P. O. (2024). Factors influencing consumer interactions with FinTech services. In Xu, X., & Liu, Y. (Eds.), *Advances in FinTech and Cybersecurity* (pp. 217–234). IGI Global., DOI: 10.4018/979-8-3693-5673-9.ch010

Antunes, M., Maximiano, M., Gomes, R., & Pinto, D. (2021). Information security and cybersecurity management: A case study with SMEs in Portugal. *Journal of Cybersecurity Practices*, *10*(2), 12–27. DOI: 10.3390/jcp1020012

Asiryan, S. (2023). Legislative practice of Singapore on the use of artificial intelligence. *Journal of Legislative Studies*, *3*(57), 92–105. DOI: 10.24144/2788-6018.2023.03.57

Badsha, S., Vakilinia, I., & Sengupta, S. (2019). Privacy-preserving cyber threat information sharing and learning for cyber defense. *Proceedings of the IEEE 9th Annual Computing and Communication Workshop and Conference (CCWC)*, 204-210. https://doi.org/DOI: 10.1109/CCWC.2019.8666477

Bae, J. K., & Hong, G. H. (2023). A study on digital financial security threats and cybersecurity policies. *Asian Journal of Banking and Accounting*, *20*(6), 133–149. DOI: 10.38115/asgba.2023.20.6.133

Carmi, G., & Bouhnik, D. (2020). The Effect of Rational Based Beliefs and Awareness on Employee Compliance with Information Security Procedures: A Case Study of a Financial Corporation in Israel. Informing Science. *The International Journal of an Emerging Transdiscipline*, *23*, 189–206. DOI: 10.28945/4596

Chilaka, O. (2024). *The Growing Importance of Cybersecurity in a Digital World.* Retrieved from https://doi.org/DOI: 10.13140/RG.2.2.20886.56641

Chowdhary, S. K., Kumar, P., Mittal, R., Gumber, I., Jangra, V., & Srivastava, P. (2024). Phishing detection tool for financial emails. *Journal of Information Security and Applications*, *11*(4), 2442002. Advance online publication. DOI: 10.1142/S2424786324420027

Dorairajan, V. (2024). Cybersecurity and organizational performance – the interplay. *Acta Cybernetica (Szeged)*, *7*, e129255. DOI: 10.3897/aca.7.e129255

Fenton, A. J. (2024). Preventing catastrophic cyber-physical attacks on the global maritime transportation system: A case study of hybrid maritime security in the Straits of Malacca and Singapore. *Journal of Marine Science and Engineering*, *12*(3), 510–526. DOI: 10.3390/jmse12030510

Fenton, A. J. (2024). Preventing catastrophic cyber-physical attacks on the global maritime transportation system: A case study of hybrid maritime security in the Straits of Malacca and Singapore. *Preprints*. https://doi.org/DOI: 10.20944/preprints202401.1609.v1

Hassan, A., Abatcha, M., & Dada, E. G. (2024). Ensemble machine learning algorithm for Telegram spam detection. *International Journal of Cybersecurity Research*, *10*(8), 123–140.

Herath, H. S. B., & Herath, T. (2006). Justifying spam and e-mail virus security investments: A case study. *Journal of Information Systems Security*, *4*(1), 123–135.

Hezam, I. M., Ali, A. M., Sallam, K. M., Hameed, I. A., & Božanić, D. (2024). *Evaluation based on multi-criteria decision-making methods and spherical fuzzy framework for security and privacy in metaverse technologies: A case study*. American Institute of Physics., DOI: 10.1063/5.0217439

Imron, I., Fridianto, T., & Nugroho, D. H. (2023). Identifikasi bahaya keamanan siber pada perizinan bahan nuklir online di Indonesia. *Jurnal Pengawasan Energi dan Teknologi Nuklir*, [Identification of cybersecurity hazards in online nuclear material licensing in Indonesia. Journal of Nuclear Energy and Technology Supervision]. 3(2), 49-67. https://doi.org/DOI: 10.53862/jupeten.v3i2.003

Joglekar, P., Rajurkar, J., Shinde, M., Tayde, P., & Gadmade, V. (2024). Machine learning based email spam detection: Achieving high accuracy and efficiency. *International Journal for Research in Applied Science and Engineering Technology, 12*(5), 189–202. DOI: 10.22214/ijraset.2024.62390

Josten, M., & Weis, T. (2024). Investigating the effectiveness of Bayesian spam filters in detecting LLM-modified spam mails. *arXiv*. https://doi.org//arXiv.2408.14293DOI: 10.48550

Kankwende, P. (2024). Cybersecurity in the modern age: Protecting digital assets. *Journal of Information Security, 19*(2), 145–160.

Kim, I., Susilo, W., Baek, J., Kim, J., & Chow, Y. W. (2023). PCSF: Privacy-preserving content-based spam filter. *IEEE Transactions on Information Forensics and Security, 18*, 3245–3257. DOI: 10.1109/TIFS.2023.3255172

Kumar, H. S., & Madan, S. (2021). A study on Aadhar privacy and personal security issues in India. *Zenodo*. https://doi.org/DOI: 10.5281/zenodo.4641658

Lahtinen, T., Costin, A., & Suarez-Tangil, G. (2024). *Brain-Computer Interface Integration With Extended Reality (XR)*. Future, Privacy, And Security Outlook., DOI: 10.34190/eccws.23.1.2284

Li, F. (2024). Application and challenges of artificial intelligence in cybersecurity. *Cybersecurity and AI Journal, 14*(3), 135–153. DOI: 10.54254/2755-2721/47/20241480

Muley, T., Sudheer, G., Sinha, K., Narayan, A., Agrawal, R., & Gandhala, S. P. (2024, September). Enhancing Email Spam Detection through Ensemble Learning: A Combined Approach of LSTM and Neural Network. In *2024 Asian Conference on Intelligent Technologies (ACOIT)* (pp. 1-6). IEEE.

Patil, N. (2024). Spam mail detection using blockchain. *International Journal of Scientific Research and Engineering Management, 9*(2), 72–83. DOI: 10.55041/IJSREM34520

Prokopowicz, D. (2023). *How does the development of generative artificial intelligence technology affect the development of cybercrime techniques and the improvement of cybersecurity systems?* Research Proposal, https://doi.org/DOI: 10.13140/RG.2.2.34354.00962

Sharma, D. P., Lashkari, A. H., & Parizadeh, M. (2024). *Understanding Cybersecurity Management in Healthcare: Challenges, Strategies and Trends*. Springer., DOI: 10.1007/978-3-031-68034-2

Shawky, M. (2023). *13 Types of Cyber Attacks You Should Know in 2023*.

Siew, R. (2024). Strengthening big data security and privacy in libraries: A review of ISO standards and real-world cyberattack case studies. *Journal of Information Security and Technology, 11*(2), 123–138. DOI: 10.5339/jist.2024.11

Styoutomo, Y. A., & Ruldeviyani, Y. (2023). Information Security Awareness Raising Strategy Using Fuzzy AHP Method with HAIS-Q and ISO/IEC 27001: 2013: A Case Study of XYZ Financial Institution. *CommIT (Communication and Information Technology). Journal, 17*(2), 133–149. DOI: 10.21512/commit.v17i2.8272

Thapaliya, S. (2024). *Examining the Influence of AI-Driven Cybersecurity in Financial Sector Management.* Banking and Technology Journal., DOI: 10.3126/batuk.v10i2.68147

Thapliyal, S., Wazid, M., & Singh, D. P. (2022, June). Defining the Convergence of Artificial Intelligence and Cyber Security with a Case Study of Email Spam Detection. In *International Conference on Soft Computing and Signal Processing* (pp. 181-190). Singapore: Springer Nature Singapore. https://doi.org/DOI: 10.1007/978-981-19-8669-7_17

Venčkauskas, A., Toldinas, J., Morkevicius, N., & Sanfilippo, F. (2024). An email cyber threat intelligence method using domain ontology and machine learning. *Electronics (Basel), 13*(14), 2716. DOI: 10.3390/electronics13142716

Wang, J., & Yishake, G. (2024). *Along the Deep Interface of Digital Food: Islanding and Networking amidst the Territorialization of Uygur Cuisine.* Retrieved from https://doi.org/DOI: 10.13140/RG.2.2.20712.07683

Wang, Y. (2024). Realistic dilemma and path optimization of online personal information protection. *Journal of Information Protection, 39*(1), 728–740. DOI: 10.51251/2753 7048/39/20240728

Wisdom, D. D., Vincent, O. R., Igulu, K., Arowolo, M. O., & Hyacinth, E. A. (2023). *Mitigating Cyber Threats in Healthcare Systems: The Role of Artificial Intelligence and Machine Learning.* In *Cybersecurity for Healthcare Systems* (pp. 299-318). IET. DOI: 10.1049/PBHE061E_ch13

Chapter 3
Security Management Practices in Social Sciences and Humanities: Safeguarding Research Integrity and Data

Andi Asrifan
https://orcid.org/0000-0002-9934-6129
Universitas Negeri Makassar, Indonesia

Chirapat Kaewnaknaew
https://orcid.org/0009-0004-5027-5990
City University, Klongtoey, Malaysia

ABSTRACT

Social science and humanities (SSH) security management for research integrity and ethical data handling is covered in this chapter. Due to its different ethnic and socioeconomic participants, SSH research requires confidentiality, informed permission, and anonymity. The qualitative investigation used Google Scholar, Scopus, and Web of Science papers. The chapter discusses how digitalization and online data collection have exacerbated cybersecurity threats like data leaks and illegal access. It stresses ethical oversight, including IRB and GDPR compliance. In interdisciplinary and transnational SSH research, scholars must traverse numerous legal regimes and collaborate across boundaries. Use encryption, secure storage, and strict data management to safeguard sensitive data. Institutions should support comprehensive cybersecurity and ethical research policies and training, the chapter says. Security precautions are essential for public trust, study validity, and participant rights and well-being.

DOI: 10.4018/979-8-3693-9720-6.ch003

1. INTRODUCTION

1.1 Overview of Research Security in Social Sciences and Humanities

Social sciences and humanities (SSH) research often involves human participants, sensitive cultural and societal data, and a range of methods. This compromises research and data security. The hard sciences rely on controlled experiments and quantitative data, whereas SSH areas research complex, context-sensitive phenomena, making security management problematic. Protecting sensitive data is a significant issue in SSH research. Interviews with vulnerable groups, ethnographic studies of marginalized communities, and sensitive archive research are examples. Researchers often face ethical challenges, including obtaining informed consent, maintaining anonymity, and ensuring confidentiality. People trust researchers with personal data—trust breaches, whether due to data protection issues or misuse, can impact research and communities. The integrity of SSH research must also assure reproducibility and transparency. Data from qualitative research is interpretative and difficult to standardize or share. Transparency and participant anonymity present security challenges for researchers. Complexity increases when SSH research uses more digital tools and platforms. Researchers are increasingly using digital archives, internet surveys, and social media data collection. This increases cybersecurity, data breach, and unauthorized access risks. Data protection is crucial for maintaining research integrity, particularly in the face of cyberattacks and hacking. Interdisciplinary social sciences and humanities research usually involves cross-institutional, cross-border, and cross-sector collaboration. Research data security is complicated by the interplay of legal and regulatory frameworks, mainly when working with global partners. To prevent legal and ethical concerns, researchers must follow data privacy regulations in various jurisdictions (Schinagl & Shahim, 2020; Josa & Aguado, 2021; Bonaccorsi et al., 2021; Carter et al., 2021; Eakin & Gladstone, 2020; King et al., 2021; Nadji, 2021; Zarour et al., 2021).

1.2 Importance of Safeguarding Research Integrity

Academic research demands integrity for credibility, trustworthiness, and ethical standards. Due to the complex and subjective nature of data and its impact on policy, education, and society, researchers in the social sciences and humanities (SSH) must maintain research integrity. SSH research validity and effect depend on research integrity, not just academic quality. First, research process integrity determines credibility—academic honesty, transparency, and accountability foster trust among colleagues, politicians, and the public. Researchers at SSH examine human behavior, civilizations, and social issues. Therefore, trust matters. Data manipulation, plagiarism, and ethical infractions can contaminate study results and undermine the reputations of researchers and organizations. SSH research is subjective and interpretive, making precise criteria even more important to avoid bias and distortion. Second, SSH research fosters honesty socially. These studies have a significant impact on public policy, education, and social interventions. Sociology, political science, and history influence legislation, policies, and social initiatives. Research corruption can result in inefficient or harmful policy. Poor sociological research can affect disadvantaged populations and propagate stereotypes (Misra & Agarwal, 2020; Holden et al., 2021; Bhaskar & Ola; Cairns et al., 2021; Amoah & Steyn, 2023).

Therefore, maintaining the integrity of SSH research is crucial for precise and effective societal contributions. Moreover, research integrity bolsters the scholarly function of academic institutions. Educators utilize credible research to instruct pupils, who then maintain these principles in their academic pursuits. Students and emerging scholars cultivate sincerity, robust technique, and reverence for intellectual property by adhering to academic integrity. Safeguarding research integrity has a profound influence on future researchers and scholars.

1.3 Defining Security Management in Academic Research

Academic research security management encompasses various methods for ensuring data integrity, confidentiality, and accessibility. Research integrity and ethics in the social sciences and humanities (SSH) necessitate security management due to the sensitive nature of human subjects, personal data, and complex ethical challenges. In SSH, qualitative data, such as interviews, ethnographic field notes, and personal histories, are sensitive and require protection. This data must be protected from unauthorized access, breaches, and leaks. Examples include data security audits, file encryption, and secure physical and digital storage. For collection, storage, disposal, and archiving, researchers must construct detailed data management plans (DMPs). These preparations must comply with the European Union's General Data Protection Regulation (GDPR) regarding the handling of personal data. Security research necessitates ethical principles that extend beyond technical security considerations. SSH research emphasizes ethical security management, stressing the rights and well-being of participants. This procedure requires informed consent, anonymity, and an explanation of data usage. IRBs assess research proposals for ethics. The researcher must follow these guidelines from data collection to publication. Research security requires secure methodologies. These demand rigorous data collecting, processing, and storage tools and methodologies. Online survey researchers require secure technology and robust privacy protections. Before fieldwork, researchers should understand secure data gathering practices to avoid theft. Software tools should follow security requirements during analysis to prevent data tampering or unauthorized access (Puputti, 2022; Muhonen et al., 2020; Leng et al., 2020; Hantrais & Lenihan, 2021; Resnik, 2021; Lynch et al., 2022; Smyth et al., 2024; Cochrane et al., 2024).

This section discusses data protection, ethical norms, and secure procedures that support the security management of academic research.

2. LITERATURE REVIEW

2.1 Principles of Research Integrity

Research integrity in the social sciences and humanities (SSH) is essential for ethical and professional conduct. These rules assist researchers in doing ethical research. Honesty, transparency, and accountability are crucial for the credibility of researchers and public confidence in SSH, mainly when studies involve complex human behaviors, social dynamics, and cultural contexts. All academic research begins honestly. It requires honesty in research design, techniques, analysis, and reporting. In SSH, where data often includes personal narratives, subjective interpretations, or qualitative findings, honesty entails accurately presenting participants' voices, avoiding misrepresentation, and acknowledging study limitations and uncertainties. Researchers must not falsify, mislead, or misreport data to avoid distorting social phenomena and reaching harmful conclusions. Intellectual integrity requires giving source credit and acknowledging the work of other scholars. Transparency is another SSH research value. These groups require transparency because they involve interpretation and subjective judgment. Researchers must clearly and adequately disclose their design, methods, data collection, and analysis. Transparency enables other researchers to evaluate, replicate, and build upon the research. Transparent processes share data when possible to enable research while protecting participant privacy. SSH research transparency demands balancing ethics and openness. SSH researchers must act ethically before academics, society, participants, and funders. Investigators must follow legal, institutional, and ethical guidelines. This includes ensuring participant safety, obtaining informed consent, and maintaining confidentiality. Researchers must take responsibility for their interpretations as these may impact public policy, education, and social initiatives. Accountability includes adequate research funding, accurate progress reporting, and resolving conflicts of interest that could jeopardize the study. Honesty, transparency, and accountability underpin the ethics of research in the social sciences and humanities. They safeguard research integrity and protect participants, society, and the academic community.

Academic trust, responsible research, and the role of SSH research in social progress are promoted by these values. This chapter applies these key ideas to social science and humanities research security (Durmaz et al., 2020; Xu et al., 2020; Husband, 2020; Bonaccorsi et al., 2021; Schuijer et al., 2021; Valkenburg et al., 2021; Freese et al., 2022; Sofyani et al., 2022; Perković et al., 2024; Kolstoe & Pugh, 2023).

2.2 Ethical Guidelines and Regulations

Social sciences and humanities (SSH) scholars must adhere to ethical guidelines to ensure research integrity, respect participant rights, maintain fairness, and uphold the highest ethical standards. These national and international guidelines help researchers confront ethical difficulties in their research. SSH research involves human participants and sensitive data; therefore, following these guidelines safeguards individuals and communities while maintaining the integrity of the study. Many nations have established ethical or institutional review boards (IRBs) to oversee research involving human participants. Informed consent, confidentiality, risk minimization, and benefits are considered by these bodies when reviewing study proposals. Researchers must prioritize the rights and well-being of participants, as mandated by Institutional Review Boards (IRBs). The Common Rule ensures the ethical conduct of human subjects research in federally supported projects in countries such as the United States. International ethics standardize research across companies and boundaries. SSH research adheres to the principles outlined in the Declaration of Helsinki for biomedical research, including respect for human beings, obtaining informed consent, and minimizing harm. These principles ensure that researchers respect participants' autonomy, provide them with sufficient information to make informed decisions, and protect their privacy and well-being. The GDPR protects personal data in the EU, which in turn influences SSH research. Researchers must obtain explicit consent and be transparent when collecting, retaining, and using personal data in accordance with the GDPR. This legislation has significantly impacted how European and international academics manage data, underscoring the importance of robust security in SSH research, where personal data is sensitive and complex. Another key ethical guidance for US human subject research is the Belmont Report (1979). Respect for humans encompasses the principles of obtaining informed consent and acknowledging autonomy, beneficence (maximizing benefits while minimizing harm to participants), and justice (fairly distributing research rewards and obligations), which are its three main principles. SSH researchers apply these principles to make informed ethical decisions, particularly when studying underprivileged communities. Particular SSH disciplines adhere to ethical standards. The Code of Ethics of the American Anthropological Association advocates for informed consent, mitigates harm, and guarantees transparency with research participants. The

American Historical Association upholds ethical standards for historians that stress the appropriate utilization of archival materials, reverence for historical subjects, and the prevention of plagiarism (Shamoo & Khin-Maung-Gyi, 2021; Nagai et al., 2022; Lantos, 2020; Chatfield et al., 2021; Schmidt, 2023; Cochrane et al., 2024).

2.3 Common Integrity Issues and Misconduct

The social sciences and humanities (SSH) require research integrity to produce accurate, ethical, and reliable knowledge that benefits both academia and society. As in other academic fields, research misconduct can erode this integrity, undermining the legitimacy of studies and eroding trust in scholars. SSH integrity issues include plagiarism, data tampering, and forging. These misconducts taint research and scholarship. Academic plagiarism is perhaps the most notorious act of failing to properly credit others' ideas, discoveries, or statements. In SSH, where scholars build on previous theories and interpretations, plagiarism can occur when researchers fail to acknowledge sources or copy or paraphrase others' work. Plagiarism undermines the researcher's authority, erodes the trust of the academic community, and tarnishes the institution's reputation. Plagiarism can lead to action for IP violations. Research data tampering for a predefined objective is unethical. SSH data is qualitative and interpretable. Thus, manipulation can include publishing findings that support a hypothesis while suppressing contrary information. Selective reporting can misrepresent study results and impact policy or historical outcomes. Omitting participant responses or downplaying data anomalies can significantly impact sociological or psychological studies. Since findings no longer reflect reality, research integrity is threatened. A key research integrity issue is fabrication. It entails creating data, sources, or discoveries. SSH researchers may fake interviews, historical documents, or survey results to support their assertions. SSH falsification can distort research, policies, and education. False historical studies can damage public understanding. False data undermines peer review and replication, thereby eroding academic reputation. Researchers may exaggerate the relevance or scope of their findings. In SSH, where outcomes are interpretive, researchers may overstate the social or cultural impact of their work without evidence (Dal-Ré et al., 2020; Xie et al., 2021; De-Grendele et al., 2022; Mansoor et al., 2024; Välikangas, 2024; Smyth et al., 2024).

2.4 Ethical Data Collection Methods

Research integrity in the social sciences and humanities (SSH) necessitates ethical data collection, mainly when working with sensitive cultural or social groups. Researchers must obtain informed consent, respect privacy, and minimize harm by using sound data-gathering methods—the cornerstone of ethical data collection in delicate situations and research integrity. Informed consent supports ethical data collecting. Participants must understand the study's objectives, purpose, risks, and benefits. The researcher and participant must communicate during informed consent. In sensitive social or cultural contexts, literacy, language issues, and cultural consent must be considered. Researchers may need to modify consent methods to ensure informed consent. Some Indigenous cultures involve community leaders or elders in addition to participants to ensure that research respects collective decision-making processes. In SSH studies related to political opposition, mental health, and trauma, anonymous and discreet participation is required. Researchers must employ pseudonyms, encrypt data, and secure sensitive data to protect participants. In ethnographic studies of small communities, where people may be recognized despite efforts to remain anonymous, researchers must inform participants and obtain their consent. Cultural understanding is essential for ethical data collection. Anthropologists, sociologists, and historians study cultures with different data sharing and privacy norms. Cultural backgrounds must inform research ethics. Some Native groups share data. Thus, researchers may need to obtain group approval to collect, use, and share data. Researchers should not apply foreign ethical frameworks that contradict local practices or beliefs, as this can undermine community relationships and ethics. Another data-collecting ethical principle is minimizing harm. Researchers must ensure that their procedures do not harm participants in any way, whether mentally, emotionally, or physically. Working with refugees, trauma survivors, and the poor demands this. Researchers should address personal trauma questions and provide support if individuals are distressed during data collection. Researchers should not leverage participant interactions to benefit populations beyond academia (Appiah, 2021; Newman et al., 2021; Josa & Aguado, 2021; Derrick & Ross-Hellauer, 2024; Cochrane et al., 2024).

2.5 Data Storage and Confidentiality

Ethical social science and humanities studies involve data security and confidentiality. These researchers handle sensitive personal data, making secure storage crucial for participant privacy and legal and ethical compliance. In an era of data breaches and cyberattacks, data storage security is crucial for maintaining research integrity and fostering participant trust. Research participant confidentiality is a top priority for data preservation. Interview transcripts, field notes, and survey replies may contain sensitive SSH data. De-identifying or anonymizing data is recommended practice for researchers to ensure confidentiality. For participant privacy, this may involve erasing names and addresses and utilizing pseudonyms or codes. Anonymous research with disadvantaged groups or in politically sensitive contexts is necessary to protect participants. Safe digital storage requires encryption. Data is encrypted for authorized users. Researchers should encrypt sensitive data at rest and in transit. Encrypted file storage with passwords and two-factor authentication can protect data. Researchers should store encrypted data backups in secure locations to prevent data loss due to technical failures or accidents. Paper records, audio recordings, and artifacts need encryption and physical security. Only authorized staff should access locked cabinets or protected rooms with sensitive data. Only authorized researchers should access secure interview tapes and handwritten field notes. This protection prevents unauthorized access or theft, which could compromise the confidentiality of studies. Maintaining data confidentiality requires compliance with data protection regulations, such as the GDPR in Europe or HIPAA in the US. These guidelines require participants to consent to data collection and storage and be informed of their rights. They can also seek data withdrawal or deletion. Institutional norms, IRB data management, and regulatory compliance criteria must also be followed by researchers. The management of data exchange should also ensure privacy. Researchers should share research data with collaborators via encrypted, restricted data-sharing platforms and create complete data management plans (DMPs) for data access, storage, and disposal after the study (Surmiak, 2020; Fiero & Beier, 2022; Campbell et al., 2023; Fisher, 2023).

2.6 Data Sharing and Access Control

To foster transparency and collaboration, researchers in the social sciences and humanities must share their data. Data sharing must strike a balance between participant anonymity and intellectual property rights. Data sharing and access management ensure the privacy of sensitive data while enabling academics to benefit from their research. This section discusses data sharing with participant anonymity and IP rights in mind. When sharing research data in SSH, participant anonymity is important because studies sometimes involve personal or sensitive information. Before sharing data, researchers should anonymize names, addresses, and other personal information. A qualitative study with narratives or situations that expose participants' identities must be re-identified. Instead of using direct identities, pseudonyms or coding techniques hide potentially revealing data while keeping analytical usefulness. To achieve consent, researchers must tell participants about data sharing and privacy protection. Researchers can restrict access to critical datasets to protect participants. Researchers or supervisory bodies must authorize access to secure repositories. These repositories often require secondary users to handle data in an ethical manner. Data-use agreements (DUAs) can regulate application limitations, participant anonymity, and the daily use of data. IP protection is another crucial aspect of data transmission. SSH researchers must protect their theories, analyses, and interpretations. Researchers should utilize licensing agreements to specify how others can utilize their data and intellectual contributions, thereby avoiding potential IP infringement. Open-access research platforms often utilize Creative Commons licenses that require attribution and the reuse of data. Researchers must also adhere to data privacy rules, such as the GDPR, when sharing personal data. These policies often require participant consent for data sharing and prohibit the migration of data between businesses and across borders. Researchers must adhere to institutional and national laws when transferring data, particularly when it crosses jurisdictions with differing privacy laws. DMPs must store, safeguard, and distribute data during and after research for responsible data sharing. DMPs should indicate data reuse, anonymity, and access. Researchers can avoid ethical and legal concerns when sharing data by planning these aspects (Ducato, 2020; Tamburri, 2020; Fecher et al., 2021; Thapa & Camtepe, 2021; Manral & Somani, 2021; Fadlelmola et al., 2021).

2.7 Cybersecurity Threats in Research

Social science and humanities researchers are increasingly concerned about cybersecurity as they increasingly utilize digital tools and platforms. Data breaches, hacking, and phishing attacks pose a significant threat to the security, integrity, and availability of research data. These threats compromise the privacy of study participants and undermine the legitimacy of the program. Research data must be protected in a connected internet world by understanding cybersecurity issues. Hacking is a significant cybersecurity risk for researchers. To steal data or disrupt operations, hackers target research databases, digital archives, and personal accounts. Interviews, participant surveys, and ethnographic field notes may contain sensitive personal or political information. Hence, SSH researchers assume substantial risks. Hackers can damage the credibility of participants and researchers with this data. Cybercriminals may steal unpublished discoveries or data analysis methods from institutional networks or poorly secured research environments. Phishing—a cyberattack that steals passwords, login credentials, or personal data—is another significant research issue. Academic research often involves phishing emails from colleagues, funders, or administrators. Hackers can modify data, steal sensitive information, and infiltrate research databases by deceiving researchers into sharing their accounts. Phishing that exposes participant data or sensitive research information can jeopardize the project and the organization. Data breaches—unauthorized access to research data—are another cybersecurity hazard. Security holes, insecure databases, and compromised accounts can trigger data leaks. Personal or sensitive SSH research data breaches might be damaging. A breach revealing the identities of politically sensitive study subjects could inflict legal, social, or physical harm. Data breaches can damage the reputations of researchers and organizations, thereby diminishing public trust in research. Researchers also confront malware and ransomware threats that can disrupt operations or steal data. Hackers charge researchers to unlock their systems. Such attacks can hamper SSH researchers, especially when years of work or sensitive data are at stake. State-sponsored hacking groups may try to suppress conflict and human rights research. SSH researchers must adhere to digital security best practices to mitigate cybersecurity threats. This includes strong, unique passwords and 2FA for research databases and email. Software and security must be updated to close hacker vulnerabilities. Another security precaution is encrypting sensitive data at rest and in transit. Researchers should also recognize phishing and social engineering frauds (Alabdan, 2020; Parti & Szigeti, 2021; Dupont & Whelan, 2021; Van de Sandt, 2021; Kaur et al.., 2022; Bellini & Degl'Innocenti, 2024).

2.8 Encryption and Secure Communication Tools

In the digital age, social scientists and humanists must protect data and communication. From interviewing vulnerable communities to handling politically sensitive material, SSH research requires strong digital security. Research data and researcher communications must be protected by encryption and secure communication methods regarding online research protection tools and strategies. Encryption protects data well. Decryption keys are needed to read encrypted data. The main encryption methods are rest and transit. Research files on desktops and in the cloud are protected by encryption at rest. To protect vital data on devices and in the cloud, researchers should use AES-256. Data in transit is encrypted to prevent unscrupulous actors from intercepting online communications, file transfers, and surveys. Researchers use SSL and TLS to encrypt data shared between participants and collaborators. Researchers require secure communication tools when discussing sensitive topics or sharing confidential information. Research communications can be compromised by email and messaging network hacking. Researchers' end-to-end encrypted messages should only be read by intended receivers. End-to-end encryption protects Signal and WhatsApp messages from third parties. These strategies are suitable for communicating with colleagues or politically sensitive research participants when secrecy is important. Tresorit, Sync.com, and SpiderOak enable encrypted file sharing in the cloud. Keeping important research information encrypted at rest and in transit prevents illegal access. Researchers should also distribute files with password-protected URLs or access controls to prevent unwanted viewing and downloading. Multi-factor authentication (MFA) for cloud storage accounts helps prevent hackers from accessing research materials using compromised passwords. Researchers should encrypt their internet connections with VPNs, especially when using public Wi-Fi or in areas prone to surveillance. VPNs encrypt all internet traffic between a researcher's device and the VPN server, preventing hackers from monitoring online activity (Gentile et al., 2021; Adee & Mouratidis, 2022; Shaik & Natarajan, 2022).

2.9 Protecting Participant Privacy Online

In the digital age, research ethics in the social sciences and humanities (SSH) require respect for participant privacy. Researchers must safeguard participants' data as online surveys, video interviews, and cloud-based storage platforms become more widespread. It emphasizes data anonymization, secure platforms, and informed consent to ensure participant privacy when utilizing digital tools. Participant privacy requires data anonymization. Names, addresses, and other identifying information are removed during the anonymization process. Context-driven qualitative research can involve pseudo-anonymization. Pseudonyms or unique codes can protect participants' identities without compromising data quality. Researchers should only acquire data essential for their research and not personal data. Inform participants of the limits and allow them to withdraw if anonymization is impossible. Protecting privacy involves collecting secure digital data. Hacking or data breaches can jeopardize sensitive participant data in online surveys, interviews, and data-sharing technology. Researchers should transit and store data using end-to-end encryption. Qualtrics, SurveyMonkey, and Google Forms encrypt responses. Zoom and Signal are good encrypted video interview services. Researchers should also ensure that all digital instruments comply with the strict European General Data Privacy Regulation (GDPR). Ethical research requires informed consent, and the online setting complicates this process. Researchers must disclose how personal data will be used, stored, and safeguarded when collecting data online. It encompasses digital tools, privacy, and mitigation strategies. Researchers should also obtain express consent for the collection and use of digital data and inform participants of their right to withdraw and request the deletion of their data. Digital permission forms must disclose data usage and storage practices, just like traditional ones. Protecting participant privacy involves access management. Researchers should only share sensitive participant data with authorized users. Manage data viewing and downloading with encrypted cloud storage. Google Drive, Dropbox, and Tresorit access controls allow researchers to restrict data accessibility and participant privacy. Data theft can be prevented using account MFA (Facca et al., 2020; Gesualdo et al., 2021; Tomás et al., 2022; Smyth et al., 2024; Rooney et al., 2024).

3. METHODOLOGY

3.1 Data Collection

Narrative synthesis involves the systematic review and integration of data from multiple investigations, utilizing textual material to summarize and clarify the findings.

A comprehensive literature review was conducted using search phrases such as "qualitative," "qualitative research," and "qualitative data analysis (Kraiwanit et al., 2023; Phuangsuwan et al., 2024). According to the data collection and analysis, this qualitative study employed a narrative review based on scholarly papers in Google Scholar, Scopus, and Web of Science (WOS). Three reviewers evaluated the chapter, and revisions have been made to ensure its quality. Grammarly has been used for grammar and plagiarism. The results show that plagiarism is 1%, and grammar is 96% for appropriateness. A word cloud is used to identify keywords and content related to this chapter.

3.2 Data Analysis

This chapter employed a systematic review based on the studies of

Content analysis was employed to examine the data. Content analysis is a qualitative methodology for systematically and objectively delineating and measuring particular occurrences derived from spoken, visual, or written data (Kraiwanit et al., 2023; Phuangsuwan et al., 2024).

4. RESULTS

Figure 1. Plagiarism checking using Grammarly

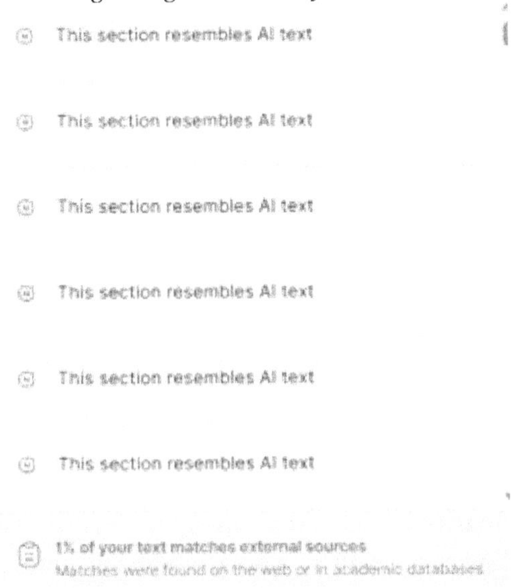

Figure 2. Word cloud generator (2025)

https://www.freewordcloudgenerator.com/generatewordcloud

5. DISCUSSIONS

5.1 Crisis Management in Research: Responding to Breaches and Misconduct

5.1.1 Identifying Breaches of Integrity and Data Security

According to the studies by Karhulahti & Backe (2021), Armond et al. (2021), Perwej et al. (2021), Gedutis et al. (2022), Seara & Serrão (2024), and Nadji (2023). It could be discussed as follows:

Social sciences and humanities (SSH) research needs integrity and data security to build trust, safeguard participants, and verify findings. Despite significant efforts, integrity or data security breaches may compromise the study. Fixing research integrity or data security issues starts with recognition. Reviewing these critical indications helps researchers spot and address breaches promptly. Research integrity violations include plagiarism, data fabrication, and falsification. Data inconsistency may indicate an integrity breach. Abnormally perfect, statistically implausible, or too close to a hypothesis research results may indicate data manipulation or falsification. Data analysis that provides drastically divergent outcomes or an ambiguous study method may reveal malfeasance. Discrepancies between raw data and findings from peer review or collaboration may compromise the integrity of the data. Plagiarism detection methods reveal similarities in uncited text or ideas, another integrity breach. Unauthorized access, deletion, or exposure of research data may compromise participants' privacy and undermine the validity of the study. Access to research databases or cloud storage platforms from unknown IP addresses or at irregular times may signal data security breaches. Researchers may identify altered or missing files indicating unauthorized access. Collaboration or team members reporting that they are unable to access encrypted or password-protected files may indicate an access control vulnerability. Alerts from cybersecurity monitoring services regarding suspicious activity, such as firewall bypasses or multiple failed login attempts, pose significant security hazards. Leaking confidential data is another symptom of a data breach. Public forums, social media, and illegal access may expose sensitive research data including participant responses and unpublished results. Concerned participants contacting researchers about their data may reveal data security breaches. Researchers should utilize continuous monitoring systems to track the use of digital research tools and access to data repositories, thereby mitigating these risks. Compare raw and processed data, validate metadata, and utilize version control systems to track changes and identify vulnerabilities early. Researchers should also monitor cybersecurity warnings and discover suspicious activity in real time.

5.1.2 Reporting and Handling Misconduct

According to the studies by Barnes et al. (2020), Perera et al. (2022), Hughes et al. (2022), El-Adaway and Jennings (2022), Rucz (2022), and Smith and Walsh (2023). It could be discussed as follows;

Research integrity and data security breaches necessitate immediate crisis management to safeguard participants, maintain research credibility, and protect institutional reputation. There are precise procedures for reporting and escalating SSH research misconduct. Researchers and institutions should address data security and integrity breaches with transparency, responsibility, and ethics. Internal reporting for misconduct should adhere to institutional norms. Most universities and research institutions have Research Integrity Offices or ethics review boards (IRBs) that oversee research ethics. Researchers must promptly report instances of plagiarism, data fabrication, and security breaches to their supervisors. Many organizations offer anonymous reporting methods for researchers and whistleblowers to report potential breaches. Reporting misconduct early can reduce damage and prevent it. The institution frequently investigates misconduct to assess its severity. A formal Research Integrity Office or special committee probe is usually used for this method. To protect the accuser and the accused until a verdict is reached, confidentiality is necessary. The inquiry may involve reviewing research records, interviewing relevant parties, and evaluating data files for manipulation or inconsistencies. For justice, institutions should safeguard privacy and be honest. The institution must impose disciplinary repercussions for wrongdoing, which may include formal reprimands, publication retraction, suspension of research funding, or termination of the contract. If a data breach violates participant privacy, the institution must notify affected participants and provide identity protection or legal support. If internal resolution fails, other entities may be necessary, especially if the violation involves significant ethical concerns. These can include funding agencies, professional groups, or regulatory bodies, such as the US Office of Research Integrity (ORI) or similar organizations abroad. Funding agencies have strict research ethics criteria and expect prompt reporting of any violations to ensure grant compliance. If the wrongdoing violates privacy laws, such as the GDPR, authorities may take action. Researchers must adhere to journal and professional organization retraction standards to remove erroneous research from the public domain. This protects academic records and reduces damage to the scientific community from fake or compromised research.

5.1.3 Restoring Trust After Integrity Breaches

According to the studies of Kirya, 2020; Di et al., 2021; Gonzalez-Granadillo et al., 2021; Cvitanovic et al., 2021; Canfield et al., 2022; Sofyani et al., 2022; Newcomb et al., 2021; Bowen et al., 2022; Ferretti et al., 2022; and Saeed et al., 2024. It could be discussed as follows:

Research integrity and data security breaches are the primary issues. Restoring trust with stakeholders—research participants, academic colleagues, funding bodies, and the public—is crucial but challenging. The researcher, institution, and field may suffer reputational damage due to misconduct or data security breaches. After an integrity violation, researchers and organizations can restore trust by being transparent, responsible, and proactive with affected parties. Trust restoration begins with breach admission. After discovering and investigating the compromise, researchers and their institutions must promptly and openly notify stakeholders. Ethics and accountability are shown by transparency. Report data security breaches, participant privacy violations, and research misconduct, such as data manipulation or plagiarism, to stakeholders. Downplaying or suppressing disaster details may damage the trust of researchers and institutions. Admit it and take responsibility. Researchers who have been hacked must retract articles, modify their methods, or protect their data. Repeated breaches may necessitate substantial internal investigations, accountability measures, and process adjustments. Publicly accepting responsibility demonstrates that researchers and the institution value research integrity. Communication with research participants, funders, and partners is crucial. Participants, especially those whose data was taken, need incident and mitigation details. Identity protection, legal advice, and future data protection may be provided. Funders require assurances that corrective actions have been implemented and that future research will be conducted ethically and securely. Collaborators should be aware of how the breach impacts their joint efforts and what steps are being taken. Science must be corrected to restore academic credibility. Researchers must contact academic journals and agencies to retract or change data-fabricated work. Retraction is crucial for research integrity, despite its short-term impacts. Rewriting history demonstrates that academics acknowledge the importance of transparency and intellectual honesty, as valued by researchers and institutions. An honest retraction and explanation of the infringement let academics move forward without fear of ruined research. Institutions and scholars must do more to restore confidence. Higher data security standards, research ethics training, and internal audits may prevent recurrence. Institutions may adopt new data management policies or routinely examine research procedures to learn from past breaches.

5.2 Building Institutional Support for Research Security

5.2.1 Developing Institutional Policies and Protocols

According to the studies of Favaretto et al. (2020), Degn (2020), Sefcik et al. (2020), Sørensen et al. (2021), Hakimi et al. (2021), Stoesz & Eaton (2022), Atenas et al. (2023), and Risi et al. (2023). It could be discussed as follows:

Research integrity and data protection rules at institutions are crucial to the credibility and ethics of social science and humanities research. SSH research is increasingly utilizing digital tools and online data collection methods. Thus, institutions must protect sensitive data, prevent misbehavior, and assure ethical research. Institutions can establish transparent, responsible, and well-trained research integrity and data security policies. Making institutional policy starts with clarifying research integrity norms. These guidelines should address informed consent, confidentiality, data quality, and transparency in research. International frameworks, such as the Declaration of Helsinki and the Belmont Report, can help organizations meet their ethical requirements. With clear consequences, policies should handle plagiarism, data manipulation, and conflict of interest. All researchers must have access to these rules, which should be included in the onboarding process and updated to reflect new ethical challenges, such as those arising from digital research contexts. Institutional policymaking demands data security. Institutions need data security rules to prevent cyberattacks, data breaches, and unauthorized access. These approaches should encrypt, protect, and restrict sensitive data during and after the study. Institutions should store data on secure, encrypted servers or cloud platforms that comply with the GDPR and other relevant data protection regulations. Policies should cover data retention, secure destruction, and sharing/transfer. Institutional research security requires accountability. Create Research Integrity Offices or Ethical Review Boards (IRBs) to manage ethics and security. These bodies should review research proposals, monitor compliance, investigate infractions, and discipline where necessary. Institutions should also assess data security and research integrity using internal audits. Transparent and impartial structures foster confidence among researchers and stakeholders, reinforcing the institution's commitment to ethical research. Training and education have a significant influence on the success of institutional policies. Researchers handling sensitive data or digital technologies must know how to maintain research integrity and data security. Institutions should mandate training in cybersecurity, data protection, ethical research, and secure communication. Researchers' professional development should include ongoing training for emerging threats and new technologies. Institutions should prioritize ongoing education to ensure researchers are familiar with the appropriate methods and can effectively address ethical and security challenges. Institutions must promote research security, integrity, and transparency. Policies should let researchers report misconduct without fear of punishment. Hide-and-seek can be prevented with anonymous reporting and defect detection technologies. Researchers, ethical review boards, and institutional leadership must communicate to maintain research integrity. Practical institutional research integrity and data security policies and procedures require a diverse approach. Establishing explicit ethical principles, implementing robust data security measures, establishing accountability systems, and providing thorough training programs can create a research climate that values integrity, protects sensitive data, and promotes the highest ethical standards. Maintaining the validity, trustworthiness, legality, and ethics of SSH research requires adherence to these policies.

5.2.2 Training and Education for Researchers

According to the studies of Moher et al. 2020, Hantrais & Lenihan (2021), Armond et al. (2021), Foulds et al. (2022), and Labadie & Legner (2023). It could be discussed as follows:

As social science and humanities research employs more digital tools and sensitive data, researchers must be trained to tackle complex ethical and security challenges. Researchers need continual education and training to stay current on best practices and regulations. As mentioned, continuous education increases research security and integrity. The fast growth of digital tools and cybersecurity dangers require ongoing education. SSH researchers use digital platforms for data collection, communication, and analysis, increasing their hacking, phishing, and data breach risk. In cybersecurity workshops, researchers can learn how to encrypt storage, safeguard communication, and restrict access. This training can cover MFA, phishing, and safe data sharing with coworkers. Regular training keeps researchers informed about emerging threats and how to address them, thereby protecting sensitive data and maintaining research integrity. Training helps researchers comply with data protection and privacy laws, such as GDPR and HIPAA. These policies limit data collection, storage, and dissemination, especially in human participant research. Legal compliance training enables researchers to understand complex regulations and prevent legal issues. For legal and ethical compliance, these courses should cover informed permission for digital data collection, anonymization, and cross-border data transfers. Training and instruction prioritize ethical research. Mental health, politics, and poor communities are common SSH topics. Participants' rights and well-being necessitate training for researchers. Workshops on ethics can cover topics such as informed consent, confidentiality, and working with vulnerable groups. These training programs help researchers examine ethical issues and make informed decisions that prioritize participant safety and dignity. Institutions can provide researchers with online guidelines, case studies, and toolkits, in addition to workshops. Online research integrity, data security, and ethics lessons help researchers learn optimal practices quickly. SSH disciplines can customize these tools to provide helpful training. Training promotes institutional honesty. Institutions continually address ethics, security, and compliance with researchers. Well-trained researchers report misconduct, maintain high standards, and collaborate with ethical review boards and institutional leadership. Researchers should receive ongoing training throughout their careers. Early-career and graduate students may get research integrity and security training. Renewal courses and advanced workshops on emerging threats and technology can help expert researchers upgrade their methods.

5.2.3 Institutional Oversight and Ethics Committees

According to the studies of Ferretti et al. (2020), Head (2020). Xu et al. (2020), Bovens & Wille (2021), Hakimi et al. (2021), Resnik (2021), Bovens & Wille (2021), and Anderson et al. (2023). It could be discussed as follows:

Ethics and responsible social science and humanities research require institutional oversight and ethics committees. Research Integrity Offices, IRBs, and Data Protection Committees evaluate applications, programs, and ethics. Organized oversight by these committees assures research integrity, participant protection, and legal and ethical compliance. Critical is how these oversight panels safeguard research security and integrity. Before implementation, oversight bodies assess research proposals. Personal, sensitive, or data research requires ethical permission. IRBs evaluate researchers' risk mitigation, informed consent, and protection activities. These reviews are crucial for preventing participant damage in disadvantaged populations or sensitive social research. To prevent unethical research, oversight committees assess design, data collection, and consent. After the initial evaluation, monitoring authorities assure ethical and legal research. Evaluations show data mismanagement, confidentiality, and protocol violations. IRB mid-project evaluations may ensure that researchers are keeping participant pledges and protecting sensitive data. Long-term research or programs that collect and transmit data digitally must be monitored owing to emerging threats. Regular monitoring helps committees identify and handle issues. Ethics committees promote institutional responsibility. These bodies regularly prosecute research misconduct and integrity infractions. Ethics committees check researchers and organizations for plagiarism, data falsification, and security breaches. It may involve investigating complaints, assessing evidence, and punishing or withdrawing. An independent and open investigation agency is needed to maintain public faith in research and resolve ethical infractions. Supervisory authorities must follow GDPR and national data protection regulations. These restrictions limit personal data collection, storage, and dissemination. Ethics committees must require data management procedures to ensure participant privacy in sensitive data research. Oversight agencies protect participants and institutions. Institutional oversight committees teach researchers ethics and optimal practices. The seminars, lectures, and training address research ethics, data security, and informed permission. Researchers learn new ethics, norms, and best practices through education. Oversight bodies promote ethical research by encouraging researchers to handle ethical issues proactively rather than as bureaucratic impediments.

6. CONCLUSION

This chapter concludes that the management of security is a crucial component in maintaining the credibility of research in the social sciences and humanities. Because social science research involves people and sensitive issues related to culture or society, it is essential to obtain informed consent, maintain confidentiality, and ensure anonymity. The research conducted by SSH employs interpretative and qualitative approaches, which makes it challenging to maintain data security and openness. Researchers are required to strike a compromise between the openness of their methodology and the confidentiality of their participants. There is an increase in concerns about cybersecurity, data breaches, and unauthorized access when digital tools and platforms are used for data collection, storage, and analysis. To mitigate these risks, this chapter emphasizes the importance of implementing encryption, secure storage, and rigorous data management practices. There is a requirement for legal and ethical compliance with the General Data Protection Regulation (GDPR) in research that is conducted across international borders and between disciplines. The integrity of research depends on Institutional Review Boards (IRBs) and other bodies responsible for ethical oversight. To ensure that research programs adhere to ethical standards and protect the rights of participants, these systems provide guidance and oversight. Furthermore, the chapter suggests that institutions should facilitate the establishment of transparent policies and procedures that promote ethical research. To keep pace with the ever-evolving threats posed by digital technology, researchers require ongoing training in cybersecurity and ethical data management.

Effective management of security safeguards ensures that participants in the study, academic peers, and the general public continue to have confidence in the organization. Researchers in the social sciences can advance society while respecting participants' rights, privacy, and dignity by adhering to best practices for research security and integrity. This chapter is a systematic review and may not include respondents. Therefore, it is recommended to include questionnaires or interview surveys in further studies.

7. DECLARATION

The authors declare that there is no conflict of interest.

REFERENCES

Adee, R. & Mouratidis, H. (2022). A dynamic four-step data security model for data in cloud computing based on cryptography and steganography. Sensors. mdpi.com

Alabdan, R. (2020). Phishing attacks survey: Types, vectors, and technical approaches. Future internet. mdpi.com

Amoah, C., & Steyn, D. (2023). Barriers to unethical and corrupt practices avoidance in the construction industry. [emerald.com]. *International Journal of Building Pathology and Adaptation*, *41*(6), 85–101. DOI: 10.1108/IJBPA-01-2022-0021

Anderson, E. E., Hurley, E. A., Serpico, K., Johnson, A., Rowe, J., Singleton, M., Bierer, B. E., Cholka, B., Chaudhari, S., & Fernandez Lynch, H. (2023). Engaging key stakeholders to overcome barriers to studying the quality of research ethics oversight. [sagepub.com]. *Research Ethics*, *19*(1), 62–77. DOI: 10.1177/17470161221138028

Appiah, R. (2021). Gurus and Griots: Revisiting the research informed consent process in rural African contexts. BMC medical Ethics. springer.com

Armond, A. C. V., Gordijn, B., Lewis, J., Hosseini, M., Bodnár, J. K., Holm, S., & Kakuk, P. (2021). A scoping review of the literature featuring research ethics and research integrity cases. [springer.com]. *BMC Medical Ethics*, *22*(1), 50. DOI: 10.1186/s12910-021-00620-8 PMID: 33931043

Atenas, J., Havemann, L., & Timmermann, C. (2023). Reframing data ethics in research methods education: A pathway to critical data literacy. [springer.com]. *International Journal of Educational Technology in Higher Education*, *20*(1), 11. DOI: 10.1186/s41239-023-00380-y PMID: 36846483

Barnes, M., Carrithers, J., & Sugarman, J. (2020). Ethical and practical concerns about IRB restrictions on the use of research data. [HTML]. *Ethics & Human Research*, *42*(6), 29–34. DOI: 10.1002/eahr.500072 PMID: 33136330

Bellini, E., & Degl'Innocenti, E. (2024, September). Transitioning SSH European Research Infrastructures to Critical Infrastructure Through Resilience. In *2024 IEEE International Conference on Cyber Security and Resilience (CSR)* (pp. 801-806). IEEE. [HTML] DOI: 10.1109/CSR61664.2024.10679383

Bhaskar, R., & Ola, M. (2024). Publication Misconduct, Plagiarism, and Research Integrity. In Principles of Research Methodology and Ethics in Pharmaceutical Sciences (pp. 271-310). CRC Press.

Bonaccorsi, A., Chiarello, F., & Fantoni, G. (2021). SSH researchers make an impact differently. Looking at public research from the perspective of users. [HTML]. *Research Evaluation*, *30*(3), 269–289. DOI: 10.1093/reseval/rvab008

Bovens, M. & Wille, A. (2021). Indexing watchdog accountability powers a framework for assessing the accountability capacity of independent oversight institutions. Regulation & Governance. wiley.com

Bowen, F. R., Epps, F., Lowe, J., & Guilamo-Ramos, V. (2022). Restoring trust in research among historically underrepresented communities: A call to action for antiracism research in nursing. Nursing outlook. sciencedirect.com

Cairns, A. C., Linville, C., Garcia, T., Bridges, B., Tanona, S., Herington, J., & Laverty, J. T. (2021). A phenomenographic study of scientists' beliefs about the causes of scientists' research misconduct. [sagepub.com]. *Research Ethics*, *17*(4), 501–521. DOI: 10.1177/17470161211042658

Campbell, R., Javorka, M., Engleton, J., Fishwick, K., Gregory, K., & Goodman-Williams, R. (2023). Open-Science guidance for qualitative research: An empirically validated approach for de-identifying sensitive narrative data. [sagepub.com]. *Advances in Methods and Practices in Psychological Science*, *6*(4), 25152459231205832. DOI: 10.1177/25152459231205832

Canfield, K. N., Mulvaney, K., & Chatelain, C. D. (2022). Using researcher and stakeholder perspectives to develop promising practices to improve stakeholder engagement in the solutions-driven research process. [springer.com]. *Socio-Ecological Practice Research*, *4*(3), 189–203. DOI: 10.1007/s42532-022-00119-5 PMID: 35855106

Carter, S. M., Shih, P., Williams, J., Degeling, C., & Mooney-Somers, J. (2021). Conducting qualitative research online: Challenges and solutions. [springer.com]. *Patient*, *14*(6), 711–718. DOI: 10.1007/s40271-021-00528-w PMID: 34114170

Chatfield, K., Schroeder, D., Guantai, A., Bhatt, K., Bukusi, E., Adhiambo Odhiambo, J., Cook, J., & Kimani, J. (2021). Preventing ethics dumping: The challenges for Kenyan research ethics committees. [sagepub.com]. *Research Ethics*, *17*(1), 23–44. DOI: 10.1177/1747016120925064

Cochrane, L., Drummond, O., & Jordan, E. (2024). Improving ethical assurance for non-university researchers in crisis settings: an early vision based on democratic norms. Research Ethics. sagepub.com

Cvitanovic, C., Shellock, R. J., Mackay, M., Van Putten, E. I., Karcher, D. B., Dickey-Collas, M., & Ballesteros, M. (2021). Strategies for building and managing 'trust'to enable knowledge exchange at the interface of environmental science and policy. [HTML]. *Environmental Science & Policy*, *123*, 179–189. DOI: 10.1016/j.envsci.2021.05.020

Dal-Ré, R., Bouter, L. M., Cuijpers, P., Gluud, C., & Holm, S. (2020). Should research misconduct be criminalized? [sagepub.com]. *Research Ethics*, **•••**, 174701611989840.

Degn, L. (2020). Integrating integrity: The organizational translation of policies on research integrity. [HTML]. *Science and Engineering Ethics*, *26*(6), 3167–3182. DOI: 10.1007/s11948-020-00262-w PMID: 32840718

DeGrendele, C. J., Kazakov, J. A., & Reuter, M. G. (2022). Interpreting non-semielliptical complex bands. [HTML]. *Journal of Physics Condensed Matter*, *34*(26), 265501. DOI: 10.1088/1361-648X/ac655b PMID: 35390781

Derrick, G. E., & Ross-Hellauer, T. (2024). De-legitimising the social sciences and humanities through peer review. Handbook of Meta-Research. [HTML] DOI: 10.4337/9781839105722.00027

Di Minin, E., Fink, C., Hausmann, A., Kremer, J., & Kulkarni, R. (2021). How to address data privacy concerns when using social media data in conservation science. [wiley.com]. *Conservation Biology*, *35*(2), 437–446. DOI: 10.1111/cobi.13708 PMID: 33749044

Ducato, R. (2020). Data protection, scientific research, and the role of information. Computer Law & Security Review. sciencedirect.com

Dupont, B. & Whelan, C. (2021). Enhancing relationships between criminology and cybersecurity. Journal of criminology. sagepub.com

Durmaz, A., Dursun, İ., & Kabadayi, E. T. (2020). Mitigating the effects of social desirability bias in self-report surveys: Classical and new techniques. In *Applied social science approaches to mixed methods research* (pp. 146–185). IGI Global. [HTML] DOI: 10.4018/978-1-7998-1025-4.ch007

Eakin, J. M., & Gladstone, B. (2020). "Value-adding" analysis: Doing more with qualitative data. [sagepub.com]. *International Journal of Qualitative Methods*, *19*, 1609406920949333. DOI: 10.1177/1609406920949333

El-Adaway, I. H. & Jennings, M. (2022). Professional and organizational leadership role in ethics management: Avoiding reliance on ethical codification and nurturing ethical culture. Science and Engineering Ethics. springer.com

Facca, D., Smith, M. J., Shelley, J., Lizotte, D., & Donelle, L. (2020). Exploring the ethical issues in research using digital data collection strategies with minors: A scoping review. Plos one. plos.org

Fadlelmola, F. M., Zass, L., Chaouch, M., Samtal, C., Ras, V., Kumuthini, J., Panji, S., & Mulder, N. (2021). Data Management Plans in the genomics research revolution of Africa: Challenges and recommendations. [sciencedirect.com]. *Journal of Biomedical Informatics*, *122*, 103900. DOI: 10.1016/j.jbi.2021.103900 PMID: 34506960

Favaretto, M., De Clercq, E., Gaab, J., & Elger, B. S. (2020). First do no harm: An exploration of researchers' ethics of conduct in Big Data behavioral studies. Plos one. plos.org

Fecher, B., Kuper, F., Sokolovska, N., Fenton, A., Hornbostel, S., & Wagner, G. G. (2021). Understanding the societal impact of the social sciences and humanities: Remarks on roles, challenges, and expectations. [frontiersin.org]. *Frontiers in Research Metrics and Analytics*, *6*, 696804. DOI: 10.3389/frma.2021.696804 PMID: 34278206

Ferretti, A., Ienca, M., Hurst, S., & Vayena, E. (2020). Big data, biomedical research, and ethics review: New challenges for IRBs. [wiley.com]. *Ethics & Human Research*, *42*(5), 17–28. DOI: 10.1002/eahr.500065 PMID: 32937036

Ferretti, A., Ienca, M., Velarde, M. R., Hurst, S., & Vayena, E. (2022). The challenges of big data for research ethics committees: A qualitative Swiss study. [sagepub.com]. *Journal of Empirical Research on Human Research Ethics; JERHRE*, *17*(1-2), 129–143. DOI: 10.1177/15562646211053538 PMID: 34779661

Fiero, A. W. & Beier, E. (2022). New global developments in data protection and privacy regulations: Comparative analysis of European Union, United States, and Russian legislation. Stan. J. Int'l L.. [HTML]

Fisher, M. T. (2023). *Stability of Cultural Information in Unstable Environments: Data Management for Digital Preservation of Immovable Cultural Heritage against Natural Hazards*. Managing Disaster Risks to Cultural Heritage. [HTML] DOI: 10.4324/9781003263647-4

Foulds, C., Royston, S., Berker, T., Nakopoulou, E., Bharucha, Z. P., Robison, R., Abram, S., Ančić, B., Arapostathis, S., Badescu, G., Bull, R., Cohen, J., Dunlop, T., Dunphy, N., Dupont, C., Fischer, C., Gram-Hanssen, K., Grandclément, C., Heiskanen, E., & Živčič, L. (2022). An agenda for future Social Sciences and Humanities research on energy efficiency: 100 priority research questions. [nature.com]. *Humanities & Social Sciences Communications*, *9*(1), 1–18. DOI: 10.1057/s41599-022-01243-z PMID: 35791377

Freese, J., Rauf, T., & Voelkel, J. G. (2022). Advances in transparency and reproducibility in the social sciences. [HTML]. *Social Science Research*, *107*, 102770. DOI: 10.1016/j.ssresearch.2022.102770 PMID: 36058608

Gedutis, A., Biagetti, M. T., & Ma, L. (2022). The challenges for research evaluation ethics in the social sciences. In *Handbook on Research Assessment in the Social Sciences* (pp. 367–385). Edward Elgar Publishing. [HTML] DOI: 10.4337/9781800372559.00032

Gentile, A. F., Fazio, P., & Miceli, G. (2021). A Survey on the Implementation and Management of Secure Virtual Private Networks (VPNs) and Virtual LANs (VLANs) in Static and Mobile Scenarios. Telecom. mdpi.com

Gesualdo, F., Daverio, M., Palazzani, L., Dimitriou, D., Diez-Domingo, J., Fons-Martinez, J., Jackson, S., Vignally, P., Rizzo, C., & Tozzi, A. E. (2021). Digital tools in the informed consent process: A systematic review. [springer.com]. *BMC Medical Ethics*, *22*(1), 1–10. DOI: 10.1186/s12910-021-00585-8 PMID: 33639926

Gonzalez-Granadillo, G., Menesidou, S. A., Papamartzivanos, D., Romeu, R., Navarro-Llobet, D., Okoh, C., Nifakos, S., Xenakis, C., & Panaousis, E. (2021). Automated cyber and privacy risk management toolkit. [mdpi.com]. *Sensors (Basel)*, *21*(16), 5493. DOI: 10.3390/s21165493 PMID: 34450935

Hakimi, L., Eynon, R., & Murphy, V. A. (2021). The ethics of using digital trace data in education: A thematic review of the research landscape. [sagepub.com]. *Review of Educational Research*, *91*(5), 671–717. DOI: 10.3102/00346543211020116

Hantrais, L., & Lenihan, A. T. (2021). Social dimensions of evidence-based policy in a digital society. [HTML]. *Contemporary Social Science*, *16*(2), 141–155. DOI: 10.1080/21582041.2021.1887508

Head, G. (2020). Ethics in educational research: Review boards, ethical issues and researcher development. European Educational Research Journal. sagepub.com

Holden, O. L., Norris, M. E., & Kuhlmeier, V. A. (2021). Academic integrity in online assessment: A research review. Frontiers in Education. frontiersin.org

Hughes, R., Rose, A., Lozano, J. S., Garguilo, S., & Knight, D. (2022). A Model of Misconduct, Accusations, and Institution Response at US Colleges and Universities: Synthesis of the Literature and an Agenda for Future Research. Higher Education: Handbook of Theory and Research: Volume 37, 457-517. [HTML]

Husband, G. (2020). Ethical data collection and recognizing the impact of semi-structured interviews on research respondents. Education Sciences. mdpi.com

Josa, I. & Aguado, A. (2021). Social sciences and humanities in the education of civil engineers: Current status and proposal of guidelines. Journal of Cleaner Production. sciencedirect.com

Karhulahti, V. M. & Backe, H. J. (2021). Transparency of peer review: a semi-structured interview study with chief editors from social sciences and humanities. Research Integrity and Peer Review. springer.com

Kaur, S., Kaur, G., & Shabaz, M. (2022). A Secure Two-Factor Authentication Framework in Cloud Computing. [wiley.com]. *Security and Communication Networks*, *2022*(1), 7540891. DOI: 10.1155/2022/7540891

King, G., Keohane, R. O., & Verba, S. (2021). Designing social inquiry: Scientific inference in qualitative research. [HTML]

Kirya, M. T. (2020). Promoting anti-corruption, transparency and accountability in the recruitment and promotion of health workers to safeguard health outcomes. Global health action. tandfonline.com

Kolstoe, S. E. & Pugh, J. (2023). The trinity of good research: Distinguishing between research integrity, ethics, and governance. Accountability in Research. tandfonline.com

Kraiwanit, T., Limna, P., & Siripipatthanakul, S. (2023). NVivo for social sciences and management studies: A systematic review. *Advance Knowledge for Executives*, *2*(3), 1–11.

Labadie, C. & Legner, C. (2023). Building data management capabilities to address data protection regulations: Learnings from EU-GDPR. Journal of Information Technology. sagepub.com

Lantos, J. D. (2020). The Belmont Report and innovative clinical research. [HTML]. *Perspectives in Biology and Medicine*, *63*(2), 389–400. DOI: 10.1353/pbm.2020.0026 PMID: 33416660

Leng, J., Zhou, M., Zhao, J. L., Huang, Y., & Bian, Y. (2020). Blockchain security: A survey of techniques and research directions. [HTML]. *IEEE Transactions on Services Computing, 15*(4), 2490–2510. DOI: 10.1109/TSC.2020.3038641

Lynch, H. F., Eriksen, W., & Clapp, J. T. (2022). "We measure what we can measure": Struggles in defining and evaluating institutional review board quality. [HTML]. *Social Science & Medicine, 292*, 114614. DOI: 10.1016/j.socscimed.2021.114614 PMID: 34861569

Manral, B., & Somani, G. (2021). Establishing forensics capabilities in the presence of superuser insider threats. [HTML]. *Forensic Science International Digital Investigation, 38*, 301263. DOI: 10.1016/j.fsidi.2021.301263

Mansoor, F., Ameen, K., & Arshad, A. (2024). An exploratory study of university librarians' perceptions on causes and deterrents of plagiarism: A Pakistani perspective. [HTML]. *Global Knowledge, Memory and Communication, 73*(4/5), 634–649. DOI: 10.1108/GKMC-04-2022-0074

Misra, D. P., & Agarwal, V. (2020). Integrity of clinical research conduct, reporting, publishing, and post-publication promotion in rheumatology. [HTML]. *Clinical Rheumatology, 39*(4), 1049–1060. DOI: 10.1007/s10067-020-04965-0 PMID: 32026178

Moher, D., Bouter, L., Kleinert, S., Glasziou, P., Sham, M. H., Barbour, V., Coriat, A.-M., Foeger, N., & Dirnagl, U. (2020). The Hong Kong Principles for assessing researchers: Fostering research integrity. [plos.org]. *PLoS Biology, 18*(7), e3000737. DOI: 10.1371/journal.pbio.3000737 PMID: 32673304

Muhonen, R., Benneworth, P., & Olmos-Peñuela, J. (2020). From productive interactions to impact pathways: Understanding the key dimensions in developing SSH research societal impact. [oup.com]. *Research Evaluation, 29*(1), 34–47.

Nadji, B. (2024). Data Security, Integrity, and Protection. In *Data, Security, and Trust in Smart Cities* (pp. 59–83). Springer Nature Switzerland.

Nagai, H., Nakazawa, E., & Akabayashi, A. (2022). The creation of the Belmont Report and its effect on ethical principles: a historical study. Monash bioethics review. springer.com

Newcomb, T. J., Simonin, P. W., Martinez, F. A., Chadderton, W. L., Bossenbroek, J. M., Cudmore, B., Hoff, M. H., Keller, R. P., Ridenhour, B. D., Rothlisberger, J. D., Rutherford, E. S., Van Egeren, S., & Lodge, D. M. (2021). A best practices case study for scientific collaboration between researchers and managers. [wiley.com]. *Fisheries (Bethesda, Md.), 46*(3), 131–138. DOI: 10.1002/fsh.10536 PMID: 33888934

Newman, A., Bavik, Y. L., Mount, M., & Shao, B. (2021). Data collection via online platforms: Challenges and recommendations for future research. [HTML]. *Applied Psychology*, *70*(3), 1380–1402. DOI: 10.1111/apps.12302

Newman, P. A., Guta, A., & Black, T. (2021). Ethical considerations for qualitative research methods during the COVID-19 pandemic and other emergency situations: Navigating the virtual field. [sagepub.com]. *International Journal of Qualitative Methods*, *20*, 16094069211047823. DOI: 10.1177/16094069211047823

Parti, K. & Szigeti, A. (2021). The future of interdisciplinary research in the digital era: Obstacles and perspectives of collaboration in social and data sciences-an empirical study. Cogent Social Sciences. tandfonline.com

Perera, S., Jin, X., Maurushat, A., & Opoku, D. G. J. (2022). Factors affecting reputational damage to organisations due to cyberattacks. Informatics. mdpi.com

Perković Paloš, A., Roje, R., Tomić, V., & Marušić, A. (2024). Creating research ethics and integrity country report cards: Case study from Europe. [tandfonline.com]. *Accountability in Research*, *31*(6), 620–654. DOI: 10.1080/08989621.2022.2163632 PMID: 36635978

Perwej, Y., Abbas, S. Q., Dixit, J. P., Akhtar, N., & Jaiswal, A. K. (2021). A systematic literature review on the cyber security. International Journal of scientific research and management, 9(12), 669-710. hal.science

Phuangsuwan, P., Siripipatthanakul, S., Limna, P., & Siripipattanakul, S. (2024). Grammar and Plagiarism Checking Using Grammarly for English Learners: A Systematic Review. *SSRN*, *7*(3), 1–20. DOI: 10.2139/ssrn.4861177

Puputti, H. (2022). Positioning social sciences and humanities actors in the ninth European Union Framework Programme: a discourse analysis of Horizon Europe reference documents. oulu.fi

Resnik, D. B. (2021). Standards of evidence for institutional review board decision-making. Accountability in research. nih.gov

Risi, D., Vigneau, L., Bohn, S., & Wickert, C. (2023). Institutional theory-based research on corporate social responsibility: Bringing values back in. [wiley.com]. *International Journal of Management Reviews*, *25*(1), 3–23. DOI: 10.1111/ijmr.12299

Rooney, M. J., Levy, Y., Li, W., & Kumar, A. (2024). Comparing experts' and users' perspectives on the use of password workarounds and the risk of data breaches. [HTML]. *Information and Computer Security*. Advance online publication. DOI: 10.1108/ICS-05-2024-0116

Rucz, M. (2022). SLAPPed by the GDPR: protecting public interest journalism in the face of GDPR-based strategic litigation against public participation. Journal of Media Law. tandfonline.com

Saeed, M. M. A., Saeed, R. A., & Ahmed, Z. E. (2024). Data Security and Privacy in the Age of AI and Digital Twins. In Digital Twin Technology and AI Implementations in Future-Focused Businesses (pp. 99-124). IGI Global. [HTML] DOI: 10.4018/979-8-3693-1818-8.ch008

Schinagl, S. & Shahim, A. (2020). What do we know about information security governance? "From the basement to the boardroom": towards digital security governance. Information & Computer Security. emerald.com

Schmidt, U. (2023). From Nuremberg to Helsinki: Historicizing the Codification of Post-War Research Ethics. In Ethical Innovation for Global Health: Pandemic, Democracy and Ethics in Research (pp. 149-174). Singapore: Springer Nature Singapore. [HTML]

Schuijer, J. W., Broerse, J., & Kupper, F. (2021). Juggling roles, experiencing dilemmas: The challenges of SSH scholars in public engagement. NanoEthics. springer.com

Seara, J. P. & Serrão, C. (2024). Automation of System Security Vulnerabilities Detection Using Open-Source Software. Electronics. mdpi.com

Sefcik, L., Striepe, M., & Yorke, J. (2020). Mapping the landscape of academic integrity education programs: What approaches are effective? [HTML]. *Assessment & Evaluation in Higher Education*, *45*(1), 30–43. DOI: 10.1080/02602938.2019.1604942

Shaik, V., & Natarajan, K. (2022). Flexible and cost-effective cryptographic encryption algorithm for securing unencrypted database files at rest and in transit. [sciencedirect.com]. *Methods (San Diego, Calif.)*, •••, X. PMID: 36438858

Shamoo, A., & Khin-Maung-Gyi, F. A. (2021). *Ethics of the Use of Human Subjects in Research*. Practical Guide. [HTML] DOI: 10.1201/9780203110744

Siripipatthanakul, S., & Siripipattanakul, S. (2025). Rural Dental Health Transformation by Adopting Digital Technologies. *Transforming Dental Health in Rural Communities: Digital Dentistry*, 47-80. DOI: DOI: 10.4018/979-8-3693-7165-7.ch003

Siripipatthanakul, S., & Siripipattanakul, S. (2025). Online Gambling of Higher Education Learners. In *International Academic Transformations and Cross-Border Collaborations* (pp. 377–400). IGI Global Scientific Publishing., DOI: 10.4018/979-8-3373-0508-0.ch015

Smith, M., & Walsh, P. (2023). Security sensitive research: Balancing research integrity, academic freedom and national interest. [HTML]. *Journal of Higher Education Policy and Management, 45*(5), 495–510. DOI: 10.1080/1360080X.2023.2202328

Smyth, B. M., Martin, M. A., & Downing, M. (2024). *The Routledge Handbook of Human Research Ethics and Integrity in Australia.* [HTML] DOI: 10.4324/9781003319733

Sofyani, H., Pratolo, S., & Saleh, Z. (2022). Do accountability and transparency promote community trust? Evidence from village government in Indonesia. [HTML]. *Journal of Accounting & Organizational Change, 18*(3), 397–418. DOI: 10.1108/JAOC-06-2020-0070

Sørensen, M. P., Ravn, T., Marušić, A., Elizondo, A. R., Kavouras, P., Tijdink, J. K., & Bendtsen, A. K. (2021). Strengthening research integrity: Which topic areas should organisations focus on? [nature.com]. *Humanities & Social Sciences Communications, 8*(1), 1–15. DOI: 10.1057/s41599-021-00874-y PMID: 38617731

Stoesz, B. M. & Eaton, S. E. (2022). Academic integrity policies of publicly funded universities in western Canada. Educational Policy. sagepub.com

Surmiak, A. (2020). Should we maintain or break confidentiality? The choices made by social researchers in the context of law violation and harm. Journal of Academic Ethics. springer.com

Tamburri, D. A. (2020). Design principles for the General Data Protection Regulation (GDPR): A formal concept analysis and its evaluation. Information Systems. sciencedirect.com

Thapa, C., & Camtepe, S. (2021). Precision health data: Requirements, challenges and existing techniques for data security and privacy. [PDF]. *Computers in Biology and Medicine, 129*, 104130. DOI: 10.1016/j.compbiomed.2020.104130 PMID: 33271399

Tomás, J., Rasteiro, D., & Bernardino, J. (2022). Data anonymization: an experimental evaluation using open-source tools. Future Internet. mdpi.com

Välikangas, A. (2024). The Limited Role of Social Sciences and Humanities in Interdisciplinary Funding: What are Its Effects?. Social Epistemology. tandfonline.com

Valkenburg, G., Dix, G., Tijdink, J., & de Rijcke, S. (2021). Expanding research integrity: A cultural-practice perspective. [springer.com]. *Science and Engineering Ethics, 27*(1), 10. DOI: 10.1007/s11948-021-00291-z PMID: 33559767

Van de Sandt, E. H. A. (2021). The deviant security practices of cyber crime. [HTML]

Xie, Y., Wang, K., & Kong, Y. (2021). Prevalence of research misconduct and questionable research practices: A systematic review and meta-analysis. Science and engineering ethics. springer.com

Xu, A., Baysari, M. T., Stocker, S. L., Leow, L. J., Day, R. O., & Carland, J. E. (2020). Researchers' views on, and experiences with, the requirement to obtain informed consent in research involving human participants: A qualitative study. [springer.com]. *BMC Medical Ethics*, *21*(1), 1–11. DOI: 10.1186/s12910-020-00538-7 PMID: 33008387

Zarour, M., Alenezi, M., Ansari, M. T. J., Pandey, A. K., Ahmad, M., Agrawal, A., Kumar, R., & Khan, R. A. (2021). Ensuring data integrity of healthcare information in the era of digital health. [wiley.com]. *Healthcare Technology Letters*, *8*(3), 66–77. DOI: 10.1049/htl2.12008 PMID: 34035927

Chapter 4
Challenges and Management Practices in Protecting Employee Personal Data in the Digital Era

Syamsul Hadi
https://orcid.org/0000-0001-7226-4978
Sarjanawiyata Tamansiswa, Indonesia

Eni Purnasari
https://orcid.org/0009-0003-1778-7663
Independent Researcher, Indonesia

Riskin Hidayat
https://orcid.org/0000-0002-2697-6947
University of Sarjanawiyata Tamansiswa, Indonesia

Ambar Lukitaningsih
https://orcid.org/0009-0002-9847-9242
University of Sarjanawiyata Tamansiswa, Indonesia

Kusuma Chandra Kirana
University of Sarjanawiyata Tamansiswa, Indonesia

Supaprawat Siripipatthanakul
https://orcid.org/0000-0001-6671-2682
Bangkok Thonburi University, Thailand

ABSTRACT

This study aims to identify the key challenges in managing employee personal data in the digital transformation era and explore effective management practices to protect such data through a systematic review of the current literature. This study employs a systematic literature review (SLR) approach based on the PRISMA protocol. The articles analyzed are sourced from the Emerald Insight database with the following criteria: published between 2020 and 2025, written in English, and presenting empirical findings related to the management of employee personal data. This study

DOI: 10.4018/979-8-3693-9720-6.ch004

found that personal data management practices are closely linked to technological innovation, sustainability, ethics, and risk management. Key issues include cyber threats, technological infrastructure limitations, and employees' lack of cybersecurity literacy. Clear policies, employee training, and investments in advanced technologies such as encryption and intrusion detection must address these.

1. INTRODUCTION

In the context of data privacy, global trends indicate that businesses across various industries are becoming increasingly aware of the importance of establishing proactive data management policies to address challenges arising from the digital transformation era. Across various industries, people are becoming increasingly aware of the importance of establishing proactive data management policies to address challenges arising from the digital transformation era. For organizations to effectively respond to the ever-evolving threats, they need to incorporate a risk-based strategy into their data protection policies. Furthermore, to formulate comprehensive security rules, the Information Technology (IT) and Human Resources (HR) divisions must collaborate across departments. This problem becomes even more critical due to the rapid adoption of information technology, which requires businesses to protect employee data, including sensitive information such as employment history and health records, from the risk of leakage or misuse. Companies are required to re-evaluate their data management policies and procedures to comply with increasingly stringent data protection regulations, such as the General Data Protection Regulation (GDPR) in the European Union and the Personal Data Protection Law (UU PDP) in Indonesia. These regulations have further complicated the management of personal data (Amoo et al., 2024; Carmi et al., 2022; Ducato, 2020; Hoofnagle et al., 2019; Marikyan et al., 2024; Koneru, 2024).

Recent technological advancements, such as cloud-based HRIS systems and AI-driven performance monitoring, also heighten the challenge of striking a balance between operational efficiency and the protection of personal data. It is essential to emphasize that advanced human resource management systems must be equipped with robust data security solutions to address the continually evolving cyber threats (Murugesan et al., 2023; Palos-Sánchez et al., 2022; Abrahams et al.. 2024; Watini et al., 2024).

Although security technologies such as multi-factor authentication (MFA) and blockchain have been implemented to enhance data protection, the application of these technologies in employee data management across various sectors still faces significant challenges. Data reported by IBM (2024), shows that the human resources (HR) sector is one of the primary targets for cyberattacks, with the average data breach cost reaching USD 4.45 million per incident globally. Furthermore, despite 100% of companies having implemented Endpoint Security and most having Network Security (94%), Cloud Security (83%), and Security Services (75%), only 53% focus on Security Training. Many organizations still overlook a critical aspect of protection: employee training. Human error and social engineering remain the primary threats, and without adequate training, even advanced technological defenses can be easily compromised (Kaspersky, 2024). The implementation of data protection regulations, such as Indonesia's Personal Data Protection Law, also faces significant challenges. Employees are the greatest asset of a company and one of its most significant vulnerabilities regarding personal data, such as stolen passwords, personnel falling for phishing scams, and misuse errors, which account for 82% of breaches (Deloitte Indonesia, 2024). Research by Quach et al. (2022) Furthermore, the existing literature on adapting data protection policies in local contexts is limited, underscoring the need to establish a robust compliance strategy to ensure adequate data protection at the organizational level.

Furthermore, employee trust in managing their data has become a key issue. While cloud attacks are a primary concern in the cybersecurity world, approximately one-third of organizations lack a risk management plan to address the challenges associated with cloud service providers. Only half of the organizations feel "very satisfied" with their technological capabilities in key cybersecurity areas. Over 30% of companies fail to consistently implement standard practices that should be part of their cybersecurity defenses, leaving employees concerned about how the company manages their data. This can damage working relationships and decrease employee trust in the organization (Gara & Porte, 2020; Mileros & Forchheimer, 2024; Sean Joyce, 2024).

Based on these findings, this study aims to fill the gaps in the existing literature by conducting a Systematic Literature Review (SLR) meta-synthesis (Hadi et al., 2020), related to privacy and data security management practices in the context of human resources (HR). This research will provide a more comprehensive analysis by identifying and synthesizing existing findings across various sectors and the technologies used to manage employee personal data. The urgency of this study stems from the pressing need for organizations to gain a more precise and comprehensive understanding of the increasingly complex challenges associated with managing employees' data. It is expected to enrich the literature on Human Resource privacy and data security management. Practically, the results of this research are expected to help companies design more effective policies and procedures to safeguard and protect employees' data.

2. LITERATURE REVIEW

In the context of managing personal data about employees during the digital transformation era, management practices can be defined as a collection of policies and processes implemented by businesses to ensure the proper protection of personal data while complying with existing legislation. These practices encompass the actions that businesses take to manage and secure their employees' data, with the goal of ensuring transparency and accountability in the handling of that data. There is a tight connection between the management of these practices and an organization's dynamic capability to respond to changes and challenges brought about by technological breakthroughs and evolving data protection regulations. As a result, the practices of data protection management need to be flexible and adaptable in order to accommodate the ever-increasing expectations of regulatory agencies and technological advancements (Otoo et al., 2025; Ranasinghe et al., 2025).

2.1 The Theory of Planned Behavior (TPB)

The Theory of Planned Behavior (TPB), developed by Ajzen (1991), explains that an individual's behavior is influenced by intention, which is shaped by three key factors: attitude, subjective norms, and perceived behavioral control. Attitude reflects beliefs about the outcomes of a behavior, whether positive or negative. Subjective norms involve social pressure or environmental expectations that influence an individual's decision to engage in a particular behavior. At the same time, perceived behavioral control refers to an individual's perception of their ability or resources to carry out the behavior. TPB asserts that behavior results from intention and is influenced by experience, knowledge, and other background factors that shape attitudes, norms, and perceived control. In this context, a positive attitude toward managing employee personal data can increase their compliance with company-implemented policies (Mileros & Forchheimer, 2024). Transparency in managing personal data can enhance employee trust in the company, thus supporting more effective data protection management practices. Additionally, subjective norms, which include employees' perceptions of expectations from supervisors or colleagues, also influence their decisions to comply with personal data protection policies (Kaspersky, 2024). It is confirmed that when companies establish norms that prioritize personal data protection, employees are more likely to adhere to existing policies and procedures, thereby representing a significant challenge in data management practices within organizations. Finally, perceived behavioral control is also crucial in management practices. Individuals are more likely to act if they feel they have the ability or control over the action. In this case, the implementation of technologies such as cloud-based HRIS systems and artificial intelligence offers operational efficiency but also introduces new challenges in managing employees' data (Patil & Priya, 2024; Shahreki & Lee, 2024).

In the modern era of digital technology, effective management practices for preserving employee personal information include implementing standards that ensure data protection and compliance with applicable requirements. The Theory of Planned Behavior (TPB), developed in the 20th century, posits that attitudes, social norms, and perceived control all contribute to determining employee behavior. It is beneficial to have a positive attitude toward data protection in terms of compliance, and maintaining transparency and strong societal norms also helps strengthen employee commitment. In addition, the management of data is simplified by technologies such as cloud-based human resource information systems; however, these technologies also introduce new challenges. As a consequence, companies are required to implement a management plan that is adaptable and responsive to the ever-evolving technological landscape and changing regulatory requirements. This can be accomplished primarily through the provision of adequate training to employees in order to improve their perception of control over the management of personal data, as well as through the development of more stringent policies regarding data protection. In light of this, the Theory of Planned Behavior provides a relevant foundation for formulating rules that protect the personal data of employees, which is especially important when considering the ever-changing dynamics of digital transformation.

2.2 Digitalization, Digital Transformation, and Digital Intelligence

Data and processes that are analog are converted into digital formats through the process of digitalization, which is a strategic process. The utilization of digital technologies automates and simplifies the company's procedures. The process of digital transformation differs from digitalization, which is a crucial step. Although digitalization has the potential to reduce costs, increase productivity, and enhance data management, it may not be necessary to undergo a comprehensive organizational transformation. To achieve digital maturity, digitalization is necessary; however, to achieve true digital transformation, a business must undergo a more fundamental organizational change (Huang, 2018; Cosa, 2024).

The digitalization of all industries and society is undergoing a transformation. The fact that it is a strong generator of innovation and disruption means that it poses an equally challenging challenge to both public and private institutions. All facets of the economy and society are being influenced by the digital economy, which is simultaneously dynamic and competitive. It enables firms that have received venture capital funding worth billions of dollars to leverage digital technology and generate new value propositions. In addition to being extremely scalable, data-driven, and software-centric, their operating paradigms coincide with those of incumbents, which poses a threat to their lives. Take, for example, Apple's iOS and Google's Android operating systems. Due to the efforts of both companies, growing ecosystems of third-party app developers were consolidated onto a consistent digital platform. As a result, Nokia went from being the dominant player in the phone industry to being irrelevant. The following are examples of threats that are emerging across the economy: cloud computing services from Amazon, Microsoft, and Google are posing a challenge to traditional software and hardware providers; online marketplaces offered by Amazon and Alibaba are competing with on-demand services offered by Walmart; and Netflix and Hulu are poised to disrupt pay-TV providers. Airbnb and Booking.com are two notable examples of companies that are disrupting well-established hotel chains, such as Marriott, Hilton, and Hyatt, by streamlining the booking process and offering personalized travel experiences. It is necessary for existing organizations, whether public or private, to incorporate digital technologies into their ecosystem to enhance their product and service portfolios through digital transformation, thereby capitalizing on the benefits of digital technology. Organizations that were not "born digital" are required to undergo significant business changes, which may involve rethinking job designs and internal business processes, as well as necessitating new ways of thinking and collaborating. This is in contrast to organizations such as Amazon, Google, Microsoft, and others (Lang, 2021; Vrana & Singh, 2021).

Digital Transformation, digital technologies, and digital intelligence are used to equip professionals with a comprehensive and practical understanding of how they are shaping the competitive landscape of the modern organization environment. The fundamental aspects of digital transformation include artificial intelligence (AI), the Internet of Things (IoT), big data, blockchain technology, and cybersecurity. The process of digital transformation is not merely a transitional phase; rather, it encompasses a shift in the way organizations perceive the world today. To make progress in a modern organizational environment, it is essential that the organization investigates changes at every stage. Organizational managers, project managers, and information technology professionals who are adopting new technologies could gain a more in-depth understanding of the developing technologies and their impact on organizations and must prioritize digital technology. Organizations and employees have acquired the knowledge and abilities necessary to navigate and lead in a world that is becoming increasingly digital, driven by technologies and digital intelligence. If the organization successfully achieves its goals, it will empower organizations and employees to become agents of change in the digital era. Digital Transformation, digital technologies, and digital intelligence will enable organizations and employees to capitalize on the changes occurring in technology, thereby gaining a competitive advantage in today's market. Changes are occurring continuously, and organizations and their employees need to prepare for them now. The time to begin is now for digital transformation and the adoption of digital intelligence in modern organizations and companies.

2.3 Keyterms and Definitions

2.3.1 Digitalization: Strategic digitalization converts analog data and processes to digital ones. Digital technologies automate and simplify company processes. Digital transformation is different from digitalization, a vital stage. Digitalization can save costs, boost productivity, and improve data management, but an organizational revolution may not be needed. Digitalization is essential for achieving digital maturity; however, true digital transformation requires a more profound organizational change.

2.3.2 Data Privacy Management: Global trends indicate that organizations across various industries are recognizing the importance of proactive data management strategies in addressing the challenges of digital transformation. People across various sectors are recognizing the need for proactive data management strategies to address the challenges of digital transformation. For enterprises to respond effectively to shifting risks, data protection strategies must be risk-based.

2.3.3 The Theory of Planned Behavior (TPB): The TPB model was created by Ajzen (1991). It states that attitude, subjective norms, and perceived behavioral control influence behavioral intention, which, in turn, influences behavior. Attitude reflects positive or negative perceptions of the outcomes of behavior. Subjective norms influence conduct through social pressure or environmental expectations. Perceived behavioral control refers to a person's belief in their ability or resources to perform a behavior. The TPB states that intention drives action and that experience, knowledge, and other background elements determine attitudes, norms, and perceived control.

2.3.4 Data Protection and Compliance: The implementation of standards that ensure data protection and compliance with legal regulations is an essential component of effective management practices for the preservation of personal information related to employees.

2.3.5 Systematic Review: A systematic review is a process that entails analyzing, evaluating, classifying, and categorizing evidence-based material that has been published. The procedures for a systematic review include many steps, such as the formulation of the background and objectives, the formulation of research questions, the conduct of a literature search, the establishment of selection criteria, the application of practical screening, the evaluation of quality, the extraction of data, and the development of strategies for data synthesis.

2.3.6 Personal Data Management: With the help of Personal Data Management, you will be able to identify which categories of data contain personal information, thereby enhancing your ability to fulfill your obligations to safeguard personal data. Data categorized as Personal or Sensitive Personal contains information that is included in other processes involving personal data. According to the Personal Data Protection Act, you are required to categorize the various types of data properly. Tools for management that allow for efficient work. Some data cannot be categorized as personal data.

3. METHODOLOGY

3.1 Data Collection

By conducting a comprehensive analysis of the existing body of literature, this study aims to identify the primary issues associated with managing employee data during the digital transformation era and to investigate effective management strategies for protecting such data. This investigation employs a systematic literature review (SLR) method guided by the PRISMA protocol. Based on the following criteria, the papers evaluated were obtained from the Emerald Insight database: they were published between 2020 and 2025, written in English, and presented empirical findings relevant to the management of employee personal data. According to the findings of this study, the implementation of personal data management policies is closely tied to technical innovation, sustainability, ethics, and risk management. Some of the most significant challenges include the presence of cyber threats, limitations in technology infrastructure, and a lack of cybersecurity knowledge among personnel. This issue needs to be addressed by establishing clear regulations, providing employees with training, and making investments in cutting-edge technologies such as encryption and intrusion detection.

The findings of this study can help organizations design more effective data protection policies and procedures. By integrating cybersecurity training, advanced technologies, and comprehensive Bring Your Own Device (BYOD) policies, organizations can strengthen the security of employees' data while building internal trust. This study contributes to the literature by applying the Theory of Planned Behavior (TPB) in the context of employee management of personal data. It also systematically synthesizes recent findings, creating new insights that various industry sectors can adapt.

This study employs a descriptive analysis approach, a component of qualitative research. The purpose of this method is to describe the data sources derived from the literature review of previous studies. The analysis process is conducted through a

Systematic Literature Review (SLR) using the PRISMA method (Preferred Reporting Items for Systematic Reviews and Meta-Analyses) (Hadi et al., 2020).

A systematic review is an approach that involves reviewing, evaluating, classifying, and categorizing evidence-based data that has been published. The procedures for a systematic review encompass several steps, including formulating the background and objectives, research questions, conducting a literature search, establishing selection criteria, applying practical screening, assessing quality, extracting data, and developing data synthesis strategies. In this study, the first step is to prepare the Background and Objectives in the introduction, which aims to uncover the challenges and management practices in protecting employee personal data in the digital transformation era. The literature search utilizes the Emerald Insight database, covering publication periods from 2020 to January 2025.

The following process is the selection of articles to ensure the alignment of the literature with the established criteria, which are:

a) Journal articles discussing management practices
b) Published within the period from 2020 to 2025
c) Written in English
d) Presenting empirical research findings

The literature is identified and screened using the PRISMA procedure, which involves both inclusion and exclusion stages.

3.2 Data Analysis

It is recommended that valid sources and scholarly papers from reputable databases, such as Google Scholar, Web of Science (WOS), and Scopus, be considered for the literature review (Rakpathum et al., 2025; Siripipatthanakul, 2011). The PRISMA method is based on PRISMA (2020), Siripipipatthanakul and Phuangsuwan (2024).

Figure 1. Systematic literature review information flow using PRISMA

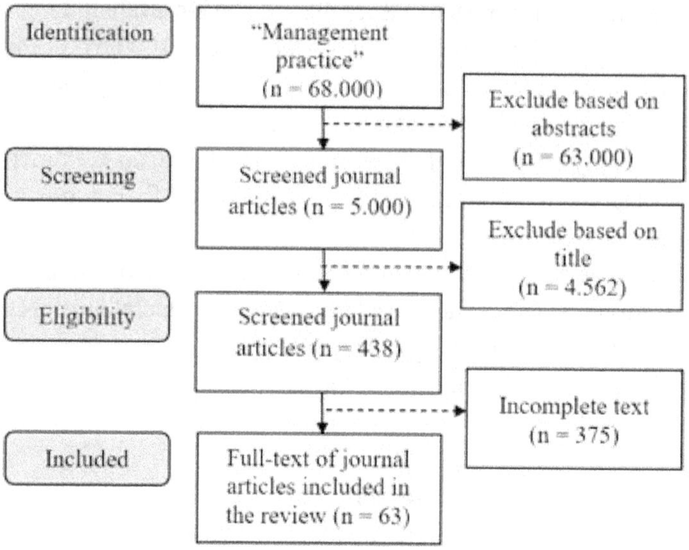

Based on the PRISMA Method (Prisma, 2020).

The purpose of this study is to identify the most significant issues associated with managing the personal data of employees in this era of digital transformation and to investigate the management strategies that are the most successful for preserving such data. Accomplishing this goal requires doing a thorough analysis of the existing body of literature. For the purpose of this inquiry, a systematic literature review (SLR) approach is utilized, which is directed by the PRISMA protocol, which stands for Preferred Reporting Items for Systematic Reviews and Meta-Analyses. The articles that were assessed were collected from the Emerald Insight database and were evaluated based on the following criteria: they were published between the years 2020 and 2025, they were written in English, and they presented empirical findings that were relevant to the management of employee personal data. When it comes to the implementation of personal data management policies, the findings of this study indicate that there is a direct connection between the execution of these policies and technical innovation, sustainability, ethics, and risk management. The presence of cyber threats, limitations in technology infrastructure, and a lack of cybersecurity expertise among staff are among the most critical challenges being faced. Establishing clear standards, providing personnel with training, and investing in cutting-edge technologies such as encryption and intrusion detection are all necessary steps to address this issue.

To determine whether the chapter is relevant to the book's overall theme, it has been examined. Following the suggestions given by the three reviewers, adjustments have been made in response to those comments. The results of Grammarly indicate that the grammatical correctness is 93%, while the percentage of plagiarism is 2%.

4. RESULTS

4.1 Number of Articles and Publication Year

This study analyzed 63 articles to explore the relationship between "management practice" and various key themes, including sustainability, technological innovation, risk management, and organizational ethics. Additionally, the distribution of articles based on year, publication title, and country provides insights into research priorities and global contributions. The following are the results of the analysis.

Figure 2. Number of articles and publication year

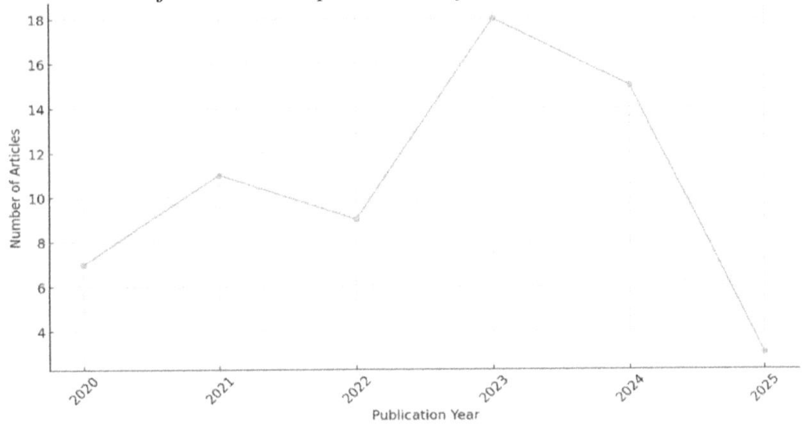

(Authors generated, 2024)

According to Figure 2, the graph that illustrates the distribution of articles by publication year, the year 2023 had the highest number of articles, contributing 28.57% of the total publications, while the year 2025 had the lowest number, contributing just 4.76% of the total publications. The following is a breakdown of the distribution over the past five years: 2023 (28.57%), 2024 (23.81%), 2021 (17.46%), 2022 (14.29%), 2020 (11.11%), and 2025 (4.76%). This discovery suggests that there will be a substantial increase in 2023, which may be the result of a strong emphasis on research or an increase in the number of journals that are published during that year. The poor contribution in 2025, on the other hand, is likely due to incomplete data, considering that we are only in the early stages of that year.

4.2 Distribution of Articles by Publication Title

Figure 3. Distribution of articles by publication title

(Author generated, 2024)

As shown in Figure 3, the graph illustrating the distribution of articles by publication title reveals that specific titles have a significantly higher number of articles than others. This demonstrates that a significant number of contributions have been made to particular titles, which may indicate the popularity or significance of the topics published in those journals. On the other hand, specific titles appear to have a smaller number of articles, which may be associated with more specialized topics or a more limited audience focus. Using these facts, one can gain a better understanding of publishing trends and the central focus of individual publications.

4.3 Number of Publications by Country

Figure 4. Number of publications by country

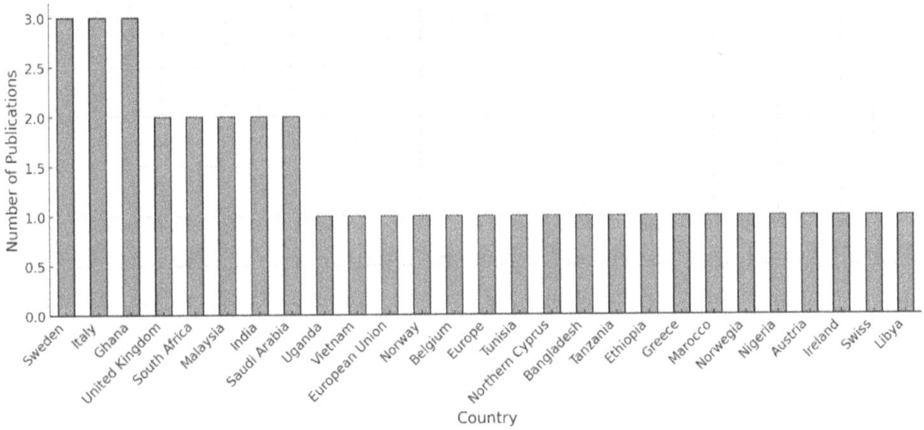

(Author generated, 2024)

As shown in Figure 4, the chart illustrates the number of publications classified by country. According to the distribution, Sweden is the country that contributes the highest percentage of publications (7.89%), followed by Italy (7.89%), Ghana (7.89%), the United Kingdom (5.26%), South Africa (5.26%), Malaysia (5.26%), India (5.26%), Saudi Arabia (5.26%), and other countries such as Uganda (2.63%), Vietnam (2.63%), European Union (2.63%), and many others, each of which contributes a smaller proportion. Although the bulk of publications comes from a small number of nations, this illustrates the diverse contributions made by publications from various countries.

4.4 Distribution of Articles by Key Themes

Figure 5. Distribution of articles by key themes

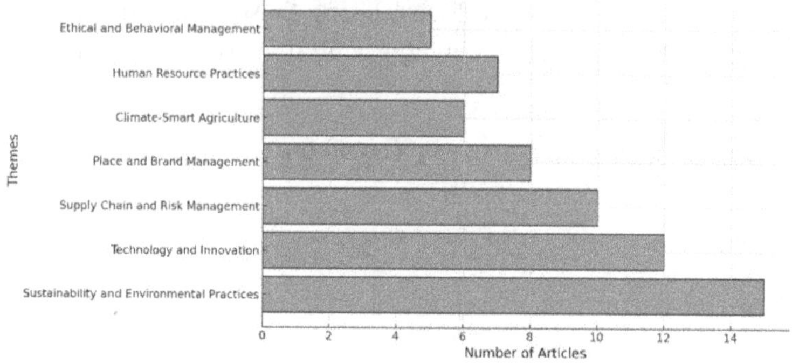

(Author generated, 2024)

Figure 5 illustrates that the concept of "management practice" is closely tied to several key topics, as identified from the 63 publications examined. Management practices in the field of sustainability and environmental practices provide an emphasis on environmental sustainability through waste management, sustainable supply chains, and land conservation. Technology and innovation highlight the role that technologies, such as artificial intelligence (AI) and algorithms, play in enhancing management efficiency, particularly in areas like record management and digital transformation. The integration of logistics and risk management can significantly enhance a company's competitive edge, as illustrated by examples from supply chain and risk management. The management of global and local branding, such as that which occurs within UNESCO Creative City networks, is facilitated by these methods, which include brand management. The concept of climate-smart agriculture emphasizes the importance of a strategic plan for integrating climate-based technologies into the operations and policies of local communities. The methods of human resource management emphasize mentoring, training, and transparency to optimize business effectiveness and cultivate trust. Ethical and behavioral management, on the other hand, emphasizes the significance of risk management methods in the process of developing a framework that is simultaneously ethical and transparent. Generally, efficient management methods provide a crucial foundation for ensuring sustainability, innovation, and efficiency across various industries.

5. DISCUSSIONS

5.1 Challenges in Protecting Employee Personal Data

When it comes to protecting employee data in the era of digital transformation, there are numerous significant challenges to address. Cloud computing and artificial intelligence (AI) are examples of technological developments that improve operational efficiency. However, these advancements often overlook the risks to their users' privacy and security. Data theft and ransomware attacks are two examples of the types of cyber threats that can be made more vulnerable to firms that place an excessive emphasis on efficiency. The ever-increasing complexity of cyber attacks is one of the most significant challenges. In their study, Frei et al. (2023) explain that the quickly shifting digital world raises the risk of phishing, malware, and the exploitation of human resources (HR) management systems. Furthermore, a significant number of businesses are faced with limitations in their technological infrastructure. There is a dearth of investment in security technologies, which increases the likelihood of data breaches, despite the potential for digital transformation to yield economic benefits. As a primary contributing element to data breach occurrences, the lack of cybersecurity awareness among employees is a crucial factor. Highlight the fact that human carelessness, such as using weak passwords or sharing sensitive information without adequate protection, increases the likelihood of data breaches occurring. Therefore, it is essential to provide ongoing training in order to enhance knowledge about cybersecurity (Cherrafi et al., 2022; Ifeanyi-Obi et al., 2022; Frei et al., 2023; Schmitter et al., 2024).

As a result of the COVID-19 pandemic, an additional challenge has arisen from the acceleration of remote work. A significant number of policies regarding remote work are regularly introduced without enough preparedness for security. The lack of clear standards is a contributing factor to the increased risk of data leakage caused by policies such as Bring Your Own Device (BYOD). The application of data protection legislation, such as the General Data Protection Regulation (GDPR), often becomes a barrier, despite these policies providing an essential legal basis. Lack of expertise and limited resources are two factors that frequently hinder organizations, particularly those in developing nations, from meeting the standards of regulatory agencies. The Internet of Things (IoT) and artificial intelligence (AI) are two examples of emerging technologies that pose additional challenges to privacy. The Internet of Things often collects data without employees' awareness, raising ethical concerns and privacy issues. In addition, the data that is collected from Internet of Things devices is frequently not appropriately encrypted, which increases the likelihood of security breaches (Cherrafi et al., 2022; Schmitter et al., 2024; Lundin et al.. 2025)

In order to effectively address these difficulties, a comprehensive strategy that emphasizes the enhancement of technology, policies, training, and organizational culture is required. Especially in the context of working remotely, it is very necessary to make investments in cutting-edge technology like encryption, firewalls, and intrusion detection systems in order to safeguard information that is personally identifiable. It is necessary to increase the level of cybersecurity literacy among personnel through regular training programs in order to reduce the likelihood of human mistake. In addition, a complete Bring Your Own Device (BYOD) policy that is helped along by Mobile Device Management (MDM) technology can assist in the management and protection of personal devices that are used for work. Compliance with legislation such as the General Data Protection Regulation (GDPR) and the California Consumer Privacy Act (CCPA) should be ensured by routine security audits in order to detect weaknesses and enhance data management. In conjunction with the implementation of AI and IoT, there should be methods for transparency as well as stringent controls on the gathering and utilization of data. In conclusion, it is imperative for enterprises to establish a culture that promotes data security by means of proactive leadership and transparent policy. Through the implementation of an integrated strategy, organizations have the ability to solve difficulties related to the protection of personal data, thereby enhancing the trust of their employees and adhering to the applicable legal criteria.

(Jakubik, 2021; Cherrafi et al., 2022; Ifeanyi-Obi et al., 2022; Frei et al., 2023; Schmitter et al., 2024; Schmitter et al., 2024; Lundin et al., 2025).

5.2 Management Practices for Employee Data Protection

Effective management procedures for preserving employee personal data are essential to ensure the security of sensitive information in today's digital age. A comprehensive approach incorporates cutting-edge technology, open and transparent policies, staff training, and an organizational culture that has a strong commitment to security. It has been suggested that the first step in good data management is the formulation of detailed internal privacy policies. These policies should incorporate guidelines for the collection, storage, and use of employee data, while also complying with international standards, such as the General Data Protection Regulation (GDPR) and the California Consumer Privacy Act (CCPA), which provide a legal framework for protecting personal data. The utilization of technology is at the center of the practices that are used for data protection management. it is essential to underline the significance of deploying encryption technology in order to safeguard data while it is being transmitted and stored. In addition, firewalls and intrusion detection systems must to be incorporated into the system in order to safeguard it against cyberattacks. Artificial intelligence-based technology can also be utilized by organizations in order to identify anomalies and suspicious behaviors within their systems. When it comes to ensuring the safety of employees' network connections, the utilization of Virtual Private Networks (VPNs) is essential in the context of remote work (Alonso-Muñoz et al., 2022; Cherrafi et al., 2022; Frei et al., 2023; Schmitter et al., 2024; Lundin et al., 2025).

Employee training is another critical element in data protection management practices. Ifeanyi-Obi et al. (2022) confirms that many data breaches occur due to human error, such as using weak passwords or clicking on phishing links. Therefore, organizations must provide regular training programs covering cyber threats, the importance of multi-factor authentication, and best practices for safeguarding personal data. Chaity and Islam (2022) summarize that such training enhances security and strengthens employee trust in the organization. Clear Bring Your Own Device (BYOD) policies are essential, given that many employees use personal devices. Frei et al. (2023) suggest using Mobile Device Management (MDM) technology to ensure personal devices meet the organization's security standards. Effective BYOD policies should include rules on data access, app usage, and protocols for handling data breaches.

Periodic security audits are another important element in data protection management practices. These audits help organizations identify weaknesses in their systems and ensure compliance with regulations (Lundin et al., 2025). Additionally, organizations need to develop a comprehensive incident response plan outlining steps to detect, respond to, and mitigate the impact of data breaches (Cherrafi et al., 2022)This step protects employee data and enhances the organization's reputation. Organizational culture also plays a key role in data protection management practices. Jakubik (2021), highlighted that proactive leadership in creating a security culture can help employees understand the importance of protecting personal data. Organizational leaders must prioritize data security as an integral part of their management strategy and set a good example for employees to foster collective awareness.

Effective employee data protection management necessitates a comprehensive approach that encompasses proactive leadership, integrated policies, employee training, advanced technologies, and adherence to relevant regulations. Organizational leaders play a crucial role in fostering a culture that supports data security by establishing clear policies and setting a positive example for employees (Jakubik, 2021). Comprehensive internal privacy policies must be developed to comply with regulations such as GDPR and CCPA, ensuring secure data management through periodic security audits (Lundin et al., 2025). Furthermore, regular training for employees is essential to raise awareness of cybersecurity threats and equip them with skills in best practices, such as password management and phishing prevention (Ifeanyi-Obi et al., 2022). To support BYOD policies, organizations need to adopt MDM technology to ensure personal devices meet security standards (Frei et al., 2023). From a technological perspective, adopting data encryption, intrusion detection systems, and AI-based technologies can help prevent breaches by detecting anomalies in systems (Schmitter et al., 2024). Quickly responding to security incidents, including isolating affected systems and notifying relevant parties, is essential to minimize damage. By implementing this approach, organizations can effectively protect employees' personal data, build trust, and ensure operational continuity in the digital era.

5.3 Digital Transformation and Its Impact on Data Protection

The digital transformation has brought about changes in how organizations manage data, but it has also introduced new challenges in securing personal data, mainly information about employees. The adoption of contemporary technologies, such as cloud computing, big data, artificial intelligence (AI), and the Internet of Things (IoT), presents significant opportunities for efficiency and innovation; however, it also raises concerns about data security risks. A significant number of firms are adopting digital technologies without including proper security measures, which increases their susceptibility to data breaches and cyberattacks. Real-time data access is made possible by cloud computing; nevertheless, cloud computing is sometimes not equipped with adequate encryption. Data breaches are more likely to occur as a result of this phenomenon, particularly when access is gained over insecure networks. When working from a remote location, the hazards become more significant. The likelihood of cyberattacks increases when employees use their devices without a transparent Bring Your Own Device (BYOD) policy. Virtual Private Networks (VPNs) and multi-factor authentication are two examples of technologies that organizations must utilize to prevent unauthorized access to sensitive data. Additionally, organizations need to embrace Mobile Device Management (MDM) technologies in order to manage personal devices (Cherrafi et al., 2022; Frei et al., 2023; Schmitter et al., 2024)

Digital transformation introduces additional complexities in data protection, particularly with the integration of AI and IoT technologies. Although AI can identify anomalous trends and mitigate cyber hazards, non-transparent algorithms provide ethical dilemmas about the acquisition and utilization of employee data. Conversely, IoT devices often lack stringent security protocols, making them vulnerable to data breaches through unencrypted devices. Regulations and compliance pose considerable hurdles in the age of the digital revolution. Emphasized that swift technology advancements hinder firms' ability to adhere to standards such as GDPR and CCPA. This difficulty is particularly pronounced in underdeveloped nations that may lack adequate or nonexistent data protection laws. To resolve this issue, it is advisable to conduct regular audits and establish adaptable internal policies that comply with international standards. Despite the considerable hurdles, digital transformation also presents an opportunity to enhance data protection. Technologies such as blockchain are being utilized to improve data transparency and integrity. Blockchain can establish an unalterable audit trail, guaranteeing that only authorized individuals can access confidential information. Moreover, this technology enables firms to transparently monitor every data access transparently, hence enhancing employee trust in data management practices. Organizational culture is essential for data protection in the era of digital transformation. Proactive leadership can enhance employee understanding regarding the protection of personal data security. Organizational leaders must prioritize data security as a fundamental component of their digital transformation plan. This encompasses routine employee training to identify and address cyber hazards, including phishing and malware (Frei et al., 2023; Schmitter et al., 2024)

An integrated approach that encompasses technology, policies, organizational culture, and strategic partnerships with technology service providers is crucial for effectively protecting employee data. Organizations must adopt advanced technologies, such as encryption, intrusion detection systems, artificial intelligence, and blockchain, to prevent data breaches. A clear BYOD policy, supported by MDM technology and multi-factor authentication, must be implemented to address risks arising from remote work (Cherrafi et al., 2022). Regular security audits are also necessary to identify system gaps and ensure compliance with global regulations, such as GDPR and CCPA. This approach can help organizations enhance data security, foster trust, and safeguard their reputations in the digital transformation era.

5.4 Importance of Employee Personal Data Protection

In the current digital era, protecting employees' data has become an essential component of organizations' operations worldwide. Information that is considered to be sensitive is gathered and processed by businesses. This includes personal identities, health records, financial information, and employee performance records. If it is not adequately safeguarded, this data is highly susceptible to misuse and vulnerable to cyber threats. For this reason, the protection of personal data is not only a legal need but also an essential precondition for the establishment of trust between businesses and their staff members (Chaity & Islam, 2022; Jakubik, 2021).

Protecting employee personal data is also key to meeting compliance with international data privacy regulations. Regulations such as the General Data Protection Regulation (GDPR) in the European Union and similar laws in various countries require companies to implement stringent measures in managing personal data. Non-compliance with these regulations can result in significant financial penalties and substantial reputational damage, ultimately affecting the organization's sustainability. Furthermore, compliance with these regulations provides a competitive edge, particularly in international business relationships, by demonstrating commitment to global standards. Protecting employees' data is important in building a positive organizational culture. Employees' trust in the organization's ability to manage their data influences engagement and job satisfaction. Organizations that prioritize data protection tend to have higher levels of internal trust, which positively impacts productivity. Conversely, data breaches can trigger dissatisfaction, lower employee morale, and even increase turnover rates (Alonso-Muñoz et al., 2022; Schmitter et al., 2024; Golandaj & Kallihal, 2021).

The protection of employees' data has become increasingly challenging due to the proliferation of digital transformation. It was discovered that the effectiveness of digital technology deployment is mainly dependent on an organization's ability to manage data security effectively. This is because the adoption of technologies such as cloud computing, big data, and digital collaboration tools raises the risks of cyberattacks. Businesses need to implement advanced security measures to mitigate the impact of these threats. These measures should include data encryption, frequent vulnerability testing, and staff privacy training. Not only do these steps enhance the organization's security, but they also add to the efficiency with which functions are carried out. The protection of personal data is consistent with the values of human rights and respect for individual dignity. The improper use of personal information can result in severe repercussions, including identity theft, discrimination, and financial loss. Within the scope of this discussion, the highlights the significance of the organization's dedication to data security as an element of its corporate social responsibility framework. In addition to enhancing the organization's reputation in the eyes of the general public and strengthening connections with employees and other stakeholders, adequate data protection embodies the ethical ideals on which the business was founded. In today's digital age, it is crucial for an organization to protect the personal information of its employees to maintain trust, ensure compliance, and cultivate a positive reputation. Through the implementation of modern security technology, effective compliance procedures, and a demonstrated commitment to ethical values, organizations can transform their working environments into trustworthy and secure ones. As a result of this endeavor, employee data is safeguarded, organizational culture is strengthened, productivity is increased, and operational sustainability is supported in the face of continual problems in the ever-evolving digital world (Alonso-Muñoz et al., 2022; Chaity & Islam, 2022; Kallihal, 2021).

6. CONCLUSIONS

The conclusions of this study can help firms develop more effective policies and processes for data protection, ultimately benefiting their operations. Enterprises can enhance the security of their employees' data while fostering a culture of trust within the organization by incorporating cybersecurity training, advanced technologies, and comprehensive Bring Your Own Device (BYOD) policies. The application of the Theory of Planned Behavior (TPB) to the setting of employee management of personal data is the significant contribution that this study makes to the existing body of research. In addition, it generates new insights by methodically synthesizing recent findings, which can be applied across various industry sectors.

This study emphasizes the importance of protecting employee personal data in the era of digital transformation, characterized by technological advancements such as cloud computing, artificial intelligence (AI), and Human Resource Information Systems (HRIS), which present both opportunities and challenges. The integration of technological, organizational, and regulatory methods is essential for implementing effective data security management practices. Through the application of the Theory of Planned Behavior (TPB), this study makes a theoretical contribution by explaining how attitudes, subjective norms, and perceived behavioral control influence the degree to which employees comply with data protection laws. When it comes to data protection, digital transformation provides a number of serious issues, but it also offers specific benefits. The usage of blockchain technology is helping to improve the integrity and transparency of data. Unauthorized access to sensitive data is prevented by the immutable audit trail that blockchain technology provides. Additionally, this technology enables businesses to track data access transparently, thereby increasing employee trust in data management. The culture of a business is also a crucial factor in ensuring data security in the era of digital transformation. The workforce could be educated about data security if the leadership takes the initiative. Within their digital transformation strategy, businesses need to place a strong emphasis on data protection. Phishing and malware awareness training for employees is conducted on a regular basis. It is essential to integrate technology, norms, company culture, and strategic relationships with technology service providers to maintain the confidentiality of employee information. To prevent data breaches, organizations are required to implement encryption, intrusion detection, artificial intelligence, and blockchain technology. There is a need for a specified Bring Your Own Device (BYOD) strategy that incorporates mobile device management (MDM) and multi-factor authentication to reduce the risks associated with remote work. Regular security audits are necessary to identify system flaws and ensure compliance with the General Data Protection Regulation (GDPR) and the California Consumer Privacy Act (CCPA). Within the context of the digital transformation era, this strategy has the potential to enhance data security, trust, and reputation. The findings highlight how important it is for firms to adopt thorough internal policies that are in line with worldwide standards, such as the General Data Protection Regulation (GDPR), invest in modern security technologies, provide continuing employee training, and cultivate a culture that places a priority on data protection. When combined with specific regulations regarding bring-your-own-device (BYOD) and remote work, these techniques have the potential to significantly reduce risks and establish trust between enterprises and their employees.

At any given organization, the information pertaining to its staff members is a highly significant asset. Additionally, it is a key component of talent management and compliance, assisting with HR functions such as payroll and benefits administration. This data, on the other hand, is more susceptible to theft than it has ever been previously as a result of the rising digitization of workplace practices. Cybercriminals frequently target employee information on the dark web because of its substantial value. Consequently, enterprises must implement robust security measures. In a workplace that places a high priority on digital technology, one of the most significant challenges that presents itself is the enormous volume of data that is being generated and stored. The attack surface has significantly increased because employees are accessing company networks from various locations and using portable storage devices. Due to the complexity of the scenario, it is crucial to implement security measures that comprise multiple layers. These measures should include encryption, access controls, and continual monitoring. As an illustration, working together with competent persons who are experts in the field of information technology outsourcing would be an excellent choice because it offers a practical approach to enhancing data safety. Establishing collaborations with knowledgeable information technology service providers enables organizations to gain access to cutting-edge security solutions that are customized to meet their unique requirements

As technological developments continue to occur, the way corporations manage and preserve data is continually evolving. When it comes to managing people data, technology has evolved into an integral tool in the field of human resources (HR). This technical innovation, on the other hand, comes with the obligation to safeguard employees' information. Within the scope of this comprehensive book, the significance of data privacy in human resource technology, the risks and challenges associated with employee data privacy, and the most effective methods for protecting employee data in HR technology have been examined. When it comes to Human Resources (HR) systems, which are responsible for managing a wide range of sensitive employee information, the need to secure personal data has increased substantially in today's highly digitalized workplace. This is especially true in the context of HR systems. Concerns regarding unauthorized access to data, breaches, and the sharing of data with third parties have arisen as a result of the ongoing evolution of human resource management systems to leverage extensive data analytics. Today's modern businesses face significant data privacy concerns, underscored by the extensive employee data maintained by HR systems. To be considered a comprehensive data privacy framework, specific necessary components must be present. The need to maintain current knowledge of global data privacy rules, implement thorough data protection policies, and cultivate a culture that prioritizes data privacy is emphasized more than ever before. Therefore, the design serves as a comprehensive guide, providing human resource professionals and organizations with actionable insights that enable them to protect employee data proactively, particularly in an era where data privacy has become a fundamental concern.

7. LIMITATIONS AND RECOMMENDATIONS

On the other hand, the research had some shortcomings, most notably that it relied on a Systematic Literature Review (SLR), a method that summarizes previous research without collecting primary data. This could potentially restrict the extent to which the findings can be generalized. In addition, the scope is further limited by the use of a single database and a focus on research conducted between 2020 and 2025. In addition, the research does not adequately address the difficulties that are specific to a particular industry or the variances in regulatory frameworks that differ from one region to another. Primary data should be incorporated into future research through interviews or surveys to address these gaps, broaden the study's scope to include a broader range of sources and earlier studies, and investigate industry-specific differences as well as disparities that exist between different cultures. Investigations into emerging technologies, such as blockchain and the Internet of Things, in conjunction with longitudinal research on the long-term implications of data protection policies, would also provide more comprehensive insights. The implementation of these procedures would enhance both awareness of and adherence to appropriate data protection practices in various administrative settings. Given that this is a systematic evaluation, it is possible that respondents were omitted. Therefore, to conduct additional research, it is suggested that either quantitative questionnaire surveys or qualitative interviews be conducted.

REFERENCES

Abrahams, T. O., Ewuga, S. K., Dawodu, S. O., Adegbite, A. O., & Hassan, A. O.Temitayo Oluwaseun AbrahamsSarah Kuzankah EwugaSamuel Onimisi Dawodu-Abimbola Oluwatoyin AdegbiteAzeez Olanipekun Hassan. (2024). A Review of Cybersecurity Strategies in Modern Organization; Examining the Evolution and Effectiveness of Cybersecurity Measures for Data Protection. *Computer Science & IT Research Journal*, *5*(1), 1–25. Advance online publication. DOI: 10.51594/csitrj.v5i1.699

Ajzen, I. (1991). The theory of planned behavior. *Organizational Behavior and Human Decision Processes*, *50*(2), 179–211. DOI: 10.1016/0749-5978(91)90020-T

Alonso-Muñoz, S., García-Muiña, F. E., Medina-Salgado, M.-S., & González-Sánchez, R. (2022). Towards circular economy practices in food waste management: A retrospective overview and a research agenda. *British Food Journal*, *124*(13), 478–500. DOI: 10.1108/BFJ-01-2022-0072

Amoo, O. O., Atadoga, A., Osasona, F., Abrahams, T. O., Ayinla, B. S., & Farayola, O. A. (2024). GDPR's impact on cybersecurity: A review focusing on USA and European practices. *International Journal of Science and Research Archive*, *11*(1), 1338–1347. DOI: 10.30574/ijsra.2024.11.1.0220

Carmi, L., Zohar, M., & Riva, G. M. (2022). The European General Data Protection Regulation (GDPR) in mHealth: Theoretical and practical aspects for practitioners' use. *Medicine, Science, and the Law*. Advance online publication. DOI: 10.1177/00258024221118411 PMID: 35950240

Chaity, N. S., & Islam, K. M. Z. (2022). Bank efficiency and practice of earnings management: A study on listed commercial banks of Bangladesh. *Asian Journal of Accounting Research*, *7*(2), 114–128. DOI: 10.1108/AJAR-09-2020-0080

Cherrafi, A., Chiarini, A., Belhadi, A., El Baz, J., & Chaouni Benabdellah, A. (2022). Digital technologies and circular economy practices: Vital enablers to support sustainable and resilient supply chain management in the post-COVID-19 era. *The TQM Journal*, *34*(7), 179–202. DOI: 10.1108/TQM-12-2021-0374

Cosa, M. (2024). Business digital transformation: Strategy adaptation, communication and future agenda. *Journal of Strategy and Management*, *17*(2), 244–259. DOI: 10.1108/JSMA-09-2023-0233

Deloitte Indonesia. (2024). *Deloitte Indonesia Perspectives*. Deloitte. https://www2.deloitte.com/content/dam/Deloitte/id/Documents/about-deloitte/id-about-dip-4th-edition-sept2024-id.pdf

Ducato, R. (2020). Data protection, scientific research, and the role of information. *Computer Law & Security Review*, *37*, 105412. DOI: 10.1016/j.clsr.2020.105412

Frei, J., Greiling, D., & Schmidthuber, J. (2023). Reconciling field-level logics and management control practices in research management at Austrian public universities. *Qualitative Research in Accounting & Management*, *20*(1), 117–143. DOI: 10.1108/QRAM-10-2020-0167

Gara, G. L., & Porte, J. M. L. (2020). Processes of building trust in organizations: Internal communication, management, and recruiting. *Church, Communication and Culture*. https://www.tandfonline.com/doi/abs/10.1080/23753234.2020.1824581

Golandaj, J. A., & Kallihal, K. G. (2021). Awareness, attitude and practises of biomedical waste management amongst public health-care staff in Karnataka, India. *Journal of Humanities and Applied Social Sciences*, *3*(1), 49–63. DOI: 10.1108/JHASS-08-2019-0041

Hadi, S., Tjahjono, H. K., & Palupi, M. (2020). *Systematic Review: Meta Sintesis Untuk Riset Perilaku Organisasional*. Viva Victory Abadi. https://pak.uii.ac.id/wp-content/uploads/2023/03/Buku-Ajar-2019-Systematic-Review-Meta-Sintesis-Untuk-Riset-Perilaku-Organisasional_ok.pdf

Hoofnagle, C. J., van der Sloot, B., & Borgesius, F. Z. (2019). The European Union general data protection regulation: What it is and what it means*. *Information & Communications Technology Law*. https://www.tandfonline.com/doi/abs/10.1080/13600834.2019.1573501

Huang, J. (2018). Building intelligence in digital transformation. *Journal of Integrated Design & Process Science*, *21*(4), 1–4. DOI: 10.3233/jid-2018-0006

IBM. (2024, August 12). *What Is Cybersecurity? | IBM*. What Is Cybersecurity? https://www.ibm.com/think/topics/cybersecurity

Ifeanyi-Obi, C. C., Issa, F. O., Aderinoye-Abdulwahab, S. O., Ayinde, A. F., Umeh, O. J., & Tologbonse, E. B. (2022). Promoting uptake and integration of climate smart agriculture technologies, innovations and management practices into policy and practice in Nigeria. *International Journal of Climate Change Strategies and Management*, *14*(4), 354–374. DOI: 10.1108/IJCCSM-09-2021-0101

Jakubik, M. (2021). How can practical wisdom manifest itself in five fundamental management and leadership practices? *Vilakshan - XIMB. Journal of Management*, *18*(1), 3–25. DOI: 10.1108/XJM-08-2020-0078

Kaspersky. (2024). *IT Security Economics*. IT Security Economics. https://www.kaspersky.com/blog/it-security-economics-2024/

Koneru, G. (2024). *The Evolving World of Data Privacy: Trends and Strategies*. The Evolving World of Data Privacy: Trends and Strategies. https://www.isaca.org/resources/news-and-trends/industry-news/2024/the-evolving-world-of-data-privacy-trends-and-strategies

Lang, V. (2021). Digitalization and digital transformation. In *Digital Fluency: Understanding the Basics of Artificial Intelligence, Blockchain Technology, Quantum Computing, and Their Applications for Digital Transformation* (pp. 1-50). Berkeley, CA: Apress. DOI: 10.1007/978-1-4842-6774-5_1

Lundin, K., Skytt, B., Silén, M., Engström, M., & Strömberg, A. (2025). First-line managers' experiences of and reflections on structural conditions for management practice in hospital settings. *Leadership in Health Services*, *38*(5), 1–15. https://studenttheses.uu.nl/handle/20.500.12932/46593. DOI: 10.1108/LHS-07-2024-0060 PMID: 39692171

Marikyan, D., Papagiannidis, S., Rana, O. F., & Ranjan, R. (2024). General data protection regulation: A study on attitude and emotional empowerment. *Behaviour & Information Technology*. https://www.tandfonline.com/doi/abs/10.1080/0144929X.2023.2285341

Mileros, M. D., & Forchheimer, R. (2024). Free for you and me? Exploring the value users gain from their seemingly free apps. *Digital Policy. Regulation & Governance*, *27*(2), 239–257. DOI: 10.1108/DPRG-01-2024-0009

Murugesan, U., Subramanian, P., Srivastava, S., & Dwivedi, A. (2023). A study of Artificial Intelligence impacts on Human Resource Digitalization in Industry 4.0. *Decision Analytics Journal*, *7*, 100249. DOI: 10.1016/j.dajour.2023.100249

Otoo, F. N. K., Junior, P. N. A., Agyeman, G. A., & Bekoe, R. (2025). Examining the relationship between human resource management practices and employee creativity: The mediating role of organizational learning capability. *African Journal of Economic and Management Studies, ahead-of-print*(ahead-of-print). DOI: 10.1108/AJEMS-08-2024-0434

Palos-Sánchez, P. R., Baena-Luna, P., Badicu, A., & Infante-Moro, J. C. (2022). Artificial Intelligence and Human Resources Management: A Bibliometric Analysis. *Applied Artificial Intelligence*. https://www.tandfonline.com/doi/abs/10.1080/08839514.2022.2145631

Patil, B. S., & Priya, M. R. S. R. (2024). HR data analytics and evidence based practice as a strategic business partner. *Vilakshan - XIMB. Journal of Management*, *21*(1), 114–125. DOI: 10.1108/XJM-07-2023-0148

Phuangsuwan, P., Siripipatthanakul, S., Praesri, S., & Rakpathum, W. (2025). The Relationship Between Good Governance and Organizational Performance Through the Mediating Role of Employee Satisfaction. *Journal of Governance and Regulation/Volume, 14*(1).

Prisma (2020). Prisma 2020 Statement. https://www.prisma-statement.org/prisma-2020

Quach, S., Thaichon, P., Martin, K. D., Weaven, S., & Palmatier, R. W. (2022). Digital technologies: Tensions in privacy and data. *Journal of the Academy of Marketing Science*, *50*(6), 1299–1323. DOI: 10.1007/s11747-022-00845-y PMID: 35281634

Rakpathum, W., Siripipatthanakul, S., Phuangsuwan, P., & Charoenporn, C. (2025). Enhancing Sustainable Development Goals (SDGs) for Rural Tourism Communities: The Case of Mae Kampong Village, Chiang Mai, Thailand. *Journal of Lifestyle and SDGs Review*, *5*(1), e04755–e04755. DOI: 10.47172/2965-730X.SDGsReview.v5.n01.pe04755

Ranasinghe, U. C., Ennis, S. F., Monteiro, J., & Malagueño, R. (2025). Global value chains, trade facilitation and the use of environmental management practices in SMEs. *International Journal of Operations & Production Management, ahead-of-print*(ahead-of-print). DOI: 10.1108/IJOPM-03-2024-0261

Schmitter, P., Shahgholian, A., & Tucker, M. (2024). Towards an understanding of the digital transformation of facility management in healthcare: Perspectives from practice. *Digital Transformation and Society*, *3*(4), 395–409. DOI: 10.1108/DTS-10-2023-0098

Sean Joyce. (2024). *Putting security at the epicenter of innovation* (2024 Global Digital Trust Insights, pp. 1–20). PricewaterhouseCoopers (PwC).

Shahreki, J., & Lee, J. Y. (2024). Adopting human resource information system and work-related outcomes in emerging market SMEs: Unified theory of acceptance and use of technology. *Cross Cultural &amp. Cross Cultural & Strategic Management*, *31*(1), 116–142. DOI: 10.1108/CCSM-09-2022-0144

Siripipatthanakul, S. (2011). Development of a Model for Administration of Student Dental Health Promotion Work for Basic Education Schools in Thailand. *International Journal of Learning*, *17*(12), 137–150. DOI: 10.18848/1447-9494/CGP/v17i12/47373

Siripipatthanakul, S., & Phuangsuwan, P. (2024). Salutogenic Marketing in Preventive Dentistry. In *Leveraging Digital Technology for Preventive Dentistry* (pp. 255–278). IGI Global., DOI: 10.4018/979-8-3693-3872-8.ch009

Vrana, J., & Singh, R. (2021). Digitization, digitalization, and digital transformation. *Handbook of nondestructive evaluation 4.0*, 1-17.

Watini, S., Davies, G., & Andersen, N. (2024). Cybersecurity in Learning Systems: Data protection and privacy in educational information systems and digital learning environments. [ITEE]. *International Transactions on Education Technology*, *3*(1), 1. Advance online publication. DOI: 10.33050/itee.v3i1.665

Chapter 5
The Determinants of FDI Attraction in Creating a Foreign Firm's Competitive Advantage:
An Extended Model for Data Protection in Privacy and Security

Seng Loong Kok
https://orcid.org/0009-0006-0997-7960
Manipal GlobalNxt University, Malaysia

Patcharavadee Sriboonruang
https://orcid.org/0000-0002-2171-2387
Kasetsart University, Thailand

ABSTRACT

Data privacy and security are crucial to competitiveness in the information age, especially for Foreign Direct Investment (FDI) and firm-level competitive advantage. A systematic review and content analysis were conducted based on scientific publications. This chapter explains the intricate relationship between factor conditions, supporting industries, policies, and regulatory frameworks that contribute to its competitiveness in attracting Foreign Direct Investment (FDI). The institutional stability of data protection boosts employees' trust and reduces geopolitical and cybersecurity concerns. The approach enhances competitiveness in attracting technology-driven Foreign Direct Investment (FDI) and enables enterprises to maintain long-term profitability through secure and transparent data ecosystems. According to research, compelling data governance and privacy enable organizations

DOI: 10.4018/979-8-3693-9720-6.ch005

to capitalize on market opportunities and mitigate risks. The chapter provides a framework for corporate leaders to integrate privacy, security, and FDI competitiveness in digital globalization.

1. INTRODUCTION

1.1 Foreign Direct Investment (FDI) Overview

Both scholars and policymakers have long recognized FDI as a crucial catalyst of economic growth, globalization, and sustainable development. Defined by International Monetary Fund (IMF) as "a category of international investment that reflects the objective of a resident in one economy (the direct investor) obtaining a lasting interest in an enterprise resident in another economy (the direct investment enterprise)" (Armand, 2020), FDI fosters international collaboration, technological innovation, and economic dynamism.

Paul and Feliciano-Cestero (2021) suggested that FDI studies are broad and multifaceted, garnering significant interest from both scholars and practitioners over the years. Since the inception of FDI studies, focus has consistently highlighting the impact of FDI on host economies, emphasizing its ability to boost GDP, generate employment opportunities, and promote the transfer of knowledge and skills (Zang & Baimbridge, 2014; Brychka, 2018; Ma'in & Mat Isa, 2020; Okwu, 2020; Le, 2021; Norehan et al., 2021; Wang et al., 2021; Halizam et al., 2021; Yimer, 2023).

Acknowledging that FDI trends have evolved significantly over the years, reflecting changing global economic patterns and priorities, research suggests that FDI flows are increasingly influenced by innovations (Mai et al., 2021; Hintošová, 2021, 2023; Roccon, 2023; Schulzmann et al., 2023) such as digitisation, credited to the technological advancement and achievement of recent decades since the turn of the 21st centuries.

These phenomena underscore the increasing importance of non-tangible assets, such as intellectual property and data, in formulating business strategies that contribute to a firm's sustainable competitive advantage (Hunjet et al., 2022; Dahiya et al., 2022; Adewusi et al., 2024). As such, recent trends in academic studies observed the focus on examining the role of FDI in fostering sustainable competitive advantages for firms, with particular emphasis on innovation and adaptability (Chen, 2021; Kong & Suntrayuth, 2021; Huan & Qamruzzaman, 2022; Gumpert et al., 2025).

Through an FDI strategy, firms gain access to new markets, expand their operations, and leverage the resources and incentives of host countries to attain sustainable competitive advantages. These advantages can potentially include embracing sustainability, which is aligned with environmental, social, and governance (ESG) agendas. In the information era, which is broadly characterized by information-driven analytic decision-making and digital interconnectivity, FDI faces unprecedented challenges, especially in the aspect of data protection and governance. The new digital economies have led to the emergence of unconventional cross-border business practices, such as the formation of global supply chain networks, regional data processing centres, software applications centric development hubs, and cloud computing infrastructures.

1.2 Data Protection and Governance: FDI Challenges in the Information Era

As highlighted earlier, the importance of FDI to economic growth is undeniable. While the potential benefits of FDI to both the host nations and investing firms are undisputable, the challenges associated with FDI in the information era cannot be disregarded. The innovation of digital technologies, such as artificial intelligence and the Internet of Things (IoT), has brought data protection and governance to the forefront of global concerns (Maras, 2015; Nadikattu, 2018; Yanamala & Suryadevara, 2023; Martin & Zimmermann, 2024; Mooradian et al., 2025). In 2021, the World Bank reported data breaches reduce FDI inflows by 15–20% in vulnerable economies.

Firms operating across borders are faced with complex geopolitical regulations governing data protection, including policies like the European Union's General Data Protection Regulation (GDPR) (Frey & Presidente, 2024). These regulations impose stringent measures to safeguard sensitive information and prevent data breaches, thereby implying significant compliance costs on investors. Recent academic studies have explored the implications of data protection and governance on Foreign Direct Investment (FDI) (Yu, 2022; Chaisse, 2023; Cheng, 2023), advocating for a balance between innovation and regulatory adherence (Nadir & Farah, 2023; Yanamala et al., 2024).

On a separate note, the relevance of data protection and governance in forging a firm competitive advantage has become critical in the information era. Recent studies underscore the importance of data as a valuable asset in facilitating strategic decision-making and enabling firms to deliver personalized services, credited to the technological advancement such as artificial intelligence driven data analytics applications (Brynjolfsson & McElheran, 2016; Adeniran et al., 2024; Sarioguz & Miser, 2024). Nonetheless, this phenomenon poses significant challenges to data protection and governance, hindering the ability to foster a competitive advantage. As such, firms that place a strong emphasis on data protection and governance can potentially differentiate themselves from their rivals, fostering long-term business relationships and client loyalty.

Academic research that emphasizes the role of transparency (Zakutnia & Hayriyan, 2017; Liu et al., 2023), accountability (Palekhova, 2016; Omoregbe & Kurtis, 2020), and technological innovation (Yu et al., 2017; Mugo & Macharia, 2020) which form the fundamental principles of data protection and governance, which lead to the enhancement of firm competitiveness in the digital world. Recent notable studies highlight digital infrastructure as a key FDI determinant (Amirov & Avazov, 2022; Bretas et al., 2022), while cybersecurity risks affect investment flows (Kshetri & Kshetri, 2016; Zwartkruis, 2024).

While FDI remains a cornerstone of economic growth and firm success, its role in the information era requires careful consideration to address emerging challenges. Hence, this study suggests that with the ability to address data protection and governance in FDI strategy consideration, firms can potentially achieve sustainable competitive advantages that may enhance their performance, particularly in technology-driven sectors where data is of strategic importance. However, rising cyber threats and regulatory fragmentation have made data protection and governance an ongoing concern in FDI decision-making.

1.3 Objective

This chapter explains how the determinants of data privacy and security competitiveness (DPSC) influence the attraction of Foreign Direct Investment (FDI).

2. LITERATURE REVIEWS

2.1 Synopsis of FDI Theories

This study underpins the FDI decision-making theories, specifically Dunning's OLI Paradigm (1979) and institutional theory (North, 1990), which emphasize the role of location-specific advantages.

Eclectic/OLI Paradigm is widely viewed as the extension of the internalisation theory and commonly referred as the contingency (multi-theoretical) approach for studying and investigating foreign entry mode choice as it shares considerations from International Trade Theory, Resource-Based Theory, and the Transaction Cost Economics (TCE) approach (Schellenberg et al., 2018). This well-established theoretical framework remains dominant in recent studies explaining market entry choices (Chiu et al., 2015; Bezuidenhout & Kleynhans, 2018; Batschauer et al., 2022).

The Eclectic (OLI) Paradigm provides a robust framework (Figure 1) to analyse the determinants of Foreign Direct Investment (FDI). The paradigm emphasizes three key advantages—Ownership (O), Location(L), and Internalization (I), that influence a firm's decision to invest abroad. Adopting the context of data security and privacy, which are paramount in the digital era, it is suggested as the following:

Figure 1. Eclectic / OLI paradigm

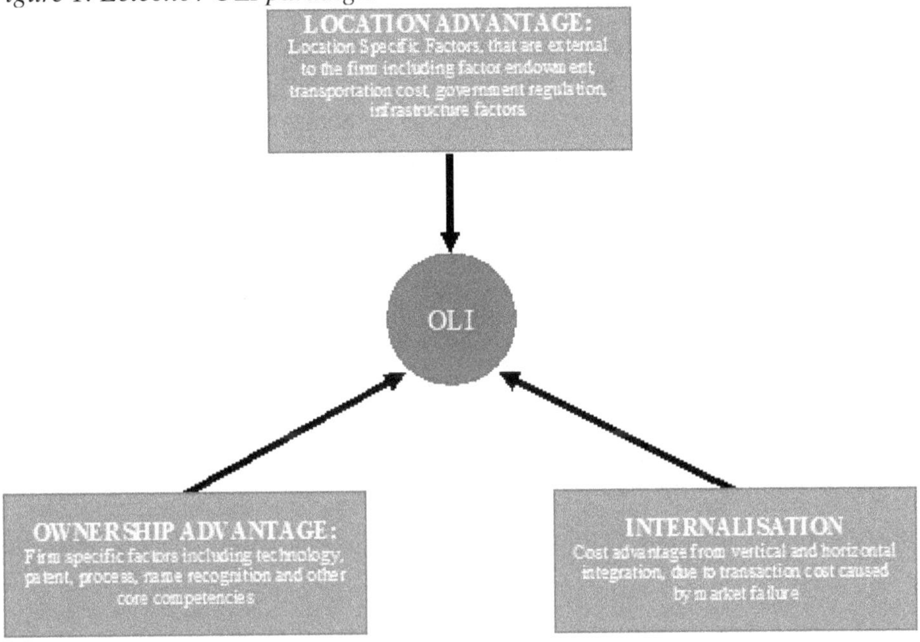

(Source: Dunning, 1973)

Institutional theory is predominantly used to explain how firms formulate strategies on entering and operating in foreign markets from an institutional context, defined by specific rules, norms, and values (Scott, 1995; Davis et al., 2000; Meyer & Nguyen, 2005). Schellenberg et al. (2018) highlight the approach is commonly adopted in conjunction with other theoretical perspectives (Roberts & Greenwood, 1997; Oliver, 1997; Arregle et al., 2006; Brouthers, 2013) contribute significantly to understanding Market Entry Modes (MEM) choice and have considerable predictive power to determine the model outcome (Canabal & White, 2008). In this context, the theory suggests that FDI decisions are influenced by a firm's desire to acquire a competitive advantage, thereby enhancing its performance.

2.2 Competitive Advantage Theory

2.2.1 Structure-Conduct-Performance (SCP) Paradigm

Mason (1939) and Bain (1959) pioneered The Structure-Conduct-Performance (SCP) paradigm (Figure 2), a foundational theory in industrial organization economics, providing a framework to understand the relationship between market structures (S), firm behaviour (conduct) (C), and market outcomes (performance) (P), which put forward the notion that the structure of an industry determines the conduct of firms, which in turn influences the overall market performance.

Figure 2. Structure conduct performance (SCP) model

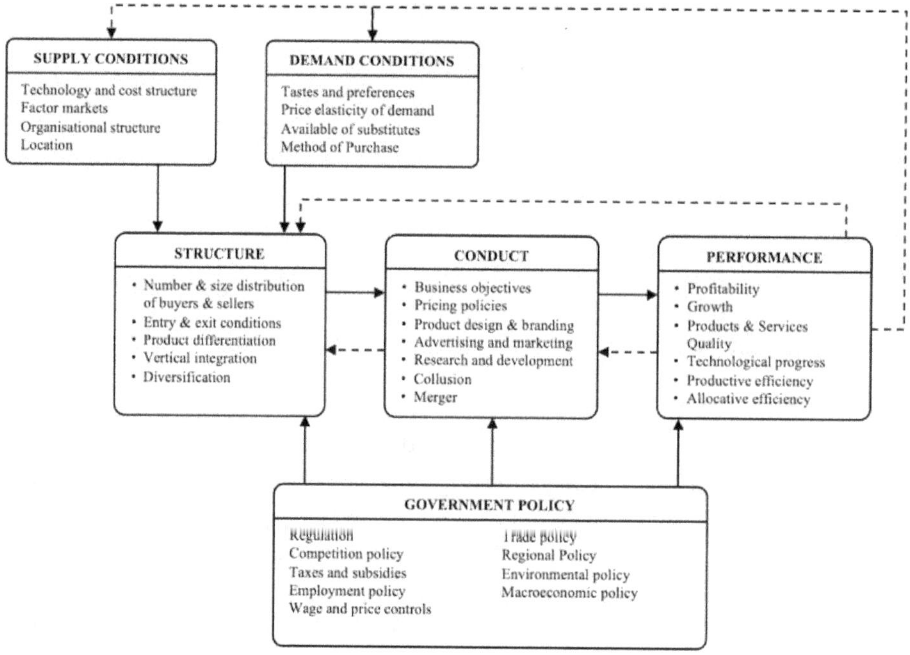

Source: Stojanović, and Kostić (2013).

The framework advocates the role of market governance, suggesting that appropriate measures to regulate market structures, such as reducing entry barriers or limiting monopolistic practices, can influence competitive behaviors and performance outcomes (Jusmadi & Armando, 2024; Bouraj et al., 2024)

2.2.2 Resource-Based View (RBV)

The concept of the RBV framework (Barney, 1991; Penrose, 1959) emphasizes the importance of firm-specific resources in achieving and sustaining competitive advantage (Wernerfelt, 1984). Barney (1991) advocates that these resources must be valuable, rare, imperfectly imitable, and imperfectly substitutable to acquire a sustainable competitive advantage, which is often referred to as VRIO: Value, Rarity, Inimitability, and Organizational support. Amit and Schoemaker (1993) define a resource as "stocks of available factors that are owned or controlled by the firm," which can be tangible and intangible. Amit and Schoemaker (1993) further expand the concept of resources to capabilities, defined as the firm's ability to utilize its resources to achieve a desired end.

2.2.3 Porter Diamond Model

Porter (1990) introduced the concept of competitive advantage, which posits that differences in national values, culture, economic structure, institutions, and history influence the success of an industry in competition. Porter's Diamond Model focuses on the competitive advantage of nations. It is well established in the literature that Porter's (1990) Diamond Framework, along with his subsequent work on clusters and competition (Porter, 1998, 2000, 2004), provides a structured framework for analyzing the competitive advantage of nations and industries. It seeks to explain the rationale of certain industries achieving higher levels of success in specific countries and identifies key determinants that drive this competitiveness.

The model (Figure 3) consists of four interrelated factors that define the rules of competition in a sector, which are vital in achieving long-term competitiveness (Sun et al., 2010):

- **Factor Conditions:** Refers to a nation's resources, such as skilled labor and infrastructure, which influence industry performance.
- **Demand Conditions:** The sophistication and size of local demand drive innovation and quality improvement.
- **Related and Supporting Industries:** Competitive supplier industries and complementary sectors foster collaboration and innovation.
- **Firm Strategy, Structure, and Rivalry:** A nation's business practices, organizational culture, and domestic competition shape strategic approaches.

The model also suggests two other factors, namely "**Government**" and "**Chance**" (exogenous shocks), which are known as supporting factors of the four attributes, affecting the competitiveness that supports and complements the system of national competitiveness but does not create lasting competitive advantages. Kuah and Day (2005) conclude that the determinants, although irrelevant to the model, can have a significant impact on the model's functions. These factors comprise the necessary assets and skills that are vital for the industry's competitive advantage, as well as information that identifies opportunities and facilitates the management and deployment of assets and skills. They also encompass the goals of all stakeholders and the ability of firms to invest and innovate (Cini & Nater, 2009).

Figure 3. The determining factors of the diamond model (Porter, 1990).

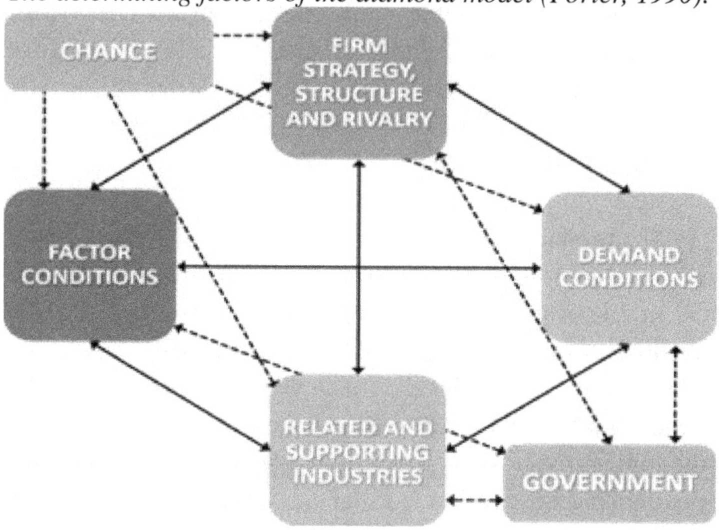

The framework is presumed to be constantly in motion due to the changes and interactions of its effects, both positive and negative. Therefore, the appearance of the competitive advantage depends on the system's renewal rate and the level of innovation that occurs. While the nature and intensity of mutual interaction in the entire system can be broad and familiar, the presence of the dynamics of a competitive environment affected by the emergence of new knowledge, technologies, and talented players also contributed to the shift in global competitive advantage (Bakan & Doğan, 2012).

2.3 The Theoretical Background

The study's theoretical framework (Figure 4) underpinned the following theoretical lenses:

Figure 4. The study's theoretical foundation (Author, 2025)

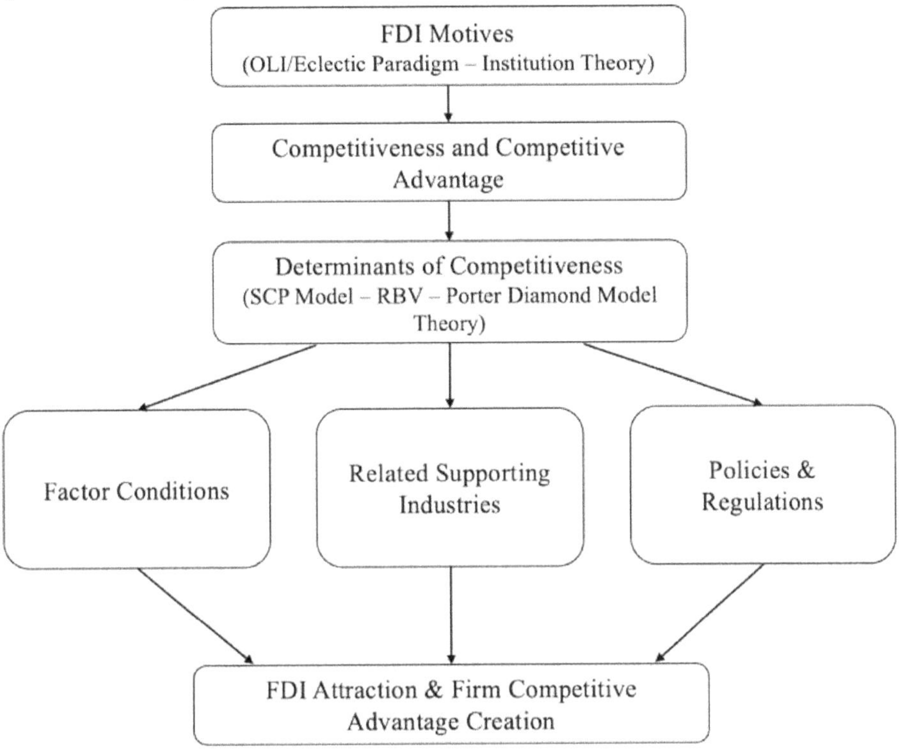

2.3.1 Eclectic (OLI) Paradigm

1) **Ownership Advantage** refers to the unique assets or capabilities that a firm possesses, allowing it to outperform its rivals (Ogundare & Merwe, 2024; Malhotra et al., 2025). Firms with strong cybersecurity protocols exemplify this advantage by ensuring the protection of sensitive data and intellectual property as opposed to their rivals. Such features foster stakeholders' trust as they enhance security and reliability in stakeholders' operations, particularly in light of data breach risks (Mmango & Gundu, 2024; Ogborigbo et al., 2024). This assurance of secure and reliable features will emerge as a compelling competitive advantage, enabling firms to capture market opportunities, neutralize threats, and establish long-term credibility.
2) **Location Advantage** highlights the gains derived from operating in a specific geographical area (Luo, 2021). In host countries with robust data protection laws and regulatory frameworks, adequate resources and infrastructure will foster a conducive ecosystem that is appealing to Foreign Direct Investment (FDI),

particularly in technology and data-driven sectors. Locations that offer legal protection, robust cybersecurity regulations, and compliance assurance aligned with international practices will tend to position themselves as favorable choices for prospective investors (Cristani, 2023; Diep et al., 2023; Qian, 2024).

3) **Internalization Advantage** refers to the benefits of managing operations internally, which mitigate both transaction costs and risks. An environment that provides assurance of data protection, where firms can maintain direct control over data management and security, exemplifies this advantage. Via the ability to internalize operations, firms can streamline processes, minimize vulnerabilities, and enhance operational efficiency, which augments overall performance.

2.3.2 Institutional Theory

Institutional theory analyses how defined norms, rules, and structures influence the behaviours of multinational enterprises (MNEs) (Scott, 1995; Davis et al., 2000; Meyer & Nguyen, 2005). Strong data governance, which implies the presence of policies and practices that ensure data accuracy, security, and compliance, is increasingly recognized as a key indicator of institutional quality (Díaz, 2016; Janssen et al., 2020; Sargiotis, 2024). Under the institutional theory framework, strong data governance is an indication to MNEs, reducing perceived risks and strengthening the confidence on the host country's institutional framework.

While robust data protection regulations represent the host country's strength and legitimacy in its institutional framework (Amoo et al., 2024), it also indicate the substance of well-established norms, regulatory consistency, and the presence of an effective enforcement mechanism, thereby mitigating uncertainties in host country, such as regulatory ambiguities, legal disputes, or reputational risks arising from data breaches. This suggests a robust data regulatory framework mitigates the transaction costs and risks associated with cross-border operations, fostering a more conducive institutional environment for FDI.

Compliance and alignment with global data protection standards, such as the European Union's General Data Protection Regulation (GDPR), enhance the institution's credibility (Gao, 2024; Prastyanti & Sharma, 2024). Conformity with international norms enhances institutional legitimacy and signals a commitment to transparency, accountability, and technological resilience. In summary, a robust data protection regulatory framework fosters market confidence, which in turn attracts sustainable FDI.

2.3.3 Resource-Based View (RBV)

Barney (1991) suggests that valuable resources allow the firm to exploit opportunities or neutralize threats; rare resources are not widely available among competitors; inimitable resources cannot be easily replicated, attributed to the unique historical, social, or organizational conditions; and organizational support ensures that the firm effectively utilizes these resources. By leveraging unique resources that competitors cannot replicate or substitute, firms can establish sustainable market advantages. For example, a company with proprietary technology or a well-regarded brand can differentiate itself and maintain profitability even in highly competitive industries. In the digital era, data security is considered both a resource (protecting IP) and a capability (ensuring operational resilience) (Ogborigbo et al., 2024; Tahseen et al., 2024). Data security is considered a **VRIO** (Valuable, Rare, Inimitable, Organized) resource that sustains competitive advantage (Simamora et al., 2024)

2.3.4 SCP Paradigm and Porter Diamond Model

2.3.4.1 SCP Paradigm

As data protection and governance form a critical aspect of organizational strategy in the digital era, the SCP paradigm provides a comprehensive framework for evaluating how market structures and firm behavior influence economic outcomes, serving as a significant driver of competitive advantage (Tan, 2009). This chapter suggests that by ensuring robust data protection and governance measures, firms can enhance their market positioning while fostering long-term trust and sustainability.

Structure: In markets characterized by high digital penetration and stringent regulatory landscapes, firms are required to adapt and comply with regulations like the General Data Protection Regulation (GDPR). These regulations pose challenges for firms in formulating robust data governance frameworks (Farhad, 2024; Oyewole et al., 2024), potentially allowing compliant rival firms to gain a competitive advantage. The presence of adequate data protection implies that the firm is aligned with institutional expectations, further reinforcing its legitimacy and competitive standing within stringent, regulated sectors.

Conduct: Firms leveraging strong data protection practices exhibit proactive conduct through transparent operations, adherence to global standards, and the deployment of advanced cybersecurity technologies. This conduct builds consumer trust, mitigates reputational risks, and differentiates firms from competitors with inferior security measures (Islam et al., 2024; Ogborigbo et al., 2024). By prioritizing data protection, firms foster customer loyalty and further reinforce their market position.

Performance: Robust data protection and governance enhance firm performance by mitigating the risks of data breaches, regulatory penalties, and associated financial losses (Naguib et al., 2024). This capability portrays the firms as reliable and ethical market players, enhancing consumer experience and fostering sustainable competitive advantage (Famoti et al., 2025). Firms excelling in data governance can also leverage innovation to develop secure digital products, thereby capturing more outstanding market share and ensuring profitability (Pala, 2020).

Hence, from the lens of the SCP paradigm, data protection and governance emerge as critical determinants of competitive advantage, enabling firms to navigate complex regulatory landscapes while achieving superior economic outcomes.

2.3.4.2 Porter's Diamond Model

The original Porter Diamond Model offers a comprehensive framework for understanding the competitive advantage of nations and industries, which can be applied to data protection and governance—a critical factor in the digital era. The model enables the analysis of competitiveness determinants and elucidates the role of robust data protection frameworks and governance mechanisms in enhancing national and firm performance.

- **Factor Conditions:** Strong data protection and governance require advanced infrastructure, skilled professionals, and robust legal frameworks. Countries investing in these areas create a conducive environment for innovation, compliance, and cybersecurity. High-quality factor conditions, such as sophisticated technological infrastructure and regulatory expertise, enable firms to implement robust data governance measures, enhancing their global competitiveness (Cristani, 2023; Diep et al., 2023; Qian, 2024; Naguib et al., 2024; Agboola, 2025).
- **Demand Conditions:** A high level of demand for data privacy and security among consumers and businesses drives innovation and the establishment of standards in data governance. Societies with heightened awareness of data protection, influenced by scandals and regulatory reforms, prompt organizations and governments to implement robust governance measures, which in turn foster trust and promote a competitive advantage (Lynskey, 2023; Farhad, 2024; Oyewole et al., 2024).
- **Related and Supporting Industries:** The presence of a vibrant ecosystem of cybersecurity firms, legal consultancies, and technology providers strengthens data governance. Collaboration among these industries facilitates the cre-

ation of innovative solutions, ensuring comprehensive data protection and bolstering competitiveness (Pala, 2020; Kamara, 2025)

- **Firm Strategy, Structure, and Rivalry:** Intense competition compels organizations to prioritize data governance as a strategic imperative. Firms adopting superior data protection frameworks differentiate themselves as trustworthy and reliable, gaining a competitive edge (Lynskey, 2023; Islam et al., 2024; Ogborigbo et al., 2024).
- **Government and Chance Factors:** Proactive regulations, such as the General Data Protection Regulation (GDPR), reinforce data governance frameworks. Governments that implement stringent standards attract investment and foster innovation, positioning their economies as global leaders in data protection (Cristani, 2023; Diep et al., 2023; Qian, 2024).

The Porter Diamond Model emphasizes how robust data protection and governance enhance competitive advantage, driving growth and fostering trust in the digital age. It highlights the factors that determine the competitiveness of data protection and governance in the FDI attraction context, thereby creating a firm's competitive advantage.

3. METHODOLOGY

This chapter employed a narrative and systematic review based on scholarly papers in Google Scholar, Scopus, and Web of Science (WOS). Mainly, papers were published in English between 2020 and 2025.

Narrative synthesis is a method that involves carefully reviewing and combining the data from numerous investigations. This method relies on textual information to summarize and explain the findings. A comprehensive literature review was conducted using search terms such as “qualitative,” “qualitative research,” and “qualitative data analysis.” Keywords include

Data Protection, Privacy, Cybersecurity, Foreign Direct Investment (FDI), Competitive Advantage, Digital Economy. The Prisma Method and Narrative synthesis were adopted and applied based on the previous studies by Kraiwanit et al. (2023), Siripipatthanakul and Phuangsuwan (2024), and Siripipatthanakul and Siripipattanakul (2025).

For inclusion, the criteria were studies written in English and published between 2020 and 2025. To analyze the data, a content analysis approach was employed. For systematically and objectively describing and measuring particular events based on verbal, visual, or written data, content analysis is a qualitative method.

4. RESULTS

4.1 FDI Determinants, FDI Attraction, and Firms' Competitive Advantage

While the majority acknowledge the Eclectic/OLI Paradigm as an established and robust framework for FDI studies, it remains a challenge to identify a comprehensive set of measures on the primary constructs in the paradigm and the interaction between the policy environment and the firm (Kok et al., 2023). Therefore, integrating the competitive advantage aspect to complement the Eclectic/OLI Paradigm framework will form a sound theoretical foundation to address these limitations.

Porter's diamond model, also viewed as an extension of the IO view, creates a structure that determines the rules of competition (Porter, 1998). Each dimension of the model is discussed in the previous section of the literature review. Mehrizi and Pakneiat (2008) suggested that the Diamond model is suitable for analysing production-related and market-intensive aspects of sectoral development. From a review of literature studies on Porter's diamond and competitiveness, Sun et al. (2010) provided a model arguing that the four variables of the diamond model—factor conditions, demand conditions, related and supporting industries, and the government—each affect the competitiveness factor. Bakan and Doğan (2012) adopted and modified the model to examine the impact of diamond model variables (the factor conditions, the demand conditions, the related and supportive industries and the government) on competitiveness by uncovering the relationship between the variables of the diamond model and competitiveness of the specific sectors to describe the current appearance of the industries. In the context of FDI studies, Bailey and Li (2015) dispute the relevance of demand conditions as they found no evidence supporting the presence of a significant effect of host country demand on FDI. This notion is also echoed by Sahiti et al. (2018), which shows that market size does not ultimately determine FDI inflows. Consequently, countries such as Singapore and Malaysia have been able to compete well, despite being smaller economies, compared to other larger economies. Kyereboah-Coleman and Agyire-Tettey (2008) argue that the relevance of market size dissipates for export-based multinational companies (MNCs) that do not have the prime target marketplaces in the host countries when deciding to invest abroad, as these MNCs may engage in FDI to access other intermediate markets for export-related purposes.

The "firm strategy, structure and rivalry" as an essential attribute of the Model has drawn its fair share of criticism (Öz, 2002). Grant (1991) found that firm strategy, structure, and rivalry are instead an "awkward catch-all" category. The criticisms intensified regarding the emphasis Porter (1990) attributes to the relationship between domestic rivalry and international competitiveness (Dobson & Starkey, 1992;

Smith, 1993). Dunning (1993) argues that Porter does not sufficiently consider the "globalisation of economic activity" and the effects of FDI on national competitiveness, given that a firm engages in cross-border activities to capitalise on its specific ownership advantages. Hence, the importance of FDI effects on national competitiveness, which are not adequately considered by the facet of "firm strategy, structure, and rivalry."

Porter's model's treatment of the government, which is limited to only intervening to support the development of emerging companies, underrates the role of government and policymakers, which could form a competitive advantage for nations and develop alternative strategies to maintain it (Esen & Uyar, 2012). Tuna (2006) argues that a national competitive advantage will likely be insufficient if government policy remains the sole source of competitiveness. While special attraction efforts do not guarantee the creation of a country differential advantage in the context of convergence towards best practices in policy and promotion, these efforts likely lead to an overall increase in investment flows to developing countries. Furthermore, a country that discontinues its special attraction efforts is likely to suffer a differential disadvantage in attracting FDI (Wint & Williams, 2002). In conclusion taking into account the arguments and criticisms on the original Diamond Model (Grant, 1991, Dobson and Starkey, 1992; Smith, 1993; Dunning 1993; Öz, 2002; Kyereboah-Coleman and Agyire-Tettey, 2008; Bailey and Li, 2015; Sahiti et al., 2018;), the variables of "Demand Condition" and "Firms' strategy, structure and rivalry" are discarded in the proposed conceptual model. The "government" is introduced as an attribute, given its significant role as a determinant of FDI and the creation of competitive advantage (Wint & Williams, 2002; Esen & Uyar, 2012), referred to as "policies and regulations."

This chapter suggest a conceptual model (Figure 4.1) underpinned on the theoretical principle of OLI/SCP/PDM framework, adopted from Kok and colleagues (2023) study to uncover the relationship between the main determinants of Data Protection and Governance competitiveness and the mediating role of FDIs' attractions and their effect on a firm's competitive advantage.

4.2 The Proposed Conceptual Model

Figure 5 shows the proposed conceptual model in this chapter. The model includes determinant factors (factor conditions, related supporting industries, policy, and regulations), FDI attraction, and the firm's competitive advantage, which is integrated with privacy and security protection.

Figure 5. The proposed conceptual model

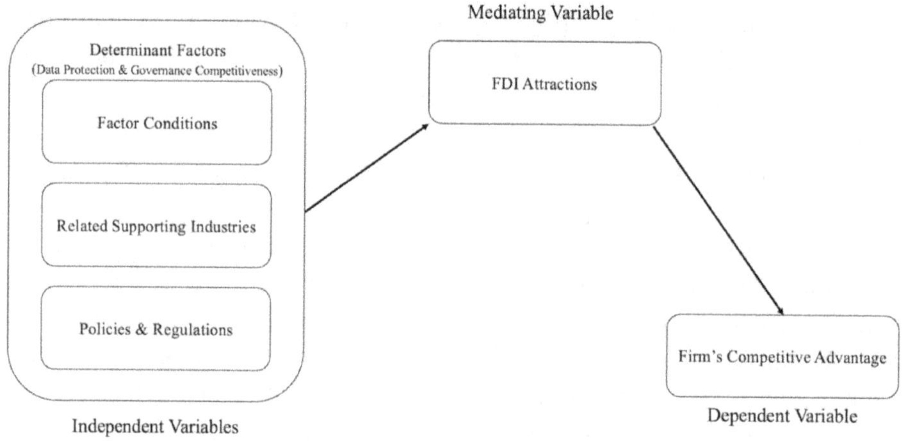

5. DISCUSSIONS

5.1 Defining Competitive Advantage and How to Measure

Kok et al. (2023) emphasize that while the concept of competitive advantage is widely employed in strategic management, extensive theoretical and empirical discussions highlight the need for more precise semantic content. The strategic management literature provides numerous definitions of competitive advantage, which often vary in meaning, making a precise and universally accepted definition elusive (Ma, 2000; Rumelt, 2003; Arend, 2003; O'Shanassy, 2008). This challenge is referred to as the "definitional problem of competitive advantage" (Sigalas et al., 2013).

Furthermore, Sigalas and Pekka Economou (2013) highlight the "Interchangeability Problem of Competitive Advantage Propositions," emphasizing that defining and operationalizing competitive advantage solely based on performance leads to tautological research propositions when these constructs are used interchangeably.

Sigalas (2015) further illustrates the real-world implications of the "definitional problem," which can lead to cognitive errors and misinterpretation among practicing managers. When managers conflate competitive advantage with their firms' idiosyncratic resources and capabilities, their decisions may deviate from the true objectives of business strategy. Consequently, resource-based strategies are often applied mechanically, failing to produce superior performance outcomes due to erroneous conceptual foundations.

While prevailing strategic management literature frequently posits a direct link between competitive advantage and superior performance (Barney, 1997; Dyer & Singh, 1998; Grant, 1998; Roberts, 1999; Zander & Zander, 2005), emerging research challenges this assumption. Scholars argue that competitive advantage does not guarantee above-industry-average performance and remains conceptually distinct (Ma, 2000; Newbert, 2008; Ambrosini & Bowman, 2010; Sigalas & Papadakis, 2018). It is acknowledged that superior performance can exist independently of competitive advantage, underscoring the need for refined conceptual clarity.

Aligned with the focus on determinants of competitive advantage, the study emphasizes the importance of identifying valid and reliable operational measures. Ambiguities in theoretical, stipulative, and operational definitions hinder the scientific falsifiability and reliability of competitive advantage theories (Popper, 1959; Sigalas et al., 2013). Accordingly, the study adopts the variable of firm competitiveness, based on the stipulative and operational definitions proposed by Sigalas et al. (2013), to ensure empirical validity and reliability.

Sigalas et al. (2013) offer a stipulative definition of competitive advantage as "the above industry average manifested exploitation of market opportunities and neutralization of competitive threats." Cognitive interviews and prior studies further refine the operational definition as "the above industry average manifested exploitation of (a) all market opportunities and (b) full exploitation of market opportunities, and the neutralization of (a) all competitive threats and (b) full neutralization of competitive threats." These definitions establish empirical indicators of competitive advantage, capturing its latent nature through phenomena such as opportunity exploitation and threat neutralization.

Significantly, these indicators exclude performance-related judgments, addressing the tautologies and fallacies inherent in existing conceptualizations of competitive advantage (Sigalas & Pekka Economou, 2013). Additionally, Newbert's (2008) empirical investigation into the resource-based view further reinforces the separation of competitive advantage from firm performance, ensuring conceptual and operational distinction. This approach lays the groundwork for more rigorous and meaningful research into competitive advantage within the field of strategic management.

In assessing a firm's competitive advantage, the predictors (determinants/constructs) identified in the conceptual model are used to explain the impact of these factors on a firm's competitive advantage (Butt et al., 2019). These predictors encompass both tangible and intangible elements (Jawed & Siddiqui, 2019). Although it is common practice in competitive advantage studies to use the construct of competitive advantage interchangeably with firm performance, Ma (2000) argues that these are distinct constructs. Competitive advantage, unlike firm performance,

vacy and security risk management into their foreign direct investment (FDI) policies to ensure compliance and mitigate the risk of cyber threats.

4. Regulatory Frameworks That Affect Foreign Direct Investment Privacy Regulations Investors are required to comply with country-specific privacy regulations, such as the General Data Protection Regulation (GDPR) in Europe, the Personal Data Protection Act (PDPA) in Singapore, and the Law on the Protection of Personal Data (LGPD) in Brazil, in order to avoid fines and harm to their reputation. National Security Screening: If privacy and security concerns are identified, governments may opt to restrict or further investigate foreign direct investment (FDI) in key industries, such as telecommunications, defense, and finance. Specialized Regulations for the Industry: FDI decisions are impacted by the fact that specific industries have more stringent criteria, such as HIPAA for the healthcare industry and PCI DSS for the banking industry. Data Localization Regulations: Some nations require businesses to store their data within their borders, which can impact investment decisions and operating expenses.

6. CONCLUSION

As the world continues to embrace the arrival of the digital economy, data protection and governance have evolved from being merely auxiliary concerns to being the critical success factors that are transforming the landscapes of national and firm-level competitiveness. Instead of merely mitigating risks and adhering to the legal framework, these phenomena underscore the importance of addressing concerns surrounding data protection and governance, as they symbolize the institutional quality that multinational companies (MNEs) desire, radiating trust and stability in a phenomenon that is unprecedented on a global scale. Robust governance frameworks represent not only the stringent rules surrounding the General Data Protection Regulation (GDPR), ensuring compliance with global norms, but they also enhance a nation's status as a stronghold of regulatory excellence, which in turn appeals to technology- and data-driven Foreign Direct Investment (FDI). The features of such ecosystems resound as safe havens, which assured investors not only business opportunities but also certainty. From a firm perspective, the commitment to robust data governance and cybersecurity represents more than just a slogan; it embodies a proclamation of ethical stewardship, good corporate citizenship, and operational excellence, which leads to enhanced profitability and market relevance.

When it comes to foreign direct investment (FDI), privacy and security have a direct impact on resource allocation, supporting systems, policies, and regulations. Strong privacy and security frameworks tend to attract investors because they provide a stable business environment. On the other hand, poor regulations or excessive restrictions may deter investment due to the risks associated with compliance and the operational difficulties they create.

Lastly, the proposed conceptual model in this study, which will serve as a vital foundation for advancing research and studies on foreign direct investment and competitiveness, provides reason for optimism. The purpose of this model is to encourage rigorous academic inquiry by offering a systematic framework. This will enable a more in-depth understanding of the global economy's dynamics and the procedures involved in making strategic decisions.

REFERENCES

Adeniran, I. A., Efunniyi, C. P., Osundare, O. S., & Abhulimen, A. O.Ibrahim Adedeji AdeniranChristianah Pelumi EfunniyiOlajide Soji OsundareAngela Omozele Abhulimen. (2024). Data-Driven Decision-Making in Healthcare: Enhancing Patient Outcomes through Predictive Modeling. *Engineering Science & Technology Journal, 5*(8), 059–067. Advance online publication. DOI: 10.56781/ijsrms.2024.5.1.0040

Adewusi, A. O., Okoli, U. I., Adaga, E., Olorunsogo, T., Asuzu, O. F., & Daraojimba, D. O. (2024). Business Intelligence in the Era of Big Data: A Review of Analytical Tools and Competitive Advantage. *Computer Science & IT Research Journal, 5*(2), 415–431. DOI: 10.51594/csitrj.v5i2.791

Agboola, D. (2025). The Evolving Landscape of Data Privacy: How Regulations are Shaping the Digital World (February 13, 2025). Available at *SSRN*: https://ssrn .com/abstract=5187183 or http://dx.doi.org/DOI: 10.2139/ssrn.5187183

Ambrosini, V., & Bowman, C. (2010). The impact of causal ambiguity within the firm on competitive advantage and rent appropriation. *British Journal of Management, 21*(4), 939–953. DOI: 10.1111/j.1467-8551.2009.00644.x

Amirov, L., & Avazov, N. (2022). The Impact of Digital Infrastructure, Foreign Direct Investment and Trade Openness on Economic Growth: In the Case of Uzbekistan. In International Conference on Next Generation Wired/Wireless Networking (pp. 322-332). Cham: Springer Nature Switzerland. DOI: 10.1007/978-3-031-30258-9_27

Amit, R., & Schoemaker, P. J. (1993). Strategic assets and organisational rent. *Strategic Management Journal, 14*(1), 33–46. DOI: 10.1002/smj.4250140105

Amoo, O. O., Atadoga, A., Osasona, F., Abrahams, T. O., Ayinla, B. S., & Farayola, O. A. (2024). GDPR's impact on cybersecurity: A review focusing on USA and European practices. *International Journal of Science and Research Archive, 11*(1), 1338–1347. DOI: 10.30574/ijsra.2024.11.1.0220

Arend, R. J. (2003). Revisiting the Logical and Research Considerations of Competitive Advantage. *Strategic Management Journal, 24*(3), 279–284. DOI: 10.1002/smj.285

Armand, J. (2020). Establishing Economic Independence in Haiti Through Public-Private Partnerships and Foreign Direct Investments. *Northwestern Journal of International Law & Business, 40*(3), 363–390.

Arregle, J. L., Hébert, L., & Beamish, P. W. (2006). Mode of international entry: The advantages of multilevel methods. *MIR. Management International Review, 46*(5), 597–618. DOI: 10.1007/s11575-006-0117-3

Bailey, N., & Li, S. (2015). Cross-national distance and FDI: The moderating role of host country local demand. *Journal of International Management*, *21*(4), 267–276. DOI: 10.1016/j.intman.2014.11.002

Bain, J. S. (1959). *Industrial Organization*. John Wiley.

Bakan, İ., & Doğan, İ. (2012). Competitiveness of the industries based on the Porter's diamond model: An empirical study. *International Journal of Research and Reviews in Applied Sciences*, *11*(3).

Barney, J. B. (1991). Firm resources and sustained competitive advantage. *Journal of Management*, *17*(1), 99–120. DOI: 10.1177/014920639101700108

Barney, J. B. (1997). *Gaining and Sustaining Competitive Advantage*. Addison-Wesley.

Batschauer da Cruz, C. B., Eliete Floriani, D., & Amal, M. (2022). The OLI Paradigm as a Comprehensive Model of FDI Determinants: A Sub-National Approach. *International Journal of Emerging Markets*, *17*(1), 145–176. DOI: 10.1108/IJOEM-07-2019-0517

Bezuidenhout, H., & Kleynhans, E. P. (2018). Modern Trends in Chinese Foreign Direct Investment in Africa: An OLI Approach. International Research Journal, 16(3), 279-300. https://www.hippocampus.si/ISSN/1854-6935/16_3.pdf#page=89

Bourai, S., Arora, R., & Yadav, N. (2024). Structure-Conduct-Performance (SCP) Paradigm in Digital Platform Competition: A Conceptual Framework. *Journal of Strategy and Management*, *17*(2), 322–347. DOI: 10.1108/JSMA-07-2023-0184

Bretas, V. P. G., Alon, I., Paltrinieri, A., & Chawla, K. (2022). Bibliometric review on FDI attractiveness factors. *European Journal of International Management*, *17*(2–3), 469–499. DOI: 10.1504/EJIM.2022.120721

Brouthers, K. D. (2013). A Retrospective on Institutional, Cultural, and Transaction Cost Influences on Entry Mode Choice and Performance. *Journal of International Business Studies*, *44*(1), 14–22. DOI: 10.1057/jibs.2012.23

Brychka, B. B. (2018). Impact of foreign direct investment on economic growth in the world during 1975–2015. Scientific Messenger of LNU of Veterinary Medicine and Biotechnologies, 20(91).

Brynjolfsson, E., & McElheran, K. (2016). The rapid adoption of data-driven decision-making. *The American Economic Review*, *106*(5), 133–139. DOI: 10.1257/aer.p20161016

Butt, M. A., Katuse, P., & Namada, J. M. (2019). Porter's Diamond Factor Conditions Determinant: Effect on Automotive Industry of Pakistan. *European Journal of Business and Management Research, 4*(4). Advance online publication. https://www.ejbmr.org/index.php/ejbmr/article/view/78. DOI: 10.24018/ejbmr.2019.4.4.78

Canabal, A., & White, G. O.III. (2008). Entry Mode Research: Past and Future. *International Business Review, 17*(3), 267–284. DOI: 10.1016/j.ibusrev.2008.01.003

Chaisse, J. (2023). The Black Pit: Power and Pitfalls of Digital FDI and Cross-Border Data Flows. *World Trade Review, 22*(1), 73–89. DOI: 10.1017/S1474745622000337

Chen, H. J. (2021). Innovation and FDI: Does the Target of Intellectual Property Rights Protection Matter? *Journal of International Money and Finance, 118*, 102458. DOI: 10.1016/j.jimonfin.2021.102458

Cheng, B. I. A. N. (2023). Data as Assets in Foreign Direct Investment: Is China's National Data Governance Compatible with Its International Investment Agreements? *Asian Journal of International Law, 13*(2), 342–364. DOI: 10.1017/S2044251322000595

Chiu, S. K., Lo, F. Y., & Susy, Y. (2015). Taiwanese Foreign Direct Investment in Southeast Asia: An Empirical Investigation of the OLI Framework. *Journal of Economics and Management, 11*(2), 127–141.

Cini, V., & Nater, N. (2009). Porter's Diamond Model of Osijek-Baranja County Industry. *Interdisciplinary Management Research, 5*, 761–769.

Cristani, F. (2023). Designing a Governance System for Cybersecurity of Foreign Investment in Europe. *International Investment Law Journal, 3*(2), 102–120.

Dahiya, R., Le, S., Ring, J. K., & Watson, K. (2022). Big Data Analytics and Competitive Advantage: The Strategic Role of Firm-Specific Knowledge. *Journal of Strategy and Management, 15*(2), 175–193. DOI: 10.1108/JSMA-08-2020-0203

Davis, P. S., Desai, A. B., & Francis, J. D. (2000). Mode of international entry: An isomorphism perspective. *Journal of International Business Studies, 31*(2), 239–258. DOI: 10.1057/palgrave.jibs.8490904

Díaz, E. (2016). The new European Union General Regulation on Data Protection and the legal consequences for institutions. Church. *Communication and Culture, 1*(1), 206–239. DOI: 10.1080/23753234.2016.1240912

Diep, N. T., Huy, D. T. N., & Hien, D. T. N. (2023). Further discussion on investment law, cybersecurity law, and recommendations for attracting foreign investment (FDI). [IJOLS]. *International Journal of Legal Studies, 13*(1), 119–134.

Dobson, P., & Starkey, K. (2002). The competitive advantage of nations. *Journal of Management Studies*, *29*(2), 253–255.

Dunning, J. H. (1979). Toward an Eclectic Theory of International Production: Some Empirical Tests. *Journal of International Business Studies*, *11*(1), 9–31. DOI: 10.1057/palgrave.jibs.8490593

Dunning, J. H. (1993). Internationalizing Porter's diamond. [special issue]. *Management International Review*, *33*, 7–15.

Dyer, J. H., & Singh, H. (1998). The relational view: Cooperative strategy and sources of interorganizational competitive advantage. *Academy of Management Review*, *23*(4), 660–679. DOI: 10.2307/259056

Esen, S., & Uyar, H. (2012). Examining the competitive structure of Turkish tourism industry in comparison with diamond model. *Procedia: Social and Behavioral Sciences*, *62*, 620–627. DOI: 10.1016/j.sbspro.2012.09.104

Famoti, O., Ewim, C. P. M., Eloho, O., Muyiwa-Ajayi, T. P., Ezechi, O. N., & Omokhoa, H. E. (2025). Revolutionizing customer experience management through data-driven strategies in financial services. *International Journal of Advanced Multidisciplinary Research and Studies.*, *5*(1), 948–957. DOI: 10.62225/2583049X.2025.5.1.3748

Farhad, M. A. (2024). Consumer Data Protection Laws and Their Impact on Business Models in the Tech Industry. *Telecommunications Policy*, *48*(9), 102836. DOI: 10.1016/j.telpol.2024.102836

Frey, C. B., & Presidente, G. (2024). Privacy Regulation and Firm Performance: Estimating the GDPR Effect Globally. *Economic Inquiry*, *62*(3), 1074–1089. DOI: 10.1111/ecin.13213

Gao, R. Y. (2024). The diffusion of a US trade-based approach to international personal data transfers and its implications for national data privacy regulations. *International Data Privacy Law*, *14*(4), 352–376.

Grant, R. M. (1991). Porter's 'Competitive Advantage of Nations': An Assessment. *Strategic Management Journal*, *12*(7), 535–548. DOI: 10.1002/smj.4250120706

Grant, R. M. (1998). *Contemporary Strategy Analysis*. Blackwell.

Gumpert, A., Manova, K., Rujan, C., & Schnitzer, M. (2025). Multinational firms and global innovation.

Halizam, M. A., Ridzuan, A. R., Shaari, M. S., Abd Rahman, N. H., & Md Razak, M. I. (2021). Revisiting the Impact of Foreign Direct Investment on Malaysia Economic Growth. *International Journal of Academic Research in Business & Social Sciences, 11*(5). Advance online publication. DOI: 10.6007/IJARBSS/v11-i5/9755

Hintošová, A., & Bódy, G. (2023). Sustainable FDI in the digital economy. *Sustainability (Basel), 15*(14), 10794. DOI: 10.3390/su151410794

Hintošová, A. B. (2021). The digital economy in the context of foreign direct investment flows. In Fostering Innovation and Competitiveness with FinTech, RegTech, and SupTech (pp. 210-227). IGI Global Scientific Publishing.

Huan, Y., & Qamruzzaman, M. (2022). Innovation-led Foreign Direct Investment (FDI) Sustainability: Clarifying the Nexus between Financial Innovation, Technological Innovation, Environmental Innovation, and FDI in the BRIC Nations. *Sustainability, 14*(23), 15732. DOI: 10.3390/su142315732

Hunjet, A., Zagoracz, I., Milkovic, M., & Kozina, G. (2022). Intellectual Property Rights as A Source of Competitive Advantage. Economic and Social Development: Book of Proceedings, 327-339.

Islam, M., Sourav, M., & Reza, J. (2024). The Impact of Data Protection Regulations on Business Analytics

Janssen, M., Brous, P., Estevez, E., Barbosa, L. S., & Janowski, T. (2020). Data Governance: Organizing Data for Trustworthy Artificial Intelligence. *Government Information Quarterly, 37*(3), 101493. DOI: 10.1016/j.giq.2020.101493

Jawed, I., & Siddiqui, D. A. (2019). *What matters for firms' performance: Capabilities, tangible or intangible resources? Evidence from corporate sectors on Pakistan.* Evidence From Corporate Sectors on Pakistan.

Jusmadi, R., & Armando, A. (2024). Structure, Conduct, and Performance (SCP) Approach and Fairness Principle in Business Competition Law in the Era of Digital Platforms. Justitia Jurnal Hukum, 8(2).

Kamara, I. (2025), 'Two Worlds Converging in 2015: Standardization and Data Protection', Standardizing Personal Data Protection, Oxford Data Protection & Privacy Law (Oxford, 2025; online edn, Oxford Academic, 14 Mar. 2025), DOI: 10.1093/9780191997037.003.0001

Kok, S. L., Khan, H., & Siripipatthanakul, S. (2023). The Role of Foreign Direct Investment in Creating Competitive Advantage For Electronics Manufacturing Companies In Northern Malaysia, December 2023. Thesis for Doctor of Business Administration. Manipal GlobalNxt University, Malaysia. DOI: DOI: 10.13140/RG.2.2.27160.61445

Kong, Y., & Suntrayuth, S. (2021). The Causal Model of Absorptive Capacity, Strategic Flexibility, and Innovation Performance in Relation to Sustainable Competitive Advantage: An Internationalization Perspective. Thammasat Review, 24(1), 214-246. https://sc01.tci-thaijo.org/index.php/tureview/article/view/239910

Kraiwanit, T., Limna, P., & Siripipatthanakul, S. (2023). NVivo for Social Sciences and Management Studies: A Systematic Review. *Advance Knowledge for Executives*, *2*(3), 1–11.

Kshetri, N., & Kshetri, N. (2016). Cybersecurity's Effects on International Trade and Investment. The Quest to Cyber Superiority: Cybersecurity Regulations, Frameworks, and Strategies of Major Economies, 75-87. https://link.springer.com/chapter/10.1007/978-3-319-40554-4_4

Kuah, A., & Day, J. (2005). Revisiting the Porter Diamond: Applying an Importance-Performance Matrix to the Singaporean Financial Cluster. University of Bradford. School of Management. *Working Paper Series*, *5*, 1–22. https://researchonline.jcu.edu.au/28374/

Kyereboah-Coleman, A., & Agyire-Tettey, K. F. (2008). Effect of Exchange-Rate Volatility on Foreign Direct Investment in Sub-Saharan Africa: The case of Ghana. *The Journal of Risk Finance*, *9*(1), 52–70. DOI: 10.1108/15265940810842410

Le, P. N. (2021). Literature Review on the Impacts of Foreign Direct Investment in the Emerging Economy: The Case of Vietnam. Open Journal of Business and Management, 09(02).

Liu, Y., Heinberg, M., Huang, X., & Eisingerich, A. B. (2023). Building a Competitive Advantage Based on Transparency: When and Why Does Transparency Matter for Corporate Social Responsibility? *Business Horizons*, *66*(4), 517–527. DOI: 10.1016/j.bushor.2022.10.004

Luo, Y. (2021). New OLI advantages in digital globalization. *International Business Review*, *30*(2), 101797. DOI: 10.1016/j.ibusrev.2021.101797

Lynskey, O. (2023). Complete and effective data protection. *Current Legal Problems*, *76*(1), 297–344. DOI: 10.1093/clp/cuad009

Ma, H. (2000). Competitive advantage and firm performance. *Competitiveness Review*, *10*(2), 15–32. DOI: 10.1108/eb046396

Ma'in, M., & Mat Isa, S. S. (2020). The Impact of Foreign Direct Investment on Economic Growth in Malaysia. Advances In Business Research International Journal, 6(1).

Mai, N. T. T., Minh, N. T., & Ngan, D. T. (2021). Foreign direct investment in digital economy in ASEAN. Вестник Российского университета кооперации [Bulletin of the Russian University of Cooperation]. (4 (46)), 63-70.

Maras, M. H. (2015). Internet of Things: Security and Privacy Implications. *Int'l Data Priv. L.*, *5*(2), 99–104. DOI: 10.1093/idpl/ipv004

Martin, K. D., & Zimmermann, J. (2024). Artificial Intelligence and Its Implications for Data Privacy Current opinion in psychology, 101829.

Mason, E. S. (1939). Price and production policies of large-scale enterprise. *The American Economic Review*, *29*, 61–74.

Mehrizi, M. H. R., & Pakneiat, M. (2008). Comparative Analysis of Sectoral Innovation Systems and the Diamond Model: The Case of Iran's Telecom Sector. *Journal of Technology Management & Innovation*, *3*(3), 78–90. DOI: 10.4067/S0718-27242008000100008

Meyer, K. E., & Nguyen, H. V. (2005). Foreign Investment Strategies and Sub-National Institutions in Emerging Markets: Evidence from Vietnam. *Journal of Management Studies*, *42*(1), 63–93. DOI: 10.1111/j.1467-6486.2005.00489.x

Mooradian, N., Franks, P. C., & Srivastav, A. (2025). The Impact of Artificial Intelligence on Data Privacy: A Risk Management Perspective. *Records Management Journal*. Advance online publication. DOI: 10.1108/RMJ-06-2024-0013

Mugo, P., & Macharia, J. (2020). Technological Innovation and Competitive Advantage in Telecommunication Companies. *International Journal of Research in Business and Social Science*, *9*(5), 38–47. DOI: 10.20525/ijrbs.v9i5.866

Nadikattu, A. K. R. (2018). IoT and the Issue of Data Privacy. *International Journal of Innovations in Engineering Research and Technology*, *5*(10), 23–26.

Nadir, J., & Farah, J. (2023). Balancing AI Innovation and Data Protection: Regulatory Challenges and Opportunities.

Naguib, H. M., Kassem, H. M., & Naem, A. E. H. M. A. (2024).. . *The Impact of IT Governance and Data Governance on Financial and Non-Financial Performance Future Business Journal*, *10*(1), 15.

Newbert, S. L. (2008). Value, rareness, competitive advantage, and performance: A conceptual level empirical investigation of the resource-based view of the firm. *Strategic Management Journal, 29*(7), 745–768. DOI: 10.1002/smj.686

Norehan, M. A. H. Bin, Ridzuan, AR Bin, & Ismail, SB. (2021). Conceptual Framework for ICT Development and Foreign Direct Investment Inflows as Drivers for Sustainable Economic Growth: Evidence from China and Malaysia. *International Journal of Academic Research in Economics and Management Sciences, 10*(1), 123–134.

North, D. C. (1990). *Institutions, Institutional Change, and Economic Performance*. Institutions, Institutional Change, and Economic Performance., DOI: 10.1017/CBO9780511808678

O'Shannassy, T. (2008). Sustainable competitive advantage or temporary competitive advantage: Improving understanding of an important strategy construct. *Journal of Strategy and Management, 1*(2), 168–180. DOI: 10.1108/17554250810926357

Ogborigbo, J. C., Sobowale, O. S., Amienwalen, E. I., Owoade, Y., Samson, A. T., & Egerson, J. (2024). Strategic integration of cyber security in business intelligence systems for data protection and competitive advantage. World Journal of Advanced Research and Reviews, 23(1), 081-096.

Okwu, A. T., Oseni, I. O., &Obiakor, R. T. (2020). Does Foreign Direct Investment Enhance Economic Growth? Evidence from 30 Leading Global Economies. Global Journal of Emerging Market Economies.

Oliver, C. (1997). The Influence of Institutional and Task Environment Relationships on Organizational Performance: The Canadian Construction Industry. *Journal of Management Studies, 34*(1), 99–124. DOI: 10.1111/1467-6486.00044

Omoregbe, O., & Kurtis, I. U. (2020). Resource Management Accountability and Organizational Sustainable Competitive Advantage: Evidence from Nigerian Research Institutes. *Nigerian Academy of Management Journal, 15*(2), 104–114.

Oyewole, A. T., Oguejiofor, B. B., Eneh, N. E., Akpuokwe, C. U., & Bakare, S. S.Adedoyin Tolulope OyewoleBisola Beatrice OguejioforNkechi Emmanuella EnehChidiogo Uzoamaka AkpuokweSeun Solomon Bakare. (2024). Data Privacy Laws and Their Impact on Financial Technology Companies: A Review. *Computer Science & IT Research Journal, 5*(3), 628–650. DOI: 10.51594/csitrj.v5i3.911

Öz, Ö. (2002). Assessing Porter's Framework for National Advantage: The Case of Turkey. *Journal of Business Research, 55*(6), 509–515. DOI: 10.1016/S0148-2963(00)00167-3

Pala, S. K. (2020). Improving Customer Experience in Banking using Big Data Insights. International Journal of Enhanced Research in Educational Development (IJERED), ISSN, 2319–7463.

Palekhova, L. (2016). Achieving the competitiveness through public accountability on sustainable development. Науковий вісник Національного гірничого університету [Scientific Bulletin of the National Mining University]. (2), 162-167.

Paul, J., & Feliciano-Cestero, M. M. (2021). Five Decades of Research on Foreign Direct Investment by MNEs: An Overview and Research Agenda. *Journal of Business Research*, *124*, 800–812. DOI: 10.1016/j.jbusres.2020.04.017 PMID: 32292218

Penrose, E. T. (1959). *The theory of the growth of the firm*. John Wiley.

Popper, K. R. (1959). *The Logic of Scientific Discovery*. Hutchinson.

Porter, M. E. (1990). *No. 6* (Vol. 76). The Competitive Advantage of Nations. Free Press, New York. Porter, Porter, M. E. (1998). Clusters and the New Economics of Competition. Harvard Business Review.

Porter, M. E. (2000). Location, competition, and economic development: Local clusters in a global economy. *Economic Development Quarterly*, *14*(1), 15–34. DOI: 10.1177/089124240001400105

Porter, M. E. (2004). Building the Microeconomic Foundations of Prosperity: Findings from the Business Competitiveness Index. In Sala-i-Martin, X. (Ed.), *The Global Competitiveness Report 2003–2004*. Oxford University Press.

Prastyanti, R. A., & Sharma, R. (2024). Establishing Consumer Trust Through Data Protection Law as a Competitive Advantage in Indonesia and India. Journal of Human Rights. *Culture and Legal System*, *4*(2), 354–390. DOI: 10.53955/jhcls.v4i2.200

Qian, X. (2024). Redefining International Law Paradigms: Charting Cybersecurity, Trade, and Investment Trajectories within Global Legal Boundaries. *The Journal of World Investment & Trade*, *25*(3), 295–333. DOI: 10.1163/22119000-12340327

Roberts, P. (1999). Product innovation, product-market competition, and persistent profitability in the US pharmaceutical industry. *Strategic Management Journal*, *20*(7), 655–670. DOI: 10.1002/(SICI)1097-0266(199907)20:7<655::AID-SMJ44>3.0.CO;2-P

Roberts, P. W., & Greenwood, R. (1997). Integrating transaction cost and institutional theories: Toward a constrained-efficiency framework for understanding organizational design adoption. *Academy of Management Review*, *22*(2), 346–373. DOI: 10.2307/259326

Roccon, M. (2023). Foreign investment in China's Cloud Industry: A Case Study of Microsoft Azure's Expansion.

Rumelt, R. P. (2003). "What in the world is competitive advantage?", Working Paper No. 2003-105, The Anderson School, UCLA, Los Angeles, CA, August 5.

Sahiti, A., Ahmeti, S., & Ismajli, H. (2018). A Review of Empirical Studies on FDI Determinants. *Baltic Journal of Real Estate Economics and Construction Management*, *6*(1), 37–47. Advance online publication. DOI: 10.1515/bjreecm-2018-0003

Sargiotis, D. (2024). Data Quality Management: Ensuring Accuracy and Reliability. In Data Governance: A Guide (pp. 197–216). Cham: Springer Nature Switzerland. DOI: 10.1007/978-3-031-67268-2_5

Sarioguz, O., & Miser, E. (2024). Data-Driven Decision-Making: Revolutionizing Management in the Information Era. Journal of Artificial Intelligence and General Science (JAIGS), ISSN: 3006-4023, Vol. 4, No. 1, pp. 179-194. DOI: 10.60087/jaigs.v4i1.131

Schellenberg, M., Harker, M. J., & Jafari, A. (2018). International Market Entry Mode: A Systematic Literature Review. *Journal of Strategic Marketing*, *26*(7), 601–627. DOI: 10.1080/0965254X.2017.1339114

Schulzmann, D., Sinani, E., Hobdari, B., & Petersen, B. (2023). Drivers of R&D greenfield investment projects in the communications, software, and IT service industries in developing countries. *Transnational Corporations*, *30*(1), 103–133. DOI: 10.18356/2076099x-30-1-4

Scott, W. R. (1995). *Institutions and organizations*. Sage.

Sharma, A. Digital Economy's Impact on FDI and the Rise of Tech MNES. FDI and Retail Sector in India, 22.

Sigalas, C. (2015). Competitive advantage: The known unknown concept. *Management Decision*, *53*(9), 2004–2016. Advance online publication. DOI: 10.1108/MD-05-2015-0185

Sigalas, C., Economou, V. P., & Georgopoulos, N. B. (2013). Developing a measure of competitive advantage. *Journal of Strategy and Management*, *6*(4), 320–342. DOI: 10.1108/JSMA-03-2013-0015

Sigalas, C., & Papadakis, V. M. (2018). Empirical investigation of relationship patterns between competitive advantage and superior performance. *Journal of Strategy and Management*, *11*(1), 81–111. DOI: 10.1108/JSMA-01-2017-0010

Sigalas, C., & Pekka Economou, V. (2013). Revisiting the Concept of Competitive Advantage: Problems and Fallacies Arising from Its Conceptualization. *Journal of Strategy and Management*, *6*(1), 61–80. DOI: 10.1108/17554251311296567

Simamora, S., Rahayu, A., & Dirgantari, P. D. (2024). Driving Digital Transformation in Small Banks With VRIO Analysis. Jurnal Aplikasi Bisnis dan Manajemen (JABM), 10(1), 99-99.

Siripipatthanakul, S., & Phuangsuwan, P. (2024). Salutogenic Marketing in Preventive Dentistry. In *Leveraging Digital Technology for Preventive Dentistry* (pp. 255–278). IGI Global. DOI: 10.4018/979-8-3693-3872-8.ch009

Siripipatthanakul, S., & Siripipattanakul, S. (2025). Talent Management Ensuring the Safety and Cybersecurity in Schools. *Cultivating Creativity and Navigating Talent Management in Academia*, 383-402.

Smith, S. C. (1993). The competitive advantage of nations - review of the competitive advantage of nations. *Journal of Development Economics*, *40*(2), 399–404. DOI: 10.1016/0304-3878(93)90095-5

Stojanović, B., and Kostić, M. (2013). Competition policy and the impact of market structure on companies' profitability. Ekonomika preduzeća, 61(5-6), 325-338.

Sun, H., Fan, Z., Zhou, Y., & Shi, Y. (2010). Empirical Research on Competitiveness Factors Analysis of the Real Estate Industry of Beijing and Tianjin. *Engineering, Construction, and Architectural Management*, *17*(3), 240–251. DOI: 10.1108/09699981011038042

Tahseen, A., Shailaja, S. R., & Ashwini, Y. (2024). Extraction for Big Data Cyber Security Analytics. Advances in Computational Intelligence and Informatics: Proceedings of ICACII 2023, 993, 365.

Tuna, E. (2006). The Tobacco Sector in the Republic of Macedonia: Competitiveness Analysis (Doctoral dissertation, Sveriges lantbruksuniversitet).

Wang, X., Xu, Z., Qin, Y., & Skare, M. (2022). Foreign direct investment and economic growth: A dynamic study of measurement approaches and results. Economic research-. *Ekonomska Istrazivanja*, *35*(1), 1011–1034.

Wernerfelt, B. (1984). A resource-based view of the firm. *Strategic Management Journal*, *5*(2), 171–180. DOI: 10.1002/smj.4250050207

Wint, A. G., & Williams, D. A. (2002). Attracting Foreign Direct Investment to Developing Countries: A Changing Role for Governments? *International Journal of Public Sector Management*, *15*(5), 361–374. DOI: 10.1108/09513550210435719

Yanamala, A. K. Y., & Suryadevara, S. (2023). Advances in Data Protection and Artificial Intelligence: Trends and Challenges. *International Journal of Advanced Engineering Technologies and Innovations*, *1*(01), 294–319.

Yanamala, A. K. Y., Suryadevara, S., & Kalli, V. D. R. (2024). Balancing Innovation and Privacy. *The Intersection of Data Protection and Artificial Intelligence International Journal of Machine Learning Research in Cybersecurity and Artificial Intelligence*, *15*(1), 1–43.

Yimer, A. (2023). The effects of FDI on economic growth in Africa. *The Journal of International Trade & Economic Development*, *32*(1), 2–36. DOI: 10.1080/09638199.2022.2079709

Yu, C., Zhang, Z., Lin, C., & Wu, Y. J. (2017). Knowledge Creation Process and Sustainable Competitive Advantage: The Role of Technological Innovation Capabilities. *Sustainability (Basel)*, *9*(12), 2280. DOI: 10.3390/su9122280

Yu, I. (2022). Foreign Investment and National Security Challenges in the Data Age: An Assessment of the Current Regime and Recommendations. *The Hastings Law Journal*, *74*, 959.

Zakutnia, A. O., & Hayriyan, A. (2017). Transparency as a Competitive Advantage of Innovation-Driven Companies. https://essuir.sumdu.edu.ua/handle/123456789/61636

Zander, I., & Zander, U. (2005). The inside track: On the important (but neglected) role of customers in the resource-based view of strategy and firm growth. *Journal of Management Studies*, *42*(8), 1519–1548. DOI: 10.1111/j.1467-6486.2005.00555.x

Zang, W., & Baimbridge, M. (2014). Foreign Direct Investment and Economic Growth in OECD Countries. In Economic Growth in the 21st Century: Perspectives, Role of Governmental Policies, Potential and Constraints. http://hdl.handle.net/10454/13800

Zwartkruis, W. (2024). Foreign Direct Investment and Security: What is Actually the Problem? In National Security and Investment Controls (pp. 27-58). Cham: Springer Nature Switzerland. DOI: 10.1007/17280_2024_29

Chapter 6
Managing Privacy and Security in Research:
Effective Practices and Strategies

Andi Asrifan
https://orcid.org/0000-0002-9934-6129
Universitas Negeri Makassar, Indonesia

Supaprawat Siripipatthanakul
https://orcid.org/0000-0001-6671-2682
Bangkok Thonburi University, Thailand

Mohammed H. Alaqad
https://orcid.org/0000-0002-9953-5763
Hashim Sani Centre of Palestine Studies, University of Malaya, Malaysia

Syamsuardi Saodi
https://orcid.org/0000-0001-8551-9300
Universitas Negeri Makassar, Indonesia

Sadaruddin Sadaruddin
https://orcid.org/0000-0001-6890-1540
Universitas Islam Makassar, Indonesia

ABSTRACT

This chapter discusses how technology and regulatory changes have complicated research privacy and security. Researchers must balance ethics and law while safeguarding personal data. The book emphasizes risk assessment and management throughout the research process to protect participant privacy and comply with data security standards. Safe data collection, storage, and sharing and privacy-enhancing technologies like anonymization and pseudonymization are key subjects. In order

DOI: 10.4018/979-8-3693-9720-6.ch006

to maintain ethical and legal compliance, researchers and oversight agencies like Institutional Review Boards (IRBs) must work together. It also shows how proactive methods and information environment knowledge may build trust among participants, sponsors, and the public. It gives a thorough approach on balancing privacy, security, and research objectives in a data-driven world, protecting research integrity and stakeholder confidence.

1. INTRODUCTION

Introduction to Privacy and Security in Research. New technology, societal norms, and evolving legal standards have all contributed to a variety of changes in the way research is conducted and the resulting data are analyzed (Quach et al., 2022; Lazer et al., 2021; Micheli et al., 2020). While these factors challenge research practices in their own right, the dual demands of privacy and data security can make informed and considered research practices even more elusive. As participants and those interested in the research results are not always the same people, research managers often find themselves in a position of representing multiple competing interests. Researchers may need to balance the requirements and expectations of a research data management plan with the need to comply with privacy laws and data transfer or security agreements (Quach et al., 2022; Florea & Florea, 2020; Martin & Palmatier, 2020). For example, a data management plan may describe data aggregation methods. However, in doing so, it can reveal gaps between what the plan can describe and what happens in the fundamental research environment. Such challenges have substantial implications for the research enterprise, as researchers who fail to meet sponsor requirements could face funding sanctions. At the same time, other types of security or privacy violations can result in funding recapture, such as research participant identity theft, data breach notification, or regulatory fines.

Suppose you have a funded and staffed institutional review board or similar oversight committee whose expertise and prior approvals of your research activities can guide your research practices. In that case, your research group can leverage these resources to ensure baseline compliance with ethical and legal requirements for privacy, security, and data sharing (Thapa & Camtepe, 2021; Keshta & Odeh, 2021). However, as board members may have lower familiarity with the specific details of your planned computational or security practices, maintaining a close working relationship between the board and research staff is often required to ensure efficient research execution. Such interaction can occur through training sessions, pre-proposal consultations, and educational sessions that target the board specifically or a research community that subsequently interacts with board processes. When operating in such contexts, research support staff must both identify any risks that are a priority for discussion or current council guidance and develop an equally socially informed technical understanding of the risks and solutions.

2. LITERATURE REVIEW: FOUNDATIONS OF PRIVACY AND SECURITY IN RESEARCH

The use of personal information is a common component of research and evaluation (Khare et al., 2024; Li & Liu, 2021; Ismagilova et al., 2022). Researchers and evaluators have a responsibility to ensure that appropriate attention is given to matters of privacy and security in research. Privacy is about personal rights and maintaining control over the information about oneself. Security is about protecting personal information from unauthorized access or release. Using privacy and security effectively requires thoughtfulness and creativity from the research community to strike the right balance (Mylrea & Robinson, 2023). Context is key when determining how to manage privacy and security appropriately. Each information environment presents different opportunities and constraints for the privacy and security of personal data. The sensitivity and risks associated with data will vary in response to these factors, thus necessitating different privacy and security responses (Quach et al., 2022; Abdulsalam & Hedabou, 2021; Mothukuri et al., 2021). The default approach should be to understand what is known about an information environment and utilize the available knowledge, technologies, and best practices. The Role of Privacy and Security in Enhancing the Trustworthiness of Research. Practices and strategies are presented to help researchers and project managers effectively handle privacy and security. Privacy and security are sometimes folded into data protection or buried in institutional research policies. Nevertheless, handling job-critical personal information in the research context underscores the risks inherent in not directly addressing privacy and security. This consideration applies to both the research and evaluation, as well as the method and form of the data used. Given that below-the-surface conditions can change norms non-transparently and in ways beyond the scope of researchers to manage, researchers and people who commission research must understand how to handle personal data in their era's particular information environment. More data does not necessarily guarantee better research (Ismagilova et al., 2022; Dias et al., 2020; Okan et al., 2020). Data quality and value are also key.

2.1. Legal and Ethical Frameworks

The use of health records in research is subject to a complex legal and ethical protection framework, partly due to the opportunities and risks associated with computerized records. The traditional framework primarily consists of legal precedents that govern the disclosure of personal information by private enterprises (Casanovas et al., 2022; Heide & Villeneuve, 2020; Cui & Qi, 2021). These require appropriate purposes, consents, and interpretation in line with the Human Rights Act, which gives effect to the European Convention on Human Rights in domestic law. Parliament can override these common law rights, and the Data Protection Act does so to permit the disclosure and use of identifiable data in healthcare in limited circumstances, primarily for purposes that include health research. Where the common law forbids it or demands confidentiality, no individual or public body may disclose personal health information in any form. This prohibition encompasses both information stored in electronic media, particularly in computer systems, and manual records, but not general knowledge. Within these limits, consent offers the primary means of protecting privacy in health research. In several instances, one can argue that the disclosure of identifiable health data without proper consent for research purposes that are not covered by the Act breaches the regulations. The fundamental privacy risks implicit in the use of biological and genetic samples in research have attracted widespread and passionate debate (Wang et al., 2024). Regulations are ad hoc at best, and the consensus is that this seriously threatens to damage the level of trust in research. In particular, under the Act, only living individuals possess personal data about themselves, empowering the courts to hold private bodies accountable for their regulator's earlier declarations that they needed permission from donors or surrogates before selling donated markers, sequences, and cell lines for biomedical research purposes. It affects both the cost and process of obtaining those samples and data and, importantly, the confidence or goodwill of those who grant permission. Researchers themselves, however, may seek data to which they are not entitled in contexts that can include both routine care and research, perhaps to address other scientific questions (Viberg Johansson et al., 2022; Campbell et al., 2023; Solbakk et al., 2021). There are equally familiar problems of identity and consent that are common in many cases. With increasing concerns among all stakeholders regarding informed consent, a new genre of studies has emerged that can exhaust these genetic materials to learn about biological functions, create new products, and develop new treatments—thereby further complicating the understanding of capabilities that may not contain any relevant information.

2.2 Risk Assessment and Management

Risk assessment and management—determining what can go wrong and then finding ways to mitigate privacy and security risks—are increasingly recognized as essential components of research planning (Ismagilova et al., 2022; Al et al., 2022; Eling et al., 2021). Participants in earlier workshops uniformly and strongly endorsed conducting these activities early in the research process, finding that waiting until later can significantly slow down work. For example, research planning may involve surveying or observing individuals to collect data on health, crime, or other topics. Suppose data collection plans do not account for privacy and security needs. In that case, data that could potentially be used to improve human well-being might never be collected, let alone used for research and other purposes (Ribeiro-Navarrete et al., 2021; Tawalbeh et al., 2020) (Emami-Naeini et al., 2020). Such scenarios largely explain why discussions about managing privacy and security often arise in the context of conducting research. The stakes in proper risk assessment and management can be high. When things go wrong with the privacy and security of proprietary data, academic institutions, businesses, reputations, and individuals can be harmed, as well as relationships and research. Economic growth can be significantly reduced, and perhaps most fundamentally, trust vital to finding truth can be damaged (Chambers, 2021; Schwab, 2021). Researchers and their academic and institutional sponsors may also suffer. On the one hand, researchers and their institutions face increasing pressure from funding and regulatory agencies to conduct their work in ways that are likely to help protect proprietary and sensitive information from loss and misuse. Risk assessment and management can help research planners identify potential privacy and security scenarios and provide them with tools to explore alternative paths forward that are likely to better support these interests.

2.1.1 Identifying Risks

Privacy and security risks in a research setting are increasingly important. In recognition of this, researchers and research institutions are taking steps to integrate privacy and security considerations into their research practices (Marshall et al., 2022; Florea & Florea, 2020). Identifying and understanding potential privacy and security risks are key to integrating these considerations into the research process. Like the foundations of privacy and security, recognizing risks, particularly in a research context, may not be immediately apparent and often coexist with other factors. Identifying risks involves considering a range of potential positive and negative consequences that arise from conducting the research or the results of that research. The scope of these consequences can include both the personal, such as the human subject of the research, and the institutional, such as the compensation or productivity of other researchers or a sponsoring institution. Risks to a research initiative often have multiple dimensions, including the sensitivity of the data or results, the likelihood of data re-identification, and broader societal-level implications of the research or its use (Haghani et al., 2020; Behrens et al., 2021; Kuran et al., 2020). There is often a focus on population-level risks, including discrimination, stigma, or stereotype avoidance; loss of data confidentiality; loss of public trust in the use of population data for research; including groups sensitized to potential research risks, such as researchers of populations traditionally considered vulnerable or with lower proximal benefits; or the possible misuse of research products. Data-related risks, including data confidentiality loss, data enclave response biases, or user adoption of less informative or less secure data utilities, attract the most interest (Makhdoom et al., 2024; Lian et al., 2024). Misidentification or re-identification of organizations is occasionally mentioned. There are frequent recommendations for further research to mitigate or eliminate these risks, although cost is occasionally a concern.

2.2.2 Assessing Impact and Likelihood

The second foundational piece, evaluating the impact and likelihood of privacy and security risks to research participants, research projects, and the institution, is also important. It can be conducted using either a qualitative or quantitative approach. While many researchers are familiar with risk assessments used in project-specific work, a more complex project typically receives an individualized risk assessment. University-wide privacy and security risk assessments can take a single response and apply it not only to an individual sensitive data item being queried but also to subject or project researchers with the same response (Abdulrasool & Turnbull, 2020; Darwinkel et al., 2020). The questions cover broad general privacy and security issues, and individuals inevitably find some to be irrelevant to their current practice. The responses can be predetermined to reflect the consensus of the university. Privacy and security risk assessments often rely on the data that individuals provide, just as project-specific privacy or security forms or questions rely on the information researchers provide for informed decisions about the research or information (Tawalbeh et al., 2020; Emami-Naeini et al., 2020). Someone must be able to explain the relevance of the answers to the rest of the risk assessment process and the significance of the risk assessment result to the overall data management process. A standardized risk assessment form compels researchers to answer questions they may not have considered themselves. It means their specific data will be further protected by the overarching efforts made to increase institutional privacy or security measures.

2.3 Data Collection and Storage Practices

The privacy and security of research data are now inextricably linked with routine considerations of data management. The protection of research data extends beyond safeguarding research integrity and confidentiality (Ibbett & Brittain, 2020; Griffin et al., 2021). There are also critical expectations from sponsors and publishers. By protecting privacy and security in this new technological age, we also protect the ability of research institutions to continue collecting and sharing these vital data. This document provides guidance and highlights some key considerations that researchers may need to address to protect confidentiality in a technological environment. Fully addressing these topics is outside the scope of this document, and the techniques discussed are intentionally outdated and general. Electronic storage of research data is shared, but it may expose research participants to unnecessary risks (Keshta & Odeh, 2021; Grimm et al., 2020). Storage media can fail, and desirable data replication has unintentionally created numerous opportunities for unauthorized data access. The risks may be limited, but the severity can be significant. Protecting data may require storing it in multiple locations and limiting access to prevent unauthorized access. Consider whether potential research participants would be reassured by information about the degree to which their research data will remain private after initial data collection is completed.

2.4 Best Practices for Data Collection

The privacy and security of research data are among the most important issues in any research project (Keshta & Odeh, 2021; Tawalbeh et al., 2020). Collecting protected data is a means of providing the necessary protections. Once completed, this process enables an organization to maintain and utilize a data set, protecting it from unauthorized access or disclosure. Protecting it is crucial, as failure to do so can hinder an organization's relationships with individuals and with other organizations with whom the entity shares the protected data (Quach et al., 2022; Politou et al., 2022). There are many different ways to protect potential data that may be collected. Reviewing these and other fundamental best practices for data collection is a crucial first step toward establishing a secure approach for data collection and subsequent use. This chapter provides an overview of the basics of privacy and security, as well as best practices for collecting protected data. These best practices have been designed to encourage everyone involved in the data collection process to take an active role in protecting the data and ensure that efforts to maintain the data's protective status remain a priority within the organization from the outset of the data collection process. Specifically, it is essential to ensure that adequate measures are in place to prevent risks to the data. The hope is that the organization will find these best practices an efficient and helpful model for data collection.

2.5 Secure Data Storage and Management

Federal and local data protection guidelines prioritize data security from illegal access, disclosure, or loss. Institutions and researchers should actively secure data throughout its lifecycle. Secure data storage and management demand constant attention. Federal regulations require safeguards to protect personally identifiable data from unlawful use or disclosure and to maintain its security and confidentiality. Researchers should employ best practices and strategies to securely store and manage research data throughout the data lifecycle, from planning and collecting data to processing, analyzing, and sharing data, both during a project and for long-term preservation. Institutions and researchers should assess and adjust existing processes to capitalize on new opportunities and efficiencies while protecting data during the transition to new guidelines. Safe data storage and backup technologies are proliferating, and many innovative and safe solutions can quickly become project data management standards (McGraw & Mandl, 2021; Kim, 2022; Kaur et al., 2022; Akhtar et al., 2021; Thapa & Camtepe, 2021).

2.6 Access Control and Authorization

Access control refers to the process of specifying a subject's privileges to access an object or service within a system (Qiu et al., 2020; Qin et al., 2021). Authorization, or privilege management, refers to implementing and controlling user rights to demand resources governed by policies. Building and maintaining access controls over large datasets are key considerations within the realm of privacy. Strict controls are required for data that falls under specific mandates.

Specific regulations explicitly require varied controls to protect personal education records stored in systems (Keshta & Odeh, 2021). They mandate a complex two-part examination to anonymize information before releasing it to individuals conducting approved research. Access controls are also required to limit data collection and to enforce the research Data Security and Data Retention section of our policies. The selective disposal of data that is no longer needed helps reduce the risk of identity breaches resulting from long-term exposure over time. Security policies also require threat assessments of databases that contain sensitive information (Ansari et al., 2022). Network protections and data access security protocols are implemented, and user access is managed through unique data access policies tailored to time-bound roles. Analysis of access logs is also used to monitor access from user groups defined to contain only approved security personnel.

2.7 Role-Based Access Control

Researchers previously discussed methods for determining who can view or access specific data. Those methods offer a standardized approach to managing privacy and security. In contrast, role-based access control relies on determining whether an individual, based on their job responsibilities, is authorized to perform a particular activity on data. It is a familiar concept often used in privacy systems to control access to sensitive data (Quach et al., 2022). Examples include who can update records in a data system, analyze data, run specific reports, and add new individuals, among others. An additional concept implied by role-based access control is that activity logs are created to track personnel activities (de and Bandiera-Paiva, 2021).

A standard implementation of role-based access control relies on the data system to associate roles or activities with individuals (Ameer et al., 2022; Adamu et al., 2021). Then, when an individual attempts to update a record or report, the data system can check if the individual is authorized. In systems with specific role-based activities, each activity can be independently defined. Additionally, since employee roles often change, role-based access must provide clear guidance and procedures for adding or removing these role-based permissions based on a member's role. Typically, role-based access control functionality is integrated into the overall privacy access solution within the data system (Saxena & Alam, 2022). In many privacy protection implementations, access to data is achieved through the security protection afforded by the database engine.

2.8 User Authentication

Authentication is the process of determining whether someone or something is who or what it claims to be (Zimmermann & Gerber, 2020; Goldsack et al., 2020; Jiang et al., 2021). On private-sector news websites, authentication ensures that only people with a password can access proprietary information. Similarly, when handling sensitive data for privacy or security reasons, arrangements must be in place to restrict access to the data and associate it with the correct individual. The most likely approach is to assign an identifier that contains sensitive data to each user of each system. The system will then be designed to verify this identifier whenever someone attempts to access the system, ensuring that the correct person is using it. The identifier could be a password for data shared among different components or processes; however, other forms of secure authentication are also available.

Privacy, consent laws, and confidentiality standards, as well as common sense, will mean that traditional uses of the Social Security number, such as a checking account number, will be limited and that private information supplied by agencies or organizations to the public will be linked for authentication purposes only to a number or token (Tawalbeh et al., 2020; Jain et al., 2021; Keshta & Odeh, 2021). A unique number used to identify individuals known to a system that contains private information is sometimes referred to as a trusted identifier or a pseudo-identifier. Although a trusted identifier could contain actual information, such as a Social Security number, in practice, it will likely need to be a separate number (Keshta & Odeh, 2021; Jain et al., 2021). Depending on the confidentiality, integrity, and availability constraints of a study, the number may need to be unique only to the current project rather than among all studies that use sensitive data.

2.9 Data Sharing and Collaboration

Research data should ideally be shared with other investigators to enable analyses that facilitate scientific discovery and validate new findings. Collaborations can enhance the quality of scientific endeavors and often encourage the development of a more inclusive scientific research community. However, with awareness of the very real issues associated with maintaining the privacy and security of analyzed data, these considerations may preclude data sharing and collaboration. In the design of a research project, consideration of potential data-sharing requirements should be a key element of the research design and plan (Tomaszewski et al., 2020; Eyal et al., 2021). If data sharing is not possible or should be limited, a strong rationale should be provided, and agreements made and/or policies should be documented as to how concerns would be dealt with.

The rationale might be based on privacy concerns for individuals, security issues regarding the potential for data resulting from proprietary information for commercially available or company-owned technology, the desire to maintain intellectual materials to enable enhanced academic growth, or the size of the project team resulting in difficulty in coordinating the collaborative activity (Rath & Kumar, 2021; Wang et al., 2021; Smidt & Jokonya, 2021). These potential barriers may need to be addressed formally through policies developed by the researcher and/or by university, academic, or governmental research agencies. Data sharing terms may be specified in the sponsored research agreement and funding terms, in individual contracts, or specific restrictions may be implied by research funding agency data sharing policies. Data repositories may influence the information they store and make readily available, which can be unsearchable depending on factors such as attribution and recognition, copyright, or privacy restrictions. Data repositories establish procedures for access to and the security of authorized data users and track data usage. Data repositories also determine the terms upon which data releases will be made.

2.10 Secure Data Sharing Platforms

Research SDOs are implementing platforms that provide increased security when sharing research data. The platforms offer a more reliable and higher level of protection for researchers' data, as their access is encrypted and proprietary (Manzoor et al., 2021; Babun et al., 2021). These platforms enable the upload of project datasets into secure research data centers via a site's secure data transfer computer. Datasets are then segregated into appropriate secure zones to assure privacy and data security. Each dataset within the secure zone is then made available through a secure data portal, with access only allowed to pre-authorized users, as determined by the PI on the project. Files are encrypted both in transit and at rest, with the file encryption key stored outside the data center.

Research institutions and research SDOs routinely transfer, analyze, collaborate on, and share sensitive data. The SDO receives several requests annually for data sharing, data editing, and data management and classification, as well as inquiries about national and international studies (Van Atteveldt et al., 2021). Reasons for sharing research data include the intent to enable and promote secondary analysis, reassurance of data quality, a desire to improve the transparency of the original EMR data, or to facilitate speedy secondary data extraction by consulting with research SDO experts in the field.

2.11 Collaborative Tools and Practices

The opportunities for remote collaboration can promote collaboration in national and international research with the requisite levels of trust for collaborative research, but only if participants engage collaboratively to implement practices and solutions for the risks introduced by tools and the partnerships fundamental to them (Morton et al., 2022); O'Dwyer et al., 2023; Matthews et al., 2020). Confidentiality and trust derive from a shared understanding of policies, practices, and requirements in sufficiently similar settings and thus must be established through dialogue and the will and ability to adequately document the terms of engagement, even when diverging policies lead to diverging practices.

It is not about better tools, though in many cases that is a vital first draft for attention, but about transparency, trust, and understanding in their development, deployment, and use, largely from analysis of needs in the light of common principles. Policy cannot afford to leave it to others. High-value collaborative research largely involves highly trained and gifted researchers operating in environments where the risks are not incidental (Gardner, 2024; Şahin et al., 2024). High-value artifacts are the tools, data, and results that represent the collected research outcomes and have value to others, both within and outside academia.

3. METHODOLOGY

3.1 Data Collection

Narrative synthesis involves integrating qualitative data to produce a comprehensive and cohesive summary of findings. Narrative synthesis involves the systematic review and integration of data from multiple studies, utilizing literary content to synthesize and clarify the findings. A thorough literature review was conducted using search terms such as "qualitative," "qualitative research," and "qualitative data analysis." A systematic review and synthesis of data from many studies, employing textual analysis to summarize and elucidate the results. A thorough literature review was conducted using search terms such as "qualitative," "qualitative research," and "qualitative data analysis" (Kraiwanit et al., 2023; Phuangsuwan et al., 2024). According to the data collection and analysis, this qualitative study employed a narrative review based on scholarly papers in Google Scholar, Scopus, and Web of Science (WOS). Three reviewers evaluated the chapter, and revisions have been made to ensure its quality. Grammarly has been used for grammar and plagiarism.

3.2 Data Analysis

The systematic review was based on the study of Siripipatthanakul & Phuangsuwan (2024), and Siripipatthanakul & Siripipattanakul (2025). Content analysis was utilized to analyze the data. Content analysis is a qualitative method for methodically and objectively identifying and quantifying specific occurrences from spoken, visual, or written data (Kraiwanit et al., 2023; Phuangsuwan et al., 2024).

4. RESULTS

Grammarly has been used for grammar and plagiarism. The results show that plagiarism is 1%, and grammar is 92% for appropriateness. A word cloud is used to identify keywords and content related to this chapter.

Figure 1. Grammarly results (https://app.grammarly.com/)

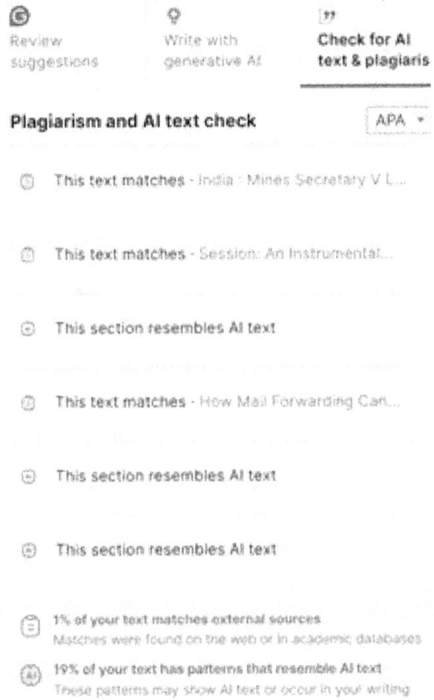

Figure 2. Word cloud

https://www.wordclouds.com

5. DISCUSSIONS

5.1 Privacy-Enhancing Technologies

Due to the sensitivity of personal information, several techniques and products are employed to minimize the likelihood that personally identifiable information can be re-identified. These are the so-called privacy-enhancing technologies. Rather than resulting from particular processes commonly used across a wide variety of research domains, these are more specialized products and techniques employed to "anonymize" (Peloquin et al., 2020; Wójcicki et al., 2022; Quach et al., 2022). These processes range from encryption of data sets, secure computational silos where data from several surveys are used but cannot be downloaded in identifiable form by a single user, protocols that allow several benefits when personal information is combined over several files, and the privacy provided when informed consent can provide willing participants. The section describes some of the key characteristics of these approaches. There is a broad range of specific privacy-enhancing technologies. Products and techniques are continuing to evolve and progress. Most U.S. federal statistical agencies have worked on and continue to work on using effective privacy-enhancing technologies, both for their own purposes and to assist the broader research community (Becher et al., 2020). Currently, one leading organization that sponsors initiatives and leads reflections in this area is the Comité Consultatif pour la Protection des Données en Matière de Recherche en Santé. Indeed, it has directed the Office of Information and Regulatory Affairs, in conjunction with other departments and agencies, to undertake a review of privacy-enhancing technologies to determine their feasibility and applicability.

5.2 Anonymization and Pseudonymization

Given the proliferation of re-identification examples, behavioral data is arguably the most challenging information to de-identify (Yogarajan et al., 2020). The general rule is that the more significant the difference in individuals, the more stringent the threshold for the number of individuals that need to be involved in the sample, as it does to each of the characteristics used to define those differences. The number and variation in characteristics used in developing a specific dataset are referred to as the dataset's dimensionality. The lower the dimensionality, the greater the leniency in thresholding the number of subjects required in the sample to prevent re-identification (Bharati & Podder, 2022; Zhang et al., 2024). That, in turn, can facilitate increased variability in the data across all characteristics, which is a primary statistical objective for study results. Similarly, more subjects are available, and there is a willingness to include and analyze the data, even when the ceiling limits replacement by random imputation instead of complete data suppression.

Anonymization replaces or removes personal identifiers from data. While seemingly straightforward, a substantial challenge inherent in the variety of attestations to data privacy that exists is that the removal of any aspect potentially revealing these personal identities is considered necessary (Tomás et al., 2022; Vokinger et al., 2020; Senavirathne & Torra, 2020). Characteristically, elements used for anonymization include protected diseases, names, addresses, Social Security numbers, and demographic characteristics. When individual privacy in data collected for a scientific study needs to be preserved, and the research is observational, formal guarantees that subject identities have been adequately protected are necessary. This requires either data anonymization or pseudonymization of the elements that can be used to identify specific persons or a merely adequate guarantee of protection. The former involves breaking the connections between the data in question and the individuals they describe, resulting in a dataset that can be safely used in specific research analytics (Sarker, 2021).

5.3 Training and Awareness

The previous sections described the roles that research institutions should play in protecting privacy and security. These roles encompassed leadership and accountability, as well as formal and informal controls on information sharing, which arise when individuals must balance the need for security and privacy with the need to share information in multifaceted and collaboratively rich research environments. Where these needs intersect, individual researchers and institutional layers must handle the complex and important tasks of privacy and security protection (Thapa & Camtepe, 2021; Gstrein & Beaulieu, 2022). Given the duties and related responsibilities that researchers and data custodians have regarding the protection of privacy and security, training and awareness are essential components of an institution's protection regimen. Each person with data management responsibilities should be given an understanding of the required safeguards commensurate with their level of responsibility.

Practical security training and awareness depend on the organization and function of government agencies, professional societies, and educational institutions (Khando et al., 2021). There are various ways to conduct training, including seminars sponsored by institutional or professional societies, presentations given by security officers, technical briefings, and notes and guidance provided by security officers. Organizations sponsor courses and training programs, and graduate research advisors should incorporate field-specific guidance to instill comprehensive security knowledge in the research culture through professional courses or briefings.

5.4 Educational Programs

Several research institutions have implemented educational workshops and programs to ensure that researchers understand and adhere to the institution's privacy and security policies, as well as relevant regulations and laws, including those under the Safe Harbor framework or other applicable private, nonprofit, public, or foreign laws. In 2002, the Privacy and Security Subcommittee of the Clinical Research Platform Committee developed an educational program designed to enhance the understanding of privacy and security of information among clinical investigators and regulatory staff (Atkinson et al., 2023; Hagedorn-Hatfield et al., 2023; Roco, 2023). This program was initially presented to departmental regulatory staff to ensure that regulations and requirements have been fully addressed by the informatics solutions underpinning the registry. The program was then presented to faculty in various settings, including Grand Rounds, divisional meetings, and sponsored lunch sessions, as well as at regulatory staff meetings.

The leaders of the Interdisciplinary Children's Research Institute have also been proactive in educational initiatives (Olsson et al., 2024; McLeod & Dulsky, 2021). As all programs are ongoing, we will provide further details about them and their impact in a future paper. Other research institutions have developed training and educational modules for clinicians. A cybersecurity session that includes topics such as passwords, patches, personal firewalls, downloads, physical access controls, and mail and web browsing has also been used (Wang et al., 2020; Dutta et al., 2022; Aslan et al., 2023). High-quality training is designed to enhance the trainee's understanding and effectiveness in applying Safe Harbor and HIPAA rules. University end users who are not yet staff or faculty and affiliated through a contract or lease agreement should also be educated. Many institutions have robust user training programs that provide money-saving options to support compliance.

5.5 Security Awareness Campaigns

Deploying, maintaining, and staffing the technology discussed in the previous subsections, while essential for providing adequate access controls to your data and resources, are not enough. Users must understand, support, and adequately use security measures to make them genuinely effective (Tawalbeh et al., 2020; Landoll, 2021). One way to achieve these goals is through the deployment of a comprehensive security awareness campaign. Such campaigns should ensure that all researchers and staff have the necessary information to safely and effectively access and utilize the data and systems employed in a research project. Furthermore, they should foster a security-conscious culture and inform researchers (and other staff) about the security measures in place. Building security into your RM-SMS system is an excellent start to an awareness campaign.

A key goal of security awareness campaigns is to raise awareness of the potential vulnerabilities in the system or research project. Researchers should have basic knowledge of common threats and attack methods (Humayun et al., 2020) (Aslan et al., 2023). They should be aware of vulnerabilities, threats, and attacks through security notifications, meetings, conference calls, annual reviews, project meetings, and regular security awareness training. Scientists also need to be aware of the major structural vulnerabilities within the infrastructure of their research project. This may concern not only the direct research infrastructure but also, perhaps more likely, the infrastructure of the institute or university.

5.6 Emerging Trends and Technologies

Technology continues to change rapidly, and along with these advances come new and often unexpected implications for privacy and security in research (Brass & Sowell, 2021; Aldabbas et al., 2020). Several of these technologies have the potential to introduce significant complexity in managing research data and assets, while others can deliver new privacy and security capabilities. Many emerging trends in technology also serve to reshape the way that individuals interact with technology, as well as the ways that we think about and approach consent and responsible use.

The privacy and security challenges of research technology do not exist in a vacuum. Ensuring privacy and security in research is a process that affects not only researchers and their technical assets but also funding sources, the research community, and the shared research environment (Newman et al., 2021; Thapa & Camtepe, 2021; Peloquin et al., 2020). Social and ethical trends and behaviors constantly shape the environment and how research is regulated and conducted. These social, funding, and policy implications – impacts that are incremental – aren't discussed in the traditional privacy and security technology literature. However, we have chosen to include them here as they remain critical to consider. As we consider technology, the environment, and policy, the importance of well-designed processes in addressing privacy and security is a common theme.

5.7 Blockchain and Distributed Ledger Technologies

Blockchain technology has been proposed as an infrastructure for data sharing between research stakeholders (Shi et al., 2021) (Yadlapalli et al., 2022). Yet, due to the technical characteristics of blockchain technology – such as immutability, lack of capacity for deleting information, and other intricacies – blockchain technology would only partially solve the security and privacy challenges researchers face. Moreover, it may even introduce new ones with data forming a permanent record and fully backed up on multiple nodes within the blockchain. Therefore, it is essential to ensure that sensitive data is never placed on-chain – public or private.

A blockchain is a distributed ledger technology that enables the secure sharing of information (Liu et al., 2020; Hellwig & Huchzermeier, 2022; Thakur, 2022). Individuals taking part in the network add a block of transaction data to the ledger, creating an ongoing list of these additions – hence the name blockchain. This process enables the creation of a timestamped, permanent, and secure record of important events and transactions, serving as valuable business and research tools. Security is provided through public-private key cryptography and is used to encrypt. Decrypt blocks to prove ownership and create a digital signature to trust those involved in the transaction. Cryptographically secure hashing is also used to link data, making it tamper-evident as each block includes the hash of the previous block.

5.8 Artificial Intelligence and Machine Learning

Artificial intelligence (AI) and machine learning (ML) methods apply to a wide range of research questions. They are being increasingly used in many fields (Cioffi et al., 2020) (Mukhamediev et al., 2022) (Kuleto et al., 2021) (Fahle et al., 2020). These methods have great potential to accelerate scientific breakthroughs, but their unique computational characteristics also pose challenges for ensuring research data privacy and security. Several AI/ML practices and strategies can help researchers manage research data privacy and security, including not unnecessarily collecting sensitive personal data, pseudonymizing personal data, using synthetic data, minimizing data sharing, implementing strong de-identification techniques, adhering to proper access controls through methods such as permissions, multi-factor authentication, and conditional access policies; and encrypt AI/ML models and other artifacts (Mylrea & Robinson, 2023) (Nankya et al., 2024). Each of these effective practices and strategies for AI/ML is discussed in detail in the text.

AI/ML methods require large amounts of training data to capture complex patterns and dependencies within the data (Wolf, 2020; Rahmani et al., 2021). Because of their need for large quantities of training data and the computational tools used to process this data, AI/ML methods are particularly well-suited to addressing scientific questions in the research fields that have access to large volumes of personally identifiable information. Although these methods have the potential to generate valuable insights and accelerate scientific breakthroughs, AI/ML methods also raise unique concerns regarding privacy and security. There is a complex interaction between the intended use of AI/ML tools, the data, the data processing methods, and the application of appropriate privacy-preserving methods. These tools should be configured with privacy and security in mind from the outset when researchers first develop their research designs. Each of the seven AI/ML practices discussed helps to address the privacy and security threats posed by AI/ML methods, and we describe them for researchers in this text.

6. CONCLUSION

In conclusion, privacy and security are crucial in modern research, particularly as technology and the use of personal data continue to grow. Researchers must balance participant privacy, data security, and regulatory legal and ethical requirements. The chapter emphasizes risk assessment as a key tool for preventing breaches and protecting sensitive data by integrating privacy and security into early research planning. Best practices—from anonymization and pseudonymization to secure data storage and access controls—offer practical techniques for diverse research situations. To maintain ethical and legal conformity, the chapter recommends closer coordination between researchers and monitoring agencies, such as institutional review boards (IRBs). Significant consequences follow these findings. For research to succeed, researchers must preserve their data and maintain the trust of participants and stakeholders by taking proactive measures to ensure privacy and security. Research methods must incorporate robust privacy and security protocols as data usage continues to increase.

7. LIMITATIONS AND RECOMMENDATIONS

This chapter employed a systematic review and may not included respondents. Therefore, questionnaires or interviews are recommended for further studies.

8. DECLARATION

The authors declare that this chapter did not utilize AI in text generation except for grammar checking, editing, and paraphrasing.

REFERENCES

Abdulrasool, F. E., & Turnbull, S. J. (2020). Exploring security, risk, and compliance driven IT governance model for universities: Applied research based on the COBIT framework. [HTML]. *International Journal of Electronic Banking*, *2*(3), 237–265. DOI: 10.1504/IJEBANK.2020.111438

Abdulsalam, Y. S. & Hedabou, M. (2021). Security and privacy in cloud computing: technical review. Future Internet. mdpi.com

Adamu, A. A., Salau, A. O., & Zhiyong, L. (2021). A Robust Context and Role-Based Dynamic Access Control for Distributed Healthcare Information Systems. [HTML]. *Internet of Things : Engineering Cyber Physical Human Systems*.

Akhtar, N., Kerim, B., Perwej, Y., Tiwari, A., & Praveen, S. (2021). A comprehensive overview of privacy and data security for cloud storage. International Journal of Scientific Research in Science Engineering and Technology. hal.science

Al Sharif, R. & Pokharel, S. (2022). Smart city dimensions and associated risks: Review of literature. Sustainable cities and society. sciencedirect.com

Aldabbas, M., Xie, X., Teufel, B., & Teufel, S. (2020, October). Future security challenges for smart societies: Overview from technical and societal perspectives. In *2020 International Conference on Smart Grid and Clean Energy Technologies (ICS-GCE)* (pp. 103-111). IEEE. [HTML] DOI: 10.1109/ICSGCE49177.2020.9275630

Ameer, S., Benson, J., & Sandhu, R. (2022). An attribute-based approach toward a secured smart-home IoT access control and a comparison with a role-based approach. Information. mdpi.com

Ansari, M. T. J., Pandey, D., & Alenezi, M. (2022). STORE: Security threat oriented requirements engineering methodology. [sciencedirect.com]. *Journal of King Saud University. Computer and Information Sciences*, *34*(2), 191–203. DOI: 10.1016/j.jksuci.2018.12.005

Aslan, Ö, Aktuğ, S. S., Ozkan-Okay, M., Yilmaz, A. A., & Akin, E. (2023). A comprehensive review of cyber security vulnerabilities, threats, attacks, and solutions. Electronics. mdpi.com

Atkinson, M. L., Mousavi, R., & Windett, J. H. (2023). Detecting diverse perspectives: Using text analytics to reveal sex differences in congressional debate about defense. [sagepub.com]. *Political Research Quarterly*, *76*(1), 75–89. DOI: 10.1177/10659129211045048

Babun, L., Denney, K., Celik, Z. B., McDaniel, P., & Uluagac, A. S. (2021). A survey on IoT platforms: Communication, security, and privacy perspectives. [sciencedirect.com]. *Computer Networks, 192*, 108040. DOI: 10.1016/j.comnet.2021.108040

Becher, S., Gerl, A., Meier, B., & Bölz, F. (2020). Big picture on privacy enhancing technologies in e-health: a holistic personal privacy workflow. Information. mdpi.com

Behrens, J., Løvholt, F., Jalayer, F., Lorito, S., Salgado-Gálvez, M. A., Sørensen, M., Abadie, S., Aguirre-Ayerbe, I., Aniel-Quiroga, I., Babeyko, A., Baiguera, M., Basili, R., Belliazzi, S., Grezio, A., Johnson, K., Murphy, S., Paris, R., Rafliana, I., De Risi, R., & Vyhmeister, E. (2021). Probabilistic tsunami hazard and risk analysis: A review of research gaps. [frontiersin.org]. *Frontiers in Earth Science (Lausanne), 9*, 628772. DOI: 10.3389/feart.2021.628772

Bharati, S. & Podder, P. (2022). Machine and deep learning for iot security and privacy: applications, challenges, and future directions. Security and communication networks. wiley.com

Brass, I. & Sowell, J. H. (2021). Adaptive governance for the Internet of Things: Coping with emerging security risks. Regulation & Governance. wiley.com

Campbell, R., Goodman-Williams, R., Engleton, J., Javorka, M., & Gregory, K. (2023). Open science and data sharing in trauma research: Developing a trauma-informed protocol for archiving sensitive qualitative data. [HTML]. *Psychological Trauma: Theory, Research, Practice, and Policy, 15*(5), 819–828. DOI: 10.1037/tra0001358 PMID: 36074633

Casanovas, P., de Koker, L., & Hashmi, M. (2022). Law, socio-legal governance, the internet of things, and industry 4.0: a middle-out/inside-out approach. J. mdpi.com

Chambers, S. (2021). Truth, deliberative democracy, and the virtues of accuracy: is fake news destroying the public sphere?. Political Studies. sagepub.com

Cioffi, R., Travaglioni, M., Piscitelli, G., Petrillo, A., & De Felice, F. (2020). Artificial intelligence and machine learning applications in smart production: Progress, trends, and directions. [mdpi.com]. *Sustainability (Basel), 12*(2), 492. DOI: 10.3390/su12020492

Cui, S., & Qi, P. (2021). The legal construction of personal information protection and privacy under the Chinese Civil Code. [HTML]. *Computer Law & Security Review, 41*, 105560. DOI: 10.1016/j.clsr.2021.105560

Darwinkel, E., Chan, A., & Sheridan, L. (2020). Tertiary concerns: Campus threat assessment and management in an Australian university. [HTML]. *Journal of Threat Assessment and Management, 7*(3-4), 173–185. DOI: 10.1037/tam0000152 de Carvalho, M. A.Junior, & Bandiera-Paiva, P. (2021). Implications of loosened Role-based Access Control session control implementation for the enforcement of Dynamic Mutually Exclusive Roles properties on Health Information Systems. [sciencedirect.com]. *Informatics in Medicine Unlocked*, *27*, 100780. DOI: 10.1016/j.imu.2021.100780

Dias Canedo, E., Toffano Seidel Calazans, A., Toffano Seidel Masson, E., Teixeira Costa, P. H., & Lima, F. (2020). Perceptions of ICT practitioners regarding software privacy. [mdpi.com]. *Entropy (Basel, Switzerland)*, *22*(4), 429. DOI: 10.3390/e22040429 PMID: 33286202

Dutta, N., Jadav, N., Tanwar, S., Sarma, H. K. D., & Pricop, E. (2022). Cyber security: Issues and current trends. [HTML]

Eling, M., McShane, M., & Nguyen, T. (2021). Cyber risk management: History and future research directions. [HTML]. *Risk Management & Insurance Review*, *24*(1), 93–125. DOI: 10.1111/rmir.12169

Emami-Naeini, P., Agarwal, Y., Cranor, L. F., & Hibshi, H. (2020, May). Ask the experts: What should be on an IoT privacy and security label? In *2020 IEEE Symposium on Security and Privacy (SP)* (pp. 447-464). IEEE. [PDF] DOI: 10.1109/SP40000.2020.00043

Eyal, P., David, R., Andrew, G., Zak, E., & Ekaterina, D. (2021). Data quality of platforms and panels for online behavioral research. [springer.com]. *Behavior Research Methods*, •••, 1–20. PMID: 34590289

Fahle, S., Prinz, C., & Kuhlenkötter, B. (2020). Systematic review on machine learning (ML) methods for manufacturing processes–Identifying artificial intelligence (AI) methods for field application. Procedia CIRP. sciencedirect.com

Florea, D. & Florea, S. (2020). Big Data and the ethical implications of data privacy in higher education research. Sustainability. mdpi.com

Gardner, H. (2024). The Essential Howard Gardner on Education. [HTML]

Goldsack, J. C., Coravos, A., Bakker, J. P., Bent, B., Dowling, A. V., Fitzer-Attas, C., & Dunn, J. (2020). Verification, analytical validation, and clinical validation (V3): The foundation of determining fit-for-purpose for Biometric Monitoring Technologies (BioMeTs). npj digital [nature.com]. *Medicine*, *3*(1), 55. PMID: 32146899

Griffin, M., Martino, R. J., LoSchiavo, C., Comer-Carruthers, C., Krause, K. D., Stults, C. B., & Halkitis, P. N. (2021). Ensuring survey research data integrity in the era of internet bots. [springer.com]. *Quality & Quantity*, •••, 1–12. PMID: 34629553

Grimm, J. J., Koehler, K., Schierenbeck, I., Saliba, I., & Lust, E. M. (2020). Safer field research in the social sciences: A guide to human and digital security in hostile environments. [HTML]

Gstrein, O. J. & Beaulieu, A. (2022). How to protect privacy in a datafied society? A presentation of multiple legal and conceptual approaches. Philosophy & Technology. springer.com

Hagedorn-Hatfield, R. L., Qamar, Z., Richards, R., Patton-López, M. M., Savoie-Roskos, M. R., Heying, E. K., Landry, M. J., Mann, G., Vogelzang, J. L., OoNorasak, K., Cuite, C. L., & Hood, L. B. (2023). Barriers and facilitators to implementing and sustaining campus food insecurity initiatives. [HTML]. *Studies in Higher Education*, *48*(8), 1273–1288. DOI: 10.1080/03075079.2023.2195414

Haghani, M., Bliemer, M. C. J., Goerlandt, F., & Li, J. (2020). The scientific literature on Coronaviruses, COVID-19 and its associated safety-related research dimensions: A scientometric analysis and scoping review. Safety science. nih.gov

Heide, M., & Villeneuve, J. P. (2020). From secrecy privilege to information management: A comparative analysis of classification reforms. [HTML]. *Government Information Quarterly*, *37*(4), 101500. DOI: 10.1016/j.giq.2020.101500

Hellwig, D. P., & Huchzermeier, A. (2022). Distributed ledger technology and fully homomorphic encryption: Next-generation information-sharing for supply chain efficiency. In *Innovative Technology at the Interface of Finance and Operations* (Vol. II, pp. 31–49). Springer International Publishing. [HTML] DOI: 10.1007/978-3-030-81945-3_2

Humayun, M., Niazi, M., Jhanjhi, N. Z., Alshayeb, M., & Mahmood, S. (2020). Cyber security threats and vulnerabilities: A systematic mapping study. [HTML]. *Arabian Journal for Science and Engineering*, *45*(4), 3171–3189. DOI: 10.1007/s13369-019-04319-2

Ibbett, H. & Brittain, S. (2020). Conservation publications and their provisions to protect research participants. Conservation Biology. wiley.com

Ismagilova, E., Hughes, L., Rana, N. P., & Dwivedi, Y. K. (2022). Security, privacy and risks within smart cities: Literature review and development of a smart city interaction framework. [springer.com]. *Information Systems Frontiers*, *24*(2), 1–22. DOI: 10.1007/s10796-020-10044-1 PMID: 32837262

Jain, A. K., Sahoo, S. R., & Kaubiyal, J. (2021). Online social networks security and privacy: comprehensive review and analysis. Complex & Intelligent Systems. springer.com

Jiang, T. A. O., Li, J. P., Haq, A. U., Saboor, A., & Ali, A. (2021). A novel stacking approach for accurate detection of fake news. IEEE Access. ieee.org

Kaur, J., Hazrati Fard, S. M., Amiri-Zarandi, M., & Dara, R. (2022). Protecting farmers' data privacy and confidentiality: Recommendations and considerations. [frontiersin.org]. *Frontiers in Sustainable Food Systems*, *6*, 903230. DOI: 10.3389/fsufs.2022.903230

Keshta, I. & Odeh, A. (2021). Security and privacy of electronic health records: Concerns and challenges. Egyptian Informatics Journal. sciencedirect.com

Khando, K., Gao, S., Islam, S. M., & Salman, A. (2021). Enhancing employees information security awareness in private and public organisations: A systematic literature review. Computers & security. sciencedirect.com

Khare, S. K., Blanes-Vidal, V., Nadimi, E. S., & Acharya, U. R. (2024). Emotion recognition and artificial intelligence [) and research recommendations. Information Fusion. sciencedirect.com]. *Systematic Reviews*, •••, 2014–2023.

Kim, L. (2022). Cybersecurity: Ensuring confidentiality, integrity, and availability of information. In *Nursing Informatics: A Health Informatics, Interprofessional and Global Perspective* (pp. 391–410). Springer International Publishing. [HTML] DOI: 10.1007/978-3-030-91237-6_26

Kraiwanit, T., Limna, P., & Siripipatthanakul, S. (2023). NVivo for social sciences and management studies: A systematic review. *Advance Knowledge for Executives*, *2*(3), 1–11.

Kuleto, V., Ilić, M., Dumangiu, M., Ranković, M., Martins, O. M., Păun, D., & Mihoreanu, L. (2021). Exploring opportunities and challenges of artificial intelligence and machine learning in higher education institutions. [mdpi.com]. *Sustainability (Basel)*, *13*(18), 10424. DOI: 10.3390/su131810424

Kuran, C. H. A., Morsut, C., Kruke, B. I., Krüger, M., Segnestam, L., Orru, K., Nævestad, T. O., Airola, M., Keränen, J., Gabel, F., Hansson, S., & Torpan, S. (2020). Vulnerability and vulnerable groups from an intersectionality perspective. [sciencedirect.com]. *International Journal of Disaster Risk Reduction*, *50*, 101826. DOI: 10.1016/j.ijdrr.2020.101826

Landoll, D. (2021). The security risk assessment handbook: A complete guide for performing security risk assessments. [HTML]

Lazer, D., Hargittai, E., Freelon, D., Gonzalez-Bailon, S., Munger, K., Ognyanova, K., & Radford, J. (2021). Meaningful measures of human society in the twenty-first century. [nature.com]. *Nature*, *595*(7866), 189–196. DOI: 10.1038/s41586-021-03660-7 PMID: 34194043

Li, Y. & Liu, Q. (2021). A comprehensive review study of cyber-attacks and cyber security; Emerging trends and recent developments. Energy Reports. sciencedirect.com

Lian, R., Zhou, A., & Zheng, Y. (2024). Towards secure and trustworthy crowdsourcing: Challenges, existing landscape, and future directions. [HTML]. *Wireless Networks*, *30*(5), 4329–4341. DOI: 10.1007/s11276-022-03015-8

Liu, H., Crespo, R. G., & Martínez, O. S. (2020). Enhancing privacy and data security across healthcare applications using blockchain and distributed ledger concepts. Healthcare. mdpi.com

Makhdoom, I., Abolhasan, M., Lipman, J., Shariati, N., Franklin, D., & Piccardi, M. (2024). Securing Personally Identifiable Information: A Survey of SOTA Techniques, and a Way Forward. IEEE Access. ieee.org

Manzoor, A., Braeken, A., Kanhere, S. S., Ylianttila, M., & Liyanage, M. (2021). Proxy re-encryption enabled secure and anonymous IoT data sharing platform based on blockchain. [sciencedirect.com]. *Journal of Network and Computer Applications*, *176*, 102917. DOI: 10.1016/j.jnca.2020.102917

Marshall, R., Pardo, A., Smith, D., & Watson, T. (2022). Implementing next generation privacy and ethics research in education technology. [HTML]. *British Journal of Educational Technology*, *53*(4), 737–755. DOI: 10.1111/bjet.13224

Martin, K. D., & Palmatier, R. W. (2020). Data privacy in retail: Navigating tensions and directing future research. [HTML]. *Journal of Retailing*, *96*(4), 449–457. DOI: 10.1016/j.jretai.2020.10.002

Matthews, K. R., Yang, E., Lewis, S. W., Vaidyanathan, B. R., & Gorman, M. (2020). International scientific collaborative activities and barriers to them in eight societies. [tandfonline.com]. *Accountability in Research*, *27*(8), 477–495. DOI: 10.1080/08989621.2020.1774373 PMID: 32515609

McGraw, D. & Mandl, K. D. (2021). Privacy protections to encourage use of health-relevant digital data in a learning health system. NPJ digital medicine. nature.com

McLeod, S. & Dulsky, S. (2021). Resilience, reorientation, and reinvention: School leadership during the early months of the COVID-19 pandemic. Frontiers in education. frontiersin.org

Micheli, M., Ponti, M., Craglia, M., & Berti Suman, A. (2020). Emerging models of data governance in the age of datafication. [sagepub.com]. *Big Data & Society*, *7*(2), 2053951720948087. DOI: 10.1177/2053951720948087

Morton, B., Vercueil, A., Masekela, R., Heinz, E., Reimer, L., Saleh, S., Kalinga, C., Seekles, M., Biccard, B., Chakaya, J., Abimbola, S., Obasi, A., & Oriyo, N. (2022). Consensus statement on measures to promote equitable authorship in the publication of research from international partnerships. [wiley.com]. *Anaesthesia*, *77*(3), 264–276. DOI: 10.1111/anae.15597 PMID: 34647323

Mothukuri, V., Parizi, R. M., Pouriyeh, S., Huang, Y., Dehghantanha, A., & Srivastava, G. (2021). A survey on security and privacy of federated learning. [HTML]. *Future Generation Computer Systems*, *115*, 619–640. DOI: 10.1016/j.future.2020.10.007

Mukhamediev, R. I., Popova, Y., Kuchin, Y., Zaitseva, E., Kalimoldayev, A., Symagulov, A., Levashenko, V., Abdoldina, F., Gopejenko, V., Yakunin, K., Muhamedijeva, E., & Yelis, M. (2022). Review of artificial intelligence and machine learning technologies: Classification, restrictions, opportunities and challenges. [mdpi.com]. *Mathematics*, *10*(15), 2552. DOI: 10.3390/math10152552

Mylrea, M. & Robinson, N. (2023). Artificial Intelligence (AI) trust framework and maturity model: applying an entropy lens to improve security, privacy, and ethical AI. Entropy. mdpi.com

Nankya, M., Mugisa, A., Usman, Y., Upadhyay, A., & Chataut, R. (2024). Security and Privacy in E-Health Systems: A Review of AI and Machine Learning Techniques. IEEE Access. ieee.org

Newman, P. A., Guta, A., & Black, T. (2021). Ethical considerations for qualitative research methods during the COVID-19 pandemic and other emergency situations: Navigating the virtual field. [sagepub.com]. *International Journal of Qualitative Methods*, *20*, 16094069211047823. DOI: 10.1177/16094069211047823

O'Dwyer, M., Filieri, R., & O'Malley, L. (2023). Establishing successful university–industry collaborations: barriers and enablers deconstructed. The Journal of Technology Transfer. springer.com

Okan, O., Bollweg, T. M., Berens, E. M., Hurrelmann, K., Bauer, U., & Schaeffer, D. (2020). Coronavirus-related health literacy: A cross-sectional study in adults during the COVID-19 infodemic in Germany. [mdpi.com]. *International Journal of Environmental Research and Public Health*, *17*(15), 5503. DOI: 10.3390/ijerph17155503 PMID: 32751484

Olsson, M., Ericson, J., Randell, E., & von Ahlefeld Nisser, D. (2024). Between an educational task and an idea for treatment: Multiprofessional collaboration for supporting children "at risk"–a coordinator role in pedagogical practice. [tandfonline.com]. *Scandinavian Journal of Educational Research*, *68*(4), 765–778. DOI: 10.1080/00313831.2023.2185809

Peloquin, D., DiMaio, M., Bierer, B., & Barnes, M. (2020). Disruptive and avoidable: GDPR challenges to secondary research uses of data. [nature.com]. *European Journal of Human Genetics : EJHG*, *28*(6), 697–705. DOI: 10.1038/s41431-020-0596-x PMID: 32123329

Phuangsuwan, P., Siripipatthanakul, S., Limna, P., & Siripipattanakul, S. (2024). Grammar and Plagiarism Checking Using Grammarly for English Learners: A Systematic Review. *SSRN*, *7*(3), 1–20. DOI: 10.2139/ssrn.4861177

Politou, E., Alepis, E., Virvou, M., & Patsakis, C. (2022). Privacy and data protection challenges in the distributed era. [HTML]

Qin, X., Huang, Y., Yang, Z., & Li, X. (2021). A blockchain-based access control scheme with multiple attribute authorities for secure cloud data sharing. [HTML]. *Journal of Systems Architecture*, *112*, 101854. DOI: 10.1016/j.sysarc.2020.101854

Qiu, J., Tian, Z., Du, C., Zuo, Q., Su, S., & Fang, B. (2020). A survey on access control in the age of internet of things. [HTML]. *IEEE Internet of Things Journal*, *7*(6), 4682–4696. DOI: 10.1109/JIOT.2020.2969326

Quach, S., Thaichon, P., Martin, K. D., Weaven, S., & Palmatier, R. W. (2022). Digital technologies: Tensions in privacy and data. [springer.com]. *Journal of the Academy of Marketing Science*, *50*(6), 1299–1323. DOI: 10.1007/s11747-022-00845-y PMID: 35281634

Rahmani, A. M., Yousefpoor, E., Yousefpoor, M. S., Mehmood, Z., Haider, A., Hosseinzadeh, M., & Ali Naqvi, R. (2021). Machine learning (ML) in medicine: Review, applications, and challenges. [mdpi.com]. *Mathematics*, *9*(22), 2970. DOI: 10.3390/math9222970

Rath, D. K. & Kumar, A. (2021). Information privacy concern at individual, group, organization and societal level-a literature review. Vilakshan-XIMB Journal of Management. emerald.com

Ribeiro-Navarrete, S., Saura, J. R., & Palacios-Marqués, D. (2021). Towards a new era of mass data collection: Assessing pandemic surveillance technologies to preserve user privacy. [nih.gov]. *Technological Forecasting and Social Change*, *167*, 120681. DOI: 10.1016/j.techfore.2021.120681 PMID: 33840865

Roco, M. C. (2023). National Nanotechnology Initiative at 20 years: enabling new horizons. Journal of Nanoparticle Research. nseresearch.org

Şahin, E., Sarı, U., & Şen, F. (2024). STEM professional development program for gifted education teachers: STEM lesson plan design competence, self-efficacy, computational thinking and…. [HTML]. *Thinking Skills and Creativity.*

Sarker, I. H. (2021). Data science and analytics: an overview from data-driven smart computing, decision-making and applications perspective. SN Computer Science. springer.com

Saxena, U. R., & Alam, T. (2022). Role based access control using identity and broadcast based encryption for securing cloud data. [HTML]. *Journal of Computer Virology and Hacking Techniques, 18*(3), 171–182. DOI: 10.1007/s11416-021-00402-1

Schwab, K. (2021). Stakeholder capitalism: A global economy that works for progress, people and planet. [HTML]

Senavirathne, N., & Torra, V. (2020, December). On the role of data anonymization in machine learning privacy. In 2020 IEEE 19th International conference on trust, security and privacy in computing and communications (TrustCom) (pp. 664-675). IEEE. [HTML] DOI: 10.1109/TrustCom50675.2020.00093

Shi, P., Wang, H., Yang, S., Chen, C., & Yang, W. (2021). Blockchain-based trusted data sharing among trusted stakeholders in IoT. [wiley.com]. *Software, Practice & Experience, 51*(10), 2051–2064. DOI: 10.1002/spe.2739

Siripipatthanakul, S., & Phuangsuwan, P. (2024). Salutogenic Marketing in Preventive Dentistry. In *Leveraging Digital Technology for Preventive Dentistry* (pp. 255–278). IGI Global., DOI: 10.4018/979-8-3693-3872-8.ch009

Siripipatthanakul, S., & Siripipattanakul, S. (2025). Talent Management Ensuring the Safety and Cybersecurity in Schools. *Cultivating Creativity and Navigating Talent Management in Academia*, 383-402. DOI: DOI: 10.4018/979-8-3693-6880-0.ch018

Smidt, H. J. & Jokonya, O. (2021). The challenge of privacy and security when using technology to track people in times of COVID-19 pandemic. Procedia Computer Science. sciencedirect.com

Solbakk, J. H., Bentzen, H. B., Holm, S., Heggestad, A. K. T., Hofmann, B., Robertsen, A., Alnæs, A. H., Cox, S., Pedersen, R., & Bernabe, R. (2021). Back to WHAT? The role of research ethics in pandemic times. [springer.com]. *Medicine, Health Care, and Philosophy, 24*(1), 3–20. DOI: 10.1007/s11019-020-09984-x PMID: 33141289

Tawalbeh, L., Muheidat, F., Tawalbeh, M., & Quwaider, M. (2020). IoT Privacy and security: Challenges and solutions. Applied Sciences. mdpi.com

Thakur, A. (2022). A comprehensive study of the trends and analysis of distributed ledger technology and blockchain technology in the healthcare industry. Frontiers in Blockchain. frontiersin.org

Thapa, C., & Camtepe, S. (2021). Precision health data: Requirements, challenges and existing techniques for data security and privacy. [PDF]. *Computers in Biology and Medicine, 129,* 104130. DOI: 10.1016/j.compbiomed.2020.104130 PMID: 33271399

Tomás, J., Rasteiro, D., & Bernardino, J. (2022). Data anonymization: an experimental evaluation using open-source tools. Future Internet. mdpi.com

Tomaszewski, L. E., Zarestky, J., & Gonzalez, E. (2020). Planning qualitative research: Design and decision making for new researchers. [sagepub.com]. *International Journal of Qualitative Methods, 19,* 1609406920967174. DOI: 10.1177/1609406920967174

Tovino, S. A. (2020). Privacy and security issues with mobile health research applications. *The Journal of Law, Medicine & Ethics, 48*(1, suppl), 154–158.

Van Atteveldt, W., Althaus, S., & Wessler, H. (2021). The trouble with sharing your privates: Pursuing ethical open science and collaborative research across national jurisdictions using sensitive data. Political Communication. tandfonline.com

Viberg Johansson, J., Bentzen, H. B., & Mascalzoni, D. (2022). What ethical approaches are used by scientists when sharing health data? An interview study. BMC Medical Ethics. springer.com

Vokinger, K. N., Stekhoven, D. J., & Krauthammer, M. (2020). Lost in anonymization—A data anonymization reference classification merging legal and technical considerations. [sagepub.com]. *The Journal of Law, Medicine & Ethics, 48*(1), 228–231. DOI: 10.1177/1073110520917025 PMID: 32342783

Wang, C., Zhang, N., & Wang, C. (2021). Managing privacy in the digital economy. Fundamental Research. sciencedirect.com

Wang, L., Yang, J., & Wan, P. J. (2020). Educational modules and research surveys on critical cybersecurity topics. [sagepub.com]. *International Journal of Distributed Sensor Networks, 16*(9), 1550147720954678. DOI: 10.1177/1550147720954678

Wang, X., Wu, Y. C., Zhou, M., & Fu, H. (2024). Beyond surveillance: privacy, ethics, and regulations in face recognition technology. Frontiers in big data. frontiersin.org

Wójcicki, K., Biegańska, M., Paliwoda, B., & Górna, J. (2022). Internet of things in industry: Research profiling, application, challenges and opportunities—a review. Energies. mdpi.com

Wolf, C. T. (2020). AI models and their worlds: Investigating data-driven, AI/ML ecosystems through a work practices lens. In Sustainable Digital Communities: 15th International Conference, iConference 2020, Boras, Sweden, March 23–26, 2020 [Springer International Publishing.]. *Proceedings*, *15*, 651–664.

Yadlapalli, A., Rahman, S., & Gopal, P. (2022). Blockchain technology implementation challenges in supply chains–evidence from the case studies of multi-stakeholders. [emerald.com]. *International Journal of Logistics Management*, *33*(5), 278–305. DOI: 10.1108/IJLM-02-2021-0086

Yogarajan, V., Pfahringer, B., & Mayo, M. (2020). A review of automatic end-to-end de-identification: Is high accuracy the only metric?. Applied Artificial Intelligence. tandfonline.com

Zhang, C., Zhang, Y., Chang, Z., & Li, C. (2024). Sperm YOLOv8E-TrackEVD: A Novel Approach for Sperm Detection and Tracking. Sensors. mdpi.com

Zimmermann, V., & Gerber, N. (2020). The password is dead, long live the password–A laboratory study on user perceptions of authentication schemes. [HTML]. *International Journal of Human-Computer Studies*, *133*, 26–44. DOI: 10.1016/j.ijhcs.2019.08.006

Chapter 7
Privacy Information Awareness:
A Case of ChatGPT Adoption

Chirapat Kaewnaknaew
https://orcid.org/0009-0004-5027-5990
City University, Klongtoey, Thailand

Patcharavadee Sriboonruang
https://orcid.org/0000-0002-2171-2387
Kasetsart University, Thailand

ABSTRACT

Everyone knows about privacy rights and how to protect them in this digital era. This chapter explains the importance of being aware of privacy information when using ChatGPT. The systematic review was synthesized through content analysis of scholarly papers, which are reliable and valid sources, from Scopus, Web of Science (WOS), and Google Scholar, using purposive sampling based on English versions and primarily published between 2020 and 2025. Findings suggest that everyone must acknowledge the importance of privacy in their daily lives as the volume of personal information exchanged online continues to rise. Personal information disclosure can pose risks. Thus, users should be aware of them and take precautions. Users' understanding of service privacy settings and policies, the importance of privacy that raises privacy concerns, the quality and quantity of personal information they disclose, and the personal consequences of potential data breaches on the technological services for information privacy awareness and sharing when using ChatGPT.

DOI: 10.4018/979-8-3693-9720-6.ch007

1. INTRODUCTION

Information, data, and privacy literacy significantly impact the community's adoption of emerging technologies, such as ChatGPT, a chatbot. Current studies demonstrate that interest in using ChatGPT to improve one's community is positively associated with information and privacy literacy skills but not data literacy skills, which is surprising considering ChatGPT's status as a data science innovation. Age, gender, education, and Internet use also affect the correlations among ChatGPT users and its adoption. It is recommended to investigate how different literacies and personal and community circumstances interact with each other's development (Lund et al., 2023). Data privacy in the digital age is crucial. It analyzes the legal and ethical dilemmas stemming from technology progress and data-centric methodologies. Essential data privacy principles are examined, including the right to privacy, consent, and secrecy. Legal frameworks influence enterprises and individuals, particularly the General Data Protection Regulation (GDPR) and analogous regulations. Concerns about ethics in personal data gathering, algorithmic biases, and upcoming technologies such as artificial intelligence (AI) and the Internet of Things (IoT) are addressed. The complex interplay between data privacy and national security is examined, emphasizing personal rights and public safety conflicts. In conclusion, the chapter underscores the importance of strong legal frameworks and ethical principles for protecting data privacy while encouraging appropriate data management practices (Renuka et al., 2025). Generative AI techniques based on massive language models (LLMs) have been utilized to analyze vast datasets, extract context and specific details, and identify information, enabling the training and answering of queries with billions of parameters. Extractions of sensitive data compromise user privacy and discourages tool use. The privacy-preserving paradigm of ChatGPT for large language models (LLMs) protects user privacy during data curation, pre-processing, private context, and training for massive datasets. To illustrate the applicability of ChatGPT, differential privacy and private Reinforcement Learning (RL) training were integrated into the LLM training model to protect user privacy. Document contents, including private contextual information and metadata, affect individuals' likelihood of exposing private information. Differential privacy causes privacy loss and unpredictability, which entropy quantifies. As additional training data is added, it recursively examines public databases, resource privacy assurances, and uncertainty. Blockchain, private information retrieval, randomization, obfuscation, anonymization, and Tor were hypothetically compared for model performance and accuracy, computational complexity, privacy versus utility, training latency, vulnerability to attacks, and resource consumption to evaluate differential privacy for private LLMs critically. Differential privacy, randomization, and obfuscation can impact the utility and performance of training models, whereas Blockchain may increase computational costs and training latency. Privacy-preserving data in generative AI tools may begin with raising awareness of privacy information (Hadi et al., 2023; Liu et al., 2023; Ullah et al., 2024).

With the implementation of ChatGPT based on the data, it was discovered that this tiredness lowers the perceived threats to users' privacy, raises their expectations of the platform, and increases their inclination to utilize ChatGPT. In order to gain a better understanding of this phenomenon, we built a novel model that incorporates the ideas of privacy fatigue and perceived risk, as well as components from the unified theory of acceptance and usage of technology. Interestingly, the desire to utilize ChatGPT was not significantly influenced by perceived risk, although possible dangers were involved. This contemporary research contributes to a better understanding of the privacy views of undergraduate students when it comes to using ChatGPT in educational settings and could imply for other sectors (Chung & Kwon, 2025).

This chapter discusses privacy rights and methods for safeguarding them in the digital age. It elucidates the significance of recognizing private information when utilizing ChatGPT.

1.1 Research Question

How important is recognizing private information when utilizing ChatGPT?

1.2 Research Objective

This chapter discussed how privacy information awareness significantly impacts the community's adoption of emerging technologies, specifically ChatGPT.

2. LITERATURE REVIEW

2.1 Privacy and Security of Online Personal Information

The term "privacy awareness" refers to the degree to which an individual is aware of their legitimate right to privacy and the measures they can take to safeguard it. As the quantity of personal information shared online continues to rise, it has become increasingly vital to recognize the importance of privacy in our daily lives. Individuals should be aware of the potential risks of disclosing their personal information and take steps to safeguard themselves. Individuals must take these precautions. Internet consumers engage in various activities daily, including surfing, e-commerce, social media, email, and more. Information privacy awareness refers to users' understanding of Internet service privacy settings and policies, the importance of privacy that raises privacy concerns, the quality and quantity of personal information they disclose, and the personal consequences of potential data breaches on the technological infrastructure supporting electronic services (Tsohou & Soumelidou, 2025; Putri & Utomo, 2025; Menard & Bott, 2025). The relationship between personal data, privacy, and security has grown increasingly intricate in the digital era. The significant difficulties related to cyber-attacks, fraud, and privacy violations have escalated recently. The function of data brokers—entities that gather, analyze, and sell personal information—and their considerable influence on individual privacy. Privacy protection frameworks and technologies are crucial. Several deficiencies include varied demographic reactions to privacy concerns, user education and training needs, the significance of summarizing privacy policies for enhanced understanding, and adherence to privacy regulations and compliance. In this digital era, the discussion is about guidelines and solutions to address these gaps, highlighting the necessity for a multifaceted strategy to improve privacy protection in the changing context of cyber risks (Ullah et al., 2024; Lokare et al., 2025). Organizations increasingly utilize artificial intelligence (AI) to analyze extensive data sets to tackle diverse business difficulties. One application entails integrating varied user data into cohesive profiles, synthesizing consumer behaviors to customize marketing strategies precisely. While AI enhances consumer convenience and enables more efficient and profitable marketing for organizations, aggregating data into behavioral profiles for machine learning algorithms raises substantial privacy concerns for users. These concerns include unexpected personal disclosures, biased outcomes affecting marginalized groups, and organizations' inability to erase data from AI systems entirely upon consumer request. While new AI implementations swiftly transform consumer perceptions of information privacy, academics have yet to establish a precise mechanism for assessing customers' privacy concerns associated with AI, including ChatGPT (Menard & Bott, 2025).

In this chapter, privacy refers to the entitlement to manage and secure personal information, whereas security involves the strategies implemented to prevent unwanted access, threats, and vulnerabilities. Safeguarding online privacy and security necessitates the formulation of robust, distinctive passwords, activating two-factor authentication, vigilance when using public Wi-Fi, and routine software patching. It also involves minimizing the information disseminated online and remaining cognizant of prospective scams.

2.2 Personal Information Awareness

The public sector culture and how national culture affects information security awareness have been discussed. In some countries, such as Sweden, France, and Tunisia, the Human Aspects of Information Security (HAIS) model has patterns and highlighted culture's influence on behavior. Incorporating Swedish employees in policy drafting is necessary to raise information security awareness. Learning from prior experiences and respecting hierarchical systems helped French employees raise awareness. In contrast, Tunisian information security programs should consider social and relational factors to raise awareness. These insights help multinational managers understand the forces and dynamics of similar countries (Riahi & Islam, 2025). The stable equilibrium options for personal information security inside the cooperative governance game framework are crucial. Digital firms' non-compliant handling of personal information might jeopardize consumers' rights and interests. The amalgamation of regulatory measures instituted by supervisory bodies and the rights protection initiatives undertaken by customers can significantly enhance digital firms' self-regulation. The reputation system constrains the participants' opportunistic behavior (Sun et al., 2025). "Personal Information" encompasses factual or subjective data about an identified individual, whether recorded or unrecorded. In the contemporary digital economy, personal information serves as the new currency. When aggregated from many individuals, tastes, likes, dislikes, and personal information help marketers and businesses refine their products and services. This information is often beneficial, as it enables organizations and consumers to inadvertently influence a product, service, or website experience; however, it can also be misused or employed detrimentally. Awareness is the state of being cognizant, characterized by the comprehension and recognition of the existence or occurrence of something. Thus, personal information awareness refers to awareness of the existence and importance of personal information protection and security (Albayrak & Bağcı, 2025; Sun et al., 2025). Among students, gender and grade did not directly influence information security awareness levels; nevertheless, participation in information security training, departmental affiliation, and technological disposition had a substantial impact. Conversely, certain human traits indirectly influence information security awareness. This investigation provided significant additions to the literature by elucidating the impact of variables on students' information security awareness comprehensively. Developing information security training programs could enhance awareness by considering personal aspects (Albayrak & Bağcı, 2025).

The comprehensive analysis of AI models' security and privacy concerns, specifically ChatGPT, is essential. Potential security threats include cyberattacks, deep fake creation, model poisoning, API, and prompt injection attacks. Privacy issues are investigated, including data leakage, misuse, and unauthorized access. User perspectives are also assessed, including public trust issues, privacy demands, and the need to balance security with innovation. The proposed mitigation strategies for these concerns have been discussed. These involve safeguards against security risks, mitigation measures for deepfakes and model poison attacks, and steps to counter API and prompt injection attacks. Furthermore, it suggests techniques for addressing privacy concerns and strategies to prevent data leakage and unauthorized access (Huang et al., 2023).

In this chapter, "Personal Information" includes recorded and unrecorded factual or subjective data about an identified individual. Personal data is the new money in the digital economy. Marketers and businesses use interests, likes, dislikes, and personal information from many people to improve their products and services. This information can help companies and customers accidentally affect a product, service, or website experience, but it can also be exploited. Awareness is the understanding and recognition of something. Personal information awareness is knowledge of security and protection of personal information. Personal information awareness and sharing are essential when using ChatGPT.

2.3 ChatGPT Adoption and Information Sharing

Generative Artificial Intelligence (AI) technology, such as Chat Generative Pre-trained Transformer (ChatGPT), constantly evolves, and its user base is rising. Organizations are now trying these technologies to leverage their potential and minimize hazards in business operations. The constant acceptance of new Generative AI technologies will help entrepreneurs gain more and more expertise with adoptions, helping them utilize the continuously shifting technical innovation landscape. However, there is a shortage of earlier studies on ChatGPT adoption in the startup setting, especially from an Entrepreneur perspective, highlighting the urgent need for a thorough examination to uncover the determinants driving this technology adoption and determining the elements that affect the absorption of ChatGPT technology by startups, foreseeing their influence on the triumph of enterprises, and offering pragmatic ideas for various stakeholders, including entrepreneurs and policymakers (Gupta & Yang, 2024). ChatGPT influences information dissemination, collaboration, and learning within the digital office environment—furthermore, ChatGPT with the tenets of Learning 3.0 and its capacity to improve individualized educational engagements. The advantages of employing ChatGPT in the digital workplace encompass personalized support, flexibility, and teamwork. It also tackles the issues related to ChatGPT, including accuracy, contextual comprehension, and ethical implications. ChatGPT benefits delineate data about cost savings, task utilization, and employee perceptions of ChatGPT in the digital workplace. It emphasizes the significance of incorporating metacognitive skills into learner applications and the capacity of ChatGPT to transform knowledge management and collaboration in the digital workplace. The significant insights into the advantages, drawbacks, and future ramifications of employing ChatGPT in the digital workplace for knowledge dissemination and collaboration (Fahad et al., 2024). Sharing information with ChatGPT is essential for organizations, policymakers, and staff regarding the awareness of privacy and cybersecurity protection.

As technology advances, generative artificial intelligence techniques are being applied in more fields, including education. ChatGPT, an Open-Source language model developed by OpenAI, is widely used in education. It examines the awareness, acceptance, and implementation of ChatGPT, OpenAI's cutting-edge language model, about the Technology Acceptance Model (TAM). It adds perceived intelligence as a crucial element in adoption. ChatGPT awareness strongly affects adoption intention. ChatGPT awareness and adoption intention are significantly mediated by perceptions of its simplicity, usefulness, and intelligence. Additionally, perceived trust strongly moderates awareness of ChatGPT and perceived ease of use, utility, and intelligence. It is suggested that ChatGPT safety be encouraged to sustain students' critical thinking and originality in assessment authoring. Therefore, educators must provide clear guidelines and instructions to ensure that artificial intelligence tools are used ethically and appropriately in evaluations (Shahzad et al., 2024).

Figure 1. Personal information sharing, awareness, and ChatGPT adoption.

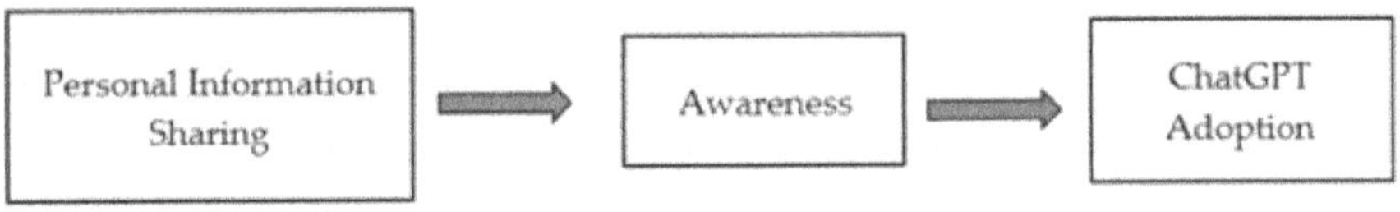

(Authers, 2025)

3. METHODOLOGY

Narrative synthesis is the systematic review and integration of findings from diverse research, predominantly utilizing language and text to summarize and elucidate the synthesized results. In purposive analysis, this procedure is termed "narrative synthesis." Researchers utilize their skills to choose the most favorable sample through sampling. They are often employed in qualitative research. The purpose of our endeavor is to attain comprehensive knowledge. Texts are often utilized as a foundation for qualitative research—analyzing the content. The aim is to condense considerable material into a succinct and structured presentation of key results. Consequently, the researchers undertook a detailed documentary study, employing content analysis to evaluate the data. Furthermore, publications were composed in English and underwent peer review for data gathering and analysis. This compilation encompasses databases like Google Scholar, Scopus, and Web of Science (WOS) (Siripipatthanakul & Siripipattanakul, 2025, a).

The methodologies and results of systematic reviews must be articulated with sufficient precision to enable users to assess the credibility of the findings and ascertain their applicability. The PRISMA statement was created to facilitate the transparent and thorough reporting of systematic reviews and meta-analyses. It has also been revised based on PRISMA 2020 and the studies of Siripipatthanakul and Siripipattanakul (2025, a, b, and c) to integrate new developments in the process and terminology of systematic reviews. This study has been utilized to elucidate the PRISMA 2020 framework.

1. Identification: The initial phase of the identification process involves selecting scholarly articles via random sampling. The selected articles for review have been determined based on their associated keywords and subjects. Selected English articles, identified by experts, were incorporated for data collection and analysis. The sources of these various papers included ScienceDirect, PubMed, Google Scholar, Scopus, and Web of Science (WOS). 12,800 scholarly articles pertinent to this subject were shown at this phase of the identification procedure.
2. Screening: Screening entails selecting papers designated for review. Furthermore, secondary data was collected and analyzed to synthesize this systematic review article via purposive sampling. This comprehensive study employs terms such as gambling, online, higher education, learners, casino, and addiction. Following the screening procedure, these academic papers were selected from the 68 papers.
3. Eligibility: The researchers removed duplicates and excluded articles for which full versions of the documents could not be obtained to ascertain eligibility. The remaining 30 selected scholarly papers are presented during the eligibility phases.
4. Inclusion: The last step in the inclusion process is finalizing the list of research to be incorporated into the systematic review of the 30 scholarly publications. Develop your academic writing under the chapter framework. Furthermore, to summarize and disseminate the findings, the research quality was assessed by five independent reviewers. Grammatical errors and instances of plagiarism were detected using Grammarly. Before submitting the final text, three experts review and certify the article's content for grammar and the chapter's contents.

4. RESULTS

4.1 The Awareness of Personal Information Sharing When Using ChatGPT

Never share any of the following six things with ChatGPT. Although ChatGPT is an excellent tool, users should not entrust private and sensitive information. Personal information should never be discussed with anybody else. Arguably, ChatGPT and other artificial intelligence (AI) chatbots are among the most helpful and time-saving technologies developed since the advent of the computer. However, there is some information that no one should ever disclose to ChatGPT unless the content poses a risk that private data will be shared with the entire world. The data that anyone inputs into chatbots is used for training purposes, which means that any input could influence the subsequent request a user receives. Although most inquiries are unlikely to result in problems, disclosing specific information may put you at risk of becoming a victim of fraud or jeopardizing employment. Some of the most important topics to avoid sharing with ChatGPT and similar platforms.

1. Confidential Information Regarding the Organization: If anyone not opted out of ChatGPT retaining your data, any information you enter into the platform is considered confidential. This information may be used to train the LLM and its artificial intelligence. Additionally, this refers to information that may not be solely yours but instead belongs to the organization for which you work. There have been previous instances where confidential company information has been inadvertently disclosed to the public through ChatGPT. Immediately upon discovering a security breach linked to an employee who shared critical company code on the platform, the company issued a note advising its employees not to use ChatGPT. Additionally, Samsung is not the only company that has blocked ChatGPT for some employees and departments; many other corporations, including Apple, have also taken similar measures. If someone is responsible for exposing sensitive data belonging to your firm, they may find themselves in an embarrassing conversation with human resources or, even worse, face termination.
2. Inventive Works and the Protection of Intellectual Property: If anyone uses ChatGPT to edit the paper, the content has the potential to be shared as the original creative work with all other users; it should never be shared with chatbots. Even works that are protected by copyright nevertheless pose a risk. Chatbots like ChatGPT are currently entangled in various legal challenges from individuals. These individuals accuse Chatbots of training their large language models (LLMs) on their published writings. If you want to avoid having your

next brilliant idea appear in the results of a ChatGPT session with a stranger, we recommend keeping it to yourself.

3. Information Regarding Finances: Just as someone would not post their social security number or financial information on a public internet forum, you should not submit those details to ChatGPT either. It is free to contact the platform for advice on finances, assistance with budgeting, or guidance on taxes; however, please do not provide the platform with sensitive financial information. If they do so, the private bank information may be exposed to the public and susceptible to misuse. Additionally, it is crucial to be vigilant for deceptive artificial intelligence chatbot systems, which may be designed to deceive users into divulging sensitive information.
4. Data on Individuals: Personal information, such as your name, address, and telephone number, as well as the name of your very first pet...Under the context of ChatGPT, all of them are major no-nos. The fact that something as intimate as this can be used to impersonate you is something that fraudsters could exploit to gain access to private accounts or carry out impersonation schemes, neither of which is beneficial to you. Therefore, it is advisable to resist the temptation of sharing your life narrative on ChatGPT. If you are adamant about having it compose your autobiography for you, you should give significant consideration to the information that you are revealing.
5. Identifying Numbers and Passwords: You should only write down passwords in one location, specifically on the website or application that requires them. There is no other place to do so. According to best practices, storing passwords in a location that does not use encryption can leave you susceptible. Therefore, if you do not want your passwords to be accessible to the general public, it is recommended that you resist the urge to allow ChatGPT to record all your passwords in a single location, making them more accessible. Alternatively, you could ask it to propose more secure passwords for you. A password manager is an excellent tool that makes it easier to remember multiple passwords simultaneously. If you have trouble remembering passwords, which is a common issue, consider using a password manager. If you wish to test the passwords you already use, numerous free and secure tools are available to perform this task for you.
6. Chats on the ChatGPT platform. So, okay, we will agree that this one is a little bit of an oxymoron, and it would not be very easy to use ChatGPT without actually talking to it. However, it does an excellent job of highlighting the significance of the risks associated with entering any information into ChatGPT. It is possible for even your own ChatGPT requests to be shared with other people, and this has occurred in the past without any problems. Additionally, there have been instances in recent times where a defect caused users of ChatGPT to view talks

conducted by other users using the chatbot. There is also evidence that Google's Bard chatbot has been indexing conversations with users, making it easy for anyone to find what they are discussing on the internet. In both instances, the firms have made assurances that they will address the problems; yet, this example demonstrates how rapidly technological advancements are occurring and that nothing, not even the requests entered into the platform, can be deemed private. This is something to keep in mind whenever you are having a conversation with a chatbot. Confidently Utilizing ChatGPT: The ChatGPT application is a powerful tool that can significantly simplify and enhance the efficiency of your personal and professional lives. Nevertheless, it is essential to remember that the information you submit may be used for training the platform and may also appear in the requests of other users in various formats. In addition to the option to opt out of ChatGPT using personal data, it is recommended that it becomes familiar with how the platform utilizes personal data. Always use chatbots cautiously rather than treating them like close friends. As a result, it is essential to be aware that any content posted in the past on the platform can be challenging to delete completely.

4.2 A Case Study of Personal Information Searching Results When Using ChatGPT

A case study using ChatGPT to search for the personal information of a well-known researcher.

Question 1: On April 8, 2025, ChatGPT was asked, "Who is Dr. Supaprawat Siripipatthanakul?"
Answer 1: ChatGPT's answer about a researcher's information is based on his profiles on ResearchGate, LinkedIn, ORCID, and Sciprofile in Figure 3.

Figure 2. ChatGPT's Result 1 (ChatGPT, 2025).

Figure 3. ChatGPT's Result 2 (ChatGPT, 2025).

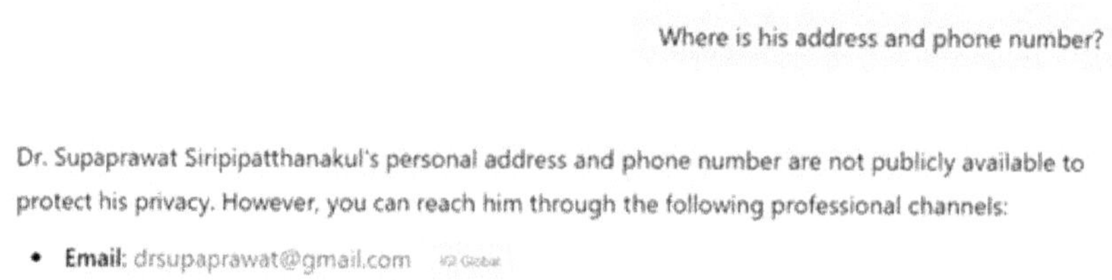

The results could be summarized as follows: "Privacy awareness" is the extent to which an individual is aware of their legitimate right to privacy and the protections they can take to protect their privacy. As the amount of personal information shared online continues to increase, it is becoming increasingly important to acknowledge the significance of privacy in our day-to-day lives. Everyone should know the potential dangers of releasing their personal information and take measures to protect themselves. Individuals are required to adopt these safety measures. Daily, anyone who uses the internet participates in various activities, such as e-commerce, social media, email, and other activities. Users' understanding of the privacy settings and policies of Internet service providers, the significance of privacy that raises privacy concerns, the quality and quantity of personal information that they disclose, and the personal consequences of potential data breaches on the technological infrastructure that supports electronic services are all examples of information privacy awareness.

"Personal Information" refers to any recorded or unrecorded data that pertains to an identified individual and may be factual or subjective. Personal information is the new money in the modern digital economy, which is characterized by its widespread use. Tastes, likes, dislikes, and personal information can assist businesses and marketers in refining their products and services when compiled from many individuals. This information is frequently advantageous since it allows businesses and customers to unintentionally impact the experience of using a product, service, or website. On the other hand, it can also be implemented in a manner that is detrimental to the firm or the customer. The knowledge and acknowledgment of the existence or occurrence of something characterizes a state of being cognizant and aware. Awareness is the state of consciousness. In this context, "personal information awareness" refers to understanding the presence of personal information protection and security and the importance of such protection and security.

Businesses increasingly turn to artificial intelligence (AI) to analyze vast amounts of data to address various challenges they face in their operations. The integration of diverse user data into cohesive profiles and the synthesis of consumer behaviors to accurately adapt marketing campaigns is one use. Even though artificial intelligence makes life easier for customers and allows businesses to conduct more effective and profitable marketing, aggregating data into behavioral profiles for machine learning algorithms poses significant privacy concerns for users. These issues include the possibility of unexpected personal disclosures, biased outcomes that damage marginalized groups, and the impossibility of enterprises completely deleting data from AI systems in response to a request from a consumer. Academics have not yet established a precise mechanism for analyzing customers' privacy issues linked with artificial intelligence, particularly ChatGPT. However, new AI implementations are rapidly transforming consumer conceptions of information privacy to a greater extent.

Data privacy is of the utmost importance in this day and age. It concerns the ethical and legal conundrums that have arisen due to the progression of technology and data-centric techniques. Considerable attention is paid to fundamental data privacy principles, such as the right to privacy, consent, and confidentiality. Legal frameworks have an impact on businesses and individuals, particularly the General Data Protection Regulation (GDPR) and other similar. Concerns are discussed regarding the ethical implications of collecting personal data, algorithmic biases, and emerging technologies such as artificial intelligence (AI) and the Internet of Things (IoT). The intricate relationship between data privacy and national security is investigated, focusing on personal rights and public safety tensions. In conclusion, the chapter emphasizes the significance of comprehensive legal frameworks and ethical standards to safeguard data privacy while promoting acceptable data management methods.

The benefits of ChatGPT include information regarding cost reductions, task utilization, and employee views of ChatGPT in the context of digital business environments. ChatGPT's capacity to alter knowledge management and collaboration in the digital workplace and to embed metacognitive abilities into learner apps are emphasized in this chapter. The key insights into the benefits, limitations, and potential future repercussions of utilizing ChatGPT in the digital workplace for knowledge sharing and collaboration: Businesses, policymakers, and staff members must share information with ChatGPT in order to raise awareness about the importance of protecting one's privacy and cybersecurity information. Sharing information via personal platforms, such as LinkedIn, ResearchGate, and other platforms where the owner has provided the information, may not cause an issue for the owners. Nevertheless, sensitive information, such as phone numbers, addresses, citizen identification, date of birth, username, and password, must be shared with awareness. This case study confirms that ChatGPT provides information from open sources, but ChatGPT's users may not get answers to some sensitive information. Nevertheless, if someone wants to share information with ChatGPT, please share with consideration, care, and awareness of privacy prevention.

5. DISCUSSION

5.1 Similarities and Arguments of Previous Studies

The findings support the studies as follows:

Chung & Kwon (2025) concluded that OpenAI's generative pre-trained transformer (GPT), specifically ChatGPT, is rapidly transforming fields such as education and becoming an integral part of our daily lives. However, its rise has sparked intense debates about privacy, raising concerns about the storage of personal information and drawing global regulatory scrutiny. ChatGPT is gaining popularity among undergraduate students owing to its personalized learning capabilities, leading many universities to provide guidelines and seminars on its use. Curiosity about the reasons for ChatGPT's popularity inspired our research. A survey of 695 undergraduate students in South Korea found that "privacy fatigue"—a feeling of hopelessness and weariness regarding privacy—was associated with these students' adoption of ChatGPT. The findings revealed that this fatigue reduces perceived privacy risks, enhances their expectations of the platform, and boosts their intention to use ChatGPT. By incorporating concepts of privacy fatigue, perceived risk, and elements from the Unified Theory of Acceptance and Use of Technology, a novel model was developed to understand this phenomenon. Interestingly, despite the potential risks, perceived risk did not significantly influence the intention to use ChatGPT. This study contributes to a better understanding of undergraduate students' privacy perceptions when leveraging ChatGPT in education.

Alshahrani and Alrodhan (2025) summarized that ChatGPT in Today's digital world increasingly relies on generative AI driven by machine learning (ML) and deep learning (DL). Generative AI shows promise across various industries, including the military, banking, education, energy, and healthcare. Given these technologies' rapid evolution and expanding impact, it is crucial to recognize their associated risks, particularly in politics, society, technology, law, and ethics. The study highlights the impact of Generative AI, specifically ChatGPT, on security, privacy, and ethics, underscoring the need for regulatory laws. Regulating ChatGPT, a Generative AI, is crucial due to the lack of precise legislation governing its secure use. Additionally, there is a lack of awareness regarding the handling and classification of sensitive data. Integrating cybersecurity controls with data management, protection, and intellectual property rights is crucial for generative AI systems and applications to prevent data leaks; protect confidentiality, privacy, and integrity; and mitigate potential threats, such as misleading information and disclosure.

Aryania et al. (2025) summarized that social robots in public settings may collect personal data. This raises privacy concerns and compels people to consider sharing their information with the robot. This research examines how privacy warnings affect people's intentions and actual sharing of personal information when engaging with a robot in public areas. Using a model, the estimation of disclosure intentions toward a robot and the evaluation of privacy warnings during interaction with over 100 participants engaging with a robot to test the model. The findings show that risk perceptions, trust, perceived enjoyment, and social influence strongly influence information disclosure intentions. A robot with privacy warnings is more accepted, and participants reveal more low-privacy information. However, disclosure is similar for people interacting with robots with and without privacy warnings. The two groups' disclosure behavior is similar, demonstrating that privacy warnings do not affect sharing.

Lee & Weber (2025) suggested that personal information trade-offs are consistent with a reasonable privacy demand. People make trade-offs across two categories of personal information sharing in an experiment to classify whether their choices fit the generalized axiom of revealed preference. They estimate the cost of sharing personal data. Sixty-three percent of individuals arrange privacy levels rationally, similar to other areas. Simple privacy trade-off inconsistency leads to more expensive preference reversals when pricing personal information exchange. Only one-third of people consistently pick and price personal information. Our findings suggest that monetizing personal information can affect welfare differently for persons with various levels of rationality in making sensible trade-offs.

Choudhury & Shamszare (2023) confirmed that trust is essential for users' acceptance of ChatGPT. It is essential to emphasize that ChatGPT was not initially intended for healthcare applications. Consequently, excessive dependence on it for health-related guidance may result in misinformation and ensuing health hazards. Efforts should concentrate on enhancing ChatGPT's capacity to differentiate between inquiries it can manage safely and those that require referral to human experts, specifically healthcare professionals. While concerns are linked to over-reliance on artificial intelligence- driven chatbots like ChatGPT, these risks can be mitigated by promoting shared accountability and encouraging collaboration among developers, subject matter experts, and human factors researchers.

Wibowo et al. (2024) concluded that the accelerating advancement of technology induces alterations in media consumption patterns. Media convergence is inevitable, driven by speed and content differentiation. The advent of ChatGPT offers a distinct evaluation for social media users. The discourse regarding Chat GPT is one of the topics addressed on social media, namely Twitter. This research aims to evaluate the social media content of Twitter's #ChatGPT as reported by the news. This study employs the notion of User Generated Content (UGC) within the framework of media convergence theory. The UGC notion manifests as content generated by ChatGPT users regarding diverse topics, presented in a textual format. This previous research employs a qualitative approach utilizing Social Network Analysis (SNA) as an effective instrument for delineating the influence of information received by the public, namely ChatGPT users in Indonesia. The research findings indicate that the SNA approach reveals the relational structure articulated by Twitter users in Indonesia about ChatGPT. Users commenced discussions regarding the emergence of ChatGPT as a consequence of feedback. The renown of the participating players is predominantly influenced by the textual discussions exchanged by ChatGPT members.

Humlum & Vestergaard (2024) investigated the adoption of ChatGPT by a large-scale survey experiment correlated with extensive registry data in Denmark. In a survey of 100,000 individuals across 11 vulnerable professions. The results show that ChatGPT is widespread: 50% of workers have utilized it, with younger, less experienced, higher-performing, and predominantly male workers at the forefront. These factors have led to certain workers adopting ChatGPT while others have refrained from using it. Employees recognize significant productivity potential in ChatGPT yet frequently encounter limitations imposed by employer constraints and mandatory training. Notifying employees about expert evaluations of ChatGPT alters their views and intentions, although it has few effects on implementation.

Gupta & Yang (2024) and Fahad et al. (2024) concluded that Generative AI technology like Chat Generative Pre-trained Transformer (ChatGPT) evolves and gains users. Businesses are experimenting with these technologies to maximize benefits and limit risks. Regularly adopting new Generative AI technologies will help entrepreneurs master adoptions and use the changing technical innovation landscape. However, there are few studies on ChatGPT adoption in startups, especially from an entrepreneur's perspective, highlighting the urgent need for a thorough examination to uncover the determinants driving this technology adoption and determining the elements that affect startups' absorption of ChatGPT technology, foreseeing their impact on enterprise success, and offering pragmatic ideas for various stakeholders, including entrepreneurs. ChatGPT affects information dissemination, cooperation, and learning in the digital office, as well as Learning 3.0 and tailored education. ChatGPT in the digital workplace provides individualized help, flexibility, and teamwork. It addresses ChatGPT's accuracy, contextual comprehension, and ethics. The benefits of ChatGPT include cost savings, task utilization, and employee attitudes in the digital workplace. It stresses the importance of metacognitive skills in learner applications and ChatGPT's ability to change digital workplace knowledge management and cooperation. The key pros, cons, and future implications of using ChatGPT in the digital workplace for knowledge distribution and collaboration. Organizations, policymakers, and staff must share privacy and cybersecurity information with ChatGPT based on their awareness of any issues.

Wu et al. (2024) suggested that ChatGPT is an AI-driven chatbot that employs topic modeling and reinforcement learning to produce coherent responses. While ChatGPT offers significant potential in diverse sectors, including customer service, education, mental health treatment, personal productivity, and content creation, it is crucial to consider its security, privacy, and ethical ramifications. The progression from GPT-1 to GPT-4 shows the model's characteristics, constraints, and prospective uses to elucidate the potential risks of integrating ChatGPT into everyday life. Emphasizing security, privacy, and ethical considerations and careful underscore these issues' obstacles to mainstream adoption. Ultimately, the unresolved issues in these domains urge collaborative initiatives to guarantee the advancement of secure and ethically responsible big language models.

Falade (2024) confirmed that technologies powered by artificial intelligence (AI), particularly chatbots that AI powers, have become essential to modern communication and task automation. As a natural language processing chatbot that is easily accessible to many people, ChatGPT, which OpenAI developed, has received a significant amount of attention. On the other hand, issues over privacy and security have accompanied its implementation and widespread adoption. Blog mining is a methodology that provides a complete analysis of the security and privacy considerations surrounding ChatGPT. The inherent vulnerabilities within the platform are extracted from pertinent blog posts and combined with examining current literature. Additionally, the prospective threats that could exploit these weaknesses. In particular, it sheds light on the dangers connected to the improper treatment of personal information, the vulnerability to cyberattacks, and the more considerable consequences for protecting human privacy and the safety of organizations. Furthermore, the insights into the legal structure governing artificial intelligence chatbots suggest future research routes to handle these difficulties properly. In conclusion, the findings of this study highlight the crucial need to develop comprehensive security measures and legislative frameworks to limit the risks connected with AI-driven chatbots and guarantee that they are deployed responsibly in the digital era.

Sebastian (2023) demonstrated that artificial intelligence (AI) and machine learning (ML) have evolved to the point where they have led to the development of sophisticated large language models (LLMs). These LLMs are utilized extensively in applications such as chatbots. There are crucial data protection issues and privacy enhancements in the context of LLM-based chatbots, particularly on OpenAI's ChatGPT. The combined challenges of protecting sensitive user information while also maintaining the efficiency of machine learning models are investigated in this paper. It evaluates the privacy-enhancing technologies (PETs) currently in use and suggests novel approaches, such as differential privacy, federated learning, and techniques for data minimization. A poll of Chatbot users is also included in the study to determine how much they are concerned about personal data privacy related to utilizing LLM-based applications. It is necessary to establish a complete guide for developers, policymakers, and researchers intending to contribute to the ongoing discussion over data protection in artificial intelligence.

Albayrak & Bağcı (2025) discussed that when it came to students, gender and grade did not directly affect the levels of information security awareness; nevertheless, involvement in information security training, departmental affiliation, and technical disposition did have a significant impact. In the opposite direction, specific human characteristics indirectly impact information security awareness. The findings of this inquiry made substantial contributions to the existing body of knowledge by providing a complete explanation of the impact that variables have on the information security awareness demonstrated by students. Greater awareness could be achieved by developing information security training programs that consider personal elements.

Thus, this discussion section also supports the study of Hua & Jiang (2024) that ChatGPT is a new discipline of artificial intelligence that holds enormous promise across various industries due to the improvements made in artificial intelligence technology. Because of its user-friendly human-machine interface, rapid response capabilities, and delivery of high-quality answers, it has garnered a significant amount of attention. A large number of people are utilizing it. ChatGPT is a new milestone in artificial intelligence, and many people consider it a revolutionary advancement. The introduction of ChatGPT, on the other hand, provides benefits and the usual security concerns and ethical issues that come with every technological evolution. The precise information about ChatGPT, including its technology, limitations, ethical issues, governance pathways, and future directions. Specifically, it began by providing a comprehensive investigation of the technical implementation details of the GPT series models. Intentional usage, invasion of privacy, and other similar issues could be incurred. In conclusion, various governance courses of action are needed to lessen the effects of ChatGPT and provide potential future possibilities. The essential information will enable users to make well-informed decisions, successfully manage potential issues that may arise when utilizing ChatGPT, and keep up with the fast-changing environment of this technology. However, it is suggested that we be aware of sharing private information with ChatGPT.

5.2 Research Implications

"Personal Information" refers to any recorded or unrecorded data that pertains to an identified individual and may be factual or subjective. Personal information is the new money in the modern digital economy, which is characterized by its widespread use. Tastes, likes, dislikes, and personal information can assist businesses and marketers in refining their products and services when compiled from many individuals. This information is frequently advantageous since it allows businesses and customers to unintentionally impact the experience of using a product, service, or website. On the other hand, it can also be implemented in a manner that is detrimental to the firm or the customer. The knowledge and acknowledgment of the existence or occurrence of something characterizes a state of being cognizant and aware. Awareness is the state of consciousness. In this context, "personal information awareness" refers to understanding the presence of personal information protection and security and the importance of such protection and security.

This chapter suggests to organizations that ChatGPT may collect personal data in public settings thanks to its ability to collect it. Because of this, users are forced to consider the possibility of revealing their personal information to the robot, which raises concerns about their privacy. The purpose of this study is to evaluate the influence that privacy warnings have on the intentions of individuals and the actual disclosure of personal information from those persons while they are engaging with a robot in public places. During interactions between users using ChatGPT, the disclosure intentions about ChatGPT and the evaluation of privacy warnings are considered. It suggests that perceptions of danger, trust, perceived enjoyment, and social influence all play a substantial role in determining intentions to share information. ChatGPT, which includes privacy warnings, is more frequently accepted, which means that users are more likely to divulge an enormous quantity of information that is not private. It is important to note that persons interacting with robots are subject to the same level of disclosure, independent of any privacy warnings. The two groups' disclosure behavior is comparable, suggesting that privacy warnings do not affect the amount of information shared. "Privacy awareness" refers to the degree to which an individual is aware of the steps they can take to safeguard their right to privacy and the amount to which they recognize their rightful claim to privacy. Because of the ever-increasing amount of private information being shared on the internet, it is necessary to recognize the relevance of privacy in daily life. The individuals are responsible for identifying the potential risks associated with disclosing their personal information and putting in place safeguards to protect themselves. These safety measures are going to be implemented by individuals. Internet users engage in various activities regularly, including sending and receiving emails, social networking, online shopping, and perusing the web. Users' comprehension of Internet service privacy settings and policies, the significance of privacy that heightens privacy concerns, the quality and quantity of personal information disclosed, and the personal ramifications of potential data breaches on the technological infrastructure that underpins electronic services are all aspects that fall under the category of information privacy awareness. When you use ChatGPT to search for personal information, the results only display online information and are based on ResearchGate, LinkedIn, ORCID, Sci-Profiles, and IGI. Information considered to be sensitive, such as an individual's address or phone number, will not be replied to safeguard personal information and privacy.

6. CONCLUSION

Within the context of the digital age, the dynamic relationship between personal data, privacy, and security has become increasingly complicated. In recent years, there has been an increase in the severity of the significant difficulties linked with cyberattacks, fraud, and invasions of privacy. Companies that gather, analyze, and sell personal information are known as data brokers. The importance of data brokers and their considerable impact on individual privacy is discussed. There has not been any discussion among academics about evaluating customers' privacy concerns about artificial intelligence, notably ChatGPT, even though recent implementations swiftly modify users' perceptions of information privacy. Implementing privacy protection technologies and regimes is essential when utilizing and distributing ChatGPT. The need for user education and training, the significance of condensing privacy rules for greater comprehension, and the necessity of complying with privacy regulations are just some of the many issues that need to be addressed. Different demographics have different attitudes to privacy concerns. Nowadays, the conversation revolves around the protocols and solutions that can be used to bridge these gaps. This highlights the necessity of adopting an all-encompassing strategy to improve privacy protection in the face of constantly increasing cyber threats. Artificial intelligence (AI) and ChatGPT are becoming increasingly utilized by organizations to evaluate massive data sets and address a variety of difficulties that are experienced by businesses and organizations. Consolidating data from a wide variety of users into uniform profiles and analyzing client behaviors to design marketing campaigns accurately are required steps. Individuals have substantial privacy concerns regarding data aggregation into behavioral profiles for machine learning algorithms.

ChatGPT can be beneficial in any field involving communication and any aspect of language processing. Because of its adaptability and versatility, it is a handy tool for companies and organizations operating in various fields. ChatGPT's performance, on the other hand, is subject to certain constraints, the majority of which are associated with privacy, security, ethics, transparency, and unexpected effects. The implementation of proper security measures, the guarantee of openness in the operation of ChatGPT, and the careful consideration of the potential repercussions of its use are all critical steps to take to solve these restrictions.

However, artificial intelligence makes life easier for consumers and makes it easier for businesses to conduct marketing that is more effective and successful. Concerns include the exposure of personal information that was not anticipated, the occurrence of prejudiced outcomes that affect underrepresented populations, and the inability of businesses to remove data from ChatGPT systems in response to user requests. It is necessary to thoroughly investigate AI models' privacy and security problems, particularly ChatGPT. Cyberattacks, deepfake creation, model poisoning, automated programming interface attacks, and prompt injection attacks are all examples of potential security issues. Investigations are conducted into privacy concerns, including data leaking, misuse, and illegal access. In addition, user views are evaluated, which includes concerns regarding public trust, requests for privacy, and the requirement to strike a balance between innovation and security. The techniques presented to alleviate these concerns have been looked at and explored. These are some examples: precautions against security risks, mitigation measures for deepfakes and model poison attacks, and methods to resist API and prompt injection attacks. As an additional point of interest, it provides recommendations for addressing privacy issues and ways to prevent data loss and unwanted access.

7. LIMITATIONS AND RECOMMENDATIONS

It is now impossible to imagine modern communication and task automation without utilizing technologies powered by artificial intelligence (AI), particularly chatbots that AI powers. ChatGPT, which OpenAI developed, has garnered substantial attention because it is a chatbot that processes natural language and is easily accessible to many individuals. On the other hand, concerns regarding privacy and security have been raised in tandem with its development and widespread acceptance. Blog mining is an approach that offers a comprehensive investigation of the security and privacy concerns associated with ChatGPT. The inherent vulnerabilities within the platform are taken from relevant blog posts and supplemented with the most recent literature. The potential dangers that could take advantage of these vulnerabilities are also considered. To be more specific, it sheds light on the dangers associated with the wrong treatment of personal information, the vulnerability to cyberattacks, and the more significant ramifications for preserving human privacy and the safety of businesses all at the same time. In addition, the insights into the legal framework that governs chatbots powered by artificial intelligence reveal potential future research avenues that could be pursued in order to address these challenges effectively. It is important to build comprehensive security measures and legislative frameworks to restrict the hazards of AI-driven chatbots and guarantee that they are employed responsibly in the digital era.

The binary response options of male and female under participant demographics prevented us from inquiring whether an individual was classified as non-binary; this facet should be addressed in further studies. Future research might involve organizations from various countries or expand their scope to include countries with diverse cultural traditions. Last but not least, considering that the new version of ChatGPT will be published later. Therefore, recommended that future research concentrate on users with more experience with ChatGPT, particularly as the platform continues to develop. However, this chapter comprehensively reviews ChatGPT and demonstrates some results regarding privacy information awareness. However, it can fail to include responses. For this reason, it is recommended that subsequent research be conducted using questionnaires or interview surveys to eliminate bias.

REFERENCES

Albayrak, E., & Bağcı, H. (2025). Modelling the effects of personal factors on information security awareness. *Journal of Information Science*, *51*(1), 20–30. DOI: 10.1177/01655515221127609

Alshahrani, H. A. A., & Alrodhan, W. A. (2025). Security and Privacy of ChatGPT: Proposed Enhancements. *IJCSNS*, *25*(2), 23.

Aryania, A., Huertas-Garcia, R., Forgas-Coll, S., Angulo, C., & Alenyà, G. (2025). Effects of Privacy Warning on the Intention to Disclose Personal Information During Interaction with a Robot in Public Spaces. *International Journal of Social Robotics*, •••, 1–19. DOI: 10.1007/s12369-025-01244-3

ChatGPT. (2025). https://chatgpt.com/

Chen, X., Wu, M., Cheng, C., & Mou, J. (2025). Weighing user's privacy calculus on personal information disclosure: The moderating effect of social media identification. *Online Information Review*, *49*(2), 353–372. DOI: 10.1108/OIR-03-2024-0135

Choudhury, A., & Shamszare, H. (2023). Investigating the impact of user trust on the adoption and use of ChatGPT: Survey analysis. *Journal of Medical Internet Research*, *25*, e47184. https://www.jmir.org/2023/1/e47184/. DOI: 10.2196/47184 PMID: 37314848

Chung, J., & Kwon, H. Y. (2025). Privacy fatigue and its effects on ChatGPT acceptance among undergraduate students: Is privacy dead? *Education and Information Technologies*, •••, 1–23. https://link.springer.com/article/10.1007/s10639-024-13198-6. DOI: 10.1007/s10639-024-13198-6

Fahad, S. A., Salloum, S. A., & Shaalan, K. (2024). The role of ChatGPT in knowledge sharing and collaboration within digital workplaces: A systematic review. *Artificial intelligence in education: The power and dangers of ChatGPT in the classroom*, 259-282. https://doi.org/DOI: 10.1007/978-3-031-52280-2_17

Falade, P. V. (2024). Investigating the security and privacy issues in ChatGPT usage and their impact on organisational and individual security. *Int. J. Sci. Res. in Multidisciplinary Studies Vol, 10*(3).

Gupta, V., & Yang, H. (2024). Study protocol for factors influencing the adoption of ChatGPT technology by startups: Perceptions and attitudes of entrepreneurs. *PLoS One*, *19*(2), e0298427. DOI: 10.1371/journal.pone.0298427 PMID: 38358993

Hadi, M. U., Qureshi, R., Shah, A., Irfan, M., Zafar, A., Shaikh, M. B., & Mirjalili, S. (2023). Large language models: a comprehensive survey of its applications, challenges, limitations, and future prospects. *Authorea Preprints, 1*, 1-26.

Hua, S., Jin, S., & Jiang, S. (2024). The limitations and ethical considerations of ChatGPT. *Data Intelligence*, *6*(1), 201–239. DOI: 10.1162/dint_a_00243

Huang, K., Zhang, F., Li, Y., Wright, S., Kidambi, V., & Manral, V. (2023). Security and privacy concerns in ChatGPT. In Beyond, A. I. (Ed.), *ChatGPT, Web3, and the Business Landscape of Tomorrow* (pp. 297–328). Springer Nature Switzerland., DOI: 10.1007/978-3-031-45282-6_11

Humlum, A., & Vestergaard, E. (2024). *The adoption of ChatGPT* (No. 16992). IZA Discussion Papers. https://www.econstor.eu/handle/10419/299920

Lee, Y. S., & Weber, R. A. (2025). Revealed privacy preferences: Are privacy choices rational? *Management Science*, *71*(3), 2657–2677. DOI: 10.1287/mnsc.2022.00807

Liu, Y., Han, T., Ma, S., Zhang, J., Yang, Y., Tian, J., He, H., Li, A., He, M., Liu, Z., Wu, Z., Zhao, L., Zhu, D., Li, X., Qiang, N., Shen, D., Liu, T., & Ge, B. (2023). Summary of chatgpt-related research and perspective towards the future of large language models. *Meta-Radiology*, *1*(2), 100017. DOI: 10.1016/j.metrad.2023.100017

Lokare, D. A., Pathan, S. M., & Dhotre, P. S. (2025, January). Exploring Privacy Challenges: A Survey of Issues, Research Gaps, and Strategies for Protection. In *2025 1st International Conference on AIML-Applications for Engineering & Technology (ICAET)* (pp. 1–6). IEEE. DOI: DOI: 10.1109/ICAET63349.2025.10932284

Lund, B., Agbaji, D., & Teel, Z. A. (2023). Information literacy, data literacy, privacy literacy, and ChatGPT: Technology literacies align with perspectives on emerging technology adoption within communities. *Human Technology*, *19*(2), 163–177. https://papers.ssrn.com/sol3/papers.cfm?abstract_id=4324580. DOI: 10.14254/1795-6889.2023.19-2.2

Menard, P., & Bott, G. J. (2025). Artificial intelligence misuse and concern for information privacy: New construct validation and future directions. *Information Systems Journal*, *35*(1), 322–367. https://onlinelibrary.wiley.com/doi/abs/10.1111/isj.12544. DOI: 10.1111/isj.12544

Putri, R. M., & Utomo, R. G. (2025, February). The Effect of Awareness, Trust, Privacy, and Security on Students Adoption of Digital Banking. In *2025 International Conference on Advancement in Data Science, E-learning and Information System (ICADEIS)* (pp. 1-6). IEEE. DOI: 10.1109/ICADEIS65852.2025.10933127

Renuka, O., RadhaKrishnan, N., Priya, B. S., Jhansy, A., & Ezekiel, S. (2025). Data Privacy and Protection: Legal and Ethical Challenges. Emerging Threats and Countermeasures in Cybersecurity, 433-465.

Riahi, E., & Islam, M. S. (2025). Employees' information security awareness (ISA) in public organisations: Insights from cross-cultural studies in Sweden, France, and Tunisia. *Behaviour & Information Technology*, *44*(1), 79–101. DOI: 10.1080/0144929X.2024.2311734

Sebastian, G. (2023). Privacy and data protection in chatgpt and other ai chatbots: Strategies for securing user information. [IJSPPC]. *International Journal of Security and Privacy in Pervasive Computing*, *15*(1), 1–14. DOI: 10.4018/IJSPPC.325475

Shahzad, M. F., Xu, S., & Javed, I. (2024). ChatGPT awareness, acceptance, and adoption in higher education: The role of trust as a cornerstone. *International Journal of Educational Technology in Higher Education*, *21*(1), 46. https://link.springer.com/article/10.1186/s41239-024-00478-x. DOI: 10.1186/s41239-024-00478-x

Siripipatthanakul, S., & Siripipattanakul, S. (2025, a). Online Gambling of Higher Education Learners. In *International Academic Transformations and Cross-Border Collaborations* (pp. 377-400). IGI Global Scientific Publishing. DOI: DOI: 10.4018/979-8-3373-0508-0.ch015

Siripipatthanakul, S., & Siripipattanakul, S. (2025, b). Rural Dental Health Transformation by Adopting Digital Technologies. *Transforming Dental Health in Rural Communities: Digital Dentistry*, 47-80.

Siripipatthanakul, S., & Siripipattanakul, S. (2025, c). Talent Management Ensuring the Safety and Cybersecurity in Schools. *Cultivating Creativity and Navigating Talent Management in Academia*, 383-402.

Sun, Y., Zhang, Y. F., Wang, Y., & Zhang, S. (2025). Cooperative governance mechanisms for personal information security: An evolutionary game approach. *Kybernetes*, *54*(1), 431–455. DOI: 10.1108/K-04-2023-0717

Tsohou, A., & Soumelidou, A. (2025). Information Privacy Awareness. In Jajodia, S., Samarati, P., & Yung, M. (Eds.), *Encyclopedia of Cryptography, Security and Privacy*. Springer., DOI: 10.1007/978-3-030-71522-9_1484

Ullah, I., Hassan, N., Gill, S. S., Suleiman, B., Ahanger, T. A., Shah, Z., Qadir, J., & Kanhere, S. S. (2024). Privacy preserving large language models: ChatGPT case study based vision and framework. *IET Blockchain*, *4*(S1), 706–724. Advance online publication. DOI: 10.1049/blc2.12091

Wibowo, G., Gunawan, I., & Sunuantari, M. (2024). Social network analysis# ChatGPT on social media. *International Journal of Innovative Research in Multidisciplinary Education*, *3*(07), 1178–1186. DOI: 10.58806/ijirme.2024.v3i7n02

Wu, X., Duan, R., & Ni, J. (2024). Unveiling security, privacy, and ethical concerns of ChatGPT. *Journal of Information and Intelligence*, *2*(2), 102–115. DOI: 10.1016/j.jiixd.2023.10.007

Chapter 8
Strategic Planning on Airport Infrastructure in the Northern Malaysia Region:
The Relevance of Privacy and Cyber Security

Seng Loong Stanley Kok
https://orcid.org/0009-0006-0997-7960
Manipal GlobalNxt University, Malaysia

Sutithep Siripipattanakul
https://orcid.org/0000-0002-5477-6723
Kasetsart University, Thailand

ABSTRACT

Academics and politicians agree that airport infrastructure boosts regional economic development, connectivity, and competitiveness. Airport infrastructure in Northern Malaysia is essential for attracting Foreign Direct Investments (FDI), tourism, trade, and logistics. Due to its proximity to Indonesia and Thailand and economic strength, northern Malaysia is well-positioned to use airport development as a regional competitive advantage. For decades, Penang International Airport (PIA) has been Northern Malaysia's main domestic and international airport. Like many others in Malaysia, the airport suffers capacity issues, obsolete infrastructure, government funding constraints, limited growth opportunities, and the need for privacy and security management for sustainable adaptations. These reasons demonstrate the urgent necessity for a comprehensive airport development plan

DOI: 10.4018/979-8-3693-9720-6.ch008

in Northern Malaysia to incorporate privacy and cyber security management for competitive advantage and sustainable development.

1. INTRODUCTION

1.1 Overview of the Malaysia Airport Industry

Malaysia's airport industry has been characterized as highly regulated due to its strategic national importance and security considerations. The regulatory framework fosters a near-monopoly market structure that has historically been dominated by Government-Linked Companies (GLCs) (MAVCOM, 2019). Before 1992, Malaysian airports were directly operated by the Directorate of Civil Aviation (DCA), providing navigation services through its Air Traffic Management Sector and other related branches. In 1991, the Airport and Aviation Service (Operating Company) Act was enacted as part of the Malaysian government's privatization initiatives. This legislation led to the division of the Department of Civil Aviation into two distinct entities: the DCA, which remained the regulatory authority overseeing airports, and a newly incorporated company tasked with the operation, management, and maintenance of Malaysian airports (ICAO, 2013).

The privatization process marked the establishment of Malaysia Airport Berhad (MAB) in 1992, which assumed the role of airport operator. In November 1999, MAB transitioned into a public limited company named Malaysia Airports Holdings Berhad (MAHB). It was subsequently listed on the Kuala Lumpur Stock Exchange, the first publicly listed airport operating company in Asia. Malaysian government retains a “Special Voting Share” in MAHB and Malaysia Sepang (the entity responsible for operating KLIA). This special share gives the government veto power to approve extraordinary transactions or significant operational changes within the two entities.

In 2020, the Transport Ministry of Malaysia introduced Malaysia's National Aviation Strategic Plan (NASP), a comprehensive framework designed to enhance the safety, efficiency, and sustainability of the nation's aviation sector. It aligns with international standards, including the Global Aviation Safety Plan (GASP) and the Asia Pacific Regional Aviation Safety Plan (AP-RASP), ensuring Malaysia's aviation policies are globally competitive. The NASP is closely integrated with Malaysia's National Transport Policy (NTP) 2019–2030, which aims to position the country as a global aviation hub. This alignment ensures that aviation development contributes to Malaysia's broader transportation and economic objectives. The NASP sets the foundation for long-term aviation safety and infrastructure development, aligning with Malaysia's broader goals of becoming a global aviation hub. However, in 2024,

Transport Minister Anthony Loke dismissed the relevance of NASP (Kamarul & Kang, 2024).

In 2025, to enhance MAHB's global competitiveness while maintaining its commitment to sustainable national airport development and passenger experience, MAHB enters a significant acquisition process led by the Gateway Development Alliance (GDA). This consortium includes Khazanah Nasional Berhad, the Employees Provident Fund (EPF), the Abu Dhabi Investment Authority (ADIA), and Global Infrastructure Partners (GIP). The consortium has made a conditional voluntary offer to acquire all remaining shares of MAHB at RM11 per share, valuing the company at RM18.4 billion to take MAHB private and delist it from the Bursa Malaysia stock exchange. Upon completion, Khazanah's stake in MAHB will increase from 33.2% to 40%, while EPF's shareholding will rise from 7.9% to 30%. ADIA and GIP will collectively hold the remaining 30%. The acquisition aims to unlock capital for infrastructure upgrades and operational improvements across MAHB's network of 39 airports, including five international hubs.

1.2 Geopolitical Landscape in Northern Regions 2000-2025

The political governance in Northern Malaysia from 2000 to 2025 reflects the region's evolving dynamics within Malaysia's domestic political landscape. This period has been marked by shifts in governance regime, electoral changes, and the interplay of regional and national interests (Figure 1.1).

2000–2010: Development Centric Policies and Shift of Electoral Support

During the early 2000s, Northern Malaysia, particularly Kedah, Penang, Perak, and Perlis, experienced political stability under the governance of the Barisan Nasional (BN) coalition led by then Prime Minister Tun Abdullah Ahmad Badawi, who succeeded the longest-serving former Prime Minister Tun Mahathir Mohammed. Before 2008, BN's dominance was characterized by policies aimed at economic development and infrastructure expansion (such as the construction of the Second Penang Bridge and the electrification of double rail tracks). As a key economic hub, Penang benefited from FDIs in manufacturing and trade, solidifying its role as a regional powerhouse. Southern Kedah experienced commendable economic growth, which observed an influx of FDIs resulting from the spillover effect from the Penang state.

However, the growing dissatisfaction with BN's governance, surrounded by corruption allegations, calls for more significant reform, transparency, and accountability. As a result, the 2008 general elections marked a shift in the governance regime.

Table 1. Major airport infrastructures in Northern Malaysia (Author created, 2025)

No.	Description	Functions	Capacity
1.	Penang International Airport (PIA) – Bayan Lepas, Penang	• *The Main Aviation Gateway for both domestic and international flights in Northern Malaysia* • *Supports Kedah & Penang's role as a global semiconductor manufacturing hub and leading destination for medical tourism.* • *Facilitates cargo operations, making it the 2nd largest air freight hub in terms of cargo tonnage after Kuala Lumpur International Airport (KLIA), highest in terms of export value in Malaysia.*	• 6.5 million passenger per annum (expansion in progress to 12.0 million passengers per annum) • Cargo Centre of 360,000 MT • In 2024, 7.6 million passengers and 103,423 MT cargo handled.
2.	Langkawi International Airport (LGK) – Langkawi Island, Kedah	• *As gateway for tourism, connecting Langkawi to major cities in Southeast Asia & beyond.* • *Supports the island's economy by facilitating international & domestic travel.* • *Main venue for the Langkawi International Maritime & Aerospace Exhibition (LIMA)*	• 4.0 million passenger per annum • 2.5 million passengers handled in 2024.
3.	Sultan Abdul Halim Airport (AOR) – Alor Setar, Kedah	• *Serving the domestic aviation connectivity needs for northern Kedah region and the state of Perlis.* • *Serve as the runway for Royal Malaysian Air Force training division.*	• 800,000 passenger capacity • 546,916 passengers handled in 2024.
4.	Sultan Azlan Shah Airport (IPH) – Ipoh, Perak.	• *Serves as a gateway for Perak's tourism and business sectors.* • *Facilitates mainly domestic aviation connectivity and limited international services.*	• 500,000 passenger capacity (expansion in progress to 700,000 passengers per annum) • 512,000 passengers handled in 2024.
5.	Pangkor Airport – Pangkor Island, Perak	• *Accessibility to the island, supporting local tourism and economic growth.*	• A small airport designed for short take-off and landing (STOL) operations, with limited passenger capacity
6.	Royal Malaysian Air Force (RMAF) Butterworth Air Base – Butterworth, Penang	• *A military airbase, with facilities for emergency and ad-hoc civilian operations.* • *Supports national security and regional defence operations.* • *Joint training support headquarter for Headquarters Integrated Area Defence System (HQIADS)*	• Military Air base for the RMAF • A Commander Integrated Area Defense System (CIADS) regional military air base under the Five Power Defence Arrangements (FPDA). • Acts as a backup for civilian air traffic during emergencies.

In summary, airports in Northern Malaysia can be described as long established (with the oldest being before the World War II era), serving civil and military purposes since their inception. Driven by the economic and defense development, most of these airports undergone various phases of expansion and upgrades, nonetheless, other than strategic defense reasons, not all these airports are operating at a commercially viable level due to the development of other logistic infrastructures (such as inter-states toll highways and electrified rail systems) within the region coupled with limitations for future expansion due to the geographical factors over the past five decades. While acknowledging the essential importance of airport development towards economic growth, airports undeniably play a significant role in contributing to carbon emissions, both directly and indirectly. Building new airports or expanding existing ones leads to emissions from construction activities and land-use changes. Emissions from ground operations, including vehicles, energy use in terminals, and auxiliary power units for aircraft. Aircraft emissions during takeoff, landing, and taxiing are also significant contributors. While these emissions are often attributed to airlines, airports facilitate these operations, associating them with the broader carbon footprint. Hence, proper strategic planning is crucial in airport development to balance sustainable economic development with climate resilience.

1.4 Northern Malaysia Airport Infrastructures Proposals

The idea of a new airport in Northern Malaysia has been discussed since the early 2000s, driven by the increasing congestion at PIA and the imminent need for a modern aviation hub in the Northern Malaysia region. Based on searches on the public domain, official press release and mainstream medias at the point of this study, there are three main airport proposals identified which aim to serve the future Northern Malaysia's aviation needs, namely the PIA expansion plan, Kulim International Airport (KXP) and the Northern Malaysia International Airport (NMIA). This overview of each of the proposals is as follows:

PIA: 12 Million Passenger Capacity Expansion Plan

The call for PIA expansion came in 2014, merely one year after the whole operation of the new 6.5 million capacity expansion, which observed that the actual passenger handling reached 6.04 million or 92.9% of the intended capacity that year. The expansion plan faces challenges and delays due to the political tension between the state and federal ruling regime, the COVID-19 pandemic, and policy uncertainty (Mok, 2020; Nambiar, 2020; MalaysiaKini, 2020).

The expansion plan was approved at the parliament's Budget 2023 session in 2023, nearly 10 years after the initial request. In 2024, the expansion costs are estimated up to RM1.5 billion, consisting of airside facility upgrades and the construction of a new terminal building on the existing PIA site with an expanded passenger handling capacity up to 12 million, which is expected to be completed by 2028 (Tan & Teng, 2024; Dermawan, 2025).

KXP: Kedah Aerotropolis – The Economic Game Changer

KXP is a proposed new international airport located in the state of Kedah. KXP was initially conceived in the 1990s as a catalyst for the development of greenfield Kulim High Tech Park to attract investment in high-tech manufacturing industries. However, the idea generally received strong opposition and criticism on its viability, especially from the Penang state. In 2014, then Menteri Besar of Kedah state reintroduce the idea with an ambitious scope, namely the KXP Airport City Plan, a 9,841 acres consists of KXP airport facilities with Passenger, Cargo and Maintenance Repair Overhaul (MRO) hub, a residential-commercial-industrial hub and Sidam Advanced Manufacturing And Logistics Hub (SLAM) focusing on high-value activities in manufacturing, logistics and aerospace (Avionics and aircraft interiors manufacturing activities) (Hashim, 2023). As of 2025, the project is estimated to cost approximately RM7.0 billion.

In 2019, KXP received its approval in principle as part of Kedah's High Impact Projects from the federal government of Malaysia (Halid, 2019). Due to the COVID-19 pandemic and policy uncertainty, KXP faced various challenges (such as funding issues and obtaining necessary approvals) and criticisms over its viability, which resulted in delays in terms of the development progress (Tay, 2023; Zulkifli, 2022; 2024). While the official statement claims KXP is not in competition with PIA, such a claim often raises doubts from the Penang state, which may adversely affect the regional economy (Dermawan, 2019).

NMIA: The Tri-state Regional International Airport

The Northern Malaysia International Airport (NMIA) plan is a strategic initiative to address the future demand for air travel in northern Malaysia, which was introduced in 2019 (Zahiid, 2019). It envisions relocating the existing Penang International Airport (PIA), which is faced with limitations due to further expansion and traffic congestion and is positioned as the Northern Malaysia regional aviation gateway. NMIA to be located at the mainland tri-state borders (Kedah-Penang-Perak), approximately 2,600 acres, with considerations for inter-connectivity to major transportation networks, including highways, seaports, and the double track electrified rail grid.

With an initial single run-way, passenger handling capacity of 16 million and a air cargo hub of 400,000 MT (with phase 2, expandable passenger capacity to 25 million and an second runway), a KTM-ETS station within the airport, and a City Check-in Terminal at Penang Island (connected to NMIA via airport transit rail link), NMIA is designed to handle a significant volume of passengers and cargo, alleviating pressure on existing PIA. Designed with sustainability principles, NMIA will adhere to Smart-Airport innovation and integrate green technologies and clean energy to minimize carbon emission footprint. The airport is designed to serve as an aviation hub for regional social-economic development in Penang state, northern Perak, and southern Kedah.

1.5 Vulnerability of Data Privacy and Cyberattack in Malaysia Airport Operations

In the information era, cyber threats to airport operations are emerging to become a primary concern, especially with the increasing use of technologies such as Wireless Fidelity (WiFi), Internet, IoT, Global Positioning System (GPS), open-source systems, virtualization and cloud computing services have been central in the optimization of aviation operations, reducing costs and response times through enhanced inter-operability (Gopalakrishnan et al., 2013; Haass et al., 2016).

Florido-Benítez (2024) studies identified 54 cyberattacks documented from 2000 to January 2024. Of the total cyberattacks in the period analysed, 35 were perpetrated at airports (65%) and 19 on airlines (35%). Distributed Denial-of-Service (DDoS) attacks are the most common in the aviation industry because they do not require significant resources and knowledge. Airports and airlines are vulnerable to DDoS attacks because they use digital technology and wireless communication in their day-to-day operations. Since safety is the most important factor in air transport for passengers and companies, cybersecurity must be a priority and not a necessity in the aviation industry, especially for airport operations.

In recent years, the cybersecurity vulnerability of Malaysia's airport infrastructure has been in the spotlight. In August 2019, KLIA (Kuala Lumpur International Airport) system failure primarily involved a network glitch affecting the airport's infrastructure. The failure was attributed to many factors, including outdated equipment and a lack of timely upgrades, ultimately leading to operational disruptions for days (Shankar, 2019). In March 2025, the cyberattack on Kuala Lumpur International Airport's (KLIA) systems caused a several-hour disruption. It rendered the airport's flight information display system, check-in counters, and baggage handling inoperative, forcing airlines and airport staff to switch to manual operations (Nizam, 2025). The initial findings suggested a cyber intrusion had compromised KLIA's critical systems, leading to the prolonged outage.

2. LITERATURE REVIEWS

2.1 Competitiveness and Sustainable Competitive Advantage Theory

Porter (1980) categorises the concept of competitiveness into three levels, namely 1) the national level, 2) the industrial level, and 3) the firm level. At the different levels of analysis, it leads to different interpretations of competitiveness, which implies the non-existence of a universal definition of competitiveness, which makes it difficult to quantify and measure. Scott and Lodge (1985) define competitiveness on a national level as "a country's ability to create, produce, distribute and/or service products in international trade while earning rising returns on its resources". Wibowo & Nurcahyo (2020) suggest the concept of competitiveness is instrumental in strategy formulation to strengthen national (region) level competitiveness by integrating macroeconomic policies. Hence, competitiveness is essential in analysing the strategic airport infrastructure planning. The region may foster a competitive advantage derived from strategic logistic infrastructures that will enable seamless access to the global supply chain and target market, improving the region's attractiveness to investors.

The concept of competitive advantage forms one of the essential pillars in strategic management that explains what accounts for differences in performance across firms (Sigalas & Papadakis, 2018) and is applied in various business and economic studies (Nilsson & Peterson, 2002). Porter (1998) highlighted the three circumstances that are pivotal in attaining a sustainable competitive advantage:

- **The source of the advantage:** Advantages derived from strategic locations such as access to resources (manpower, infrastructures, etc.), inter-connectivity to supply chain network and market (supporting industries, logistic network, etc.).
- **The number of sources of the advantage:** Strategic locations with less competitive advantage may easily be imitated by competing rivalries.
- **The upgrading and improvement of the region:** In the long run, sustained competitive advantage requires upgrading and improving the sources into more sustainable types (Porter, 1998).

2.2 Strategy and Strategic Planning

The concept of strategy can be traced back to ancient times and is commonly applied in the military. Its application in the modern era is widely adopted in all aspects of life, from business to policy-making. Mintzberg (1994) summarises four common ways strategy is applied – 1) As *plan*, a "how," a means of getting from here to there; 2) As a *pattern* in actions over time - for example, firms regularly markets premium products adopt a "high end" strategy; 3) As a *position*, which reflects decisions to offer particular products or services in particular markets; and 4) As a *perspective* - vision and direction.

Mintzberg further argues that strategy emerges over time as intentions collide with and accommodate a changing reality. Thus, one might start with a *perspective* and conclude that it calls for a specific *position*, which is to be achieved by way of a carefully crafted *plan*, with the eventual outcome and strategy reflected in a *pattern* evident in decisions and actions over time. This pattern in decisions and actions is defined as an *emergent strategy* (Nickols, 2012). Porter (1986) further suggests that strategy, from a competitive position, is about differentiating in the eyes of the customers (stakeholders) and about adding value through a mix of activities different from those deployed by competing rivalries. These form the principles of Porter's definition of competitive strategy as "a combination of the ends (goals) for which the firm is striving and the means (policies) by which it is seeking to get there".

Figure 2. Design school paradigm - strategic planning processes

(Mintzberg, 1990)

Kraus et al. (2007) suggest strategic planning is the attempt to prepare for all eventualities by abstraction and thus to account for the environment's complexity and dynamics. This entails the need to build alternative future scenarios and configurations. Pennings (1985) argues that strategic planning processes deliberately guide the course of the organization by focusing on adjusting the organization to its surroundings through a series of consecutive steps which identify SWOT, i.e. internal strengths and weaknesses and external opportunities and threats. SWOT is the initial stage of Mintzberg's (1990) framework of the conventional strategic planning process (Figure 2.1), known as the fundamental *Design School Paradigm*.

2.3 Concept of Aerotropolis

Aerotropolis is a concept of urban transformation leveraging airports as the core of its economic activities. Pioneered by Kasarda (2000), who argued that airports would have the same impact on urban development in the 21st century that seaports had in the 18th century, railroads in the 19th century, and highways in the 20th century. This concept has attracted the interest of many scholars and policymakers, given its potential to stimulate regional economic growth (Ekaputra & Simamora, 2024). Kasarda (2008) suggests that with the airport itself serving as a region-wide multimodal transportation and commercial nexus, strings and clusters of airport-linked developments such as business parks, information and communications technology complexes, retail, hotel and entertainment centres, industrial parks, logistics parks, wholesale merchandise marts and residential developments formed along airport arteries up to 20 miles outward with the economic impact potential up to 60 miles from the airports.

However, the Aerotropolis-driven development also attracts considerable criticism. These criticisms include social-economics concern surrounding overrating the significant of air transport for goods (Chohan, 2019), carbon emission (Charles et al., 2007; Huston, 2015), inflation and social repercussions tend to focus on business rather than people (Frétigny et al., 2024; Kwan, 2025), state intervention and huge fundings requirements on public infrastructures and land acquisition (Hall, 1998; Kasarda; 2008; Meckelburg, & Wardana, 2024), vulnerability to aviation demand (COVID-19 & economic downturn) (Chung, 2015; Kazda et al., 2022; Liou et al., 2024). Cidell (2015) further argues that there is insufficient evidence on the scale of the airport and its immediate surroundings to justify investing in airport-led development and that the role of the local metropolitan context in economic development associated with airports is often overlooked.

2.4 Airport Site Selection Approach

ITF-OECD (2017) describes decisions on major airport investments as often contentious and controversial due to fundamental trade-offs to consider between the national and local impacts of airport capacity expansion, which are often exacerbated by significant risks and uncertainties. While major airport investments have the potential to contribute to a host of significant social, economic, and environmental impacts, these impacts often conflict with each other (economic development at the expense of environmental preservation). These conflicting interests can trigger significant opposition and impose challenges to airport investment.

Airport infrastructure is often time-consuming and requires substantial financial considerations. Once construction commences, the process is difficult to reverse without significant losses. This implies that infrastructure investment planning is inherently exposed to considerable risks and uncertainties regarding how the project's impacts are likely to develop over the investment's lifetime. Hence, addressing the conflicting interests at play will improve the support needed from various divergent stakeholders, ensuring the successful implementation of large airport infrastructure projects. Airport site selection is a complex task that requires careful evaluation of multiple criteria, such as accessibility, environmental impact, risk assessment, and passenger demand. The selection of an appropriate airport site has significant implications for air transport's safety, efficiency, and sustainability (Rangsaritvorakarn, 2023).

Multiple Criteria Decision Analysis (MCDA)

Multiple Criteria Decision Analysis (MCDA) is a structured decision-making framework to evaluate and prioritize alternatives based on multiple criteria. MCDA is commonly used in various studies on infrastructure planning (Abdullah et al., 2021). The MCDA framework begins by identifying the decision problem and objectives and then establishing relevant criteria that reflect the decision's goals. Criteria are prioritised based on their relative importance by assigning weights to these criteria. Based on the sets of criteria, the alternatives are evaluated based on scores. Alternatives' aggregated scores are ranked by using mathematical models.

MCDA has often been used with combined techniques such as the Analytical Hierarchy Process (AHP), TOPSIS, PROMETHEE, VIKOR, and other mixed-method approaches (Sennaroglu & Celebi, 2018; Ramu et al., 2020; Abdullah et al., 2021; Rangsaritvorakarn, 2023). It provides the flexibility for integrating quantitative and qualitative data, suitable for complex, contradicting, multidisciplinary problems (Talukder et al., 2021). The MCDA framework provides transparency, structure, and rationality, which are relevant to decision-making processes (Abdullah et al.,

2021; Talukder et al., 2021). Hence, challenges remain, as subjective weight assignment and computational complexity tend to produce contrasting recommendations (Dean, 2022).

Criteria Influencing Airport Site Selection

Determining the appropriate criteria for airport site selection is a complex task that varies based on prior academic and policy regimes. In the Asia context, case study of Kansai Airport Osaka Japan, seven criteria are considered for the airport site selection in 1974, namely, 1) *flight paths and airport capacity*, 2*) convenience for users*, 3) *construction issues*, 4) *environmental impacts*, 5) *co-ordination with vested interests*, 6) *integrity with the future vision of the surrounding region*, and 7) *regional development effect* (ITF-OECD (2017). Among the seven criteria, numbers 1, 2, and 3 are mainly related to the *basic functioning of the airport*. Criteria 4, 5, 6, and 7 deal with the relationship between *airport development and the surrounding region*.

In the scenario of Youngnam airport South Korea airport site selection, Aéroports de Paris Ingénierie (ADPI) adopts a set of seven criteria considerations, namely 1) *Strategic fit* considerations based on market and expansion potential, 2) *Operational* considerations which comprise of airspace availability, Standard Instrument Departures (SID) and Standard Terminal Arrival Routes (STARs) characteristics and holding capacity, hazards and obstacles (mountains, man-made obstacles, birds, ships etc) and meteorology. 3) *Site potential* considerations include surface access such as road, rail, light rail, and metro. 4) *Socio-economic impacts* considerations which includes economic, social, 5) Ecological impact considerations on carbon emission, ecosystem (water, habitat loss, deforestation etc), 6) Financial considerations such as land acquisition and compensation, airport construction, access and utilities connections and operations, 7) Risk and deliverability consideration on technical challenges and construction risks, potential for legal challenge, potential for political/decision making hurdles, competition on nearby airports and phasing potential (ITF-OECD (2017).

Rangsaritvorakarn's (2023) study highlights five main criteria pivotal to airport site selection (figure 2.2) based on a review of 16 prior studies on airport site selection and multi-criteria decision-making techniques. The studies suggest that *environmental* criteria are the primary focus when selecting an airport site. This is followed by *geographic accessibility* criteria, which include convenience in connecting to other modes of transportation. This is followed by *topography*, which must be evaluated before analysing *safety and risk* criteria, which involves assessing natural hazards. Finally, *social* criteria which refers to accessibility to airport facilities have the least impact on airport site selection.

Table 2. The Northern Malaysia region's unique backdrop, four sets of criteria for evaluating the three options as follows:

No.	Criteria	Considerations
1	Geographic Accessibility	Proximity to transportation network, availability of land and infrastructure, and distance to nearby airport. (Palczewski & Sałabun, 2019; Erkan & Elsharida, 2019; Rangsaritvorakarn, 2023)
2	Strategic Economic Impact	Market & Expansion Potential (ITF-OECD, 2017; Erkan & Elsharida, 2019)
3	Social-Environmental Impact	Water Quality (ITF-OECD, 2017), Noise (Sennaroglu & Celebi, 2018; Ramu et al., 2020; Alves et al., 2020)
4	Risks and Deliverability	Conflict with air corridors (no-fly zone) (ITF-OECD, 2017; Sennaroglu & Celebi, 2018; Zhang et al., 2021), Delivery challenges (ITD-OECD, 2017; Rangsaritvorakarn, 2023)

2.5 Privacy and Cyber Security Management

Information technology grew rapidly in the 1980s and 1990s, but privacy received little attention. Designing to make information widely accessible without considering whether an individual had a wish or right to regulate access and usage was the priority. It expects a rising awareness of the need to handle privacy concerns in information technology, which will require knowledge of information usage regulations and developing solutions to implement them. Our research focuses on designing a privacy management workbench for policy formulation, implementation, and compliance monitoring. Identifying organizational privacy requirements, reviewing existing technology, researching alternatives to meet these requirements, and iteratively creating and validating a prototype with target users for flexible privacy technologies are essential (Brodie et al., 2005).

Urban transportation constitutes a dynamic and non-linear complicated system. This technology allows unauthorized entities in the metropolitan area to edit, monitor, forge, and access private, public, and resource information of depot staff and communication agents. Current solutions for managing the security and privacy of communication agents in an intelligent public transportation system (IPTS) fail to accommodate the dynamic nature of real-time event information. Consequently, current methods are inadequate to tackle the randomness and other attributes associated with a non-linear complex system like an intelligent transport system (ITS). Hence, the privacy and security protocol are pivotal to ensure the integrity for Intelligent Transportation System. It ensures privacy and security management in the transportation sector throughout the interchange of information related to operation management, resource allocation and preventive maintenance.

The lack of the aforementioned plan results in issues of system breach and cyber-hacking. Emergent intelligence (EI) technique to gather, evaluate, and disseminate information, facilitating dynamic decision-making pertaining to security and privacy management within the transportation sector. The EI technique offers autonomy, flexibility, adaptability, robustness, self-organization, and evolution to manage the randomness and dynamics of a non-linear complex system related to metropolitan transportation systems (Chavhan et al., 2020).

The global digitalization of services has led to the emergence of passenger Intelligent Transportation Systems (ITSs) as revolutionary elements to enhance competitiveness and passenger experience; thus, the framework for managing information security and privacy is crucial. The Intelligent Transportation Systems in some areas of the European Union offers insights into actual ITS deployments, facilitating a comprehensive comparison with the proposed cutting-edge solutions. It is suggested that Intelligent Transportation Systems need to strengthen their information security and privacy management frameworks and to reconcile the disparity between research concepts and practical execution (Bakhtina et al., 2024).

Hence, smart cities featuring integrated public transportation systems raise significant privacy issues regarding the data gathered on passengers and their travel behaviors—the assessment of security and privacy issues in Intelligent Transportation Systems (ITS). While the transportation and logistics sector is experiencing a substantial digital transformation, adopting trends redefining the industry's landscape. Internet of Things (IoT) devices optimize supply chain management through real-time tracking and monitoring of commodities, the full potential can only be attainable provided the privacy and security of data and information is protected.

The emergence of Artificial intelligence (AI) enhances routing and predictive maintenance, minimizing downtime and augmenting efficiency. Software provides scalable and adaptable management systems, whilst cloud computing supplies the essential foundation for extensive data storage and analysis. There are many primary catalysts for this digital transition. Customer anticipations for expedited and more transparent services are increasing. The competitive market environment compels organizations to innovate or face obsolescence.

Regulatory demands are increasing, necessitating increasingly rigorous compliance and reporting standards. Collectively, these elements are driving the industry toward a more computerized future. The advantages of digitalization in transportation and logistics are evident. Automation and more excellent data flow augment operational efficiency, decreasing costs and errors. The customer experience is enhanced through improved service reliability and tailored products. Furthermore, digitalization facilitates the management of heightened clientele and commodities traffic without a corresponding rise in operational expenses. Nevertheless, the implementation of digital technologies necessitates the establishment of stringent data security and privacy protocols. A digital-centric landscape introduces novel threats, necessitating enterprises allocate resources towards cybersecurity and data protection methods. Securing consumer and operational data is not merely a legislative obligation but a fundamental element of trust in the digital world.

3. METHODOLOGY

The data collection in this chapter was based on scholarly papers validated with peer reviews and published on reliable sources, such as Scopus, Web of Science (WOS), and Google Scholarly. The publication years are mainly between 2020 and 2025, and the articles are in English.

The narrative and systematic review was based on the studies of Siripipatthanakul & Siripipattanakul (2025, a &b), and Lim (2023), who suggested a narrative summary accompany this lengthy literature assessment. Narrative synthesis aims to summarize and explain synthesis results in academic writing. The qualitative research process comprises four steps: research design, data collecting, analysis, and report writing. Whereas, the PRISM method was used to select the papers in four steps; identification, screening, eligibility assessment, and inclusion of studies Content analysis is a qualitative method that organizes verbal, visual, or written material to describe phenomena and draw appropriate conclusions objectively. This method of data analysis is appropriate for systematized qualitative reviews. To find knowledge and theory, systematic qualitative evaluators must adjust content analysis methodologies to match highly organized and contextualized information.

Finally, this study used qualitative content analysis. Purposive sampling of secondary data employed terms such as Infrastructure Development, Airport Planning, Strategic Planning, Competitive Advantage, Privacy, and Cyber Security Management. The data analysis in this chapter is based on analysis and synthesis, which also uses principles of the SWOT-MCDA framework.

4. RESULTS

Table 3. Analysis of the airport site options based on the criteria framework

No.	Domains	PIA	KXP	NMIA
1.	Geographic Accessibility	• Located at an approximately 800-acre land area in the southeastern area of Penang Island. • Surrounded by a well-developed free trade industrial zone with an established international logistic network. (InvestPenang, 2025) • Connect with the proposed new LRT mass transit network. (Malay Mail, 2025) • 2 cross-strait bridges served as the main connectivity to the mainland region. • Within a 49 km radius of central industrial hubs in Northern Malaysia (Bayan Lepas, Kulim, Batu Kawan) • Approximately 29 km from the Butterworth, Penang seaport and rail station.	• Located at the Siram Kiri district of Kedah, occupying 5,114 acres of land area. (part of the 9,841-acre KXP Airport city plan) • The proposed site is currently a palm oil plantation estate. • Approximately 20 km away from the nearest North-South Highway (PLUS) toll – Sungai Petani • Approximately 46km away from Butterworth-Kulim Expressway (BKE) • Approximately 17 km away from the Sungai Petani Rail Station. • Approximately 40 km from Kulim High Tech Park, 70 km from Bayan Lepas Industrial Zone, 75 km from Batu Kawan Industrial Park • Approximately 50 km from the Butterworth, Penang seaport and rail station.	• Located in the vicinity of Nibong Tebal (Penang) - Parit Buntar (Perak) - Bandar Baharu (Kedah) (Tri State Border Area). • To occupy approximately 2,600 acres of land area. • The proposed site is mainly a paddy field plantation. • Approximately 10 km from the nearest PLUS toll (Jawi and Bandar Baharu). • Approximately 5 km from the Nibong Tebal and Parit Buntar Rail Station. • Approximately 23 km from Batu Kawan Industrial Park, 36 km from Kulim High Tech Park, 45 km from Bayan Lepas Industrial Zone. • Approximately 38 km from the Butterworth, Penang seaport and rail station.

Table 4.

2.	Strategic Economic Impact	• Proven track record in serving the air cargo needs for high-value industries such as Electrical and electronics, Medical Devices, Aerospace / Avionics, Precision Engineering, and equipment. • proximity with high-tech industrial park development at Penang Mainland, Kedah, and Perak (MIDA, 2023). • Main Aviation Gateway for Tourism and Healthcare Tourism • The expansion plan will elevate the existing PIA infrastructure to accommodate the demand, up to a 12 million passenger handling capacity. • A pivotal component for Penang state vision to become a regional financial centre.	• Greenfield development proposal: It is in Close proximity to high-tech industrial park development at Penang Mainland, Kedah, and Perak (MIDA, 2023). • Potential economic development for the region of Kulim-Sungai Petani - Baling - Kepala Batas-Bukit Mertajam - Seberang Jaya (Hanan et al., 2022). • Strive to become the main international gateway to Malaysia within the Indonesia—Malaysia- Thailand Growth Triangle (IMT-GT) and the Northern Corridor Economic Region (NCER). • Position to be the Kedah Aerotropolis as "Memphis of ASEAN".	• Proximity to high-tech industrial parks in Penang, Kedah, and Perak (MIDA, 2023). • A strategic proximity with the regional logistic infrastructures (seaport, highways, and rail grid) • Relocate the existing PIA and make way for new development on the existing PIA site. • Potential uplift and accelerate the under-developed clusters of the Tri-State Border region. • Strategic alignment to the Kedah-Penang-Perak state development vision for the industrial development in the mainland northern region. • Wider impact outreach with the potential of fostering more balanced economic growth between the Northern Malaysia states. • City Check-In Terminal with Airport Express Transit Link will potentially foster a new CBD district on the existing PIA site.

continued on following page

Table 4. Continued

3.	**Social-Environmental Impact**	• The surrounding of PIA is described as a matured eco-system with fully developed industrial zone, coupled with rapid residential and commercial development. • Lack of natural land for further expansion (without massive land reclamation) • Climate change coupled with rapid development within 5 km radius of PIA, has experienced flash flood incidents (Basyir, 2018; Dermawan, 2022) & worsening traffic congestion (Liew & Lee, 2024). • With the industrial development shift towards mainland, the dependence on the 2 cross-straits bridges may poses traffic congestions and disruption on cargo handling. • The aging PIA facilities may not be operational effective on addressing carbon footprint issues. Major overhaul on the existing facilities may impose high investments than anticipated.	• KXP development is planned on existing palm oil plantation estates, given its remote location, substantial infrastructure is required (road access, public utilities). • The designated development area is located along the river bank of Muda River – the main water source for water supply to Penang & Kedah state. • Deforestation (clearing the palm oil plantation) and relocation of local community is needed to make way for the development. • The massive industrial-logistic centric development of KXP airport city will required substantial skilled manpower in the respective expertise. • Active engagement with regional stakeholders especially Penang state (both public and private sectors) are essential for the success of the development.	• NMIA development is planned on existing paddy field area, while the fundamental logistics infrastructures are within its vicinity, considerable upgrade and last-mile integration is required (road access, public utilities etc). • Deforestation (clearing the paddy field) and relocation of local community is needed to make way for the development. • The existence of massive mangrove areas along the shoreline are within 2km radius of the proposed area. • Active engagement with regional stakeholders between Kedah-Penang-Perak states (both public and private sectors) are essential for the success of the development. • Noise pollution and traffic congestion is pivotal consideration of the proposed site.

continued on following page

Table 4. Continued

4.	**Risks and Deliverability**	• High rise real estate development potentials is restricted by building heights limits regulations and pose a potential operating risk. • Lack of future expansion growth given the massive developments – competing for land resources. • While expansion plan is on the way, construction work poses challenges as the airport is still operational during constructions which may results in costs overrun and delay in deliveries. • With the expanded capacity, it potentially worsen the traffic congestion conditions if the surrounding infrastructures are not upgraded at par with the expansion.	• Land acquisition may take longer timeframe depending on negotiation with the affected stakeholders. • The Muda River is the critical water source to the regional water supply. Water contamination during construction & operation may risk major water disruption as faced in other region. (Raihan et al., 2023) • The 9,841 acres KXP airport city development maybe potentially too ambitious which may impose challenges and uncertainties in raising the financial commitment needed for the project (Tay, 2023; Zulkifli, 2022; 2024). • The idea of a Air Cargo, Aerospace & MRO centric development might not have the needed essential criteria as opposed to KLIA which has the similar strategic plan - RtS 2020 (MAHB, 2018) • Lack of active engagement with the regional stakeholders may impose challenges in realising the project full potentials	• Land acquisition may take longer timeframe depending on negotiation with the affected stakeholders. • The 2,600 acres NMIA development maybe potentially face challenges and uncertainties in addressing the environmental (natural habitat preservation – mangrove) and noise pollution issues. • The viability of NMIA is highly dependence on the agreement of the respective authorities to relocate PIA to NMIA rather than co-exist. • Lack of active engagement with the regional stakeholders (both states and federal level) may impose challenges in obtaining the necessary approvals.

Source: (Author created, 2025)

5. DISCUSSIONS

Airport site selection is hard. Choices have advantages and cons and must consider all stakeholders' interests, compromise, transparency, and impartiality. In the previous session, our research found that addressing aviation needs is overdue but problematic due to regional geopolitics and a lack of national policy clarity. The criteria framework suggests that PIA may fix short-term concerns. However, this solution may not be sustainable enough for medium-term development and regional competitiveness. KXP's goal may be politically motivated rather than economically justified, but PIA's long-term expandability limits will make Northern Malaysia's development mainland-centric. Airport infrastructure affects sustainability and climate change. Aviation certainly increases connection and economic growth. A strategic airport infrastructure planning site boosts regional sustainability. KXP and NMIA may succeed as regional air transport gateway catalysts. KXP's lofty goal may not explain PIA's survival. North of PIA may hinder the Northern Region's holistic progress. KXP may need to reduce its ambition and focus on high-tech, high-value manufacturing. From its tri-state border location, NMIA can affect Kedah-Penang-Perak, making it a good regional aviation gateway contender. However, NMIA struggles to convince Tri-state stakeholders and federal policymakers to move PIA. The major development principles must comprehensively address sustainability and environmental challenges to reduce risks and uncertainties. Scholars and politicians say airport infrastructure enhances regional economic growth, connections, and competitiveness. Northern Malaysia's FDI, tourism, trade, and logistics depend on airport infrastructure. Northern Malaysia may exploit airport development as a regional competitive advantage due to its proximity to Indonesia and Thailand and economic fundamentals. Northern Malaysia has relied on Penang International Airport (PIA) for domestic and international aviation travel for decades. Northern Malaysia needs a strategic airport infrastructure plan to address capacity constraints, aging infrastructure, government financial constraints, limited expansion space, and sustainable practices upgrades to address climate change, as do many other Malaysian airports. These issues require a diversified solution that supports national development, equitable regional development, and privacy-security management practices for sustainable growth. Three strategic option to increase regional competitiveness are discussed, and how a strategic planning framework affects airport infrastructure design in Northern Malaysia with high confidence in privacy and security management. The regional development potentials and issues, accessibility and connection, competitive edge and limitations of each choice, privacy-security management, and geopolitical agenda alignment with the national development agenda. SWOT and MCDA, well-established strategic planning tools, determine each option's advantages and cons. It shows how well-planned airport infrastructure may improve inclusive regional economic growth and Northern Malaysia's worldwide competitiveness. Improving airport infrastructure requires regional perspectives beyond state-level planning. Economic collaboration, sustainable development, and resource optimization require strategic regional planning. By addressing interconnected states' capabilities and needs, such planning gives regions and nations an edge. It helps airports serve local interests and enhance national and regional connectivity, economic integration, and global competitiveness. An effective regional strategy stops governments from wastefully competing and achieving little. It facilitates regional infrastructure planning through state collaboration, resource pooling, and synergy. Airport cargo and tourist services can be integrated to boost efficiency and local economies. Sustainable national growth requires non-partisan strategic planning. This method reduces political prejudices and advances national interests by remaining neutral and focusing on long-term goals. It focuses on resources, sets goals, engages stakeholders, and privacy-security management. Thus, regional airport infrastructure development can strengthen Malaysia's global aviation position and economic and sustainability aims. This study assesses airport placement theoretically, not commercially. Hence, it does not calculate airport goods, services, passenger movement, logistics, or supply chain. Regional strategic planning unites state-level competencies and priorities to create airport infrastructure for equitable growth, environmental sustainability, and competitiveness.

6. CONCLUSION AND RECOMMENDATIONS

6.1 Importance of Privacy and Cyber Security Management

Managing privacy and security for airport infrastructure is intricately connected to strategic planning for airport infrastructure. In this manner:

1. Airport Infrastructure Planning with Privacy & Cyber Security as key element of consideration: To ensure the safety (beyond physical risks) of airport infrastructure, it is imperative that strategic planning incorporate cyber-security considerations from the very beginning of the design phase. The cyber-security protocols on terminals, the positioning of security checkpoints, the incorporation of smart surveillance systems, access control mechanisms, other aspects of airport operations are essential to ensure the system's integrity. Additionally, privacy concerns must be incorporated into the design of systems responsible for collecting and processing passenger data (for example, biometrics and passenger flow management). Alternatives in Technology: Decisions made at the strategic level regarding which technologies to employ (for example, biometric scanners, surveillance systems powered by artificial intelligence, and data analytics platforms) have direct implications for both the efficiency of security and data privacy. It is necessary to analyse the potential privacy threats linked with each technology thoroughly and implement suitable safeguards.
2. Data management and governance: Data Collection and Storage: An airport's infrastructure depends on the collection and storage of vast amounts of data, including information about passengers, flight details, surveillance footage, and operational data. To ensure compliance with privacy rules, strategic planning must establish transparent policies and procedures about the data acquired, how

it is stored, the individuals who have access to it, and the length of time it is kept.

3. Sharing of Information and Integration: Integrating various airport systems can improve the operational efficiency and security of the airport. On the other hand, strategic planning must guarantee proper data protection measures and handle the privacy issues associated with data sharing between systems. Compliance: Strategic plans must consider the ever-changing data privacy rules (such as the General Data Protection Regulation) and security regulations. In order to avoid non-compliance and the possibility of incurring penalties, the development of infrastructure and the adoption of technology must be per specific legislative frameworks.
4. Protocols and procedures for operational procedures: Security Screening Procedures The design and implementation of security screening procedures are influenced by strategic planning during the screening process. These procedures must efficiently identify potential dangers while causing as little disruption as possible to passengers' privacy (for example, by employing screening technologies that protect passengers' privacy). Response to events: Strategic plans must incorporate methods for appropriately handling security events and data breaches. At the same time, as these protocols should specify methods for containment, eradication, recovery, and notification, they should also ensure that security and privacy are adequately maintained both during and after an occurrence. Awareness and Training: The strategic planning process ought to incorporate thorough training programs for airport staff on the policies and procedures of data privacy and security standards. When it comes to maintaining a safe and privacy-conscious environment, having a well-informed team is necessary.
5. Collaboration and communication among stakeholders are essential: The strategic planning process must entail close engagement with aviation security authorities and data protection agencies to guarantee that the rules and best practices follow it. To address privacy concerns and establish confidence with passengers, it is vital to communicate openly and honestly about the security measures already in place and how their data is being used. In addition to Other Partners, Airlines: To achieve a cohesive and efficient strategy, it is essential to have strategic alignment with international airlines and other airport partners about data handling and security procedures.

To achieve the following goals, strategic planning for airport infrastructure must fully incorporate privacy and security management: Ensure the infrastructure is secure and respectful of individuals' privacy. Put technology that improves safety without unreasonably jeopardizing individuals' right to privacy into practice. Establish efficient structures for the governance of data by rules. Establish operational processes that strike a balance between the effectiveness of security and the right to privacy. Create an environment that encourages collaboration and open communication with all stakeholders. When airports take into account privacy and security as key pillars in the process of strategic planning, they can design infrastructure that is not only effective and secure but also respects the rights and data of the individuals who use it.

REFERENCES

Abdullah, M. F., Siraj, S., & Hodgett, R. E. (2021). An overview of multi-criteria decision analysis (MCDA) application in managing water-related disaster events: Analyzing 20 years of literature for flood and drought events. *Water (Basel), 13*(10), 1358. https://www.mdpi.com/2073-4441/13/10/1358. DOI: 10.3390/w13101358

Alves, C. J. P., da Silva, E. J., Müller, C., Borille, G. M. R., Guterres, M. X., Arraut, E. M., & dos Santos, R. J. (2020). Towards an objective decision-making framework for regional airport site selection. *Journal of Air Transport Management, 89*, 101888. DOI: 10.1016/j.jairtraman.2020.101888

Bakhtina, M., Matulevičius, R., & Malina, L. (2024). *Information Security and Privacy Management in Intelligent Transportation Systems.* Complex Systems Informatics and Modeling Quarterly., DOI: 10.7250/csimq.2024-38.04

Basyir, M. (2018). State govt calls on MAHB to solve flash floods at PIA. New Straits Times. 28 October 2018. https://www.nst.com.my/news/nation/2018/10/425956/state-govt-calls-mahb-solve-flash-floods-pia#google_vignette Retrieved on 10 April 2025.

Brodie, C., Karat, C. M., Karat, J., & Feng, J. (2005, July). Usable security and privacy: a case study of developing privacy management tools. In *Proceedings of the 2005 symposium on Usable privacy and security* (pp. 35-43). https://dl.acm.org/doi/abs/10.1145/1073001.1073005

Charles, M. B., Barnes, P., Ryan, N., & Clayton, J. (2007). Airport futures: Towards a critique of the aerotropolis model. *Futures, 39*(9), 1009–1028. DOI: 10.1016/j.futures.2007.03.017

Chavhan, S., Gupta, D., Garg, S., Khanna, A., Choi, B. J., & Hossain, M. S. (2020). Privacy and security management in intelligent transportation system. *IEEE Access : Practical Innovations, Open Solutions, 8*, 148677–148688. DOI: 10.1109/ACCESS.2020.3015096

Chohan, U. W. (2019). The concept of the aerotropolis: A review. https://papers.ssrn.com/sol3/papers.cfm?abstract_id=3412543

Chung, L. H. (2015). Impact of pandemic control over airport economics: Reconciling public health with airport business through a streamlined approach in pandemic control. *Journal of Air Transport Management, 44*, 42–53. DOI: 10.1016/j.jairtraman.2015.02.003 PMID: 32572319

Cidell, J. (2015). The role of major infrastructure in subregional economic development: An empirical study of airports and cities. *Journal of Economic Geography, 15*(6), 1125–1144. DOI: 10.1093/jeg/lbu029

Dean, M. (2022). *A practical guide to multi-criteria analysis.* UCL.

Dermawan, A. (2019), No reason for PIA to fear competition from KXP. New Straits Times. 5 November 2019. https://www.nst.com.my/news/nation/2019/11/535956/no-reason-pia-fear-competition-kxp Retrieved on 8 April 2025.

Dermawan, A. (2022). Flash floods also strike Penang International Airport. New Straits Times, 24 September 2022. https://www.nst.com.my/news/nation/2022/09/834000/flash-floods-also-strike-penang-international-airport Retrieved on 10 April 2025.

Dermawan, A. (2025). Penang airport to expand parking bays to accommodate 12mil annual passengers. New Straits Times. 2 April 2025. https://www.nst.com.my/business/corporate/2025/04/1196365/penang-airport-expand-parking-bays-accommodate-12mil-annual Retrieved on 8 April 2025.

Ekaputra, V. D., & Simamora, S. C. (2024). Systematic Literature Review on Aerotropolis.

Erkan, T. E., & Elsharida, W. M. (2019). Overview of airport location selection methods. *International Journal of Applied Engineering Research: IJAER, 14*(7), 1613–1618.

Florido-Benítez, L. (2024). The types of hackers and cyberattacks in the aviation industry. *Journal of Transportation Security, 17*(1), 13. https://link.springer.com/article/10.1007/s12198-024-00281-9. DOI: 10.1007/s12198-024-00281-9

Frétigny, J. B., Magnan, M., Maulat, J., & Pedro, M. (2024). "Airport city" or "VIP" urbanism? Questioning the market-led land development strategies of airports. *Human Geographies, 17*(3), 262–277. DOI: 10.1177/19427786241251723

Gopalakrishnan, K., Govindarasu, M., Jacobson, D. W., & Phares, B. M. (2013). Cyber security for airports. *IJTTE. International Journal for Traffic and Transport Engineering, 3*(4), 365–376. DOI: 10.7708/ijtte.2013.3(4).02

Haass, J., Sampigethaya, R., & Capezzuto, V. (2016). Aviation and cybersecurity: opportunities for applied research. Tr News, (304), 39. https://commons.erau.edu/publication/299/

Halid, S. (2019). Kerajaan lulus bina Lapangan Terbang Antarabangsa Kulim, lebuh raya Berita Harian [Government approves construction of Kulim International Airport, highway Berita Harian]. Retrieved on 8 April 2025.

Hall, P. G. (1998). *Cities in civilization* (Vol. 21). Pantheon Books.

Hanan, S. A., Osman, N. H., Abidin, R., Zahari, F. M., & Noordin, A. (2022). Location Planning of Airport Facilities: Case Study of KXP International Airport. UUM 7th International Case Study Conference (ICSC) 2022. Universiti Utara Malaysia (UUM). e-ISSN: 2756-8482

Hashim, R. (2023). KXP untuk keperluan kargo, bukan bersaing dengan [LTAPP KXP for cargo needs, not competing with LTAPP]. Sinar Harian. 10 March 2023. https://www.sinarharian.com.my/article/249010/edisi/utara/kxp-untuk-keperluan-kargo-bukan-bersaing-dengan-ltapp Retrieved on 8 April 2025.

Huston, S. (2015). The Aerotropolis Development Catalyst or Distraction.

ITF-OECD. (2017). Airport Site Selection. Organisation for Economic Co-operation and Development - International Transport Forum (OECD-ITF)_https://www.itf-oecd.org/sites/default/files/docs/airport-site-selection.pdf

Kamarul, A., & Kang, S. L. (2024). Cover Story: No urgent need for national policy on airport and seaport development, says Loke. 24 December 2024. The Edge Malaysia. Retrieved from https://theedgemalaysia.com/node/737973

Kasarda, J. D. (2000). Logistics & the rise of aerotropolis. *Real Estate Issues*, *25*(4), 43–43.

Kasarda, J. D. (2008). *The evolution of airport cities and the aerotropolis. Dalam JD Kasarda, Airport Cities, The Evolution*. Insight Media.

Kazda, A., Badanik, B., & Serrano, F. (2022). Pandemic vs. Post-pandemic airport operations: Hard impact, slow recovery. *Aerospace (Basel, Switzerland)*, *9*(12), 810. DOI: 10.3390/aerospace9120810

Kraus, S., Reiche, B. S., & Reschke, C. H. (2007, September). The role of strategic planning in SMEs: Literature review and implications. In Conference proceedings of the Annual Meeting of the British Academy of Management.

Kwan, C. (2025, March). Land rush at Sydney's Aerotropolis with $450m government site on offer. *Financial Review*, •••, 10. Retrieved April 9, 2025, from

Liew, J. T., & Lee, E. (2024). Cover Story: Penang's infrastructure playing catch-up with its industrial boom. The Edge Malaysia. 10 October 2024. https://theedgemalaysia.com/node/728632 Retrieved on 10 April 2024.

Lim, L. (2023). Digital Marketing Strategies: A Case of Charles & Keith. *Advance Knowledge for Executives*, *2*(2), 1–11.

Liou, J. J., Chien, C. W., Gudiel Pineda, P. J., Li, C. S. J., & Hsu, C. C. (2024). Exploring the Impact of Pandemic Measures on Airport Performance. *Aerospace (Basel, Switzerland)*, *11*(5), 373. https://www.mdpi.com/2226-4310/11/5/373. DOI: 10.3390/aerospace11050373

Malaysiakini. (2020). Penang in no hurry for airport expansion project – CM. Mkini Dotcom Sdn Bhd. https://www.malaysiakini.com/news/536412. 28 July 2020. Retrieved on 8 April 2024.

MAVCOM. (2019). Malaysia's Airports Industry Structure. Position Paper. Malaysian Aviation Commission. December 2019. https://www.mavcom.my/wp-content/uploads/2019/12/191204-Position-Paper-Malaysias-Airports-Industry-Stucture.pdf Retrieved on 8 April 2025.

Meckelburg, R., & Wardana, A. (2024). The political economy of land acquisition for development in the public interest: The case of Indonesia. *Land Use Policy*, *137*, 107017. DOI: 10.1016/j.landusepol.2023.107017

MIDA. (2023). Budget 2024 focus on Perak's high-tech industrial area will boost sector – Analysts. Malaysian Investment Development Authority (MIDA). https://www.mida.gov.my/mida-news/budget-2024-focus-on-peraks-high-tech-industrial-area-will-boost-sector-analysts/Retrieved on 10 April 2025.

Mintzberg, H. (1990). The Design School: Reconsidering the Basic Premises of Strategic Management. *Strategic Management Journal*, *11*(3), 171–195. DOI: 10.1002/smj.4250110302

Mintzberg, H. (1994). The rise and fall of strategic planning, Prentice Hall, 1994.

Mok, O. (2020). CM: Penang airport expansion on hold pending strategic study. Malay Mail. 13 August 2020. https://www.malaymail.com/news/malaysia/2020/08/13/cm-penang-airport-expansion-on-hold-pending-strategic-study/1893577 Retrieved on 8 April 2025.

Nambiar, P. (2020). Politics in the way of Penang airport expansion, says Chow. Free Malaysia Today (FMT). 25 August 2020. https://www.freemalaysiatoday.com/category/nation/2020/08/25/politics-in-the-way-of-penang-airport-expansion-says-chow/ Retrieved on 8 April 2025.

Nickols, F. (2012). Definitions & meanings. *Distance Consulting*, *200*, 2–10.

Nizam, F. (2025). Cyberattack on MAHB: Hackers yet to be identified.https://www.nst.com.my/news/nation/2025/03/1193233/cyberattack-mahb-hackers-yet-be-identified

Palczewski, K., & Sałabun, W. (2019). Influence of various normalization methods in PROMETHEE II: An empirical study on the selection of the airport location. *Procedia Computer Science*, *159*, 2051–2060. DOI: 10.1016/j.procs.2019.09.378

Pennings, J. (1985). *Organizational strategy and change*. Jossey-Bass.

Porter, M. E. (1986). *Competitive Strategy (1986)*. Harvard Business School Press.

Raihan, A., Pereira, J. J., Begum, R. A., & Rasiah, R. (2023). The economic impact of water supply disruption from the Selangor River, Malaysia. *Blue-Green Systems*, *5*(2), 102–120. DOI: 10.2166/bgs.2023.031

Ramu, P., Srinivasarao, T., Lalith Nandan, K., & Keshav, M. (2020). Fuzzy AHP, RS & GIS based hybrid approach for airport site selection-Kothagudem district. *International Journal of Advanced Science and Technology*, *29*(1), 1645–1653. http://sersc.org/journals/index.php/IJAST/article/view/3731

Rangsaritvorakarn, N. (2023). A Decision-making Criteria in Airport Site Selection: A Systematic Review. *Journal for Strategy and Enterprise Competitiveness*, *2*(5), 78–94. https://so07.tci-thaijo.org/index.php/STECOJournal/article/view/2916

Sennaroglu, B., & Celebi, G. V. (2018). A military airport location selection by AHP integrated PROMETHEE and VIKOR methods. *Transportation Research Part D, Transport and Environment*, *59*, 160–173. DOI: 10.1016/j.trd.2017.12.022

Shankar, A.C. (2019). What MAHB now faces after the unprecedented systems outage at KLIA. theedgemarkets.com. 24 Aug 2019. Retrieved on 10 April 2025.

Siripipatthanakul, S., & Siripipattanakul, S. (2025, a). Rural Dental Health Transformation by Adopting Digital Technologies. *Transforming Dental Health in Rural Communities: Digital Dentistry*, 47-80. DOI: DOI: 10.4018/979-8-3693-7165-7.ch003

Siripipatthanakul, S., & Siripipattanakul, S. (2025, b). Online Gambling of Higher Education Learners. In *International Academic Transformations and Cross-Border Collaborations* (pp. 377-400). IGI Global Scientific Publishing. DOI: DOI: 10.4018/979-8-3373-0508-0.ch015

Talukder, B., & Hipel, K. W. (2021). Review and selection of multi-criteria decision analysis (MCDA) technique for sustainability assessment. In Energy Systems Evaluation (Volume 1) Sustainability Assessment (pp. 145-160). Cham: Springer International Publishing. https://doi.org/DOI: 10.1007/978-3-030-67529-5_7

Tan, D., & Teng, A. (2024, March). Tender out for Penang airport's RM1.5bil expansion project. *The Star*, *14*, ●●●. Retrieved April 8, 2025, from https://www.thestar.com.my/news/nation/2024/03/14/tender-out-for-penangs-airports-rm15bil-expansion-project

Tay, C. (2023). Syed Mokhtar tells Anwar he can't afford to support whopping RM7 bil Kulim International Airport project. The Edge Malaysia. 9 March 2023. https://theedgemalaysia.com/node/658521. Retrieved on 8 April 2025.

Zahiid, S.J. (2019). Two firms in rival bids for international airports in north of peninsula. Malay Mail. 10 June 2019. Retrieved on 8 April 2025.

Zhang, W., Zhong, Y., Wang, Z., Luo, Z., & Wang, B. (2021). Influence on distributed airport site selection from ground-effect wind field of UAV. In 2021 2nd International Symposium on Computer Engineering and Intelligent Communications (ISCEIC), 322-329. DOI: 10.1109/ISCEIC53685.2021.00074

Zulkifli, A. (2022) ECK's axing from KXP nothing to do with Musang King plantation, says Sanusi. New Straits Times. 13 July 2022. https://www.nst.com.my/news/nation/2022/07/813127/ecks-axing-kxp-nothing-do-musang-king-plantation-says-sanusi Retrieved on 8 April 2025.

Zulkifli, A. (2024). Opposition rep raises doubt on Kedah high-impact project. New Straits Times. (26 November 2024). https://www.nst.com.my/news/nation/2024/11/1140094/opposition-rep-raises-doubt-kedah-high-impact-projects Retrieved on 8 April 2025.

Conclusion

This book, "Privacy and Security Management Practices for Organizations," explains how businesses and organizations can determine the most effective management and strategies. Companies and organizations can use this versatility to resolve security and privacy concerns while satisfying the responsible due diligence criteria. Following management practices, the security and privacy in businesses and organizations could be ensured.

The book "Privacy and Security Management Practices for Organizations" explores the influence that recent legal changes in data privacy, environmental standards, and labor constraints have had on corporations' management practices and tactics. The following are some examples of the fundamentals of privacy and security management practices that are significant for online markets, remote work, cyber terrorism, and other activities. Corporate leaders, managers, cybersecurity professionals, data scientists, researchers, scholars, and academics will find it invaluable. Accounting Systems, Cloud Computing, Computer Science, Cyber Terrorism, Cybersecurity, Digital Economy, FinTech, Logistics Information Systems, Online Marketplaces, Privacy Information Sharing, Public Organizations, Remote Working, and Security Management are just some of the many academic fields that are covered in privacy and security management practices. However, this list is not exhaustive. To inspire academics and researchers to adopt collaboration, creativity, communication, and critical thinking among researchers, professors, organizations, and industries, the book contains comprehensive guidance that might empower academic leaders and strategic planners for privacy and security management practices.

The fundamentals of protecting personal information and cybersecurity in the digital economy are discussed. Cybersecurity, privacy, and data security are all concerned with protecting against cyberattacks and computer infections. Digital privacy protects customer information, personal information, online communication, and online behavior. Digital platforms generate enormous volumes of personal data, which may include records of financial transactions and medical conditions. The use of digital privacy can prevent data theft.

Email spam, WhatsApp, and Telegram affect privacy, cybersecurity, financial security, and personal invasion, exploring the hazards to privacy, the high phishing rates, and the unwelcome messages sent through these mobile messaging platforms. Younger people who use digital devices are more susceptible to these dangers. In contrast, adults with greater levels of education are more aware of the risks and more inclined to take measures. Anxiety among users is demonstrated by the perceived risks to their privacy and the requests for stronger cybersecurity solutions. Enhanced cybersecurity, more stringent regulatory monitoring, and focused public education are all necessary to address the identified platform security and user awareness gaps. To preserve user privacy and prevent financial fraud and data breaches in modern digital communication platforms, a proposal has been made to increase encryption, introduce automated spam detection, and modify the regulatory framework for cybersecurity.

Social science and humanities (SSH) security management for research integrity and ethical data handling is included in "Security Management Practices in Social Sciences and Humanities: Safeguarding Research Integrity and Data." Because participants in SSH research come from various socioeconomic and ethnic backgrounds, confidentiality, informed consent, and anonymity are all required. The proliferation of digital technology and data collection online has made cybersecurity dangers such as leaks and unauthorized access even more severe. To conduct interdisciplinary and transnational SSH research, academics must navigate many legal regimes and work together across boundaries. When it comes to protecting sensitive data, researchers should make use of encryption, secure storage, and stringent data management. The institutions must provide support for comprehensive cybersecurity and ethical research policies, training, and education. The public's trust, the study's validity, and the participants' rights and well-being depend on implementing security precautions.

Challenges and Management Practices in Protecting Employee Personal Data discusses the most significant challenges in managing employee personal data in the digital transformation era. Additionally, the effective management practices in protecting such data are crucial. Personal data management techniques are intricately connected to new technical developments, ethical considerations, environmental sustainability, and risk management. Some of the most critical problems include cyber threats, limits in technology infrastructure, and a lack of cybersecurity knowledge among personnel. This issue must be addressed by establishing clear regulations, training employees, and investing in cutting-edge technologies such as encryption and intrusion detection.

The Determinants of FDI Attraction in Creating a Foreign Firm's Competitive Advantage: An Extended Model for Data Protection in Privacy and Security" focuses on the importance of data privacy and security for competitiveness in the information age, particularly regarding Foreign Direct Investment (FDI) and firm-level competitive advantage. It was determined through the use of scientific publications that a systematic review and content analysis were carried out. This chapter explains the complex link between the factors, circumstances, supporting industries, policies, and regulatory frameworks contributing to its competitiveness in attracting Foreign Direct Investment from other countries. Increasing the institutional consistency of data protection increases employees' trust and eliminates concerns over geopolitics and cybersecurity. The strategy improves competitiveness in recruiting technology-driven Foreign Direct Investment (FDI). It enables businesses to retain long-term profitability by utilizing data ecosystems that are both secure and transparent. Research indicates that firms could successfully capitalize on market possibilities and avoid risks if they had persuasive data governance and privacy policies. Within digital globalization, this chapter offers a framework that corporate leaders can use to integrate privacy, security, foreign direct investment competitiveness, effective practices, and strategies for managing privacy and security in research operations.

Technological advancements and regulatory shifts have made achieving research privacy and security more difficult. When protecting personal information, researchers have to strike a compromise between ethics and the law. Throughout the entire research process, it is essential to conduct risk assessment and management to protect participants' privacy and adhere to data security requirements. Important topics include the secure gathering, storage, and exchange of data and the development of technologies that enhance privacy, such as anonymization and pseudonymization. Researchers and oversight bodies such as Institutional Review Boards (IRBs) must collaborate to ensure that ethical and legal standards are continuously met. In addition to this, it demonstrates how proactive tactics and awareness of the information environment may be used to develop trust among participants, sponsors, and the general public. Furthermore, it provides a comprehensive strategy for achieving a balance between privacy, security, and research objectives in a world driven by data, thereby safeguarding research integrity and the confidence of stakeholders.

Privacy information awareness for ChatGPT adoption explores the significance of awareness of one's private information when using ChatGPT. As the amount of personal information shared online increases, everyone must recognize the importance of upholding their privacy in their day-to-day dealings. The exposure of personal information can be fraught with danger. By understanding the service privacy settings and policies, the importance of confidentiality that raises privacy concerns, the quality and quantity of personal information that users disclose, and the personal consequences of potential data breaches on the technological services for information privacy awareness and sharing when using ChatGPT, users should be aware of these things and take precautions to protect themselves.

Strategic planning on airport infrastructure in the context of privacy and cybersecurity discusses how infrastructure contributes to regional economic development, connectivity, and competitiveness. The airport infrastructure development is critical for luring Foreign Direct Investments (FDI) and facilitating tourism, commerce, and logistics. Over several decades, there has been infrastructure no longer in use, restrictions on government funding, restricted opportunities for growth, and the requirement for privacy and security management to facilitate sustainable modifications. It is of utmost importance to construct a comprehensive airport development plan incorporating privacy and cybersecurity management to achieve sustainable growth and a competitive advantage.

"Privacy and Security Management Practices for Organizations" is a publication created by academics and professors who collaborated carefully on various topics. It provides academic leaders and strategic planners with strategies to improve corporate privacy and security policies.

With the advent of the digital revolution, businesses and organizations have improved their ability to streamline their operations and manage vast volumes of data, including information on customers, medical records, users, and financial evidence. Nevertheless, it does not provide complete protection against the dangers posed by cyber terrorists. A cyberattack can result in significant damage, including the theft of personal information, the exploitation of private information, and fraudulent financial transactions.

Consequently, businesses and organizations must build plans for dealing with data and implement protections for information and cybersecurity. By implementing a risk policy, a company or an organization can safeguard its digital data against unauthorized access, utilization, and disclosure. Disruption, modification, and deletion of data are also prevented within the system. Data is essential for every organization. This necessitates the implementation of safeguards. A comprehensive set of data security procedures is required to guarantee data availability, integrity, and confidentiality. Data security is essential to protect assets, meet regulatory obligations, and maintain consumer and user confidence regarding data security and privacy. Data protection in businesses and organizations can articulate the privacy and security policies that they have in place, and raise awareness of privacy and security concerns involving personal information.

Compilation of References

Abadi, M., Chu, A., Goodfellow, I., McMahan, H. B., Mironov, I., Talwar, K., & Zhang, L. (2016, October). Deep learning with differential privacy. In *Proceedings of the 2016 ACM SIGSAC Conference on Computer and Communications Security* (pp. 308–318). DOI: 10.1145/2976749.2978318

Abbas, Z., & Robbins, S. (2024). Cybersecurity protocols in human resources: Ensuring legal compliance and ethical standards. *ResearchGate*. https://doi.org/DOI: 10.13140/RG.2.2.17080.76809

Abdullah, M. F., Siraj, S., & Hodgett, R. E. (2021). An overview of multi-criteria decision analysis (MCDA) application in managing water-related disaster events: Analyzing 20 years of literature for flood and drought events. *Water (Basel)*, *13*(10), 1358. https://www.mdpi.com/2073-4441/13/10/1358. DOI: 10.3390/w13101358

Abdulrasool, F. E., & Turnbull, S. J. (2020). Exploring security, risk, and compliance driven IT governance model for universities: Applied research based on the COBIT framework. [HTML]. *International Journal of Electronic Banking*, 2(3), 237–265. DOI: 10.1504/IJEBANK.2020.111438

Abdulsalam, Y. S. & Hedabou, M. (2021). Security and privacy in cloud computing: technical review. Future Internet. mdpi.com

Abrahams, T. O., Ewuga, S. K., Dawodu, S. O., Adegbite, A. O., & Hassan, A. O.Temitayo Oluwaseun AbrahamsSarah Kuzankah EwugaSamuel Onimisi Dawodu-Abimbola Oluwatoyin AdegbiteAzeez Olanipekun Hassan. (2024). A Review of Cybersecurity Strategies in Modern Organization; Examining the Evolution and Effectiveness of Cybersecurity Measures for Data Protection. *Computer Science & IT Research Journal*, *5*(1), 1–25. Advance online publication. DOI: 10.51594/csitrj.v5i1.699

Adamu, A. A., Salau, A. O., & Zhiyong, L. (2021). A Robust Context and Role-Based Dynamic Access Control for Distributed Healthcare Information Systems. [HTML]. *Internet of Things : Engineering Cyber Physical Human Systems.*

Adee, R. & Mouratidis, H. (2022). A dynamic four-step data security model for data in cloud computing based on cryptography and steganography. Sensors. mdpi.com

Adeniran, I. A., Efunniyi, C. P., Osundare, O. S., & Abhulimen, A. O.Ibrahim Adedeji AdeniranChristianah Pelumi EfunniyiOlajide Soji OsundareAngela Omozele Abhulimen. (2024). Data-Driven Decision-Making in Healthcare: Enhancing Patient Outcomes through Predictive Modeling. *Engineering Science & Technology Journal*, *5*(8), 059–067. Advance online publication. DOI: 10.56781/ijsrms.2024.5.1.0040

Adewusi, A. O., Okoli, U. I., Adaga, E., Olorunsogo, T., Asuzu, O. F., & Daraojimba, D. O. (2024). Business Intelligence in the Era of Big Data: A Review of Analytical Tools and Competitive Advantage. *Computer Science & IT Research Journal*, *5*(2), 415–431. DOI: 10.51594/csitrj.v5i2.791

Adeyoju, F. I. P. (2020). Financial Technology and Privacy: Evaluating the Approach to Consumer Data. *Available atSSRN* 3558810. https://doi.org/DOI: 10.2139/ssrn.3558810

Afzal, J. (2024). Best practice of digital laws and digital justice. In Zhang, X., & Liu, S. (Eds.), *Global Digital Laws and Justice* (pp. 105–121). Springer., DOI: 10.1007/978-981-97-7106-6_5

Agboola, D. (2025). The Evolving Landscape of Data Privacy: How Regulations are Shaping the Digital World (February 13, 2025). Available at *SSRN*: https://ssrn.com/abstract=5187183 or http://dx.doi.org/DOI: 10.2139/ssrn.5187183

Ajzen, I. (1991). The theory of planned behavior. *Organizational Behavior and Human Decision Processes*, *50*(2), 179–211. DOI: 10.1016/0749-5978(91)90020-T

Akhtar, N., Kerim, B., Perwej, Y., Tiwari, A., & Praveen, S. (2021). A comprehensive overview of privacy and data security for cloud storage. International Journal of Scientific Research in Science Engineering and Technology. hal.science

Akkaya, F. D. (2023). HES: A case study on cybersecurity and privacy risks in health surveillance systems. *In L. Santiago & M. Chen (Eds.), Cybersecurity Challenges in Health Systems* (pp. 112-137). IGI Global. DOI: 10.4018/978-1-6684-9018-1.ch006

Al Sharif, R. & Pokharel, S. (2022). Smart city dimensions and associated risks: Review of literature. Sustainable cities and society. sciencedirect.com

Alabdan, R. (2020). Phishing attacks survey: Types, vectors, and technical approaches. Future internet. mdpi.com

Albayrak, E., & Bağcı, H. (2025). Modelling the effects of personal factors on information security awareness. *Journal of Information Science*, *51*(1), 20–30. DOI: 10.1177/01655515221127609

Aldabbas, M., Xie, X., Teufel, B., & Teufel, S. (2020, October). Future security challenges for smart societies: Overview from technical and societal perspectives. In *2020 International Conference on Smart Grid and Clean Energy Technologies (ICSGCE)* (pp. 103-111). IEEE. [HTML] DOI: 10.1109/ICSGCE49177.2020.9275630

Aldboush, H. H., & Ferdous, M. (2023). Building trust in fintech: An analysis of ethical and privacy considerations in the intersection of big data, ai, and customer trust. *International Journal of Financial Studies*, *11*(3), 90. DOI: 10.3390/ijfs11030090

Alibeigi, A., & Munir, A. B. (2023). Public health data and international privacy rules and practices: A case study of Singapore. In Xu, X., & Liu, Y. (Eds.), *Digital Health Governance* (pp. 57–77). Springer., DOI: 10.1007/978-3-031-39841-4_4

Alkhdour, T., Alrawashdeh, R., Almaiah, M. A., Al-Ali, R., & Salloum, S. A. (2024). A new technique for detecting email spam risks using LSTM-particle swarm optimization algorithms. *Journal of Information Security and Applications*, *65*, 103–119.

Alonso-Muñoz, S., García-Muiña, F. E., Medina-Salgado, M.-S., & González-Sánchez, R. (2022). Towards circular economy practices in food waste management: A retrospective overview and a research agenda. *British Food Journal*, *124*(13), 478–500. DOI: 10.1108/BFJ-01-2022-0072

Aloumi, D., Malik, S., Alkhaldi, A., & de Pablos, P. O. (2024). Factors influencing consumer interactions with FinTech services. In Xu, X., & Liu, Y. (Eds.), *Advances in FinTech and Cybersecurity* (pp. 217–234). IGI Global., DOI: 10.4018/979-8-3693-5673-9.ch010

Alperovitch, D. (2011). *Revealed: Operation Shady RAT. McAfee Apple. Apple's approach to privacy.*

Alshahrani, H. A. A., & Alrodhan, W. A. (2025). Security and Privacy of ChatGPT: Proposed Enhancements. *IJCSNS*, *25*(2), 23.

Alves, C. J. P., da Silva, E. J., Müller, C., Borille, G. M. R., Guterres, M. X., Arraut, E. M., & dos Santos, R. J. (2020). Towards an objective decision-making framework for regional airport site selection. *Journal of Air Transport Management*, *89*, 101888. DOI: 10.1016/j.jairtraman.2020.101888

Ambrosini, V., & Bowman, C. (2010). The impact of causal ambiguity within the firm on competitive advantage and rent appropriation. *British Journal of Management, 21*(4), 939–953. DOI: 10.1111/j.1467-8551.2009.00644.x

Ameer, S., Benson, J., & Sandhu, R. (2022). An attribute-based approach toward a secured smart-home IoT access control and a comparison with a role-based approach. Information. mdpi.com

Amirov, L., & Avazov, N. (2022). The Impact of Digital Infrastructure, Foreign Direct Investment and Trade Openness on Economic Growth: In the Case of Uzbekistan. In International Conference on Next Generation Wired/Wireless Networking (pp. 322-332). Cham: Springer Nature Switzerland. DOI: 10.1007/978-3-031-30258-9_27

Amit, R., & Schoemaker, P. J. (1993). Strategic assets and organisational rent. *Strategic Management Journal, 14*(1), 33–46. DOI: 10.1002/smj.4250140105

Amoah, C., & Steyn, D. (2023). Barriers to unethical and corrupt practices avoidance in the construction industry. [emerald.com]. *International Journal of Building Pathology and Adaptation, 41*(6), 85–101. DOI: 10.1108/IJBPA-01-2022-0021

Amoo, O. O., Atadoga, A., Osasona, F., Abrahams, T. O., Ayinla, B. S., & Farayola, O. A. (2024). GDPR's impact on cybersecurity: A review focusing on USA and European practices. *International Journal of Science and Research Archive, 11*(1), 1338–1347. DOI: 10.30574/ijsra.2024.11.1.0220

Anderson, E. E., Hurley, E. A., Serpico, K., Johnson, A., Rowe, J., Singleton, M., Bierer, B. E., Cholka, B., Chaudhari, S., & Fernandez Lynch, H. (2023). Engaging key stakeholders to overcome barriers to studying the quality of research ethics oversight. [sagepub.com]. *Research Ethics, 19*(1), 62–77. DOI: 10.1177/17470161221138028

Ansari, M. T. J., Pandey, D., & Alenezi, M. (2022). STORE: Security threat oriented requirements engineering methodology. [sciencedirect.com]. *Journal of King Saud University. Computer and Information Sciences, 34*(2), 191–203. DOI: 10.1016/j.jksuci.2018.12.005

Antunes, M., Maximiano, M., Gomes, R., & Pinto, D. (2021). Information security and cybersecurity management: A case study with SMEs in Portugal. *Journal of Cybersecurity Practices, 10*(2), 12–27. DOI: 10.3390/jcp1020012

Appiah, R. (2021). Gurus and Griots: Revisiting the research informed consent process in rural African contexts. BMC medical Ethics. springer.com

Arend, R. J. (2003). Revisiting the Logical and Research Considerations of Competitive Advantage. *Strategic Management Journal, 24*(3), 279–284. DOI: 10.1002/smj.285

Armand, J. (2020). Establishing Economic Independence in Haiti Through Public-Private Partnerships and Foreign Direct Investments. *Northwestern Journal of International Law & Business, 40*(3), 363–390.

Armond, A. C. V., Gordijn, B., Lewis, J., Hosseini, M., Bodnár, J. K., Holm, S., & Kakuk, P. (2021). A scoping review of the literature featuring research ethics and research integrity cases. [springer.com]. *BMC Medical Ethics, 22*(1), 50. DOI: 10.1186/s12910-021-00620-8 PMID: 33931043

Arregle, J. L., Hébert, L., & Beamish, P. W. (2006). Mode of international entry: The advantages of multilevel methods. *MIR. Management International Review, 46*(5), 597–618. DOI: 10.1007/s11575-006-0117-3

Aryania, A., Huertas-Garcia, R., Forgas-Coll, S., Angulo, C., & Alenyà, G. (2025). Effects of Privacy Warning on the Intention to Disclose Personal Information During Interaction with a Robot in Public Spaces. *International Journal of Social Robotics*, •••, 1–19. DOI: 10.1007/s12369-025-01244-3

Asiryan, S. (2023). Legislative practice of Singapore on the use of artificial intelligence. *Journal of Legislative Studies, 3*(57), 92–105. DOI: 10.24144/2788-6018.2023.03.57

Aslan, Ö, Aktuğ, S. S., Ozkan-Okay, M., Yilmaz, A. A., & Akin, E. (2023). A comprehensive review of cyber security vulnerabilities, threats, attacks, and solutions. Electronics. mdpi.com

Atenas, J., Havemann, L., & Timmermann, C. (2023). Reframing data ethics in research methods education: A pathway to critical data literacy. [springer.com]. *International Journal of Educational Technology in Higher Education, 20*(1), 11. DOI: 10.1186/s41239-023-00380-y PMID: 36846483

Atkinson, M. L., Mousavi, R., & Windett, J. H. (2023). Detecting diverse perspectives: Using text analytics to reveal sex differences in congressional debate about defense. [sagepub.com]. *Political Research Quarterly, 76*(1), 75–89. DOI: 10.1177/10659129211045048

Axelsson, S. (2013). Intrusion detection systems: A survey and taxonomy. *Journal of Computer Networks, 34*(4), 476–491.

Babun, L., Denney, K., Celik, Z. B., McDaniel, P., & Uluagac, A. S. (2021). A survey on IoT platforms: Communication, security, and privacy perspectives. [sciencedirect.com]. *Computer Networks, 192*, 108040. DOI: 10.1016/j.comnet.2021.108040

Badsha, S., Vakilinia, I., & Sengupta, S. (2019). Privacy-preserving cyber threat information sharing and learning for cyber defense. *Proceedings of the IEEE 9th Annual Computing and Communication Workshop and Conference (CCWC)*, 204-210. https://doi.org/DOI: 10.1109/CCWC.2019.8666477

Bae, J. K., & Hong, G. H. (2023). A study on digital financial security threats and cybersecurity policies. *Asian Journal of Banking and Accounting*, *20*(6), 133–149. DOI: 10.38115/asgba.2023.20.6.133

Bailey, N., & Li, S. (2015). Cross-national distance and FDI: The moderating role of host country local demand. *Journal of International Management*, *21*(4), 267–276. DOI: 10.1016/j.intman.2014.11.002

Bain, J. S. (1959). *Industrial Organization*. John Wiley.

Bakan, İ., & Doğan, İ. (2012). Competitiveness of the industries based on the Porter's diamond model: An empirical study. *International Journal of Research and Reviews in Applied Sciences*, *11*(3).

Bakhtina, M., Matulevičius, R., & Malina, L. (2024). *Information Security and Privacy Management in Intelligent Transportation Systems*. Complex Systems Informatics and Modeling Quarterly., DOI: 10.7250/csimq.2024-38.04

Balasubramanian, R., Prakash, E., Khan, I., & Platts, J. (2021, May). Blockchain technology for healthcare. In *AMI 2021-The 5th Advances in Management and Innovation Conference 2021*.

Barnes, M., Carrithers, J., & Sugarman, J. (2020). Ethical and practical concerns about IRB restrictions on the use of research data. [HTML]. *Ethics & Human Research*, *42*(6), 29–34. DOI: 10.1002/eahr.500072 PMID: 33136330

Barney, J. B. (1991). Firm resources and sustained competitive advantage. *Journal of Management*, *17*(1), 99–120. DOI: 10.1177/014920639101700108

Barney, J. B. (1997). *Gaining and Sustaining Competitive Advantage*. Addison-Wesley.

Basyir, M. (2018). State govt calls on MAHB to solve flash floods at PIA. New Straits Times. 28 October 2018. https://www.nst.com.my/news/nation/2018/10/425956/state-govt-calls-mahb-solve-flash-floods-pia#google_vignette Retrieved on 10 April 2025.

Batschauer da Cruz, C. B., Eliete Floriani, D., & Amal, M. (2022). The OLI Paradigm as a Comprehensive Model of FDI Determinants: A Sub-National Approach. *International Journal of Emerging Markets*, *17*(1), 145–176. DOI: 10.1108/IJOEM-07-2019-0517

Becher, S., Gerl, A., Meier, B., & Bölz, F. (2020). Big picture on privacy enhancing technologies in e-health: a holistic personal privacy workflow. Information. mdpi.com

Behrens, J., Løvholt, F., Jalayer, F., Lorito, S., Salgado-Gálvez, M. A., Sørensen, M., Abadie, S., Aguirre-Ayerbe, I., Aniel-Quiroga, I., Babeyko, A., Baiguera, M., Basili, R., Belliazzi, S., Grezio, A., Johnson, K., Murphy, S., Paris, R., Rafliana, I., De Risi, R., & Vyhmeister, E. (2021). Probabilistic tsunami hazard and risk analysis: A review of research gaps. [frontiersin.org]. *Frontiers in Earth Science (Lausanne)*, *9*, 628772. DOI: 10.3389/feart.2021.628772

Bellini, E., & Degl'Innocenti, E. (2024, September). Transitioning SSH European Research Infrastructures to Critical Infrastructure Through Resilience. In *2024 IEEE International Conference on Cyber Security and Resilience (CSR)* (pp. 801-806). IEEE. [HTML] DOI: 10.1109/CSR61664.2024.10679383

Bezuidenhout, H., & Kleynhans, E. P. (2018). Modern Trends in Chinese Foreign Direct Investment in Africa: An OLI Approach. International Research Journal, 16(3), 279-300. https://www.hippocampus.si/ISSN/1854-6935/16_3.pdf#page=89

Bharati, S. & Podder, P. (2022). Machine and deep learning for iot security and privacy: applications, challenges, and future directions. Security and communication networks. wiley.com

Bhaskar, R., & Ola, M. (2024). Publication Misconduct, Plagiarism, and Research Integrity. In Principles of Research Methodology and Ethics in Pharmaceutical Sciences (pp. 271-310). CRC Press.

Bonaccorsi, A., Chiarello, F., & Fantoni, G. (2021). SSH researchers make an impact differently. Looking at public research from the perspective of users. [HTML]. *Research Evaluation*, *30*(3), 269–289. DOI: 10.1093/reseval/rvab008

Bourai, S., Arora, R., & Yadav, N. (2024). Structure-Conduct-Performance (SCP) Paradigm in Digital Platform Competition: A Conceptual Framework. *Journal of Strategy and Management*, *17*(2), 322–347. DOI: 10.1108/JSMA-07-2023-0184

Bovens, M. & Wille, A. (2021). Indexing watchdog accountability powers a framework for assessing the accountability capacity of independent oversight institutions. Regulation & Governance. wiley.com

Bowen, F. R., Epps, F., Lowe, J., & Guilamo-Ramos, V. (2022). Restoring trust in research among historically underrepresented communities: A call to action for antiracism research in nursing. Nursing outlook. sciencedirect.com

Brass, I. & Sowell, J. H. (2021). Adaptive governance for the Internet of Things: Coping with emerging security risks. Regulation & Governance. wiley.com

Bretas, V. P. G., Alon, I., Paltrinieri, A., & Chawla, K. (2022). Bibliometric review on FDI attractiveness factors. *European Journal of International Management, 17*(2–3), 469–499. DOI: 10.1504/EJIM.2022.120721

Brodie, C., Karat, C. M., Karat, J., & Feng, J. (2005, July). Usable security and privacy: a case study of developing privacy management tools. In *Proceedings of the 2005 symposium on Usable privacy and security* (pp. 35-43). https://dl.acm.org/doi/abs/10.1145/1073001.1073005

Brouthers, K. D. (2013). A Retrospective on Institutional, Cultural, and Transaction Cost Influences on Entry Mode Choice and Performance. *Journal of International Business Studies*, *44*(1), 14–22. DOI: 10.1057/jibs.2012.23

Brychka, B. B. (2018). Impact of foreign direct investment on economic growth in the world during 1975–2015. Scientific Messenger of LNU of Veterinary Medicine and Biotechnologies, 20(91).

Brynjolfsson, E., & McElheran, K. (2016). The rapid adoption of data-driven decision-making. *The American Economic Review*, *106*(5), 133–139. DOI: 10.1257/aer.p20161016

Butt, M. A., Katuse, P., & Namada, J. M. (2019). Porter's Diamond Factor Conditions Determinant: Effect on Automotive Industry of Pakistan. *European Journal of Business and Management Research*, *4*(4). Advance online publication. https://www.ejbmr.org/index.php/ejbmr/article/view/78. DOI: 10.24018/ejbmr.2019.4.4.78

Cairns, A. C., Linville, C., Garcia, T., Bridges, B., Tanona, S., Herington, J., & Laverty, J. T. (2021). A phenomenographic study of scientists' beliefs about the causes of scientists' research misconduct. [sagepub.com]. *Research Ethics*, *17*(4), 501–521. DOI: 10.1177/17470161211042658

Campbell, R., Goodman-Williams, R., Engleton, J., Javorka, M., & Gregory, K. (2023). Open science and data sharing in trauma research: Developing a trauma-informed protocol for archiving sensitive qualitative data. [HTML]. *Psychological Trauma: Theory, Research, Practice, and Policy*, *15*(5), 819–828. DOI: 10.1037/tra0001358 PMID: 36074633

Campbell, R., Javorka, M., Engleton, J., Fishwick, K., Gregory, K., & Goodman-Williams, R. (2023). Open-Science guidance for qualitative research: An empirically validated approach for de-identifying sensitive narrative data. [sagepub.com]. *Advances in Methods and Practices in Psychological Science*, *6*(4), 25152459231205832. DOI: 10.1177/25152459231205832

Canabal, A., & White, G. O.III. (2008). Entry Mode Research: Past and Future. *International Business Review, 17*(3), 267–284. DOI: 10.1016/j.ibusrev.2008.01.003

Canfield, K. N., Mulvaney, K., & Chatelain, C. D. (2022). Using researcher and stakeholder perspectives to develop promising practices to improve stakeholder engagement in the solutions-driven research process. [springer.com]. *Socio-Ecological Practice Research, 4*(3), 189–203. DOI: 10.1007/s42532-022-00119-5 PMID: 35855106

Carmi, G., & Bouhnik, D. (2020). The Effect of Rational Based Beliefs and Awareness on Employee Compliance with Information Security Procedures: A Case Study of a Financial Corporation in Israel. Informing Science. *The International Journal of an Emerging Transdiscipline, 23*, 189–206. DOI: 10.28945/4596

Carmi, L., Zohar, M., & Riva, G. M. (2022). The European General Data Protection Regulation (GDPR) in mHealth: Theoretical and practical aspects for practitioners' use. *Medicine, Science, and the Law*. Advance online publication. DOI: 10.1177/00258024221118411 PMID: 35950240

Carter, S. M., Shih, P., Williams, J., Degeling, C., & Mooney-Somers, J. (2021). Conducting qualitative research online: Challenges and solutions. [springer.com]. *Patient, 14*(6), 711–718. DOI: 10.1007/s40271-021-00528-w PMID: 34114170

Casanovas, P., de Koker, L., & Hashmi, M. (2022). Law, socio-legal governance, the internet of things, and industry 4.0: a middle-out/inside-out approach. J. mdpi.com

Chaisse, J. (2023). The Black Pit: Power and Pitfalls of Digital FDI and Cross-Border Data Flows. *World Trade Review, 22*(1), 73–89. DOI: 10.1017/S1474745622000337

Chaity, N. S., & Islam, K. M. Z. (2022). Bank efficiency and practice of earnings management: A study on listed commercial banks of Bangladesh. *Asian Journal of Accounting Research, 7*(2), 114–128. DOI: 10.1108/AJAR-09-2020-0080

Chambers, S. (2021). Truth, deliberative democracy, and the virtues of accuracy: is fake news destroying the public sphere?. Political Studies. sagepub.com

Charles, M. B., Barnes, P., Ryan, N., & Clayton, J. (2007). Airport futures: Towards a critique of the aerotropolis model. *Futures, 39*(9), 1009–1028. DOI: 10.1016/j.futures.2007.03.017

Chatfield, K., Schroeder, D., Guantai, A., Bhatt, K., Bukusi, E., Adhiambo Odhiambo, J., Cook, J., & Kimani, J. (2021). Preventing ethics dumping: The challenges for Kenyan research ethics committees. [sagepub.com]. *Research Ethics, 17*(1), 23–44. DOI: 10.1177/1747016120925064

ChatGPT. (2025). https://chatgpt.com/

Chavhan, S., Gupta, D., Garg, S., Khanna, A., Choi, B. J., & Hossain, M. S. (2020). Privacy and security management in intelligent transportation system. *IEEE Access : Practical Innovations, Open Solutions, 8*, 148677–148688. DOI: 10.1109/ACCESS.2020.3015096

Cheng, B. I. A. N. (2023). Data as Assets in Foreign Direct Investment: Is China's National Data Governance Compatible with Its International Investment Agreements? *Asian Journal of International Law, 13*(2), 342–364. DOI: 10.1017/S2044251322000595

Chen, H. J. (2021). Innovation and FDI: Does the Target of Intellectual Property Rights Protection Matter? *Journal of International Money and Finance, 118*, 102458. DOI: 10.1016/j.jimonfin.2021.102458

Chen, X., Li, N., & Zhang, L. (2021). Privacy-preserving machine learning: A survey on techniques and applications. *IEEE Transactions on Knowledge and Data Engineering, 33*(5), 1955–1971.

Chen, X., Wu, M., Cheng, C., & Mou, J. (2025). Weighing user's privacy calculus on personal information disclosure: The moderating effect of social media identification. *Online Information Review, 49*(2), 353–372. DOI: 10.1108/OIR-03-2024-0135

Cherrafi, A., Chiarini, A., Belhadi, A., El Baz, J., & Chaouni Benabdellah, A. (2022). Digital technologies and circular economy practices: Vital enablers to support sustainable and resilient supply chain management in the post-COVID-19 era. *The TQM Journal, 34*(7), 179–202. DOI: 10.1108/TQM-12-2021-0374

Chilaka, O. (2024). *The Growing Importance of Cybersecurity in a Digital World.* Retrieved from https://doi.org/DOI: 10.13140/RG.2.2.20886.56641

Chiu, S. K., Lo, F. Y., & Susy, Y. (2015). Taiwanese Foreign Direct Investment in Southeast Asia: An Empirical Investigation of the OLI Framework. *Journal of Economics and Management, 11*(2), 127–141.

Chohan, U. W. (2019). The concept of the aerotropolis: A review. https://papers.ssrn.com/sol3/papers.cfm?abstract_id=3412543

Choo, K. K. R., Liu, J., & Choo, R. (2023). A Comprehensive Review of Future Threat Landscapes in Cyberspace. *IEEE Transactions on Emerging Topics in Computing.*

Choudhury, A., & Shamszare, H. (2023). Investigating the impact of user trust on the adoption and use of ChatGPT: Survey analysis. *Journal of Medical Internet Research, 25*, e47184. https://www.jmir.org/2023/1/e47184/. DOI: 10.2196/47184 PMID: 37314848

Chowdhary, S. K., Kumar, P., Mittal, R., Gumber, I., Jangra, V., & Srivastava, P. (2024). Phishing detection tool for financial emails. *Journal of Information Security and Applications*, *11*(4), 2442002. Advance online publication. DOI: 10.1142/S2424786324420027

Chukwunweike, J. N., Yussuf, M., Okusi, O., & Oluwatobi, T. (2024). The role of deep learning in ensuring privacy integrity and security: Applications in AI-driven cybersecurity solutions. *World Journal of Advanced Research and Reviews*, *23*(2), 2550.

Chung, J., & Kwon, H. Y. (2025). Privacy fatigue and its effects on ChatGPT acceptance among undergraduate students: Is privacy dead? *Education and Information Technologies*, •••, 1–23. https://link.springer.com/article/10.1007/s10639-024-13198-6. DOI: 10.1007/s10639-024-13198-6

Chung, L. H. (2015). Impact of pandemic control over airport economics: Reconciling public health with airport business through a streamlined approach in pandemic control. *Journal of Air Transport Management*, *44*, 42–53. DOI: 10.1016/j.jairtraman.2015.02.003 PMID: 32572319

Cidell, J. (2015). The role of major infrastructure in subregional economic development: An empirical study of airports and cities. *Journal of Economic Geography*, *15*(6), 1125–1144. DOI: 10.1093/jeg/lbu029

Cini, V., & Nater, N. (2009). Porter's Diamond Model of Osijek-Baranja County Industry. *Interdisciplinary Management Research*, *5*, 761–769.

Cioffi, R., Travaglioni, M., Piscitelli, G., Petrillo, A., & De Felice, F. (2020). Artificial intelligence and machine learning applications in smart production: Progress, trends, and directions. [mdpi.com]. *Sustainability (Basel)*, *12*(2), 492. DOI: 10.3390/su12020492

Cochrane, L., Drummond, O., & Jordan, E. (2024). Improving ethical assurance for non-university researchers in crisis settings: an early vision based on democratic norms. Research Ethics. sagepub.com

Cosa, M. (2024). Business digital transformation: Strategy adaptation, communication and future agenda. *Journal of Strategy and Management*, *17*(2), 244–259. DOI: 10.1108/JSMA-09-2023-0233

Cristani, F. (2023). Designing a Governance System for Cybersecurity of Foreign Investment in Europe. *International Investment Law Journal*, *3*(2), 102–120.

Cui, S., & Qi, P. (2021). The legal construction of personal information protection and privacy under the Chinese Civil Code. [HTML]. *Computer Law & Security Review*, *41*, 105560. DOI: 10.1016/j.clsr.2021.105560

Curti, F., Ivanov, I., Macchiavelli, M., & Zimmermann, T. (2023). City hall has been hacked! the financial costs of lax cybersecurity. SSRN *Electronic Journal*. DOI: 10.2139/ssrn.4465071

Cvitanovic, C., Shellock, R. J., Mackay, M., Van Putten, E. I., Karcher, D. B., Dickey-Collas, M., & Ballesteros, M. (2021). Strategies for building and managing 'trust'to enable knowledge exchange at the interface of environmental science and policy. [HTML]. *Environmental Science & Policy*, *123*, 179–189. DOI: 10.1016/j.envsci.2021.05.020

Dahiya, R., Le, S., Ring, J. K., & Watson, K. (2022). Big Data Analytics and Competitive Advantage: The Strategic Role of Firm-Specific Knowledge. *Journal of Strategy and Management*, *15*(2), 175–193. DOI: 10.1108/JSMA-08-2020-0203

Dal-Ré, R., Bouter, L. M., Cuijpers, P., Gluud, C., & Holm, S. (2020). Should research misconduct be criminalized? [sagepub.com]. *Research Ethics*, •••, 174701611989840.

Darwinkel, E., Chan, A., & Sheridan, L. (2020). Tertiary concerns: Campus threat assessment and management in an Australian university. [HTML]. *Journal of Threat Assessment and Management*, *7*(3-4), 173–185. DOI: 10.1037/tam0000152

Davis, P. S., Desai, A. B., & Francis, J. D. (2000). Mode of international entry: An isomorphism perspective. *Journal of International Business Studies*, *31*(2), 239–258. DOI: 10.1057/palgrave.jibs.8490904

de Carvalho, M. A.Junior, & Bandiera-Paiva, P. (2021). Implications of loosened Role-based Access Control session control implementation for the enforcement of Dynamic Mutually Exclusive Roles properties on Health Information Systems. [sciencedirect.com]. *Informatics in Medicine Unlocked*, *27*, 100780. DOI: 10.1016/j.imu.2021.100780

Dean, M. (2022). *A practical guide to multi-criteria analysis*. UCL.

Degn, L. (2020). Integrating integrity: The organizational translation of policies on research integrity. [HTML]. *Science and Engineering Ethics*, *26*(6), 3167–3182. DOI: 10.1007/s11948-020-00262-w PMID: 32840718

DeGrendele, C. J., Kazakov, J. A., & Reuter, M. G. (2022). Interpreting non-semielliptical complex bands. [HTML]. *Journal of Physics Condensed Matter*, *34*(26), 265501. DOI: 10.1088/1361-648X/ac655b PMID: 35390781

Deloitte Indonesia. (2024). *Deloitte Indonesia Perspectives*. Deloitte. https://www2.deloitte.com/content/dam/Deloitte/id/Documents/about-deloitte/id-about-dip-4th-edition-sept2024-id.pdf

Dermawan, A. (2019), No reason for PIA to fear competition from KXP. New Straits Times. 5 November 2019. https://www.nst.com.my/news/nation/2019/11/535956/no-reason-pia-fear-competition-kxp Retrieved on 8 April 2025.

Dermawan, A. (2022). Flash floods also strike Penang International Airport. New Straits Times, 24 September 2022. https://www.nst.com.my/news/nation/2022/09/834000/flash-floods-also-strike-penang-international-airport Retrieved on 10 April 2025.

Dermawan, A. (2025). Penang airport to expand parking bays to accommodate 12mil annual passengers. New Straits Times. 2 April 2025. https://www.nst.com.my/business/corporate/2025/04/1196365/penang-airport-expand-parking-bays-accommodate-12mil-annual Retrieved on 8 April 2025.

Derrick, G. E., & Ross-Hellauer, T. (2024). De-legitimising the social sciences and humanities through peer review. Handbook of Meta-Research. [HTML] DOI: 10.4337/9781839105722.00027

Di Minin, E., Fink, C., Hausmann, A., Kremer, J., & Kulkarni, R. (2021). How to address data privacy concerns when using social media data in conservation science. [wiley.com]. *Conservation Biology*, *35*(2), 437–446. DOI: 10.1111/cobi.13708 PMID: 33749044

Dias Canedo, E., Toffano Seidel Calazans, A., Toffano Seidel Masson, E., Teixeira Costa, P. H., & Lima, F. (2020). Perceptions of ICT practitioners regarding software privacy. [mdpi.com]. *Entropy (Basel, Switzerland)*, *22*(4), 429. DOI: 10.3390/e22040429 PMID: 33286202

Díaz, E. (2016). The new European Union General Regulation on Data Protection and the legal consequences for institutions. Church. *Communication and Culture*, *1*(1), 206–239. DOI: 10.1080/23753234.2016.1240912

Diep, N. T., Huy, D. T. N., & Hien, D. T. N. (2023). Further discussion on investment law, cybersecurity law, and recommendations for attracting foreign investment (FDI). [IJOLS]. *International Journal of Legal Studies*, *13*(1), 119–134.

Dinev, T., & Hart, P. (2006). An extended privacy calculus model for e-commerce transactions. *Information Systems Research*, *17*(1), 61–80. DOI: 10.1287/isre.1060.0080

Dobson, P., & Starkey, K. (2002). The competitive advantage of nations. *Journal of Management Studies*, *29*(2), 253–255.

Dorairajan, V. (2024). Cybersecurity and organizational performance – the interplay. *Acta Cybernetica (Szeged)*, *7*, e129255. DOI: 10.3897/aca.7.e129255

Dorfleitner, G., Hornuf, L., & Kreppmeier, J. (2023). Promise not fulfilled: FinTech, data privacy, and the GDPR. *Electronic Markets*, *33*(1), 33. DOI: 10.1007/s12525-023-00622-x

Ducato, R. (2020). Data protection, scientific research, and the role of information. Computer Law & Security Review. sciencedirect.com

Ducato, R. (2020). Data protection, scientific research, and the role of information. *Computer Law & Security Review*, *37*, 105412. DOI: 10.1016/j.clsr.2020.105412

Dunning, J. H. (1979). Toward an Eclectic Theory of International Production: Some Empirical Tests. *Journal of International Business Studies*, *11*(1), 9–31. DOI: 10.1057/palgrave.jibs.8490593

Dunning, J. H. (1993). Internationalizing Porter's diamond. [special issue]. *Management International Review*, *33*, 7–15.

Dupont, B. & Whelan, C. (2021). Enhancing relationships between criminology and cybersecurity. Journal of criminology. sagepub.com

Durmaz, A., Dursun, İ., & Kabadayi, E. T. (2020). Mitigating the effects of social desirability bias in self-report surveys: Classical and new techniques. In *Applied social science approaches to mixed methods research* (pp. 146–185). IGI Global. [HTML] DOI: 10.4018/978-1-7998-1025-4.ch007

Dutta, N., Jadav, N., Tanwar, S., Sarma, H. K. D., & Pricop, E. (2022). Cyber security: Issues and current trends. [HTML]

Dwork, C., & Roth, A. (2014). The algorithmic foundations of differential privacy. Foundations and Trends® in Theoretical Computer Science, 9(3–4), 211-407.

Dyer, J. H., & Singh, H. (1998). The relational view: Cooperative strategy and sources of interorganizational competitive advantage. *Academy of Management Review*, *23*(4), 660–679. DOI: 10.2307/259056

Eakin, J. M., & Gladstone, B. (2020). "Value-adding" analysis: Doing more with qualitative data. [sagepub.com]. *International Journal of Qualitative Methods*, *19*, 1609406920949333. DOI: 10.1177/1609406920949333

Ekaputra, V. D., & Simamora, S. C. (2024). Systematic Literature Review on Aerotropolis.

El-Adaway, I. H. & Jennings, M. (2022). Professional and organizational leadership role in ethics management: Avoiding reliance on ethical codification and nurturing ethical culture. Science and Engineering Ethics. springer.com

Eling, M., McShane, M., & Nguyen, T. (2021). Cyber risk management: History and future research directions. [HTML]. *Risk Management & Insurance Review*, *24*(1), 93–125. DOI: 10.1111/rmir.12169

Emami-Naeini, P., Agarwal, Y., Cranor, L. F., & Hibshi, H. (2020, May). Ask the experts: What should be on an IoT privacy and security label? In *2020 IEEE Symposium on Security and Privacy (SP)* (pp. 447-464). IEEE. [PDF] DOI: 10.1109/SP40000.2020.00043

Erkan, T. E., & Elsharida, W. M. (2019). Overview of airport location selection methods. *International Journal of Applied Engineering Research: IJAER*, *14*(7), 1613–1618.

Esen, S., & Uyar, H. (2012). Examining the competitive structure of Turkish tourism industry in comparison with diamond model. *Procedia: Social and Behavioral Sciences*, *62*, 620–627. DOI: 10.1016/j.sbspro.2012.09.104

European Parliament & Council of the European Union. (2016). *Regulation (EU) 2016/679 of the European Parliament and of the Council.*

Eyal, P., David, R., Andrew, G., Zak, E., & Ekaterina, D. (2021). Data quality of platforms and panels for online behavioral research. [springer.com]. *Behavior Research Methods*, •••, 1–20. PMID: 34590289

Facca, D., Smith, M. J., Shelley, J., Lizotte, D., & Donelle, L. (2020). Exploring the ethical issues in research using digital data collection strategies with minors: A scoping review. Plos one. plos.org

Fadlelmola, F. M., Zass, L., Chaouch, M., Samtal, C., Ras, V., Kumuthini, J., Panji, S., & Mulder, N. (2021). Data Management Plans in the genomics research revolution of Africa: Challenges and recommendations. [sciencedirect.com]. *Journal of Biomedical Informatics*, *122*, 103900. DOI: 10.1016/j.jbi.2021.103900 PMID: 34506960

Fahad, S. A., Salloum, S. A., & Shaalan, K. (2024). The role of ChatGPT in knowledge sharing and collaboration within digital workplaces: A systematic review. *Artificial intelligence in education: The power and dangers of ChatGPT in the classroom*, 259-282. https://doi.org/DOI: 10.1007/978-3-031-52280-2_17

Fahle, S., Prinz, C., & Kuhlenkötter, B. (2020). Systematic review on machine learning (ML) methods for manufacturing processes–Identifying artificial intelligence (AI) methods for field application. Procedia CIRP. sciencedirect.com

Falade, P. V. (2024). Investigating the security and privacy issues in ChatGPT usage and their impact on organisational and individual security. *Int. J. Sci. Res. in Multidisciplinary Studies Vol, 10*(3).

Famoti, O., Ewim, C. P. M., Eloho, O., Muyiwa-Ajayi, T. P., Ezechi, O. N., & Omokhoa, H. E. (2025). Revolutionizing customer experience management through data-driven strategies in financial services. *International Journal of Advanced Multidisciplinary Research and Studies.*, *5*(1), 948–957. DOI: 10.62225/2583049X.2025.5.1.3748

Farhad, M. A. (2024). Consumer Data Protection Laws and Their Impact on Business Models in the Tech Industry. *Telecommunications Policy*, *48*(9), 102836. DOI: 10.1016/j.telpol.2024.102836

Favaretto, M., De Clercq, E., Gaab, J., & Elger, B. S. (2020). First do no harm: An exploration of researchers' ethics of conduct in Big Data behavioral studies. Plos one. plos.org

Fecher, B., Kuper, F., Sokolovska, N., Fenton, A., Hornbostel, S., & Wagner, G. G. (2021). Understanding the societal impact of the social sciences and humanities: Remarks on roles, challenges, and expectations. [frontiersin.org]. *Frontiers in Research Metrics and Analytics*, *6*, 696804. DOI: 10.3389/frma.2021.696804 PMID: 34278206

Fenton, A. J. (2024). Preventing catastrophic cyber-physical attacks on the global maritime transportation system: A case study of hybrid maritime security in the Straits of Malacca and Singapore. *Journal of Marine Science and Engineering*, *12*(3), 510–526. DOI: 10.3390/jmse12030510

Fenton, A. J. (2024). Preventing catastrophic cyber-physical attacks on the global maritime transportation system: A case study of hybrid maritime security in the Straits of Malacca and Singapore. *Preprints*. https://doi.org/DOI: 10.20944/preprints202401.1609.v1

Ferretti, A., Ienca, M., Hurst, S., & Vayena, E. (2020). Big data, biomedical research, and ethics review: New challenges for IRBs. [wiley.com]. *Ethics & Human Research*, *42*(5), 17–28. DOI: 10.1002/eahr.500065 PMID: 32937036

Ferretti, A., Ienca, M., Velarde, M. R., Hurst, S., & Vayena, E. (2022). The challenges of big data for research ethics committees: A qualitative Swiss study. [sagepub.com]. *Journal of Empirical Research on Human Research Ethics; JERHRE, 17*(1-2), 129–143. DOI: 10.1177/15562646211053538 PMID: 34779661

Fiero, A. W. & Beier, E. (2022). New global developments in data protection and privacy regulations: Comparative analysis of European Union, United States, and Russian legislation. Stan. J. Int'l L.. [HTML]

Fisher, M. T. (2023). *Stability of Cultural Information in Unstable Environments: Data Management for Digital Preservation of Immovable Cultural Heritage against Natural Hazards*. Managing Disaster Risks to Cultural Heritage. [HTML] DOI: 10.4324/9781003263647-4

Florea, D. & Florea, S. (2020). Big Data and the ethical implications of data privacy in higher education research. Sustainability. mdpi.com

Floridi, L., Cowls, J., Beltrametti, M., Chatila, R., Chazerand, P., Dignum, V., Luetge, C., Madelin, R., Pagallo, U., Rossi, F., Schafer, B., Valcke, P., & Vayena, E. (2018). AI4People—an ethical framework for a good AI society: Opportunities, risks, principles, and recommendations. *Minds and Machines, 28*(4), 689–707. DOI: 10.1007/s11023-018-9482-5 PMID: 30930541

Florido-Benítez, L. (2024). The types of hackers and cyberattacks in the aviation industry. *Journal of Transportation Security, 17*(1), 13. https://link.springer.com/article/10.1007/s12198-024-00281-9. DOI: 10.1007/s12198-024-00281-9

Foulds, C., Royston, S., Berker, T., Nakopoulou, E., Bharucha, Z. P., Robison, R., Abram, S., Ančić, B., Arapostathis, S., Badescu, G., Bull, R., Cohen, J., Dunlop, T., Dunphy, N., Dupont, C., Fischer, C., Gram-Hanssen, K., Grandclément, C., Heiskanen, E., & Živčič, L. (2022). An agenda for future Social Sciences and Humanities research on energy efficiency: 100 priority research questions. [nature.com]. *Humanities & Social Sciences Communications, 9*(1), 1–18. DOI: 10.1057/s41599-022-01243-z PMID: 35791377

Freese, J., Rauf, T., & Voelkel, J. G. (2022). Advances in transparency and reproducibility in the social sciences. [HTML]. *Social Science Research, 107*, 102770. DOI: 10.1016/j.ssresearch.2022.102770 PMID: 36058608

Frei, J., Greiling, D., & Schmidthuber, J. (2023). Reconciling field-level logics and management control practices in research management at Austrian public universities. *Qualitative Research in Accounting & Management, 20*(1), 117–143. DOI: 10.1108/QRAM-10-2020-0167

Frétigny, J. B., Magnan, M., Maulat, J., & Pedro, M. (2024). "Airport city" or "VIP" urbanism? Questioning the market-led land development strategies of airports. *Human Geographies, 17*(3), 262–277. DOI: 10.1177/19427786241251723

Frey, C. B., & Presidente, G. (2024). Privacy Regulation and Firm Performance: Estimating the GDPR Effect Globally. *Economic Inquiry, 62*(3), 1074–1089. DOI: 10.1111/ecin.13213

Gao, R. Y. (2024). The diffusion of a US trade-based approach to international personal data transfers and its implications for national data privacy regulations. *International Data Privacy Law, 14*(4), 352–376.

Gara, G. L., & Porte, J. M. L. (2020). Processes of building trust in organizations: Internal communication, management, and recruiting. *Church, Communication and Culture*. https://www.tandfonline.com/doi/abs/10.1080/23753234.2020.1824581

Gardner, H. (2024). The Essential Howard Gardner on Education. [HTML]

Gedutis, A., Biagetti, M. T., & Ma, L. (2022). The challenges for research evaluation ethics in the social sciences. In *Handbook on Research Assessment in the Social Sciences* (pp. 367–385). Edward Elgar Publishing. [HTML] DOI: 10.4337/9781800372559.00032

Gentile, A. F., Fazio, P., & Miceli, G. (2021). A Survey on the Implementation and Management of Secure Virtual Private Networks (VPNs) and Virtual LANs (VLANs) in Static and Mobile Scenarios. Telecom. mdpi.com

Gesualdo, F., Daverio, M., Palazzani, L., Dimitriou, D., Diez-Domingo, J., Fons-Martinez, J., Jackson, S., Vignally, P., Rizzo, C., & Tozzi, A. E. (2021). Digital tools in the informed consent process: A systematic review. [springer.com]. *BMC Medical Ethics, 22*(1), 1–10. DOI: 10.1186/s12910-021-00585-8 PMID: 33639926

Ghosh, A., Thomas, M., & Chakraborty, S. (2021). 5G and IoT security: Emerging threats and countermeasures. *Journal of Ambient Intelligence and Humanized Computing, 12*(5), 5033–5047.

Golandaj, J. A., & Kallihal, K. G. (2021). Awareness, attitude and practises of biomedical waste management amongst public health-care staff in Karnataka, India. *Journal of Humanities and Applied Social Sciences, 3*(1), 49–63. DOI: 10.1108/JHASS-08-2019-0041

Goldsack, J. C., Coravos, A., Bakker, J. P., Bent, B., Dowling, A. V., Fitzer-Attas, C., & Dunn, J. (2020). Verification, analytical validation, and clinical validation (V3): The foundation of determining fit-for-purpose for Biometric Monitoring Technologies (BioMeTs). npj digital [nature.com]. *Medicine, 3*(1), 55. PMID: 32146899

Gonzalez-Granadillo, G., Menesidou, S. A., Papamartzivanos, D., Romeu, R., Navarro-Llobet, D., Okoh, C., Nifakos, S., Xenakis, C., & Panaousis, E. (2021). Automated cyber and privacy risk management toolkit. [mdpi.com]. *Sensors (Basel), 21*(16), 5493. DOI: 10.3390/s21165493 PMID: 34450935

Gopalakrishnan, K., Govindarasu, M., Jacobson, D. W., & Phares, B. M. (2013). Cyber security for airports. *IJTTE. International Journal for Traffic and Transport Engineering*, *3*(4), 365–376. DOI: 10.7708/ijtte.2013.3(4).02

Gopal, R. D., Ramesh, R., & Whinston, A. B. (2003). Microproducts in a digital economy: Trading small, gaining large. *International Journal of Electronic Commerce*, *8*(2), 9–30. DOI: 10.1080/10864415.2003.11044292

Gordon, L. A., Loeb, M. P., & Zhou, L. (2020). Integrating cost–benefit analysis into the NIST Cybersecurity Framework via the Gordon–Loeb Model. *Journal of Cybersecurity*, *6*(1), tyaa005.

Grant, R. M. (1991). Porter's 'Competitive Advantage of Nations': An Assessment. *Strategic Management Journal, 12*(7), 535–548. DOI: 10.1002/smj.4250120706

Grant, R. M. (1998). *Contemporary Strategy Analysis*. Blackwell.

Griffin, M., Martino, R. J., LoSchiavo, C., Comer-Carruthers, C., Krause, K. D., Stults, C. B., & Halkitis, P. N. (2021). Ensuring survey research data integrity in the era of internet bots. [springer.com]. *Quality & Quantity*, •••, 1–12. PMID: 34629553

Grimm, J. J., Koehler, K., Schierenbeck, I., Saliba, I., & Lust, E. M. (2020). Safer field research in the social sciences: A guide to human and digital security in hostile environments. [HTML]

Gstrein, O. J. & Beaulieu, A. (2022). How to protect privacy in a datafied society? A presentation of multiple legal and conceptual approaches. Philosophy & Technology. springer.com

Gumpert, A., Manova, K., Rujan, C., & Schnitzer, M. (2025). Multinational firms and global innovation.

Guo, Y. C. (2023). Development Opportunities, Challenges, and Strategies for Cybersecurity Insurance in the Digital Economy Era. *Global Economic Perspectives, 1*(3).

Gupta, V., & Yang, H. (2024). Study protocol for factors influencing the adoption of ChatGPT technology by startups: Perceptions and attitudes of entrepreneurs. *PLoS One*, *19*(2), e0298427. DOI: 10.1371/journal.pone.0298427 PMID: 38358993

Haass, J., Sampigethaya, R., & Capezzuto, V. (2016). Aviation and cybersecurity: opportunities for applied research. Tr News, (304), 39. https://commons.erau.edu/publication/299/

Hadi, S., Tjahjono, H. K., & Palupi, M. (2020). *Systematic Review: Meta Sintesis Untuk Riset Perilaku Organisasional*. Viva Victory Abadi. https://pak.uii.ac.id/wp-content/uploads/2023/03/Buku-Ajar-2019-Systematic-Review-Meta-Sintesis-Untuk-Riset-Perilaku-Organisasional_ok.pdf

Hadi, M. U., Qureshi, R., Shah, A., Irfan, M., Zafar, A., Shaikh, M. B., & Mirjalili, S. (2023). Large language models: a comprehensive survey of its applications, challenges, limitations, and future prospects. *Authorea Preprints, 1*, 1-26.

Hagedorn-Hatfield, R. L., Qamar, Z., Richards, R., Patton-López, M. M., Savoie-Roskos, M. R., Heying, E. K., Landry, M. J., Mann, G., Vogelzang, J. L., OoNorasak, K., Cuite, C. L., & Hood, L. B. (2023). Barriers and facilitators to implementing and sustaining campus food insecurity initiatives. [HTML]. *Studies in Higher Education*, *48*(8), 1273–1288. DOI: 10.1080/03075079.2023.2195414

Haghani, M., Bliemer, M. C. J., Goerlandt, F., & Li, J. (2020). The scientific literature on Coronaviruses, COVID-19 and its associated safety-related research dimensions: A scientometric analysis and scoping review. Safety science. nih.gov

Haislip, J., Kolev, K., Pinsker, R., & Steffen, T. (2019, June). The economic cost of cybersecurity breaches: A broad-based analysis. In *Workshop on the economics of information security (WEIS)* (Vol. 1, p. 37).

Hakimi, L., Eynon, R., & Murphy, V. A. (2021). The ethics of using digital trace data in education: A thematic review of the research landscape. [sagepub.com]. *Review of Educational Research*, *91*(5), 671–717. DOI: 10.3102/00346543211020116

Halid, S. (2019). Kerajaan lulus bina Lapangan Terbang Antarabangsa Kulim, lebuh raya Berita Harian [Government approves construction of Kulim International Airport, highway Berita Harian]. Retrieved on 8 April 2025.

Halizam, M. A., Ridzuan, A. R., Shaari, M. S., Abd Rahman, N. H., & Md Razak, M. I. (2021). Revisiting the Impact of Foreign Direct Investment on Malaysia Economic Growth. *International Journal of Academic Research in Business & Social Sciences*, *11*(5). Advance online publication. DOI: 10.6007/IJARBSS/v11-i5/9755

Hall, P. G. (1998). *Cities in civilization* (Vol. 21). Pantheon Books.

Hanan, S. A., Osman, N. H., Abidin, R., Zahari, F. M., & Noordin, A. (2022). Location Planning of Airport Facilities: Case Study of KXP International Airport. UUM 7th International Case Study Conference (ICSC) 2022. Universiti Utara Malaysia (UUM). e-ISSN: 2756-8482

Hantrais, L., & Lenihan, A. T. (2021). Social dimensions of evidence-based policy in a digital society. [HTML]. *Contemporary Social Science*, *16*(2), 141–155. DOI: 10.1080/21582041.2021.1887508

Hashim, R. (2023). KXP untuk keperluan kargo, bukan bersaing dengan [LTAPP KXP for cargo needs, not competing with LTAPP]. Sinar Harian. 10 March 2023. https://www.sinarharian.com.my/article/249010/edisi/utara/kxp-untuk-keperluan-kargo-bukan-bersaing-dengan-ltapp Retrieved on 8 April 2025.

Hassan, A., Abatcha, M., & Dada, E. G. (2024). Ensemble machine learning algorithm for Telegram spam detection. *International Journal of Cybersecurity Research*, *10*(8), 123–140.

Head, G. (2020). Ethics in educational research: Review boards, ethical issues and researcher development. European Educational Research Journal. sagepub.com

Heide, M., & Villeneuve, J. P. (2020). From secrecy privilege to information management: A comparative analysis of classification reforms. [HTML]. *Government Information Quarterly*, *37*(4), 101500. DOI: 10.1016/j.giq.2020.101500

Hellwig, D. P., & Huchzermeier, A. (2022). Distributed ledger technology and fully homomorphic encryption: Next-generation information-sharing for supply chain efficiency. In *Innovative Technology at the Interface of Finance and Operations* (Vol. II, pp. 31–49). Springer International Publishing. [HTML] DOI: 10.1007/978-3-030-81945-3_2

Herath, H. S. B., & Herath, T. (2006). Justifying spam and e-mail virus security investments: A case study. *Journal of Information Systems Security*, *4*(1), 123–135.

Hezam, I. M., Ali, A. M., Sallam, K. M., Hameed, I. A., & Božanić, D. (2024). *Evaluation based on multi-criteria decision-making methods and spherical fuzzy framework for security and privacy in metaverse technologies: A case study*. American Institute of Physics., DOI: 10.1063/5.0217439

Hintošová, A. B. (2021). The digital economy in the context of foreign direct investment flows. In Fostering Innovation and Competitiveness with FinTech, RegTech, and SupTech (pp. 210-227). IGI Global Scientific Publishing.

Hintošová, A., & Bódy, G. (2023). Sustainable FDI in the digital economy. *Sustainability (Basel)*, *15*(14), 10794. DOI: 10.3390/su151410794

Holden, O. L., Norris, M. E., & Kuhlmeier, V. A. (2021). Academic integrity in online assessment: A research review. Frontiers in Education. frontiersin.org

Hoofnagle, C. J., van der Sloot, B., & Borgesius, F. Z. (2019). The European Union general data protection regulation: What it is and what it means*. *Information & Communications Technology Law*. https://www.tandfonline.com/doi/abs/10.1080/13600834.2019.1573501

Huang, J. (2018). Building intelligence in digital transformation. *Journal of Integrated Design & Process Science*, *21*(4), 1–4. DOI: 10.3233/jid-2018-0006

Huang, K., Zhang, F., Li, Y., Wright, S., Kidambi, V., & Manral, V. (2023). Security and privacy concerns in ChatGPT. In Beyond, A. I. (Ed.), *ChatGPT, Web3, and the Business Landscape of Tomorrow* (pp. 297–328). Springer Nature Switzerland., DOI: 10.1007/978-3-031-45282-6_11

Huan, Y., & Qamruzzaman, M. (2022). Innovation-led Foreign Direct Investment (FDI) Sustainability: Clarifying the Nexus between Financial Innovation, Technological Innovation, Environmental Innovation, and FDI in the BRIC Nations. *Sustainability*, *14*(23), 15732. DOI: 10.3390/su142315732

Hua, S., Jin, S., & Jiang, S. (2024). The limitations and ethical considerations of ChatGPT. *Data Intelligence*, *6*(1), 201–239. DOI: 10.1162/dint_a_00243

Hughes, R., Rose, A., Lozano, J. S., Garguilo, S., & Knight, D. (2022). A Model of Misconduct, Accusations, and Institution Response at US Colleges and Universities: Synthesis of the Literature and an Agenda for Future Research. Higher Education: Handbook of Theory and Research: Volume 37, 457-517. [HTML]

Humayun, M., Niazi, M., Jhanjhi, N. Z., Alshayeb, M., & Mahmood, S. (2020). Cyber security threats and vulnerabilities: A systematic mapping study. [HTML]. *Arabian Journal for Science and Engineering*, *45*(4), 3171–3189. DOI: 10.1007/s13369-019-04319-2

Humlum, A., & Vestergaard, E. (2024). *The adoption of ChatGPT* (No. 16992). IZA Discussion Papers. https://www.econstor.eu/handle/10419/299920

Hunjet, A., Zagoracz, I., Milkovic, M., & Kozina, G. (2022). Intellectual Property Rights as A Source of Competitive Advantage. Economic and Social Development: Book of Proceedings, 327-339.

Husband, G. (2020). Ethical data collection and recognizing the impact of semi-structured interviews on research respondents. Education Sciences. mdpi.com

Huston, S. (2015). The Aerotropolis Development Catalyst or Distraction.

Ibbett, H. & Brittain, S. (2020). Conservation publications and their provisions to protect research participants. Conservation Biology. wiley.com

IBM. (2024, August 12). *What Is Cybersecurity? | IBM*. What Is Cybersecurity? https://www.ibm.com/think/topics/cybersecurity

Ifeanyi-Obi, C. C., Issa, F. O., Aderinoye-Abdulwahab, S. O., Ayinde, A. F., Umeh, O. J., & Tologbonse, E. B. (2022). Promoting uptake and integration of climate smart agriculture technologies, innovations and management practices into policy and practice in Nigeria. *International Journal of Climate Change Strategies and Management*, *14*(4), 354–374. DOI: 10.1108/IJCCSM-09-2021-0101

Imron, I., Fridianto, T., & Nugroho, D. H. (2023). Identifikasi bahaya keamanan siber pada perizinan bahan nuklir online di Indonesia. *Jurnal Pengawasan Energi dan Teknologi Nuklir*, [Identification of cybersecurity hazards in online nuclear material licensing in Indonesia. Journal of Nuclear Energy and Technology Supervision]. 3(2), 49-67. https://doi.org/DOI: 10.53862/jupeten.v3i2.003

Islam, M., Sourav, M., & Reza, J. (2024). The Impact of Data Protection Regulations on Business Analytics

Ismagilova, E., Hughes, L., Rana, N. P., & Dwivedi, Y. K. (2022). Security, privacy and risks within smart cities: Literature review and development of a smart city interaction framework. [springer.com]. *Information Systems Frontiers*, *24*(2), 1–22. DOI: 10.1007/s10796-020-10044-1 PMID: 32837262

ITF-OECD. (2017). Airport Site Selection. Organisation for Economic Co-operation and Development - International Transport Forum (OECD-ITF) https://www.itf-oecd.org/sites/default/files/docs/airport-site-selection.pdf

Jain, A. K., Sahoo, S. R., & Kaubiyal, J. (2021). Online social networks security and privacy: comprehensive review and analysis. Complex & Intelligent Systems. springer.com

Jakubik, M. (2021). How can practical wisdom manifest itself in five fundamental management and leadership practices? *Vilakshan - XIMB. Journal of Management*, *18*(1), 3–25. DOI: 10.1108/XJM-08-2020-0078

Jangampeta, S. (2022). Financial data security and SIEM: Protecting Sensitive Financial Information in Banking and Fintech Systems. *Turkish Journal of Computer and Mathematics Education*, *13*(2), 1185–1188. DOI: 10.61841/turcomat.v13i2.14414

Janssen, M., Brous, P., Estevez, E., Barbosa, L. S., & Janowski, T. (2020). Data Governance: Organizing Data for Trustworthy Artificial Intelligence. *Government Information Quarterly*, *37*(3), 101493. DOI: 10.1016/j.giq.2020.101493

Jawed, I., & Siddiqui, D. A. (2019). *What matters for firms' performance: Capabilities, tangible or intangible resources? Evidence from corporate sectors on Pakistan*. Evidence From Corporate Sectors on Pakistan.

Jiang, T. A. O., Li, J. P., Haq, A. U., Saboor, A., & Ali, A. (2021). A novel stacking approach for accurate detection of fake news. IEEE Access. ieee.org

Joglekar, P., Rajurkar, J., Shinde, M., Tayde, P., & Gadmade, V. (2024). Machine learning based email spam detection: Achieving high accuracy and efficiency. *International Journal for Research in Applied Science and Engineering Technology, 12*(5), 189–202. DOI: 10.22214/ijraset.2024.62390

Jordan, J., & Ellen, C. (2009). Business need, data and business intelligence. *Journal of Digital Asset Management, 5*(1), 10–20. DOI: 10.1057/dam.2008.53

Josa, I. & Aguado, A. (2021). Social sciences and humanities in the education of civil engineers: Current status and proposal of guidelines. Journal of Cleaner Production. sciencedirect.com

Josten, M., & Weis, T. (2024). Investigating the effectiveness of Bayesian spam filters in detecting LLM-modified spam mails. *arXiv*. https://doi.org//arXiv.2408.14293DOI: 10.48550

Jusmadi, R., & Armando, A. (2024). Structure, Conduct, and Performance (SCP) Approach and Fairness Principle in Business Competition Law in the Era of Digital Platforms. Justitia Jurnal Hukum, 8(2).

Kamara, I. (2025), 'Two Worlds Converging in 2015: Standardization and Data Protection', Standardizing Personal Data Protection, Oxford Data Protection & Privacy Law (Oxford, 2025; online edn, Oxford Academic, 14 Mar. 2025), DOI: 10.1093/9780191997037.003.0001

Kamarul, A., & Kang, S. L. (2024). Cover Story: No urgent need for national policy on airport and seaport development, says Loke. 24 December 2024. The Edge Malaysia. Retrieved from https://theedgemalaysia.com/node/737973

Kankwende, P. (2024). Cybersecurity in the modern age: Protecting digital assets. *Journal of Information Security, 19*(2), 145–160.

Karhulahti, V. M. & Backe, H. J. (2021). Transparency of peer review: a semi-structured interview study with chief editors from social sciences and humanities. Research Integrity and Peer Review. springer.com

Kasarda, J. D. (2000). Logistics & the rise of aerotropolis. *Real Estate Issues, 25*(4), 43–43.

Kasarda, J. D. (2008). *The evolution of airport cities and the aerotropolis. Dalam JD Kasarda, Airport Cities, The Evolution*. Insight Media.

Kaspersky. (2024). *IT Security Economics*. IT Security Economics. https://www.kaspersky.com/blog/it-security-economics-2024/

Kaur, J., Hazrati Fard, S. M., Amiri-Zarandi, M., & Dara, R. (2022). Protecting farmers' data privacy and confidentiality: Recommendations and considerations. [frontiersin.org]. *Frontiers in Sustainable Food Systems*, *6*, 903230. DOI: 10.3389/fsufs.2022.903230

Kaur, S., Kaur, G., & Shabaz, M. (2022). A Secure Two-Factor Authentication Framework in Cloud Computing. [wiley.com]. *Security and Communication Networks*, *2022*(1), 7540891. DOI: 10.1155/2022/7540891

Kazda, A., Badanik, B., & Serrano, F. (2022). Pandemic vs. Post-pandemic airport operations: Hard impact, slow recovery. *Aerospace (Basel, Switzerland)*, *9*(12), 810. DOI: 10.3390/aerospace9120810

Kehal, H. S., & Singh, V. P. (Eds.). (2005). *Digital Economy: impacts, influences, and challenges*. IGI Global. DOI: 10.4018/978-1-59140-363-0

Keshta, I. & Odeh, A. (2021). Security and privacy of electronic health records: Concerns and challenges. Egyptian Informatics Journal. sciencedirect.com

Khando, K., Gao, S., Islam, S. M., & Salman, A. (2021). Enhancing employees information security awareness in private and public organisations: A systematic literature review. Computers & security. sciencedirect.com

Khare, S. K., Blanes-Vidal, V., Nadimi, E. S., & Acharya, U. R. (2024). Emotion recognition and artificial intelligence [) and research recommendations. Information Fusion. sciencedirect.com]. *Systematic Reviews*, •••, 2014–2023.

Kim, I., Susilo, W., Baek, J., Kim, J., & Chow, Y. W. (2023). PCSF: Privacy-preserving content-based spam filter. *IEEE Transactions on Information Forensics and Security*, *18*, 3245–3257. DOI: 10.1109/TIFS.2023.3255172

Kim, L. (2022). Cybersecurity: Ensuring confidentiality, integrity, and availability of information. In *Nursing Informatics: A Health Informatics, Interprofessional and Global Perspective* (pp. 391–410). Springer International Publishing. [HTML] DOI: 10.1007/978-3-030-91237-6_26

Kindervag, J., & Balaouras, S. (2010). No more chewy centers: Introducing the zero trust model of information security. *Forestry Research*, *3*(1), 1–16.

King, G., Keohane, R. O., & Verba, S. (2021). Designing social inquiry: Scientific inference in qualitative research. [HTML]

Kirya, M. T. (2020). Promoting anti-corruption, transparency and accountability in the recruitment and promotion of health workers to safeguard health outcomes. Global health action. tandfonline.com

Kok, S. L., Khan, H., & Siripipatthanakul, S. (2023). The Role of Foreign Direct Investment in Creating Competitive Advantage For Electronics Manufacturing Companies In Northern Malaysia, December 2023. Thesis for Doctor of Business Administration. Manipal GlobalNxt University, Malaysia. DOI: DOI: 10.13140/ RG.2.2.27160.61445

Kolstoe, S. E. & Pugh, J. (2023). The trinity of good research: Distinguishing between research integrity, ethics, and governance. Accountability in Research. tandfonline.com

Koneru, G. (2024). *The Evolving World of Data Privacy: Trends and Strategies*. The Evolving World of Data Privacy: Trends and Strategies. https://www.isaca.org/ resources/news-and-trends/industry-news/2024/the-evolving-world-of-data-privacy -trends-and-strategies

Kong, Y., & Suntrayuth, S. (2021). The Causal Model of Absorptive Capacity, Strategic Flexibility, and Innovation Performance in Relation to Sustainable Competitive Advantage: An Internationalization Perspective. Thammasat Review, 24(1), 214-246. https://sc01.tci-thaijo.org/index.php/tureview/article/view/239910

Kraiwanit, T., Limna, P., & Siripipatthanakul, S. (2023). NVivo for social sciences and management studies: A systematic review. *Advance Knowledge for Executives*, *2*(3), 1–11.

Kraiwanit, T., Limna, P., & Siripipatthanakul, S. (2023). NVivo for Social Sciences and Management Studies: A Systematic Review. *Advance Knowledge for Executives*, *2*(3), 1–11.

Kraus, S., Reiche, B. S., & Reschke, C. H. (2007, September). The role of strategic planning in SMEs: Literature review and implications. In Conference proceedings of the Annual Meeting of the British Academy of Management.

Krutilla, K., Alexeev, A., Jardine, E., & Good, D. (2021). The benefits and costs of cybersecurity risk reduction: A dynamic extension of the Gordon and Loeb model. *Risk Analysis*, *41*(10), 1795–1808. DOI: 10.1111/risa.13713 PMID: 33586801

Kshetri, N., & Kshetri, N. (2016). Cybersecurity's Effects on International Trade and Investment. The Quest to Cyber Superiority: Cybersecurity Regulations, Frameworks, and Strategies of Major Economies, 75-87. https://link.springer.com/chapter/10.1007/978-3-319-40554-4_4

Kuah, A., & Day, J. (2005). Revisiting the Porter Diamond: Applying an Importance-Performance Matrix to the Singaporean Financial Cluster. University of Bradford. School of Management. *Working Paper Series*, *5*, 1–22. https://researchonline.jcu.edu.au/28374/

Kuleto, V., Ilić, M., Dumangiu, M., Ranković, M., Martins, O. M., Păun, D., & Mihoreanu, L. (2021). Exploring opportunities and challenges of artificial intelligence and machine learning in higher education institutions. [mdpi.com]. *Sustainability (Basel)*, *13*(18), 10424. DOI: 10.3390/su131810424

Kumar, H. S., & Madan, S. (2021). A study on Aadhar privacy and personal security issues in India. *Zenodo*. https://doi.org/DOI: 10.5281/zenodo.4641658

Kuran, C. H. A., Morsut, C., Kruke, B. I., Krüger, M., Segnestam, L., Orru, K., Nævestad, T. O., Airola, M., Keränen, J., Gabel, F., Hansson, S., & Torpan, S. (2020). Vulnerability and vulnerable groups from an intersectionality perspective. [sciencedirect.com]. *International Journal of Disaster Risk Reduction*, *50*, 101826. DOI: 10.1016/j.ijdrr.2020.101826

Kwan, C. (2025, March). Land rush at Sydney's Aerotropolis with $450m government site on offer. *Financial Review*, •••, 10. Retrieved April 9, 2025, from

Kyereboah-Coleman, A., & Agyire-Tettey, K. F. (2008). Effect of Exchange-Rate Volatility on Foreign Direct Investment in Sub-Saharan Africa: The case of Ghana. *The Journal of Risk Finance*, *9*(1), 52–70. DOI: 10.1108/15265940810842410

Labadie, C. & Legner, C. (2023). Building data management capabilities to address data protection regulations: Learnings from EU-GDPR. Journal of Information Technology. sagepub.com

Lahtinen, T., Costin, A., & Suarez-Tangil, G. (2024). *Brain-Computer Interface Integration With Extended Reality (XR)*. Future, Privacy, And Security Outlook., DOI: 10.34190/eccws.23.1.2284

Landoll, D. (2021). The security risk assessment handbook: A complete guide for performing security risk assessments. [HTML]

Lang, V. (2021). Digitalization and digital transformation. In *Digital Fluency: Understanding the Basics of Artificial Intelligence, Blockchain Technology, Quantum Computing, and Their Applications for Digital Transformation* (pp. 1-50). Berkeley, CA: Apress. DOI: 10.1007/978-1-4842-6774-5_1

Lantos, J. D. (2020). The Belmont Report and innovative clinical research. [HTML]. *Perspectives in Biology and Medicine*, *63*(2), 389–400. DOI: 10.1353/pbm.2020.0026 PMID: 33416660

Lazer, D., Hargittai, E., Freelon, D., Gonzalez-Bailon, S., Munger, K., Ognyanova, K., & Radford, J. (2021). Meaningful measures of human society in the twenty-first century. [nature.com]. *Nature*, *595*(7866), 189–196. DOI: 10.1038/s41586-021-03660-7 PMID: 34194043

Le, P. N. (2021). Literature Review on the Impacts of Foreign Direct Investment in the Emerging Economy: The Case of Vietnam. Open Journal of Business and Management, 09(02).

Lee, I. (2021). Cybersecurity: Risk management framework and investment cost analysis. *Business Horizons*, *64*(5), 659–671. DOI: 10.1016/j.bushor.2021.02.022

Lee, Y. S., & Weber, R. A. (2025). Revealed privacy preferences: Are privacy choices rational? *Management Science*, *71*(3), 2657–2677. DOI: 10.1287/mnsc.2022.00807

Leng, J., Zhou, M., Zhao, J. L., Huang, Y., & Bian, Y. (2020). Blockchain security: A survey of techniques and research directions. [HTML]. *IEEE Transactions on Services Computing*, *15*(4), 2490–2510. DOI: 10.1109/TSC.2020.3038641

Li, Y. & Liu, Q. (2021). A comprehensive review study of cyber-attacks and cyber security; Emerging trends and recent developments. Energy Reports. sciencedirect.com

Lian, R., Zhou, A., & Zheng, Y. (2024). Towards secure and trustworthy crowdsourcing: Challenges, existing landscape, and future directions. [HTML]. *Wireless Networks*, *30*(5), 4329–4341. DOI: 10.1007/s11276-022-03015-8

Liew, J. T., & Lee, E. (2024). Cover Story: Penang's infrastructure playing catch-up with its industrial boom. The Edge Malaysia. 10 October 2024. https://theedgemalaysia.com/node/728632 Retrieved on 10 April 2024.

Li, F. (2024). Application and challenges of artificial intelligence in cybersecurity. *Cybersecurity and AI Journal*, *14*(3), 135–153. DOI: 10.54254/2755-2721/47/20241480

Li, K., Kim, D. J., Lang, K. R., Kauffman, R. J., & Naldi, M. (2020). How should we understand the digital economy in Asia? Critical assessment and research agenda. *Electronic Commerce Research and Applications*, *44*, 101004. DOI: 10.1016/j.elerap.2020.101004 PMID: 32922241

Lim, L. (2023). Digital Marketing Strategies: A Case of Charles & Keith. *Advance Knowledge for Executives*, *2*(2), 1–11.

Liou, J. J., Chien, C. W., Gudiel Pineda, P. J., Li, C. S. J., & Hsu, C. C. (2024). Exploring the Impact of Pandemic Measures on Airport Performance. *Aerospace (Basel, Switzerland)*, *11*(5), 373. https://www.mdpi.com/2226-4310/11/5/373. DOI: 10.3390/aerospace11050373

Liu, H., Crespo, R. G., & Martínez, O. S. (2020). Enhancing privacy and data security across healthcare applications using blockchain and distributed ledger concepts. Healthcare. mdpi.com

Liu, Y., Han, T., Ma, S., Zhang, J., Yang, Y., Tian, J., He, H., Li, A., He, M., Liu, Z., Wu, Z., Zhao, L., Zhu, D., Li, X., Qiang, N., Shen, D., Liu, T., & Ge, B. (2023). Summary of chatgpt-related research and perspective towards the future of large language models. *Meta-Radiology*, *1*(2), 100017. DOI: 10.1016/j.metrad.2023.100017

Liu, Y., Heinberg, M., Huang, X., & Eisingerich, A. B. (2023). Building a Competitive Advantage Based on Transparency: When and Why Does Transparency Matter for Corporate Social Responsibility? *Business Horizons*, *66*(4), 517–527. DOI: 10.1016/j.bushor.2022.10.004

Li, Z., Lu, Q., Chen, S., Liu, Y., & Xu, X. (2019, May). A landscape of cryptocurrencies. In *2019 IEEE International Conference on Blockchain and Cryptocurrency (ICBC)* (pp. 165-166). IEEE. Available: DOI: 10.1109/BLOC.2019.8751469

Lokare, D. A., Pathan, S. M., & Dhotre, P. S. (2025, January). Exploring Privacy Challenges: A Survey of Issues, Research Gaps, and Strategies for Protection. In *2025 1st International Conference on AIML-Applications for Engineering & Technology (ICAET)* (pp. 1–6). IEEE. DOI: DOI: 10.1109/ICAET63349.2025.10932284

Lund, B., Agbaji, D., & Teel, Z. A. (2023). Information literacy, data literacy, privacy literacy, and ChatGPT: Technology literacies align with perspectives on emerging technology adoption within communities. *Human Technology*, *19*(2), 163–177. https://papers.ssrn.com/sol3/papers.cfm?abstract_id=4324580. DOI: 10.14254/1795-6889.2023.19-2.2

Lundin, K., Skytt, B., Silén, M., Engström, M., & Strömberg, A. (2025). First-line managers' experiences of and reflections on structural conditions for management practice in hospital settings. *Leadership in Health Services, 38*(5), 1–15. https://studenttheses.uu.nl/handle/20.500.12932/46593. DOI: 10.1108/LHS-07-2024-0060 PMID: 39692171

Luo, Y. (2021). New OLI advantages in digital globalization. *International Business Review, 30*(2), 101797. DOI: 10.1016/j.ibusrev.2021.101797

Lynch, H. F., Eriksen, W., & Clapp, J. T. (2022). "We measure what we can measure": Struggles in defining and evaluating institutional review board quality. [HTML]. *Social Science & Medicine, 292*, 114614. DOI: 10.1016/j.socscimed.2021.114614 PMID: 34861569

Lynskey, O. (2023). Complete and effective data protection. *Current Legal Problems, 76*(1), 297–344. DOI: 10.1093/clp/cuad009

Ma'in, M., & Mat Isa, S. S. (2020). The Impact of Foreign Direct Investment on Economic Growth in Malaysia. Advances In Business Research International Journal, 6(1).

Ma, H. (2000). Competitive advantage and firm performance. *Competitiveness Review, 10*(2), 15–32. DOI: 10.1108/eb046396

Mai, N. T. T., Minh, N. T., & Ngan, D. T. (2021). Forcign dircct invcstmcnt in digital economy in ASEAN. Вестник Российского университета кооперации [Bulletin of the Russian University of Cooperation]. (4 (46)), 63-70.

Makhdoom, I., Abolhasan, M., Lipman, J., Shariati, N., Franklin, D., & Piccardi, M. (2024). Securing Personally Identifiable Information: A Survey of SOTA Techniques, and a Way Forward. IEEE Access. ieee.org

Malaysiakini. (2020). Penang in no hurry for airport expansion project – CM. Mkini Dotcom Sdn Bhd. https://www.malaysiakini.com/news/536412. 28 July 2020. Retrieved on 8 April 2024.

Manral, B., & Somani, G. (2021). Establishing forensics capabilities in the presence of superuser insider threats. [HTML]. *Forensic Science International Digital Investigation, 38*, 301263. DOI: 10.1016/j.fsidi.2021.301263

Mansoor, F., Ameen, K., & Arshad, A. (2024). An exploratory study of university librarians' perceptions on causes and deterrents of plagiarism: A Pakistani perspective. [HTML]. *Global Knowledge, Memory and Communication, 73*(4/5), 634–649. DOI: 10.1108/GKMC-04-2022-0074

Manzoor, A., Braeken, A., Kanhere, S. S., Ylianttila, M., & Liyanage, M. (2021). Proxy re-encryption enabled secure and anonymous IoT data sharing platform based on blockchain. [sciencedirect.com]. *Journal of Network and Computer Applications, 176*, 102917. DOI: 10.1016/j.jnca.2020.102917

Maras, M. H. (2015). Internet of Things: Security and Privacy Implications. *Int'l Data Priv. L., 5*(2), 99–104. DOI: 10.1093/idpl/ipv004

Marikyan, D., Papagiannidis, S., Rana, O. F., & Ranjan, R. (2024). General data protection regulation: A study on attitude and emotional empowerment. *Behaviour & Information Technology*. https://www.tandfonline.com/doi/abs/10.1080/0144929X.2023.2285341

Marshall, R., Pardo, A., Smith, D., & Watson, T. (2022). Implementing next generation privacy and ethics research in education technology. [HTML]. *British Journal of Educational Technology, 53*(4), 737–755. DOI: 10.1111/bjet.13224

Martin, K. D., & Zimmermann, J. (2024). Artificial Intelligence and Its Implications for Data Privacy Current opinion in psychology, 101829.

Martin, K. D., & Palmatier, R. W. (2020). Data privacy in retail: Navigating tensions and directing future research. [HTML]. *Journal of Retailing, 96*(4), 449–457. DOI: 10.1016/j.jretai.2020.10.002

Mason, E. S. (1939). Price and production policies of large-scale enterprise. *The American Economic Review, 29*, 61–74.

Matthews, K. R., Yang, E., Lewis, S. W., Vaidyanathan, B. R., & Gorman, M. (2020). International scientific collaborative activities and barriers to them in eight societies. [tandfonline.com]. *Accountability in Research, 27*(8), 477–495. DOI: 10.1080/08989621.2020.1774373 PMID: 32515609

MAVCOM. (2019). Malaysia's Airports Industry Structure. Position Paper. Malaysian Aviation Commission. December 2019. https://www.mavcom.my/wp-content/uploads/2019/12/191204-Position-Paper-Malaysias-Airports-Industry-Stucture.pdf Retrieved on 8 April 2025.

McGraw, D. & Mandl, K. D. (2021). Privacy protections to encourage use of health-relevant digital data in a learning health system. NPJ digital medicine. nature.com

McLeod, S. & Dulsky, S. (2021). Resilience, reorientation, and reinvention: School leadership during the early months of the COVID-19 pandemic. Frontiers in education. frontiersin.org

Meckelburg, R., & Wardana, A. (2024). The political economy of land acquisition for development in the public interest: The case of Indonesia. *Land Use Policy, 137*, 107017. DOI: 10.1016/j.landusepol.2023.107017

Mehrizi, M. H. R., & Pakneiat, M. (2008). Comparative Analysis of Sectoral Innovation Systems and the Diamond Model: The Case of Iran's Telecom Sector. *Journal of Technology Management & Innovation*, *3*(3), 78–90. DOI: 10.4067/S0718-27242008000100008

Menard, P., & Bott, G. J. (2025). Artificial intelligence misuse and concern for information privacy: New construct validation and future directions. *Information Systems Journal*, *35*(1), 322–367. https://onlinelibrary.wiley.com/doi/abs/10.1111/isj.12544. DOI: 10.1111/isj.12544

Meyer, K. E., & Nguyen, H. V. (2005). Foreign Investment Strategies and Sub-National Institutions in Emerging Markets: Evidence from Vietnam. *Journal of Management Studies*, *42*(1), 63–93. DOI: 10.1111/j.1467-6486.2005.00489.x

Micheli, M., Ponti, M., Craglia, M., & Berti Suman, A. (2020). Emerging models of data governance in the age of datafication. [sagepub.com]. *Big Data & Society*, *7*(2), 2053951720948087. DOI: 10.1177/2053951720948087

MIDA. (2023). Budget 2024 focus on Perak's high-tech industrial area will boost sector – Analysts. Malaysian Investment Development Authority (MIDA). https://www.mida.gov.my/mida-news/budget-2024-focus-on-peraks-high-tech-industrial-area-will-boost-sector-analysts/Retrieved on 10 April 2025.

Mihus, I., & Gupta, S. G. (2023). Exploring the foundations of the digital economy: an in-depth overview. *Business model innovation in the digital economy*, 6-37.

Mileros, M. D., & Forchheimer, R. (2024). Free for you and me? Exploring the value users gain from their seemingly free apps. *Digital Policy. Regulation & Governance*, *27*(2), 239–257. DOI: 10.1108/DPRG-01-2024-0009

Mintzberg, H. (1994). The rise and fall of strategic planning, Prentice Hall, 1994.

Mintzberg, H. (1990). The Design School: Reconsidering the Basic Premises of Strategic Management. *Strategic Management Journal*, *11*(3), 171–195. DOI: 10.1002/smj.4250110302

Misra, D. P., & Agarwal, V. (2020). Integrity of clinical research conduct, reporting, publishing, and post-publication promotion in rheumatology. [HTML]. *Clinical Rheumatology*, *39*(4), 1049–1060. DOI: 10.1007/s10067-020-04965-0 PMID: 32026178

Moher, D., Bouter, L., Kleinert, S., Glasziou, P., Sham, M. H., Barbour, V., Coriat, A.-M., Foeger, N., & Dirnagl, U. (2020). The Hong Kong Principles for assessing researchers: Fostering research integrity. [plos.org]. *PLoS Biology, 18*(7), e3000737. DOI: 10.1371/journal.pbio.3000737 PMID: 32673304

Mok, O. (2020). CM: Penang airport expansion on hold pending strategic study. Malay Mail. 13 August 2020. https://www.malaymail.com/news/malaysia/2020/08/13/cm-penang-airport-expansion-on-hold-pending-strategic-study/1893577 Retrieved on 8 April 2025.

Möller, D. P. (2023). Cybersecurity in digital transformation. In *Guide to cybersecurity in digital transformation: Trends, methods, technologies, applications and best practices* (pp. 1–70). Springer Nature Switzerland. DOI: 10.1007/978-3-031-26845-8_1

Mooradian, N., Franks, P. C., & Srivastav, A. (2025). The Impact of Artificial Intelligence on Data Privacy: A Risk Management Perspective. *Records Management Journal*. Advance online publication. DOI: 10.1108/RMJ-06-2024-0013

Morton, B., Vercueil, A., Masekela, R., Heinz, E., Reimer, L., Saleh, S., Kalinga, C., Seekles, M., Biccard, B., Chakaya, J., Abimbola, S., Obasi, A., & Oriyo, N. (2022). Consensus statement on measures to promote equitable authorship in the publication of research from international partnerships. [wiley.com]. *Anaesthesia, 77*(3), 264–276. DOI: 10.1111/anae.15597 PMID: 34647323

Mothukuri, V., Parizi, R. M., Pouriyeh, S., Huang, Y., Dehghantanha, A., & Srivastava, G. (2021). A survey on security and privacy of federated learning. [HTML]. *Future Generation Computer Systems, 115*, 619–640. DOI: 10.1016/j.future.2020.10.007

Mugo, P., & Macharia, J. (2020). Technological Innovation and Competitive Advantage in Telecommunication Companies. *International Journal of Research in Business and Social Science, 9*(5), 38–47. DOI: 10.20525/ijrbs.v9i5.866

Muhonen, R., Benneworth, P., & Olmos-Peñuela, J. (2020). From productive interactions to impact pathways: Understanding the key dimensions in developing SSH research societal impact. [oup.com]. *Research Evaluation, 29*(1), 34–47.

Mukhamediev, R. I., Popova, Y., Kuchin, Y., Zaitseva, E., Kalimoldayev, A., Symagulov, A., Levashenko, V., Abdoldina, F., Gopejenko, V., Yakunin, K., Muhamedijeva, E., & Yelis, M. (2022). Review of artificial intelligence and machine learning technologies: Classification, restrictions, opportunities and challenges. [mdpi.com]. *Mathematics, 10*(15), 2552. DOI: 10.3390/math10152552

Muley, T., Sudheer, G., Sinha, K., Narayan, A., Agrawal, R., & Gandhala, S. P. (2024, September). Enhancing Email Spam Detection through Ensemble Learning: A Combined Approach of LSTM and Neural Network. In *2024 Asian Conference on Intelligent Technologies (ACOIT)* (pp. 1-6). IEEE.

Murugesan, U., Subramanian, P., Srivastava, S., & Dwivedi, A. (2023). A study of Artificial Intelligence impacts on Human Resource Digitalization in Industry 4.0. *Decision Analytics Journal, 7*, 100249. DOI: 10.1016/j.dajour.2023.100249

Mylrea, M. & Robinson, N. (2023). Artificial Intelligence (AI) trust framework and maturity model: applying an entropy lens to improve security, privacy, and ethical AI. Entropy. mdpi.com

Nadikattu, A. K. R. (2018). IoT and the Issue of Data Privacy. *International Journal of Innovations in Engineering Research and Technology, 5*(10), 23–26.

Nadir, J., & Farah, J. (2023). Balancing AI Innovation and Data Protection: Regulatory Challenges and Opportunities.

Nadji, B. (2024). Data Security, Integrity, and Protection. In *Data, Security, and Trust in Smart Cities* (pp. 59–83). Springer Nature Switzerland.

Nagai, H., Nakazawa, E., & Akabayashi, A. (2022). The creation of the Belmont Report and its effect on ethical principles: a historical study. Monash bioethics review. springer.com

Naguib, H. M., Kassem, H. M., & Naem, A. E. H. M. A. (2024).. . *The Impact of IT Governance and Data Governance on Financial and Non-Financial Performance Future Business Journal, 10*(1), 15.

Nambiar, P. (2020). Politics in the way of Penang airport expansion, says Chow. Free Malaysia Today (FMT). 25 August 2020. https://www.freemalaysiatoday.com/category/nation/2020/08/25/politics-in-the-way-of-penang-airport-expansion-says-chow/ Retrieved on 8 April 2025.

Nankya, M., Mugisa, A., Usman, Y., Upadhyay, A., & Chataut, R. (2024). Security and Privacy in E-Health Systems: A Review of AI and Machine Learning Techniques. IEEE Access. ieee.org

Newbert, S. L. (2008). Value, rareness, competitive advantage, and performance: A conceptual level empirical investigation of the resource-based view of the firm. *Strategic Management Journal, 29*(7), 745–768. DOI: 10.1002/smj.686

Newcomb, T. J., Simonin, P. W., Martinez, F. A., Chadderton, W. L., Bossenbroek, J. M., Cudmore, B., Hoff, M. H., Keller, R. P., Ridenhour, B. D., Rothlisberger, J. D., Rutherford, E. S., Van Egeren, S., & Lodge, D. M. (2021). A best practices case study for scientific collaboration between researchers and managers. [wiley.com]. *Fisheries (Bethesda, Md.)*, *46*(3), 131–138. DOI: 10.1002/fsh.10536 PMID: 33888934

Newman, A., Bavik, Y. L., Mount, M., & Shao, B. (2021). Data collection via online platforms: Challenges and recommendations for future research. [HTML]. *Applied Psychology*, *70*(3), 1380–1402. DOI: 10.1111/apps.12302

Newman, P. A., Guta, A., & Black, T. (2021). Ethical considerations for qualitative research methods during the COVID-19 pandemic and other emergency situations: Navigating the virtual field. [sagepub.com]. *International Journal of Qualitative Methods*, *20*, 16094069211047823. DOI: 10.1177/16094069211047823

Nickols, F. (2012). Definitions & meanings. *Distance Consulting*, *200*, 2–10.

Nizam, F. (2025). Cyberattack on MAHB: Hackers yet to be identified.https://www.nst.com.my/news/nation/2025/03/1193233/cyberattack-mahb-hackers-yet-be-identified

Norehan, M. A. H. Bin, Ridzuan, AR Bin, & Ismail, SB. (2021). Conceptual Framework for ICT Development and Foreign Direct Investment Inflows as Drivers for Sustainable Economic Growth: Evidence from China and Malaysia. *International Journal of Academic Research in Economics and Management Sciences*, *10*(1), 123–134.

North, D. C. (1990). *Institutions, Institutional Change, and Economic Performance*. Institutions, Institutional Change, and Economic Performance., DOI: 10.1017/CBO9780511808678

O'Flaherty, K. (2024). The rise of AI-powered surveillance. The Guardian. Available from: [URL]. Accessed 2024 Aug 20.

O'Shannassy, T. (2008). Sustainable competitive advantage or temporary competitive advantage: Improving understanding of an important strategy construct. *Journal of Strategy and Management*, *1*(2), 168–180. DOI: 10.1108/17554250810926357

O'Dwyer, M., Filieri, R., & O'Malley, L. (2023). Establishing successful university–industry collaborations: barriers and enablers deconstructed. The Journal of Technology Transfer. springer.com

Ogborigbo, J. C., Sobowale, O. S., Amienwalen, E. I., Owoade, Y., Samson, A. T., & Egerson, J. (2024). Strategic integration of cyber security in business intelligence systems for data protection and competitive advantage. World Journal of Advanced Research and Reviews, 23(1), 081-096.

Okan, O., Bollweg, T. M., Berens, E. M., Hurrelmann, K., Bauer, U., & Schaeffer, D. (2020). Coronavirus-related health literacy: A cross-sectional study in adults during the COVID-19 infodemic in Germany. [mdpi.com]. *International Journal of Environmental Research and Public Health, 17*(15), 5503. DOI: 10.3390/ijerph17155503 PMID: 32751484

Okwu, A. T., Oseni, I. O., &Obiakor, R. T. (2020). Does Foreign Direct Investment Enhance Economic Growth? Evidence from 30 Leading Global Economies. Global Journal of Emerging Market Economies.

Oliver, C. (1997). The Influence of Institutional and Task Environment Relationships on Organizational Performance: The Canadian Construction Industry. *Journal of Management Studies, 34*(1), 99–124. DOI: 10.1111/1467-6486.00044

Olsson, M., Ericson, J., Randell, E., & von Ahlefeld Nisser, D. (2024). Between an educational task and an idea for treatment: Multiprofessional collaboration for supporting children "at risk"–a coordinator role in pedagogical practice. [tandfonline.com]. *Scandinavian Journal of Educational Research, 68*(4), 765–778. DOI: 10.1080/00313831.2023.2185809

Omoregbe, O., & Kurtis, I. U. (2020). Resource Management Accountability and Organizational Sustainable Competitive Advantage: Evidence from Nigerian Research Institutes. *Nigerian Academy of Management Journal, 15*(2), 104–114.

Otoo, F. N. K., Junior, P. N. A., Agyeman, G. A., & Bekoe, R. (2025). Examining the relationship between human resource management practices and employee creativity: The mediating role of organizational learning capability. *African Journal of Economic and Management Studies, ahead-of-print*(ahead-of-print). DOI: 10.1108/AJEMS-08-2024-0434

Oyewole, A. T., Oguejiofor, B. B., Eneh, N. E., Akpuokwe, C. U., & Bakare, S. S.Adedoyin Tolulope OyewoleBisola Beatrice OguejioforNkechi Emmanuella EnehChidiogo Uzoamaka AkpuokweSeun Solomon Bakare. (2024). Data privacy laws and their impact on financial technology companies: A review. *Computer Science & IT Research Journal, 5*(3), 628–650. DOI: 10.51594/csitrj.v5i3.911

Öz, Ö. (2002). Assessing Porter's Framework for National Advantage: The Case of Turkey. *Journal of Business Research, 55*(6), 509–515. DOI: 10.1016/S0148-2963(00)00167-3

Pala, S. K. (2020). Improving Customer Experience in Banking using Big Data Insights. International Journal of Enhanced Research in Educational Development (IJERED), ISSN, 2319–7463.

Palczewski, K., & Sałabun, W. (2019). Influence of various normalization methods in PROMETHEE II: An empirical study on the selection of the airport location. *Procedia Computer Science*, *159*, 2051–2060. DOI: 10.1016/j.procs.2019.09.378

Palekhova, L. (2016). Achieving the competitiveness through public accountability on sustainable development. Науковий вісник Національного гірничого університету [Scientific Bulletin of the National Mining University]. (2), 162-167.

Palos-Sánchez, P. R., Baena-Luna, P., Badicu, A., & Infante-Moro, J. C. (2022). Artificial Intelligence and Human Resources Management: A Bibliometric Analysis. *Applied Artificial Intelligence*. https://www.tandfonline.com/doi/abs/10.1080/08839514.2022.2145631

Parti, K. & Szigeti, A. (2021). The future of interdisciplinary research in the digital era: Obstacles and perspectives of collaboration in social and data sciences-an empirical study. Cogent Social Sciences. tandfonline.com

Patil, B. S., & Priya, M. R. S. R. (2024). HR data analytics and evidence based practice as a strategic business partner. *Vilakshan - XIMB. Journal of Management*, *21*(1), 114–125. DOI: 10.1108/XJM-07-2023-0148

Patil, N. (2024). Spam mail detection using blockchain. *International Journal of Scientific Research and Engineering Management*, *9*(2), 72–83. DOI: 10.55041/IJSREM34520

Paul, J., & Feliciano-Cestero, M. M. (2021). Five Decades of Research on Foreign Direct Investment by MNEs: An Overview and Research Agenda. *Journal of Business Research*, *124*, 800–812. DOI: 10.1016/j.jbusres.2020.04.017 PMID: 32292218

Peloquin, D., DiMaio, M., Bierer, B., & Barnes, M. (2020). Disruptive and avoidable: GDPR challenges to secondary research uses of data. [nature.com]. *European Journal of Human Genetics : EJHG*, *28*(6), 697–705. DOI: 10.1038/s41431-020-0596-x PMID: 32123329

Pennings, J. (1985). *Organizational strategy and change*. Jossey-Bass.

Penrose, E. T. (1959). *The theory of the growth of the firm*. John Wiley.

Perera, S., Jin, X., Maurushat, A., & Opoku, D. G. J. (2022). Factors affecting reputational damage to organisations due to cyberattacks. Informatics. mdpi.com

Perković Paloš, A., Roje, R., Tomić, V., & Marušić, A. (2024). Creating research ethics and integrity country report cards: Case study from Europe. [tandfonline.com]. *Accountability in Research*, *31*(6), 620–654. DOI: 10.1080/08989621.2022.2163632 PMID: 36635978

Perwej, Y., Abbas, S. Q., Dixit, J. P., Akhtar, N., & Jaiswal, A. K. (2021). A systematic literature review on the cyber security. International Journal of scientific research and management, 9(12), 669-710. hal.science

Phuangsuwan, P., Siripipatthanakul, S., Praesri, S., & Rakpathum, W. (2025). The Relationship between Good Governance and Organizational Performance through the Mediating Role of Employee Satisfaction. *Journal of Governance and Regulation/Volume, 14*(1).

Phuangsuwan, P., Siripipatthanakul, S., Praesri, S., & Rakpathum, W. (2025). The Relationship Between Good Governance and Organizational Performance Through the Mediating Role of Employee Satisfaction. *Journal of Governance and Regulation/Volume, 14*(1).

Phuangsuwan, P., Siripipatthanakul, S., Limna, P., & Siripipattanakul, S. (2024). Grammar and Plagiarism Checking Using Grammarly for English Learners: A Systematic Review. *SSRN*, *7*(3), 1–20. DOI: 10.2139/ssrn.4861177

Politou, E., Alepis, E., Virvou, M., & Patsakis, C. (2022). Privacy and data protection challenges in the distributed era. [HTML]

Popper, K. R. (1959). *The Logic of Scientific Discovery*. Hutchinson.

Porter, M. E. (1986). *Competitive Strategy (1986)*. Harvard Business School Press.

Porter, M. E. (1990). *No. 6* (Vol. 76). The Competitive Advantage of Nations. Free Press, New York. Porter, Porter, M. E. (1998). Clusters and the New Economics of Competition. Harvard Business Review.

Porter, M. E. (2000). Location, competition, and economic development: Local clusters in a global economy. *Economic Development Quarterly*, *14*(1), 15–34. DOI: 10.1177/089124240001400105

Porter, M. E. (2004). Building the Microeconomic Foundations of Prosperity: Findings from the Business Competitiveness Index. In Sala-i-Martin, X. (Ed.), *The Global Competitiveness Report 2003–2004*. Oxford University Press.

Pradnyawati, N. M. E., Sukandia, I. N., & Arini, D. G. D. (2021). Perjanjian Pinjaman Online Berbasis Financial Technology (Fintech). *Jurnal Konstruksi Hukum*, *2*(2), 320–325. DOI: 10.22225/jkh.2.2.3230.320-325

Prastyanti, R. A., & Sharma, R. (2024). Establishing Consumer Trust Through Data Protection Law as a Competitive Advantage in Indonesia and India. Journal of Human Rights. *Culture and Legal System*, *4*(2), 354–390. DOI: 10.53955/jhcls.v4i2.200

Prisma (2020). Prisma 2020 Statement. https://www.prisma-statement.org/prisma-2020

Prokopowicz, D. (2023). *How does the development of generative artificial intelligence technology affect the development of cybercrime techniques and the improvement of cybersecurity systems?* Research Proposal, https://doi.org/DOI: 10.13140/RG.2.2.34354.00962

Puputti, H. (2022). Positioning social sciences and humanities actors in the ninth European Union Framework Programme: a discourse analysis of Horizon Europe reference documents. oulu.fi

Putri, R. M., & Utomo, R. G. (2025, February). The Effect of Awareness, Trust, Privacy, and Security on Students Adoption of Digital Banking. In *2025 International Conference on Advancement in Data Science, E-learning and Information System (ICADEIS)* (pp. 1-6). IEEE. DOI: 10.1109/ICADEIS65852.2025.10933127

Qian, X. (2024). Redefining International Law Paradigms: Charting Cybersecurity, Trade, and Investment Trajectories within Global Legal Boundaries. *The Journal of World Investment & Trade*, *25*(3), 295–333. DOI: 10.1163/22119000-12340327

Qin, X., Huang, Y., Yang, Z., & Li, X. (2021). A blockchain-based access control scheme with multiple attribute authorities for secure cloud data sharing. [HTML]. *Journal of Systems Architecture*, *112*, 101854. DOI: 10.1016/j.sysarc.2020.101854

Qiu, J., Tian, Z., Du, C., Zuo, Q., Su, S., & Fang, B. (2020). A survey on access control in the age of internet of things. [HTML]. *IEEE Internet of Things Journal*, *7*(6), 4682–4696. DOI: 10.1109/JIOT.2020.2969326

Quach, S., Thaichon, P., Martin, K. D., Weaven, S., & Palmatier, R. W. (2022). Digital technologies: Tensions in privacy and data. *Journal of the Academy of Marketing Science*, *50*(6), 1299–1323. DOI: 10.1007/s11747-022-00845-y PMID: 35281634

Rahmani, A. M., Yousefpoor, E., Yousefpoor, M. S., Mehmood, Z., Haider, A., Hosseinzadeh, M., & Ali Naqvi, R. (2021). Machine learning (ML) in medicine: Review, applications, and challenges. [mdpi.com]. *Mathematics*, *9*(22), 2970. DOI: 10.3390/math9222970

Raihan, A., Pereira, J. J., Begum, R. A., & Rasiah, R. (2023). The economic impact of water supply disruption from the Selangor River, Malaysia. *Blue-Green Systems*, *5*(2), 102–120. DOI: 10.2166/bgs.2023.031

Rakpathum, W., Siripipatthanakul, S., Phuangsuwan, P., & Charoenporn, C. (2025). Enhancing Sustainable Development Goals (SDGs) for Rural Tourism Communities: The Case of Mae Kampong Village, Chiang Mai, Thailand. *Journal of Lifestyle and SDGs Review, 5*(1), e04755–e04755. DOI: 10.47172/2965-730X.SDGsReview.v5.n01.pe04755

Ramu, P., Srinivasarao, T., Lalith Nandan, K., & Keshav, M. (2020). Fuzzy AHP, RS & GIS based hybrid approach for airport site selection-Kothagudem district. *International Journal of Advanced Science and Technology, 29*(1), 1645–1653. http://sersc.org/journals/index.php/IJAST/article/view/3731

Ranasinghe, U. C., Ennis, S. F., Monteiro, J., & Malagueño, R. (2025). Global value chains, trade facilitation and the use of environmental management practices in SMEs. *International Journal of Operations & Production Management, ahead-of-print*(ahead-of-print). DOI: 10.1108/IJOPM-03-2024-0261

Rangsaritvorakarn, N. (2023). A Decision-making Criteria in Airport Site Selection: A Systematic Review. *Journal for Strategy and Enterprise Competitiveness, 2*(5), 78–94. https://so07.tci-thaijo.org/index.php/STECOJournal/article/view/2916

Rath, D. K. & Kumar, A. (2021). Information privacy concern at individual, group, organization and societal level-a literature review. Vilakshan-XIMB Journal of Management. emerald.com

Rawindaran, N., Jayal, A., & Prakash, E. (2021). Artificial intelligence and machine learning within the context of cyber security used in the UK SME Sector. *Proceedings of the AMI.*

Regulation, P. (2016). Regulation (EU) 2016/679 of the European Parliament and of the Council. *Regulation, 679*, 2016.

Renuka, O., RadhaKrishnan, N., Priya, B. S., Jhansy, A., & Ezekiel, S. (2025). Data Privacy and Protection: Legal and Ethical Challenges. Emerging Threats and Countermeasures in Cybersecurity, 433-465.

Resnik, D. B. (2021). Standards of evidence for institutional review board decision-making. Accountability in research. nih.gov

Riahi, E., & Islam, M. S. (2025). Employees' information security awareness (ISA) in public organisations: Insights from cross-cultural studies in Sweden, France, and Tunisia. *Behaviour & Information Technology, 44*(1), 79–101. DOI: 10.1080/0144929X.2024.2311734

Ribeiro-Navarrete, S., Saura, J. R., & Palacios-Marqués, D. (2021). Towards a new era of mass data collection: Assessing pandemic surveillance technologies to preserve user privacy. [nih.gov]. *Technological Forecasting and Social Change*, *167*, 120681. DOI: 10.1016/j.techfore.2021.120681 PMID: 33840865

Risi, D., Vigneau, L., Bohn, S., & Wickert, C. (2023). Institutional theory-based research on corporate social responsibility: Bringing values back in. [wiley.com]. *International Journal of Management Reviews*, *25*(1), 3–23. DOI: 10.1111/ijmr.12299

Rittinghouse, J. W., & Ransome, J. F. (2016). *Cloud computing: Implementation, management, and security*. CRC Press.

Roberts, P. (1999). Product innovation, product-market competition, and persistent profitability in the US pharmaceutical industry. *Strategic Management Journal*, *20*(7), 655–670. DOI: 10.1002/(SICI)1097-0266(199907)20:7<655::AID-SMJ44>3.0.CO;2-P

Roberts, P. W., & Greenwood, R. (1997). Integrating transaction cost and institutional theories: Toward a constrained-efficiency framework for understanding organizational design adoption. *Academy of Management Review*, *22*(2), 346–373. DOI: 10.2307/259326

Roccon, M. (2023). Foreign investment in China's Cloud Industry: A Case Study of Microsoft Azure's Expansion.

Roco, M. C. (2023). National Nanotechnology Initiative at 20 years: enabling new horizons. Journal of Nanoparticle Research. nseresearch.org

Roman, R., Zhou, J., & Lopez, J. (2013). On the features and challenges of security and privacy in distributed internet of things. *Computer Networks*, *57*(10), 2266–2279. DOI: 10.1016/j.comnet.2012.12.018

Rooney, M. J., Levy, Y., Li, W., & Kumar, A. (2024). Comparing experts' and users' perspectives on the use of password workarounds and the risk of data breaches. [HTML]. *Information and Computer Security*. Advance online publication. DOI: 10.1108/ICS-05-2024-0116

Rucz, M. (2022). SLAPPed by the GDPR: protecting public interest journalism in the face of GDPR-based strategic litigation against public participation. Journal of Media Law. tandfonline.com

Rumelt, R. P. (2003). "What in the world is competitive advantage?", Working Paper No. 2003-105, The Anderson School, UCLA, Los Angeles, CA, August 5.

Saeed, M. M. A., Saeed, R. A., & Ahmed, Z. E. (2024). Data Security and Privacy in the Age of AI and Digital Twins. In Digital Twin Technology and AI Implementations in Future-Focused Businesses (pp. 99-124). IGI Global. [HTML] DOI: 10.4018/979-8-3693-1818-8.ch008

Saeed, S. (2023). A Customer-Centric View of E-Commerce Security and Privacy. *Applied Sciences (Basel, Switzerland), 13*(2), 1020. DOI: 10.3390/app13021020

Saeed, S. (2023). DigitalWorkplaces and Information Security Behavior of Business Employees: An Empirical Study of Saudi Arabia. *Sustainability (Basel), 15*(7), 6019. DOI: 10.3390/su15076019

Saeed, S., Altamimi, S. A., Alkayyal, N. A., Alshehri, E., & Alabbad, D. A. (2023). Digital transformation and cybersecurity challenges for businesses resilience: Issues and recommendations. *Sensors (Basel), 23*(15), 6666. DOI: 10.3390/s23156666 PMID: 37571451

Şahin, E., Sarı, U., & Şen, F. (2024). STEM professional development program for gifted education teachers: STEM lesson plan design competence, self-efficacy, computational thinking and…. [HTML]. *Thinking Skills and Creativity*.

Sahiti, A., Ahmeti, S., & Ismajli, H. (2018). A Review of Empirical Studies on FDI Determinants. *Baltic Journal of Real Estate Economics and Construction Management, 6*(1), 37–47. Advance online publication. DOI: 10.1515/bjreecm-2018-0003

Santos, J. R. (2020). Cybersecurity and the role of traditional methods. In: *Proceedings of the International Conference on Cybersecurity*; Mar 10-12, 2020; London, UK. IEEE. p. 43-58.

Sargiotis, D. (2024). Data Quality Management: Ensuring Accuracy and Reliability. In Data Governance: A Guide (pp. 197–216). Cham: Springer Nature Switzerland. DOI: 10.1007/978-3-031-67268-2_5

Sarioguz, O., & Miser, E. (2024). Data-Driven Decision-Making: Revolutionizing Management in the Information Era. Journal of Artificial Intelligence and General Science (JAIGS), ISSN: 3006-4023, Vol. 4, No. 1, pp. 179-194. DOI: 10.60087/jaigs.v4i1.131

Sarker, I. H. (2021). Data science and analytics: an overview from data-driven smart computing, decision-making and applications perspective. SN Computer Science. springer.com

Saxena, U. R., & Alam, T. (2022). Role based access control using identity and broadcast based encryption for securing cloud data. [HTML]. *Journal of Computer Virology and Hacking Techniques, 18*(3), 171–182. DOI: 10.1007/s11416-021-00402-1

Schellenberg, M., Harker, M. J., & Jafari, A. (2018). International Market Entry Mode: A Systematic Literature Review. *Journal of Strategic Marketing*, *26*(7), 601–627. DOI: 10.1080/0965254X.2017.1339114

Schinagl, S. & Shahim, A. (2020). What do we know about information security governance? "From the basement to the boardroom": towards digital security governance. Information & Computer Security. emerald.com

Schmidt, U. (2023). From Nuremberg to Helsinki: Historicizing the Codification of Post-War Research Ethics. In Ethical Innovation for Global Health: Pandemic, Democracy and Ethics in Research (pp. 149-174). Singapore: Springer Nature Singapore. [HTML]

Schmitter, P., Shahgholian, A., & Tucker, M. (2024). Towards an understanding of the digital transformation of facility management in healthcare: Perspectives from practice. *Digital Transformation and Society*, *3*(4), 395–409. DOI: 10.1108/DTS-10-2023-0098

Schuijer, J. W., Broerse, J., & Kupper, F. (2021). Juggling roles, experiencing dilemmas: The challenges of SSH scholars in public engagement. NanoEthics. springer.com

Schulzmann, D., Sinani, E., Hobdari, B., & Petersen, B. (2023). Drivers of R&D greenfield investment projects in the communications, software, and IT service industries in developing countries. *Transnational Corporations*, *30*(1), 103–133. DOI: 10.18356/2076099x-30-1-4

Schwab, K. (2021). Stakeholder capitalism: A global economy that works for progress, people and planet. [HTML]

Scott, W. R. (1995). *Institutions and organizations*. Sage.

Sean Joyce. (2024). *Putting security at the epicenter of innovation* (2024 Global Digital Trust Insights, pp. 1–20). PricewaterhouseCoopers (PwC).

Seara, J. P. & Serrão, C. (2024). Automation of System Security Vulnerabilities Detection Using Open-Source Software. Electronics. mdpi.com

Sebastian, G. (2023). Privacy and data protection in chatgpt and other ai chatbots: Strategies for securing user information. [IJSPPC]. *International Journal of Security and Privacy in Pervasive Computing*, *15*(1), 1–14. DOI: 10.4018/IJSPPC.325475

Sefcik, L., Striepe, M., & Yorke, J. (2020). Mapping the landscape of academic integrity education programs: What approaches are effective? [HTML]. *Assessment & Evaluation in Higher Education*, *45*(1), 30–43. DOI: 10.1080/02602938.2019.1604942

Senavirathne, N., & Torra, V. (2020, December). On the role of data anonymization in machine learning privacy. In 2020 IEEE 19th International conference on trust, security and privacy in computing and communications (TrustCom) (pp. 664-675). IEEE. [HTML] DOI: 10.1109/TrustCom50675.2020.00093

Sennaroglu, B., & Celebi, G. V. (2018). A military airport location selection by AHP integrated PROMETHEE and VIKOR methods. *Transportation Research Part D, Transport and Environment*, *59*, 160–173. DOI: 10.1016/j.trd.2017.12.022

Shahreki, J., & Lee, J. Y. (2024). Adopting human resource information system and work-related outcomes in emerging market SMEs: Unified theory of acceptance and use of technology. *Cross Cultural &amp. Cross Cultural & Strategic Management*, *31*(1), 116–142. DOI: 10.1108/CCSM-09-2022-0144

Shahzad, M. F., Xu, S., & Javed, I. (2024). ChatGPT awareness, acceptance, and adoption in higher education: The role of trust as a cornerstone. *International Journal of Educational Technology in Higher Education*, *21*(1), 46. https://link.springer.com/article/10.1186/s41239-024-00478-x. DOI: 10.1186/s41239-024-00478-x

Shaik, V., & Natarajan, K. (2022). Flexible and cost-effective cryptographic encryption algorithm for securing unencrypted database files at rest and in transit. [sciencedirect.com]. *Methods (San Diego, Calif.)*, •••, X. PMID: 36438858

Shamoo, A., & Khin-Maung-Gyi, F. A. (2021). *Ethics of the Use of Human Subjects in Research*. Practical Guide. [HTML] DOI: 10.1201/9780203110744

Shankar, A.C. (2019). What MAHB now faces after the unprecedented systems outage at KLIA. theedgemarkets.com. 24 Aug 2019. Retrieved on 10 April 2025.

Sharif, M. H. U., & Mohammed, M. A.Md Haris Uddin SharifMehmood Ali Mohammed. (2022). A literature review of financial losses statistics for cyber security and future trend. *World J. Adv.Res. Rev.*, *15*(1), 138–156. DOI: 10.30574/wjarr.2022.15.1.0573

Sharma, A. Digital Economy's Impact on FDI and the Rise of Tech MNES. FDI and Retail Sector in India, 22.

Sharma, D. P., Lashkari, A. H., & Parizadeh, M. (2024). *Understanding Cybersecurity Management in Healthcare: Challenges, Strategies and Trends*. Springer., DOI: 10.1007/978-3-031-68034-2

Shawky, M. (2023). *13 Types of Cyber Attacks You Should Know in 2023*.

Shi, P., Wang, H., Yang, S., Chen, C., & Yang, W. (2021). Blockchain-based trusted data sharing among trusted stakeholders in IoT. [wiley.com]. *Software, Practice & Experience*, *51*(10), 2051–2064. DOI: 10.1002/spe.2739

Shokri, R., Stronati, M., Song, L., & Shmatikov, V. (2017). Membership inference attacks against machine learning models. *IEEE Symposium on Security and Privacy*; San Jose, CA, USA. IEEE. p. 3-18 DOI: 10.1109/SP.2017.41

Siew, R. (2024). Strengthening big data security and privacy in libraries: A review of ISO standards and real-world cyberattack case studies. *Journal of Information Security and Technology*, *11*(2), 123–138. DOI: 10.5339/jist.2024.11

Sigalas, C. (2015). Competitive advantage: The known unknown concept. *Management Decision*, *53*(9), 2004–2016. Advance online publication. DOI: 10.1108/MD-05-2015-0185

Sigalas, C., Economou, V. P., & Georgopoulos, N. B. (2013). Developing a measure of competitive advantage. *Journal of Strategy and Management*, *6*(4), 320–342. DOI: 10.1108/JSMA-03-2013-0015

Sigalas, C., & Papadakis, V. M. (2018). Empirical investigation of relationship patterns between competitive advantage and superior performance. *Journal of Strategy and Management*, *11*(1), 81–111. DOI: 10.1108/JSMA-01-2017-0010

Sigalas, C., & Pekka Economou, V. (2013). Revisiting the Concept of Competitive Advantage: Problems and Fallacies Arising from Its Conceptualization. *Journal of Strategy and Management*, *6*(1), 61–80. DOI: 10.1108/17554251311296567

Simamora, S., Rahayu, A., & Dirgantari, P. D. (2024). Driving Digital Transformation in Small Banks With VRIO Analysis. Jurnal Aplikasi Bisnis dan Manajemen (JABM), 10(1), 99-99.

Simon, J., & Omar, A. (2020). Cybersecurity investments in the supply chain: Coordination and a strategic attacker. *European Journal of Operational Research*, *282*(1), 161–171. DOI: 10.1016/j.ejor.2019.09.017

Sinaga, N. P. (2021). Perlindungan hukum bagi konsumen yang data pribadinya diperjualbelikan di aplikasi fintech peer-to-peer lending. *Nusantara Law and Opinion Journal*, *2*(2), 156–167. Advance online publication. DOI: 10.51622/njlo.v2i02.366

Siripipatthanakul, S., & Siripipattanakul, S. (2025). Rural Dental Health Transformation by Adopting Digital Technologies. *Transforming Dental Health in Rural Communities: Digital Dentistry*, 47-80. DOI: DOI: 10.4018/979-8-3693-7165-7.ch003

Siripipatthanakul, S., & Siripipattanakul, S. (2025). Talent Management Ensuring the Safety and Cybersecurity in Schools. *Cultivating Creativity and Navigating Talent Management in Academia*, 383-402.

Siripipatthanakul, S., & Siripipattanakul, S. (2025). Talent Management Ensuring the Safety and Cybersecurity in Schools. *Cultivating Creativity and Navigating Talent Management in Academia*, 383-402. DOI: DOI: 10.4018/979-8-3693-6880-0.ch018

Siripipatthanakul, S., & Siripipattanakul, S. (2025, a). Online Gambling of Higher Education Learners. In *International Academic Transformations and Cross-Border Collaborations* (pp. 377-400). IGI Global Scientific Publishing. DOI: DOI: 10.4018/979-8-3373-0508-0.ch015

Siripipatthanakul, S., & Siripipattanakul, S. (2025, b). Rural Dental Health Transformation by Adopting Digital Technologies. *Transforming Dental Health in Rural Communities: Digital Dentistry*, 47-80.

Siripipatthanakul, S., & Siripipattanakul, S. (2025, c). Talent Management Ensuring the Safety and Cybersecurity in Schools. *Cultivating Creativity and Navigating Talent Management in Academia*, 383-402.

Siripipatthanakul, S., Limna, P., Phuangsuwan, P., & Siripipattanakul, S. (2025a). Enhancing Student Satisfaction With Blended Learning Among Thai Higher Education Students. In Navigating Quality Assurance and Accreditation in Global Higher Education (pp. 293-312). IGI Global Scientific Publishing.

Siripipatthanakul, S., Limna, P., Phuangsuwan, P., & Siripipattanakul, S. (2025c). Enriching Satisfaction With Web-Based Learning (WBL) Among Higher Education Students in Thailand. In Building Organizational Capacity and Strategic Management in Academia (pp. 213 236). IGI Global

Siripipatthanakul, S., Limna, P., Siripipattanakul, S., & Phuangsuwan, P. (2025b). Modelling Problem-Based Learning, Student Satisfaction, and Effectiveness Among Higher Education Students in Thailand. In International Academic Transformations and Cross-Border Collaborations (pp. 311-332). IGI Global Scientific Publishing.

Siripipatthanakul, S. (2011). Development of a Model for Administration of Student Dental Health Promotion Work for Basic Education Schools in Thailand. *International Journal of Learning*, *17*(12), 137–150. DOI: 10.18848/1447-9494/CGP/v17i12/47373

Siripipatthanakul, S., & Phuangsuwan, P. (2024). Salutogenic Marketing in Preventive Dentistry. In *Leveraging Digital Technology for Preventive Dentistry* (pp. 255–278). IGI Global., DOI: 10.4018/979-8-3693-3872-8.ch009

Siripipatthanakul, S., & Siripipattanakul, S. (2025). Online Gambling of Higher Education Learners. In *International Academic Transformations and Cross-Border Collaborations* (pp. 377–400). IGI Global Scientific Publishing.

Smidt, H. J. & Jokonya, O. (2021). The challenge of privacy and security when using technology to track people in times of COVID-19 pandemic. Procedia Computer Science. sciencedirect.com

Smith, M., & Walsh, P. (2023). Security sensitive research: Balancing research integrity, academic freedom and national interest. [HTML]. *Journal of Higher Education Policy and Management, 45*(5), 495–510. DOI: 10.1080/1360080X.2023.2202328

Smith, S. C. (1993). The competitive advantage of nations - review of the competitive advantage of nations. *Journal of Development Economics, 40*(2), 399–404. DOI: 10.1016/0304-3878(93)90095-5

Smyth, B. M., Martin, M. A., & Downing, M. (2024). *The Routledge Handbook of Human Research Ethics and Integrity in Australia.* [HTML] DOI: 10.4324/9781003319733

Sofyani, H., Pratolo, S., & Saleh, Z. (2022). Do accountability and transparency promote community trust? Evidence from village government in Indonesia. [HTML]. *Journal of Accounting & Organizational Change, 18*(3), 397–418. DOI: 10.1108/JAOC-06-2020-0070

Solbakk, J. H., Bentzen, H. B., Holm, S., Heggestad, A. K. T., Hofmann, B., Robertsen, A., Alnæs, A. H., Cox, S., Pedersen, R., & Bernabe, R. (2021). Back to WHAT? The role of research ethics in pandemic times. [springer.com]. *Medicine, Health Care, and Philosophy, 24*(1), 3–20. DOI: 10.1007/s11019-020-09984-x PMID: 33141289

Solove, D. J. (2021). *Understanding privacy.* Harvard University Press.

Sørensen, M. P., Ravn, T., Marušić, A., Elizondo, A. R., Kavouras, P., Tijdink, J. K., & Bendtsen, A. K. (2021). Strengthening research integrity: Which topic areas should organisations focus on? [nature.com]. *Humanities & Social Sciences Communications, 8*(1), 1–15. DOI: 10.1057/s41599-021-00874-y PMID: 38617731

Stevani, W., & Sudirman, L. (2021). Urgensi Perlindungan Data Pengguna Financial Technology terhadap Aksi Kejahatan Online di Indonesia. *Journal of Judicial Review, 23*(2), 197–216. DOI: 10.37253/jjr.v23i2.5028

Stoesz, B. M. & Eaton, S. E. (2022). Academic integrity policies of publicly funded universities in western Canada. Educational Policy. sagepub.com

Stojanović, B., and Kostić, M. (2013). Competition policy and the impact of market structure on companies' profitability. Ekonomika preduzeća, 61(5-6), 325-338.

Styoutomo, Y. A., & Ruldeviyani, Y. (2023). Information Security Awareness Raising Strategy Using Fuzzy AHP Method with HAIS-Q and ISO/IEC 27001: 2013: A Case Study of XYZ Financial Institution. *CommIT (Communication and Information Technology). Journal, 17*(2), 133–149. DOI: 10.21512/commit.v17i2.8272

Sun, H., Fan, Z., Zhou, Y., & Shi, Y. (2010). Empirical Research on Competitiveness Factors Analysis of the Real Estate Industry of Beijing and Tianjin. *Engineering, Construction, and Architectural Management, 17*(3), 240–251. DOI: 10.1108/09699981011038042

Sun, Y., Zhang, Y. F., Wang, Y., & Zhang, S. (2025). Cooperative governance mechanisms for personal information security: An evolutionary game approach. *Kybernetes, 54*(1), 431–455. DOI: 10.1108/K-04-2023-0717

Surmiak, A. (2020). Should we maintain or break confidentiality? The choices made by social researchers in the context of law violation and harm. Journal of Academic Ethics. springer.com

Tahseen, A., Shailaja, S. R., & Ashwini, Y. (2024). Extraction for Big Data Cyber Security Analytics. Advances in Computational Intelligence and Informatics: Proceedings of ICACII 2023, 993, 365.

Talukder, B., & Hipel, K. W. (2021). Review and selection of multi-criteria decision analysis (MCDA) technique for sustainability assessment. In Energy Systems Evaluation (Volume 1) Sustainability Assessment (pp. 145-160). Cham: Springer International Publishing. https://doi.org/DOI: 10.1007/978-3-030-67529-5_7

Tamburri, D. A. (2020). Design principles for the General Data Protection Regulation (GDPR): A formal concept analysis and its evaluation. Information Systems. sciencedirect.com

Tan, D., & Teng, A. (2024, March). Tender out for Penang airport's RM1.5bil expansion project. *The Star, 14*, •••. Retrieved April 8, 2025, from https://www.thestar.com.my/news/nation/2024/03/14/tender-out-for-penangs-airports-rm15bil-expansion-project

Tawalbeh, L., Muheidat, F., Tawalbeh, M., & Quwaider, M. (2020). IoT Privacy and security: Challenges and solutions. Applied Sciences. mdpi.com

Tay, C. (2023). Syed Mokhtar tells Anwar he can't afford to support whopping RM7 bil Kulim International Airport project. The Edge Malaysia. 9 March 2023. https://theedgemalaysia.com/node/658521. Retrieved on 8 April 2025.

Thakur, A. (2022). A comprehensive study of the trends and analysis of distributed ledger technology and blockchain technology in the healthcare industry. Frontiers in Blockchain. frontiersin.org

Thapa, C., & Camtepe, S. (2021). Precision health data: Requirements, challenges and existing techniques for data security and privacy. [PDF]. *Computers in Biology and Medicine*, *129*, 104130. DOI: 10.1016/j.compbiomed.2020.104130 PMID: 33271399

Thapaliya, S. (2024). *Examining the Influence of AI-Driven Cybersecurity in Financial Sector Management*. Banking and Technology Journal., DOI: 10.3126/batuk.v10i2.68147

Thapliyal, S., Wazid, M., & Singh, D. P. (2022, June). Defining the Convergence of Artificial Intelligence and Cyber Security with a Case Study of Email Spam Detection. In *International Conference on Soft Computing and Signal Processing* (pp. 181-190). Singapore: Springer Nature Singapore. https://doi.org/DOI: 10.1007/978-981-19-8669-7_17

Tomás, J., Rasteiro, D., & Bernardino, J. (2022). Data anonymization: an experimental evaluation using open-source tools. Future Internet. mdpi.com

Tomaszewski, L. E., Zarestky, J., & Gonzalez, E. (2020). Planning qualitative research: Design and decision making for new researchers. [sagepub.com]. *International Journal of Qualitative Methods*, *19*, 1609406920967174. DOI: 10.1177/1609406920967174

Tovino, S. A. (2020). Privacy and security issues with mobile health research applications. *The Journal of Law, Medicine & Ethics*, *48*(1, suppl), 154–158.

Tsohou, A., & Soumelidou, A. (2025). Information Privacy Awareness. In Jajodia, S., Samarati, P., & Yung, M. (Eds.), *Encyclopedia of Cryptography, Security and Privacy*. Springer., DOI: 10.1007/978-3-030-71522-9_1484

Tufekci, Z. (2018). Algorithmic harms beyond Facebook and Google: Emergent challenges of computational agency. *Colorado Tech Law J.*, *13*(2), 203–218.

Tuna, E. (2006). The Tobacco Sector in the Republic of Macedonia: Competitiveness Analysis (Doctoral dissertation, Sveriges lantbruksuniversitet).

U.S. Department of Health & Human Services. (1966). Health Insurance Portability and Accountability Act of 1996 (HIPAA). Available from. [URL], Retrieved August 20, 2024, from.

Uddin, M.H.; Ali, M.H.; Hassan, M.K. (2020). Cybersecurity hazards and financial system vulnerability: A synthesis of literature. Risk Manag. 22, 239–309. University; 2021.

Ullah, I., Hassan, N., Gill, S. S., Suleiman, B., Ahanger, T. A., Shah, Z., Qadir, J., & Kanhere, S. S. (2024). Privacy preserving large language models: ChatGPT case study based vision and framework. *IET Blockchain*, *4*(S1), 706–724. Advance online publication. DOI: 10.1049/blc2.12091

Välikangas, A. (2024). The Limited Role of Social Sciences and Humanities in Interdisciplinary Funding: What are Its Effects?. Social Epistemology. tandfonline.com

Valkenburg, G., Dix, G., Tijdink, J., & de Rijcke, S. (2021). Expanding research integrity: A cultural-practice perspective. [springer.com]. *Science and Engineering Ethics*, *27*(1), 10. DOI: 10.1007/s11948-021-00291-z PMID: 33559767

Van Atteveldt, W., Althaus, S., & Wessler, H. (2021). The trouble with sharing your privates: Pursuing ethical open science and collaborative research across national jurisdictions using sensitive data. Political Communication. tandfonline.com

Van de Sandt, E. H. A. (2021). The deviant security practices of cyber crime. [HTML]

Venčkauskas, A., Toldinas, J., Morkevicius, N., & Sanfilippo, F. (2024). An email cyber threat intelligence method using domain ontology and machine learning. *Electronics (Basel)*, *13*(14), 2716. DOI: 10.3390/electronics13142716

Viberg Johansson, J., Bentzen, H. B., & Mascalzoni, D. (2022). What ethical approaches are used by scientists when sharing health data? An interview study. BMC Medical Ethics. springer.com

Vokinger, K. N., Stekhoven, D. J., & Krauthammer, M. (2020). Lost in anonymization—A data anonymization reference classification merging legal and technical considerations. [sagepub.com]. *The Journal of Law, Medicine & Ethics*, *48*(1), 228–231. DOI: 10.1177/1073110520917025 PMID: 32342783

Vrana, J., & Singh, R. (2021). Digitization, digitalization, and digital transformation. *Handbook of nondestructive evaluation 4.0*, 1-17.

Wang, C., Zhang, N., & Wang, C. (2021). Managing privacy in the digital economy. Fundamental Research. sciencedirect.com

Wang, X., Wu, Y. C., Zhou, M., & Fu, H. (2024). Beyond surveillance: privacy, ethics, and regulations in face recognition technology. Frontiers in big data. frontiersin.org

Wang, J., & Yishake, G. (2024). *Along the Deep Interface of Digital Food: Islanding and Networking amidst the Territorialization of Uygur Cuisine*. Retrieved from https://doi.org/DOI: 10.13140/RG.2.2.20712.07683

Wang, L., Yang, J., & Wan, P. J. (2020). Educational modules and research surveys on critical cybersecurity topics. [sagepub.com]. *International Journal of Distributed Sensor Networks*, *16*(9), 1550147720954678. DOI: 10.1177/1550147720954678

Wang, X., Xu, Z., Qin, Y., & Skare, M. (2022). Foreign direct investment and economic growth: A dynamic study of measurement approaches and results. Economic research-. *Ekonomska Istrazivanja*, *35*(1), 1011–1034.

Wang, Y. (2024). Realistic dilemma and path optimization of online personal information protection. *Journal of Information Protection*, *39*(1), 728–740. DOI: 10.54254/2753-7048/39/20240728

Watini, S., Davies, G., & Andersen, N. (2024). Cybersecurity in Learning Systems: Data protection and privacy in educational information systems and digital learning environments. [ITEE]. *International Transactions on Education Technology*, *3*(1), 1. Advance online publication. DOI: 10.33050/itee.v3i1.665

Wernerfelt, B. (1984). A resource-based view of the firm. *Strategic Management Journal*, *5*(2), 171–180. DOI: 10.1002/smj.4250050207

Wibowo, G., Gunawan, I., & Sunuantari, M. (2024). Social network analysis# ChatGPT on social media. *International Journal of Innovative Research in Multidisciplinary Education*, *3*(07), 1178–1186. DOI: 10.58806/ijirme.2024.v3i7n02

Williams, L. D. (2021). Concepts of Digital Economy and Industry 4.0 in Intelligent and information systems. *International Journal of Intelligent Networks*, *2*, 122–129. DOI: 10.1016/j.ijin.2021.09.002

Wint, A. G., & Williams, D. A. (2002). Attracting Foreign Direct Investment to Developing Countries: A Changing Role for Governments? *International Journal of Public Sector Management*, *15*(5), 361–374. DOI: 10.1108/09513550210435719

Wisdom, D. D., Vincent, O. R., Igulu, K., Arowolo, M. O., & Hyacinth, E. A. (2023). *Mitigating Cyber Threats in Healthcare Systems: The Role of Artificial Intelligence and Machine Learning*. In *Cybersecurity for Healthcare Systems* (pp. 299-318). IET. DOI: 10.1049/PBHE061E_ch13

Wójcicki, K., Biegańska, M., Paliwoda, B., & Górna, J. (2022). Internet of things in industry: Research profiling, application, challenges and opportunities—a review. Energies. mdpi.com

Wolf, C. T. (2020). AI models and their worlds: Investigating data-driven, AI/ML ecosystems through a work practices lens. In Sustainable Digital Communities: 15th International Conference, iConference 2020, Boras, Sweden, March 23–26, 2020 [Springer International Publishing.]. *Proceedings, 15*, 651–664.

Wu, X., Duan, R., & Ni, J. (2024). Unveiling security, privacy, and ethical concerns of ChatGPT. *Journal of Information and Intelligence*, *2*(2), 102–115. DOI: 10.1016/j.jiixd.2023.10.007

Wylde, V., & Prakash, E. (2021). [Crisis: Is our personal data likely to be breached?]. *COVID*, •••, 19.

Wylde, V., Rawindaran, N., Lawrence, J., Balasubramanian, R., Prakash, E., Jayal, A., Khan, I., Hewage, C., & Platts, J. (2022). Cybersecurity, data privacy and blockchain: A review. *SN Computer Science*, *3*(2), 127. DOI: 10.1007/s42979-022-01020-4 PMID: 35036930

Xie, Y., Wang, K., & Kong, Y. (2021). Prevalence of research misconduct and questionable research practices: A systematic review and meta-analysis. Science and engineering ethics. springer.com

Xu, A., Baysari, M. T., Stocker, S. L., Leow, L. J., Day, R. O., & Carland, J. E. (2020). Researchers' views on, and experiences with, the requirement to obtain informed consent in research involving human participants: A qualitative study. [springer.com]. *BMC Medical Ethics*, *21*(1), 1–11. DOI: 10.1186/s12910-020-00538-7 PMID: 33008387

Yadlapalli, A., Rahman, S., & Gopal, P. (2022). Blockchain technology implementation challenges in supply chains–evidence from the case studies of multi-stakeholders. [emerald.com]. *International Journal of Logistics Management*, *33*(5), 278–305. DOI: 10.1108/IJLM-02-2021-0086

Yanamala, A. K. Y., & Suryadevara, S. (2023). Advances in Data Protection and Artificial Intelligence: Trends and Challenges. *International Journal of Advanced Engineering Technologies and Innovations*, *1*(01), 294–319.

Yanamala, A. K. Y., Suryadevara, S., & Kalli, V. D. R. (2024). Balancing Innovation and Privacy. *The Intersection of Data Protection and Artificial Intelligence International Journal of Machine Learning Research in Cybersecurity and Artificial Intelligence*, *15*(1), 1–43.

Yimer, A. (2023). The effects of FDI on economic growth in Africa. *The Journal of International Trade & Economic Development*, *32*(1), 2–36. DOI: 10.1080/09638199.2022.2079709

Yogarajan, V., Pfahringer, B., & Mayo, M. (2020). A review of automatic end-to-end de-identification: Is high accuracy the only metric?. Applied Artificial Intelligence. tandfonline.com

Yu, C., Zhang, Z., Lin, C., & Wu, Y. J. (2017). Knowledge Creation Process and Sustainable Competitive Advantage: The Role of Technological Innovation Capabilities. *Sustainability (Basel)*, *9*(12), 2280. DOI: 10.3390/su9122280

Yu, I. (2022). Foreign Investment and National Security Challenges in the Data Age: An Assessment of the Current Regime and Recommendations. *The Hastings Law Journal*, *74*, 959.

Zahiid, S.J. (2019). Two firms in rival bids for international airports in north of peninsula. Malay Mail. 10 June 2019. Retrieved on 8 April 2025.

Zakutnia, A. O., & Hayriyan, A. (2017). Transparency as a Competitive Advantage of Innovation-Driven Companies. https://essuir.sumdu.edu.ua/handle/123456789/61636

Zander, I., & Zander, U. (2005). The inside track: On the important (but neglected) role of customers in the resource-based view of strategy and firm growth. *Journal of Management Studies*, *42*(8), 1519–1548. DOI: 10.1111/j.1467-6486.2005.00555.x

Zang, W., & Baimbridge, M. (2014). Foreign Direct Investment and Economic Growth in OECD Countries. In Economic Growth in the 21st Century: Perspectives, Role of Governmental Policies, Potential and Constraints. http://hdl.handle.net/10454/13800

Zarour, M., Alenezi, M., Ansari, M. T. J., Pandey, A. K., Ahmad, M., Agrawal, A., Kumar, R., & Khan, R. A. (2021). Ensuring data integrity of healthcare information in the era of digital health. [wiley.com]. *Healthcare Technology Letters*, *8*(3), 66–77. DOI: 10.1049/htl2.12008 PMID: 34035927

Zhang, C., Zhang, Y., Chang, Z., & Li, C. (2024). Sperm YOLOv8E-TrackEVD: A Novel Approach for Sperm Detection and Tracking. Sensors. mdpi.com

Zhang, W., Zhong, Y., Wang, Z., Luo, Z., & Wang, B. (2021). Influence on distributed airport site selection from ground-effect wind field of UAV. In 2021 2nd International Symposium on Computer Engineering and Intelligent Communications (ISCEIC), 322-329. DOI: 10.1109/ISCEIC53685.2021.00074

Zhao, H., Jiang, Q., & Yu, H. (2021). Zero-day attack detection and mitigation strategies. In: *Proceedings of the International Symposium on Information Technology*; 2021 Jul 12-14; Beijing, China. IEEE. p. 135-45

Zimmermann, V., & Gerber, N. (2020). The password is dead, long live the password–A laboratory study on user perceptions of authentication schemes. [HTML]. *International Journal of Human-Computer Studies, 133*, 26–44. DOI: 10.1016/j.ijhcs.2019.08.006

Zuboff, S. (2019). *The age of surveillance capitalism: The fight for a human future at the new frontier of power*. PublicAffairs.

Zulkifli, A. (2022) ECK's axing from KXP nothing to do with Musang King plantation, says Sanusi. New Straits Times. 13 July 2022. https://www.nst.com.my/news/nation/2022/07/813127/ecks-axing-kxp-nothing-do-musang-king-plantation-says-sanusi Retrieved on 8 April 2025.

Zulkifli, A. (2024). Opposition rep raises doubt on Kedah high-impact project. New Straits Times. (26 November 2024). https://www.nst.com.my/news/nation/2024/11/1140094/opposition-rep-raises-doubt-kedah-high-impact-projects Retrieved on 8 April 2025.

Zwartkruis, W. (2024). Foreign Direct Investment and Security: What is Actually the Problem? In National Security and Investment Controls (pp. 27-58). Cham: Springer Nature Switzerland. DOI: 10.1007/17280_2024_29

About the Contributors

Mohammed H. Alaqad is a distinguished assistant professor and researcher specializing in translation studies and applied linguistics, with over a decade of academic experience. He currently serves as a postdoctoral research fellow at the Hashim Sani Centre for Palestine Studies, University of Malaya. Dr. Alaqad has been an invited speaker and presenter at over 40 international conferences and events. He has published numerous scientific papers and book chapters globally and has authored several articles and a book chapter on Palestinians in the diaspora. Additionally, he serves on the editorial boards of the Cambridge Scholars of Language & Linguistics in the UK and the International Journal of Applied Linguistics and Translation (IJALT) in the USA. He is the founder and CEO of the Asian Federation of Translators and Interpreters, Malaysia. His research interests include applied linguistics, education technology, and translation.

Andi Asrifan, S.Pd, M.Pd, a distinguished figure in the realm of education, particularly in English Language Education, has made significant contributions through his extensive research, teaching, and leadership roles. As the Head of the Institute for Cooperation and International Affairs at Universitas Muhammadiyah Sidenreng Rappang, Dr. Asrifan's academic journey is marked by a rich tapestry of achievements, including a Doctor of Education in English Language Education. His work spans various facets of education, language, and technology, reflecting the diverse topics covered in his publications and research endeavors. These include, but are not limited to, the impact of the COVID-19 pandemic on educational practices, methodologies in English as a Foreign Language (EFL) classrooms, and the integration of technology in teaching and learning processes. Dr. Asrifan's commitment to advancing educational standards and practices is further evidenced by his active participation in international conferences, webinars, and workshops across countries like India, the Philippines, and Pakistan. These events, organized by various institutions and associations, underscore his role as a global educator and thought leader. His dedication to professional development is also highlighted through his involvement in numerous courses and certifications in personal branding, public speaking, and literacy teaching. Moreover, Dr. Asrifan's leadership extends beyond academia into organizational and educational development, where he has served in various capacities, including as an external examiner for Ph.D. dissertations and a reviewer for scientific journals. His accolades, memberships in professional organizations, and roles as an ambassador for international associations speak volumes of his influence and commitment to fostering educational excellence and sustainable development goals globally.

Kusuma Chandra Kirana is a lecturer in the Master's program in Management at Universitas Sarjanawiyata Tamansiswa (UST) and also an Associate Professor. He has an educational background in management with a primary focus on the development and application of management theories in business practices. Kusuma Chandra Kirana has contributed to various research and publications in the field of management, and he is actively involved in teaching and mentoring students in the master's program. His expertise in management makes him a respected figure in the academic community, particularly in the context of developing managerial capacities among students

Ambar Lukitaningsih is a lecturer at Universitas Sarjanawiyata Tamansiswa, specializing in management and marketing. She holds a doctoral degree in Management and focuses on marketing communication and customer behavior. Dr. Lukitaningsih has published numerous research papers and is dedicated to bridging theory and practice in business education.

Eni Purnasari is a graduate of the Master's Program in Management at Universitas Sarjanawiyata Tamansiswa Yogyakarta. With a strong background in business, she pursued further studies to deepen her expertise in management. In addition to her academic pursuits, Eni runs a fashion business with an international market. She is also actively involved in various organizational activities to enhance her leadership and communication skills. Eni aims to apply the knowledge gained from her studies to expand her business and contribute to the global industry.

Sadaruddin was born in Bone on June 15, 1980. He is a dedicated lecturer in the Early Childhood Education Teacher Training Program at the Faculty of Teacher Training and Education, Universitas Islam Makassar. He also serves as a tutor at the Open University (UPBJJT) and as an adjunct lecturer at Universitas Negeri Makassar and Universitas Islam Negeri Alauddin Makassar. Sadaruddin holds a Bachelor's degree in Automotive Engineering Education from Universitas Negeri Makassar, a Master's degree in Early Childhood Education Administration from the same university, and a Doctorate in Educational Sciences. His professional experience includes roles such as Head of Administration at the Regional Distribution Center of the Ministry of Trade and Industry, Business Development Manager at Kospermindo, and local consultant for various international projects. He has actively contributed to the academic community as an assessor for the National Accreditation Board for Early Childhood and Non-Formal Education, and as a member of the editorial boards for several journals. His research focuses on early childhood education, and he has published numerous articles and presented at national and international conferences. Sadaruddin's dedication to education and his extensive experience in teaching, research, and administration highlight his commitment to advancing the field of early childhood education.

Syamsuardi Saodi was born in Bulu, Lappariaja District, on February 10, 1983. He is the second child of H. Saodi Nuntung and Hj. Haneria Haddaning. He began his elementary education at State Elementary School 146 Bengo and continued to SLTP Negeri 2 Lappariaja and SMA Negeri 1 Lappariaja. He earned his bachelor's degree from the State University of Makassar in Automotive Engineering Education in 2000 and completed his master's degree in Language Studies with a concentration in Early Childhood Education at the same university in 2006. Dr. Syamsuardi completed his Ph.D. in Educational Sciences at the State University of Makassar in 2021. Dr. Syamsuardi is a permanent lecturer in the Early Childhood Teacher Education Study Program at the Faculty of Education, State University of Makassar. He has held various significant positions, including Head of the Early Childhood Teacher Education Study Program (2014-2018), Coordinator of the Center for Cooperation and Innovation Development in Education (2021-2022), and Head of the Curriculum and Entrepreneurship Module Center at the Institute for Innovation and Entrepreneurship Development (LIPK) from 2021 to 2025.

Index

P

R

S

T

W